FOR THE DEFENSE
OF THEMSELVES
AND THE STATE

FOR THE DEFENSE OF THEMSELVES AND THE STATE

The Original Intent and Judicial Interpretation of the Right to Keep and Bear Arms

Clayton E. Cramer

Foreword by Preston K. Covey

Westport, Connecticut
London

Library of Congress Cataloging-in-Publication Data

Cramer, Clayton E.
    For the defense of themselves and the state : the original intent
and judicial interpretation of the right to keep and bear arms /
Clayton E. Cramer ; foreword, Preston K. Covey.
       p.   cm.
    Includes bibliographical references and index.
    ISBN 0–275–94913–3 (alk. paper)
    1. Firearms—Law and legislation—United States—History.
2. United States—Constitutional law—Amendments—2nd—
Interpretation and construction.   I. Title.
KF3941.C73   1994
344.73′0533—dc20
[347.304533]   94–13728

British Library Cataloguing in Publication Data is available.

Library of Congress Catalog Card Number: 94–13728
ISBN: 0–275–94913–3

First published in 1994

Praeger Publishers, 88 Post Road West, Westport, CT 06881
An imprint of Greenwood Publishing Group, Inc.

Printed in the United States of America

The paper used in this book complies with the
Permanent Paper Standard issued by the National
Information Standards Organization (Z39.48–1984).

10 9 8 7 6 5 4 3 2

CONTENTS

FOREWORD

He who decides a case without hearing the other side...
though he decides justly, cannot be considered just. (Seneca)

I write to commend this book by Clayton Cramer to the widest possible audience, the educated citizenry of a democratic republic whose very integrity depends upon fair and informed hearings of its divisive controversies. The educated citizen has two interests in this book, both of which are also obligations for those who would be considered just.

First and foremost, we have a common interest in moral integrity and accountability. We must give account of the rights and liberties we claim for ourselves and against others. This is most fundamentally a moral, not a political or legalistic, matter. It is not a matter of "might" making "right" through due legal or political process, of playing by the rules of legal or political contest. Moral right is not a matter of contests of power, of who wins in court, who wins the votes, or who turns out, today, to have the referees of constitutional contests on their side. To be considered just, we may not simply decide an issue by due process; we must also be sure to hear the other side.

So, when it comes to the most hotly contested claim rights in our public controversies (such as the "right" to abort, the "right" to die with dignity, the "right" to adequate health care, etc.), a just people cannot hide behind constitutional, judicial or political victories. Our moral obligation to hear the other side and to give account of our claims against others remains paramount, regardless of who wins in the legal or political arena. Any fundamental claim right requires a fair and careful hearing from us all, as moral agents, regardless of how the claim is privileged or prejudiced by judicial interpretation. Our moral integrity and the justness of our public policy are not ensured by conformity to the law of the land, however that may be interpreted at the moment even in our highest courts. Nonetheless, a study of the higher law of the land, its origin and evolution, is dramatically instructive to moral inquiry, for it reveals in high relief the varied complexion and complexity of human interests whose contest we need justly hear and resolve, from the moral as well as the legal point of view.

Therefore, first and foremost, I commend this book as a vehicle for moral inquiry into our essentially contested civil rights and liberties. Perhaps none of these is so intractably disputed as the right to keep and bear arms, despite its indisputable nominal existence as a constitutional right. For even where a right is recognized, its meaning and scope will be disputed.

Underneath these disputes and our variant notions of our rights and liberties lie our respective and common interests as persons and citizens. No right can be debated absent an understanding of the interests it purports to protect as well as the interests it may abut or trump. At the moral bottom line, argument about rights is argument about human interests. No interest is more fundamental to the formation and governance of civil society than our common stake in security from harm, without which the enjoyment of every interest is threatened. There are at least three families of interests related to security from harm, in particular security against threats to life, limb, or liberty:

1. Personal security, including our paramount interest in self-defense in the gravest extreme when other protective measures have failed.

We all have an interest in protection from harm, but not all people take an interest in defending themselves or personal responsibility for protecting themselves. Some eschew personal responsibility for personal protection or self-defense and seek to delegate that function exclusively to authorities of the state. Therefore, not all people take an interest in keeping and bearing arms for the defense of themselves and others, and some would grant the state a monopoly of armed force. However, everyone who has an interest in personal protection (and, in the gravest extreme, self-defense) also has an interest in effective means and, therefore, in keeping and bearing arms. Beyond having an interest in personal protection, many argue that this is also a personal responsibility, a moral obligation as well as a right.

Thus, about this matter of personal protection, one dimension of our common interest in security from harm, there is a contest of moral views, well beyond any argument about the actual utility of keeping or bearing arms for the defense of oneself or others. The actuarial success of armed defense is one matter; the residual moral value of having the personal responsibility and prerogative of armed defense is quite another. The fundamental moral value of self-determination (personal responsibility and personal prerogative) remains salient, quite independent of the sociological question about the personal risks and benefits of armed self-defense. And the question of residual moral value remains salient, quite independent of the judicial disposition of the right to keep and bear arms.

Cramer's compendious exploration of legislative and judicial deliberations on this right reveals a rich landscape of moral controversy. Even when we view the paramount right to personal protection as enjoining the further right both to keep and to bear arms, we also recognize that the practice of "bearing" arms (carrying arms abroad in society, concealed or openly) is more problematic than the practice of "keeping" arms (in and for the security of one's home), since many perceive the interest in bearing arms for personal protection as competitive with our collective interest in public safety.

2. Public safety, involving not only personal protection but collective security through the deterrence of both misadventure and criminal harm as we attempt to live and go abroad peaceably in society.

Again, there are the empirical, actuarial, utilitarian questions: Does an armed citizenry collectively deter crime against the person and thereby provide, on balance, an effective measure of collective security from harm? Or, rather, does the keeping or bearing of arms by law-abiding citizens undermine our collective security and public safety by misadventure or inadvertence? Again, there are also the moral questions: Are citizens not morally responsible to contribute to the public safety, as well as to their own defense, by vigilance and, in the gravest extreme, by responsible armed response? Can citizens be fairly expected to fulfill this civic duty without being afforded effective means? Or, rather, is the state to be afforded a monopoly of armed force and sole responsibility for maintaining the public order and security?

Cramer's book reveals not just historic but perennial moral-philosophic views radically at odds with a state monopoly on armed force: by these lights, keeping and bearing arms for the public security is not only a civil right but a civic duty. On the contrary, some argue that an armed citizenry with a duty to respond to the "alarm" (literally, the "call to arms") of the "hue and cry" against criminals in their midst is an anachronism, long since outdated by the modern institution of professional law enforcement. However, this is but one utilitarian view on the social utility of an armed citizenry for the deterrence of crime which does not address the more fundamental moral issues: the residual moral value of distributed responsibility for the public order, the moral value of a citizenry invested and entrusted with a stake in the public security, or the moral propriety of a paternalistic state monopoly on protective force that in turn denies its citizens the means of personal protection.

3. Political security, which involves two functions in tension: (1) the protection of the polity and political order itself and (2) enforcement of the social compact, protection against governmental abuse of power in the gravest extreme.

Cramer's book is entitled "For The Defense Of Themselves And The State," a title which implies several basic functions underlying the right of "the people" to keep and bear arms: for their personal protection against law breakers, for their collective protection against law breakers, for the protection of their state against civil disorder or foreign invasion, and for their protection against "the state" lest their government ever breech the social compact. Again, there are the obvious speculative albeit empirical questions: whether an armed citizenry is any longer necessary or even useful for the protection of the state against disorder from within or invasion from without; or whether an armed citizenry is either a necessary or even viable impediment to governmental abuse of power or the gravest breech of the social compact. Be that as it may, there remain fundamental moral questions: the propriety in principle of entrusting the state with a paternalistic monopoly of coercive force, the value of methodical mistrust of government (irrespective of its actual trustworthiness), the value of sharing all manner of power with the people as part and parcel of the system of checks and balances, and the residual value of investing a measure of coercive (not just procedural) power to resist "the state" in "the people" themselves, individually as well as collectively. The residual moral value of entrusting and empowering the people is not a function of expected utility (whether it would ever be necessary or feasible in fact for the people to pose a threat of armed resistance against their government); it is rather a matter of the moral principles upon which the governance of a free people should be founded, a question of moral value rather than social utility alone.

The question of the need for an armed citizenry as a check on the abuse of governmental power strikes many as both anachronistic and anathema in our modern and high-mindedly optimistic times. But the question is relative, as the need or threat or capacity of armed resistance pertains to any level of government: federal, state, or local. In fact, our citizens have, even in recent history, incorporated themselves as a "militia" or mustered informally in order, successfully, to resist corrupt governmental authority on the local level. That an armed citizenry is a factor to be reckoned with even by a government superior in arms is shown by countless insurgency actions around the world, not the least by our own forebearers' historic war of independence. But today the very idea of a people having to take up arms against their own government invites images of anarchy and is, in any case, a discomfiting thought. Sanford Levinson in his judicious treatment of the Second Amendment controversy ("The Embarrassing Second Amendment," in the December 1989 issue of *The Yale Law Journal*, 656) also provides a judicious perspective on this sensitive moral-political issue:

> One would, of course, like to believe that the state, whether at the local or national level, presents no threat to important political values, including liberty. But our propensity to believe that this is the case may be little more than a sign of how truly different we are from our radical forebearers. I do not want to argue that the state is necessarily tyrannical; I am not an anarchist. But it seems foolhardy to assume that the armed state will necessarily be benevolent. The American political tradition is, for good or ill, based in large measure on a healthy mistrust of the state.... In any event, it is hard for me to see how one can argue that circumstances have so changed as to make mass disarmament constitutionally unproblematic.

The bottom line is that the empirical fact of the matter (whether the people *need* to be empowered so as to resist their government in the gravest breech) is quite beside the moral question (whether a free people *should* nonetheless be so empowered). Again, Cramer's book highlights the historic terrain here in a way that is instructive to modern mentalities that approach the moral questions with more complacency than inquisitiveness.

It is noteworthy that each of these three families of interests (personal security, public safety, political security) have implications for the types of arms to be kept or borne by citizens and the types of domestic arms control that are ultimately sanctioned. For example, the first and third categories of interest argue against blanket prohibitions, while the third category also argues for state-of-the-art "militia" arms. Yet, as regards the second category, public safety in the aggregate might be judged to weigh against public carry or certain types of arms. It all depends on how the facts of the matter are tried and how the contested interests are ultimately weighed and balanced.

How protection from harm is to be afforded a free people, how responsibility for our personal, public and political security is to be apportioned, and what means are to be allowed for the exercise of this responsibility remain fundamental and perennial moral questions regardless of the historic structure or substance of our laws. Competing private and public interests regarding the keeping or bearing of arms would remain salient even without the Second Amendment and its state constitutional analogues. Logically prior to the jurisprudential question of precisely what interests are afforded the politically privileged status of constitutional protection is the moral question of precisely what interests should be afforded protection. The weighing and balancing of interests is the irreducible moral burden of any system of justice irrespective of positive constitutional constraints. This is not to dismiss the importance of constitutional protections, but rather to underscore the moral obligation to take the disputed interests seriously and to weigh them carefully nonetheless. The dispute over what means citizens should be allowed for the exercise of their paramount right to self-defense, universally recognized by even the most despotic and uncivil of societies, is first and last a moral question. This is no less the case when the issue debated is that of a state monopoly of force or when the interest debated is that of a citizenry armed for both the protection of and protection against the state.

The moral weighing and balancing of the interests at stake cannot be evaded by hiding behind one or another interpretation of constitutional protections. Obdurate dogmatism is anathema to moral inquiry. Respectful regard for the interests of others is part and parcel of respect for persons. Human interests cannot be dismissed in the very debate about their status and the just resolution of their conflicts. The private and public interests at stake in the debate about the right to keep and bear arms demand a fair and rigorous hearing, on all sides. In so far as this debate is framed around a contested constitutional right, the origins and evolution of that protean right need to be understood. But, more fundamentally, the history of the judicial interpretation of the right to keep and bear arms reflects the complexion and complexity of the interests at stake, private and public. Cramer's book, therefore, provides a rich education in the interests whose conflict we must justly hear and resolve, in conscience as well as in policy. Judicial interpretation may be left to the judiciary; legislation may be left to the legislatures; but a fair hearing for competing human interests is a moral responsibility shared by us all.

Thus, the first and foremost interest that educated citizens have in reading Cramer's book is that it provides a rich landscape for moral inquiry and accounting. A second if not secondary interest is our civic education in the substance and history of the legislative and judicial issues respecting the controversial right to keep and bear arms. There is also the civic obligation to become informed about the evolution of the constitutional and judicial issues which hold sway in the current policy debate over gun control. Cramer's book enlightens the history of judicial interpretation of the right to keep and bear arms, a matter which is more often the subject of ignorant opinion than informed study. In the wake of the bicentennial of our Bill of Rights, it is timely for citizens to reflect deeply on the origins and meaning of our essentially contested rights and liberties. But the bicentennial has produced more opinionated punditry than scholarship on the right to keep and bear arms. On the judicial interpretation of not only the Second Amendment but also the several state constitutional provisions, we must also heed Seneca's caveat to give the matter a fair and rigorous hearing. Cramer's history provides the most compendious grist for this mill to date.

Pundits tell us that the "original intent" of the Framers of our Constitution as regards the right to keep and bear arms was either prescient of modern gun-control advocacy or else ignorant of the fact that times change and irrelevant today. We are thus asked to believe that on this singular issue of the canon of liberty the Framers were either preternaturally privileged or uniquely benighted. Pundits tell us that our

highest courts, federal or state, have never defended the right to keep and bear arms
as an individual right against state infringement. We are thus asked to believe that
this controversial right has for the entire history of our republic been immune from
the subtlety and acumen that afflicts or ennobles every other area of jurisprudence.
Pundits pontificate and moralize. Scholars, by contrast, adduce evidence in gener-
ous portion so that citizens can educate and make up their own minds.

Cramer provides the kind of scholarly resource that educated citizens need to
think for themselves, a rich digest of primary sources documenting—in their own
words—the views, motives and intentions of the Framers, historic commentators,
legislators and members of the federal and state judiciary who have debated the
right to keep and bear arms from the origins of our republic. Contrary to the dogmatism of latter-day pundits, we find in Cramer's digest of judicial interpretation
the fine granularity of legal and civic reasoning that is commensurate with a complex social issue. Cramer's work is unique in both the scope and the detail with
which it reports the historic case law respecting the right to keep and bear arms.
Cramer also shows us how the law is embedded in the fabric of social history, with
provocative observations on the fate of the right to keep and bear arms in the fitful
history of modern civil liberties, from the antebellum south to the labor and civil
rights movements of the Twentieth Century.

Today, gun control is lionized as a public-health measure, no longer the narrow
preserve of criminal justice. Readers wont to believe that civic-mindedness can only
sanction domestic disarmament will be surprised at the moral eloquence with which
it has long been opposed. Readers wont to believe that only civic-mindedness has
motivated domestic arms control will be surprised at the venality and partisan variety of its historic animus. In our history, if not also today, darker motives can be
found. As with all history, we are advised to heed it, lest we be condemned to repeat it witlessly.

In an age and society obsessed with its own violence, some believe it a mark of
civic virtue to dismiss the right to keep and bear arms as anathema or anachronism.
But moral inquiry and plain honesty demand better of us. For those citizens who
prefer to think for themselves, or to inquire rather than opine, Cramer provides invaluable scholarship and the higher standard of care that democracy demands of us
all.

Preston K. Covey, Director
Center for the Advancement of Applied Ethics
Carnegie Mellon University

PREFACE

This work began in 1989 as a term paper for an undergraduate history class at Sonoma State University. With Professor Daniel Markwyn's encouragement, a 29-page paper on the original intent of the Second Amendment has become the most comprehensive history of the judicial interpretation of the right to keep and bear arms yet compiled—and even this volume is just a survey of this largely unexplored topic.

When I completed research on the original intent section of this book, I intended to write another sixty or seventy pages about judicial interpretation—how many decisions could there be? There were only a half dozen decisions by the U.S. Supreme Court, and a couple dozen state supreme court decisions in the entire history of the Republic—or so I thought. In fact, judicial interpretation of the right to keep and bear arms is not merely a field rich in material, it is positively fecund. This book includes a careful analysis of more than 200 decisions of the federal and state courts. To avoid giving a false impression of the history of judicial interpretation because of unintentional bias in selecting which decisions to study, I have gathered together *all* the decisions that I could locate.

Is this a comprehensive history of American gun control? No. The social and legislative history of gun control is a much more complex research topic than finding and analyzing the decisions of the courts. The comprehensive history of American gun control laws remains to be written. I have been continually startled at how little effort has been made to bring together the essential information required for even a survey of this fascinating topic. How early did the various states adopt laws prohibiting concealed carry of handguns? There is no central source for that information, and study of current penal codes for the various states is, at best, a first approximation of this information.

What influence did racism play in the passage of gun control laws during Reconstruction? There is strong evidence that it was a powerful factor—but it appears that this subject has not been examined in the detail it deserves. Were issues of social class a factor in the passage of discretionary permit issuance laws in the twentieth century? Don Kates' work in this area would seem to indicate so—but a detailed study remains to be done. Why was the National Rifle Association a major participant in the creation of the state gun control laws adopted in the 1920s and 1930s, commonly known as the Model Uniform Firearms Act? How much actual criminal misuse of privately owned automatic weapons was there during the Roaring Twenties? Which provisions of the Gun Control Act of 1968 were intended as crime control, and which were intended to protect the economic interests of American firearms manufacturers? Why does Vermont, alone of the fifty states, remain without laws prohibiting concealed carry? These are all questions in need of detailed study, since gun control laws remain a major bone of contention in American society today. Before we pass or repeal laws, we need to understand how and why the current laws came about.

I am a partisan on the issue of gun control. I suspect it would be difficult to find anyone studying the history of such an emotionally charged and politically signifi- cant issue, who is not a partisan of one side or the other. But I am in the in- teresting position to have changed sides, partly because of my experiences, and partly because of my research.

I knew people who had lived under the Nazi terror. A teacher at my junior high school, Mirte de Boer, told us one day of her work with the Dutch Resistance dur- ing World War II, forging documents to help smuggle people out of the Nazi-oc- cupied Netherlands. Then she told us of a friend whom she had helped to escape; but he just disappeared, somewhere between the Netherlands and Switzerland, and as she told us about him, tears welled up in her eyes.

Another slight acquaintance who worked where I bought ice cream cones as a child, was a concentration camp survivor with a number tattooed on her arm. Here was a tangible reminder of the horror of totalitarianism—treating a person like a piece of expensive machinery by giving her a serial number, instead of a name. She was fortunate—her value as a working asset exceeded her "scrap value," and she survived the war.

At the time, the connection between this sort of savagery and the centralization of power was completely elusive to me. Unfortunately, my schooling had failed to educate me to an essential truth underlying the U.S. Constitution, admirably expressed by the noted Constitutional historian, Page Smith:

> I can find no major flaw in the framers' view that since all people were tainted with original sin, i.e., disposed to pursue their own selfish interests rather than the common good, it was necessary to distribute power in such a way as to minimize the dangers of its being abused, and to protect all legitimate social and economic interests from appropria- tion or exploitation. If they overstated the degree of human depravity, that was certainly a far sounder approach than to overestimate man's natural goodness as the theoreticians of the French Revolution did. Our problem today is, more than ever, how to restrain and redistribute power. The Founders' formula—human selfishness times power equals corruption—has been verified thousands of times since they framed the Constitution.[1]

In 1979 a solicitation from the National Rifle Association arrived in my mailbox. Like many urban Baby Boomers, I had no exposure to hunting, gun ownership, or the rest of what is sometimes disparaged as "redneck culture." Like many of my peers, influenced by my schooling and the popular press, my perceptions of gun owners and hunters were strongly negative; my answers to the NRA survey could only be considered cheeky and insulting. "Did I hunt? How often? What sort of game?" I responded, "Yes, daily, only people," and stuffed the survey into the business reply envelope. That'll show them!

"The only people that need guns are people that hang out with criminals," I told myself. Like most of my urban contemporaries, I assumed—based on a steady

---

1 Page Smith, *The Constitution: A Documentary and Narrative History*, (New York: William Morrow & Co., 1978), 531-2.

drumbeat of conventional wisdom—that the Second Amendment was "about the National Guard—the militia." Why did anyone want to own a gun?

Yet, within two years of my cheeky response to the NRA survey, the critical necessity of self-defense had turned my wife and I into handgun owners. (A number of acquaintances and friends of my wife and I during the period 1975-1980 were murdered, stabbed, raped, beheaded, robbed, or beaten.) I researched the laws that regulated the ownership and carrying of firearms, to make sure that I did not unintentionally become a criminal. In the midst of my research, I found myself face to face with California Military & Veterans Code §120—and suddenly, all the carefully inculcated notions about the meaning of the Second Amendment collapsed—*I* was a member of the militia, and nearly everything that I believed on the subject of the Second Amendment, was in need of more careful study.

Now, eleven years later, on the 200th anniversary of the ratification of the Bill of Rights, December 15, 1791, I find myself one of those crazy people who *actually* think the Second Amendment was intended to protect an individual right "to keep and bear arms"—and I encourage all who disagree to examine the evidence of original intent.

The latter three-quarters of this book examines the history of judicial interpretation of the right to keep and bear arms—and demonstrates that understanding original intent has not been enough to persuade the courts to uphold this right. Just as we find with the rest of the Bill of Rights, our courts have shown a frightening willingness to ignore arguments based on the literal text and original intent of the Second Amendment when issues of race, class, and cultural differences, have been raised. But along with justices who were no better than the society from which they were selected, there have been remarkable occupants of the bench with the courage to directly face the hard questions that the right to keep and bear arms raises.

Before we too quickly dispense with the protections of the Second Amendment, we owe it to future generations to examine the reasons why it was added to our Constitution, and make *quite* sure that those reasons no longer apply. When we look at the history of the twentieth century, where millions have been murdered by their own governments, we must ask ourselves: Do Patrick Henry's words on the relationship between freedom and arms still apply?

> Guard with jealous attention the public liberty. Suspect every one who approaches that jewel. Unfortunately, nothing will preserve it but downright force. Whenever you give up that force, you are inevitably ruined.[2]

---

2 Jonathan Elliot, *The Debates of the Several State Conventions on the Adoption of the Federal Constitution*, (New York: Burt Franklin, 1888), 3:45.

ACKNOWLEDGMENTS

The volume before you now represents not only my work, but also the help, suggestions, and legwork of many others, without whose assistance it would not have come together in its present form. Professor Daniel Markwyn's suggestions and pointers to primary sources have been invaluable in bringing together the rich variety of materials in the original intent chapters; even more important was his encouragement to tackle a task that was larger than either of us realized.

The process of locating up to date case law citations for the various states was a major undertaking; without the assistance of my many correspondents around the United States, this task would have been far more expensive in time and money. The following have been of assistance in locating these indispensable starting points for legal research: Kirk Webb (Colorado); Michael Plowinske (New York & Vermont); David Robinson (Tennessee); Spencer Garrett (Washington); Dave Chesler (Massachusetts); Joseph McConnell (Michigan); Mike Rose (Maryland); John Donahue (Maine); and Drew Betz (Ohio). Professor Joseph St. Sauver at the University of Oregon, Professor Preston Covey at Carnegie-Mellon University, and Jack Schudel, were kind enough to send me recent revisions to the Oregon, Pennsylvania, and Florida concealed weapons permit laws; Donald Newcomb sent me the *National Firearms Act* hearings. Andy Freeman provided me with Marcus Kavanagh's *The Criminal and His Allies*. Similarly, Wayne Warf's provision of Andrew Fletcher's works concerning the militia was much appreciated.

My colleagues Allan Clarke and Ron Kennemer looked over the manuscript at an early stage, and made useful suggestions. My wife Rhonda provided substantial assistance in locating information relating to slavery, civil rights, and racial fear, in addition to reviewing and thoroughly critiquing not only the writing, but also the organizational scheme of this book, and then assisting me in the grueling task of cutting it down to its current size. As the book reached its final form, Chris Hansen made a number of useful grammatical and stylistic suggestions. My children Hilary and James have, with good humor, accepted that all their father's spare time would be lost for a year.

I. DEFINITIONS

Two radically different interpretations of the Second Amendment are commonly espoused in the United States. One school asserts that the Second Amendment protected the right of individual states to maintain military forces independent of the national government, based on the philosophy of civic republicanism. Any individual right that was protected was only for the purpose of maintaining those state militias,[1] and is therefore irrelevant today, because those state militias have ceased to be a component of our national defense.[2] In the words of John Levin, one of the more direct proponents of a collective understanding of the Second Amendment:

> Thus, after over three centuries, the right to bear arms is becoming anachronistic. As the policing of society becomes more efficient, the need for arms for personal self-defense becomes more irrelevant; and as the society itself becomes more complex, the military power in the hands of the government more powerful, and the government itself more responsive, the right to bear arms becomes more futile, meaningless and dangerous.[3]

The other school claims that the Second Amendment protects an individual right "to keep and bear arms," derived from the emerging philosophy of classical liberalism. While acknowledging Revolutionary America's concern about the dangers of standing armies, this school asserts that an individual right was also intended, and that the individual right was essential to maintaining a counterbalance to both federal and state governmental power.[4] In 1982, the Senate Subcommittee on the Constitution staff studied this question, and declared:

> [T]he history, concept, and wording of the second amendment to the Constitution of the United States, as well as its interpretation by every major commentator and court in the first half-century after its ratification, indicates that what is protected is an individual right of a private citizen to own and carry firearms in a peaceful manner.[5]

While the terms "republican" and "liberal" have clear-cut meanings to historians, the use of these terms can be quite confusing to the uninitiated, since the

---

1 David J. Steinberg, "Other Views of the Second Amendment", in *The Right To Keep And Bear Arms*, 97th Congress, 2d Sess. (1982), 25.

2 Warren E. Burger, "The Right To Bear Arms", in *Parade*, January 14, 1990, 4-6.

3 John Levin, "The Right To Bear Arms: The Development Of The American Experience", *Chicago-Kent Law Review*, [Fall-Winter 1971], reprinted in *The Right To Keep And Bear Arms*, 129.

4 David T. Hardy, "Historical Bases of the Right To Keep and Bear Arms", in *The Right To Keep And Bear Arms*, 57-59.

5 Senate Subcommittee on The Constitution Staff, "History: Second Amendment Right To 'Keep and Bear Arms'", in *The Right To Keep And Bear Arms*, 12.

"republican" school of Second Amendment interpretation would doubtless find themselves at variance with many Republican politicians today, and the "liberal" school of Second Amendment analysis, with a few notable exceptions, would probably prefix the word "classical" before calling themselves liberals of any sort. Let us define these terms.

The *republican* school asserts that the right to keep and bear arms was an outgrowth of republicanism, intended to protect the society from the related evils of a standing army and tyranny. While the arms might be broadly distributed, they would still be possessed by the population for the purpose of collective action against a foreign army, or a domestic tyrant.

The *liberal* school asserts that the right was individual, a logical outgrowth of the right to self-defense. Such arms would be for the defense of the individual against private criminals; there was no need for a collective purpose or ownership.

The two positions are not necessarily mutually exclusive; a society might believe in both perspectives, or either, or neither. In practice, many of the advocates of the republican camp, throughout American history, have argued for the republican understanding, to the exclusion of the liberal understanding. In the modern era, there are scholars who argue that the republican understanding was the only one intended, and that even this reason is now obsolete. The historical dispute becomes simply this: did the Second Amendment include a right to keep and bear arms *only* for collective defense, or was an individual right included as well?

Is it possible, from examining contemporary documents, debates, and ideas, to determine which school is right? It appears, from the paucity of materials debating it, that the "right to keep and bear arms" was not controversial in 1780s America. By comparison, freedom of religion, the wisdom of standing armies in peacetime, and the morality of slavery were debated at great length. The lack of debate suggests that a consensus existed about the meaning of this right. Does the lack of debate show that there was consensus that this was an individual right? Or was the consensus that this was a collective right?

The Second Amendment is not just a dusty passage in the Constitution. A dramatic turnaround in attitudes about private ownership of firearms has been under way in the United States since the 1960s. At one time, gun ownership was the norm for nearly all classes and professions of Americans. Today, when private gun ownership is viewed by some segments of our society as not only a hazard to public safety, but evidence of mental disturbance,[6] and serious efforts are underway to severely limit the private ownership of not only handguns, but also some types of rifles and shotguns;[7] determining the original intent of the Second Amendment is more than an academic exercise.

---

6 Don Kates, Jr., "Handgun Prohibition and the Original Meaning of the Second Amendment", in *Michigan Law Review*, 82 [November 1983], 208, note 17 quotes psychologist Joyce Brothers that "men possess guns in order to compensate for sexual dysfunction." Kates also informs us that Dr. Brothers' husband is among the New York City elite with a concealed handgun permit.

7 The highest profile law is California's "Assault Weapons Control Act." California's law attempted to prohibit new sales or transfers of several dozen brands of semiautomatic pistols, rifles, and shotguns, while inexplicably leaving functionally equivalent firearms off the restricted list. A bewildering array of similar restrictions have been passed by individual cities across the United States, as well as by New Jersey and Connecticut.

Does a relationship exist between individual ownership of arms and resistance to tyranny? Is this a peculiarly Western idea, or peculiar only to this century? This relationship has been recognized in many cultures and centuries by those who sought to centralize power. Toyotomi Hideyoshi's efforts at centralizing power in sixteenth century Japan, and eliminating new opposition, included "the famous sword hunt of 1588 which disarmed the soldier-monks and the peasants, bound the latter firmly to the land, and henceforth distinguished clearly between the civilian population of peasants, merchants, and craftsmen and the military aristocracy which alone had the privilege to bear arms."[8]

Article 10 of the Mexican Constitution of 1857, like many of the other protections openly drawn from the U. S. Bill of Rights, guaranteed the right of all men "to possess and carry arms for their security and self-defense..." While debate about which "arms" were protected by this guarantee suggests that there was some anxiety about including all sorts of hand-carried arms, this provision survived debate as a broad individual guarantee.[9]

In our own century, the confiscation of arms by the Chinese Communists,[10] the confiscation of private arms in the various Soviet republics, and in modern Kuwait, first by the Iraqi occupation, then by the returning "legitimate" government, shows that the concern about private arms as a restraint on centralizing power retains its relevance today.[11] Perhaps the most dramatic example of tyranny, with its fear of popular uprising, is the disarmament of Germany and the occupied countries of Europe by the Nazis.[12] The Weimar Republic adopted a number of gun control laws intended to discourage the street violence of Nazis and Communists, and created a registration system for purchase of ammunition and handguns. As the chaos increased, the laws became sufficiently restrictive that the Nazis were able to use the existing licensing scheme to achieve their goals without changes to the statutes until 1938. Regulations adopted the day after *Kristallnacht* formally prohibited Jews from possessing firearms or ammunition.[13]

In spite of the apparent success of the Nazi gun control efforts, Albert Speer tells us that when, in 1939, he was drawing up the plans for Hitler's grandiose governmental complex in Berlin, Hitler's concern about popular discontent caused him to tell Speer:

---

8 Reinhard Bendix, *Kings or People: Power and the Mandate to Rule*, (Berkeley: University of California Press, 1978), 85-86.

9 Wilfrid Hardy Callcott, *Church and State in Mexico: 1822-1857*, (Duke University Press: 1926; reprinted New York, Octagon Books: 1971), 287.

10 Nien Cheng, *Life and Death In Shanghai*, (New York: Grove Press, 1986), 106.

11 "Kuwait begins search for illegal weapons", *USA Today*, July 2, 1991, 4A. With respect to the relationship between widespread distribution of arms and democratization of post-war Kuwait, see "Underground in Kuwait", *Newsweek*, December 31, 1990, 43, and "The Liberation of the Emir", *Newsweek*, March 18, 1991, 26.

12 Israel Gutman, "The Armed Struggle of the Jews in Nazi-Occupied Countries" in Leni Yahil, *The Holocaust*, transl. Ina Friedman and Haya Galai, (New York: Oxford University Press, 1990), 457-98, provides a detailed analysis of the political, social, and psychological factors, as well as the logistical problems of obtaining arms that severely hampered Jewish resistance to the Holocaust.

13 Jay Simkin and Aaron Zelman, "*Gun Control*": *Gateway to Tyranny*, (Milwaukee, Wisc.: Jews for the Preservation of Firearms Ownership, 1992), contains the full text (in German and with an English translation) of the various weapons laws and regulations adopted by the Weimar Republic and the Nazis from 1928 to 1938.

"You know it is not out of the question that I shall some day be forced to take unpopular measures. These might possibly lead to riots. We must provide for that eventuality. All the buildings on this square must be equipped with heavy steel bulletproof shutters over their windows. The doors, too, must be of steel, and there should be heavy iron gates for closing off the square. It must be possible to defend the center of the Reich like a fortress."

This remark betrayed a nervousness he had not had before. The same feeling emerged when we discussed the location of the barracks for the bodyguard, which had meanwhile grown into a fully motorized regiment armed with the most modern equipment... "Suppose there should be some disturbances!" he said. And pointing to the four hundred foot wide avenue: "If they come rolling up here in their armored vehicles the full length of the street—nobody will be able to put up any resistance."[14]

This work's first three chapters seek to determine original intent of the Second Amendment. To that end, we will explore the common law origins of the right to keep and bear arms, Enlightenment perspectives on the bearing of arms, early state constitutional analogs to the Second Amendment, and the legislative history of the Second Amendment. The remaining chapters of this work trace the development of the different judicial interpretations (and misinterpretations) of "the right of the people to keep and bear arms," in the hopes of understanding how and why the original intent has been lost, confused, and in some cases, openly and intentionally discarded, in the intervening 200 years.

Determining original intent for the Second Amendment is prone to error because most studies of it have been conducted by parties with an eye to present day public policy and an axe to grind. To a lesser degree, this has been a problem in the various analyses of the judicial interpretation of the Second Amendment as well. In some cases, reading the primary sources cited (and miscited) by the various authors has demonstrated the hazards of relying on secondary sources, and the dangers of quoting out of context. As a consequence, the greatest possible care has been taken to quote entire paragraphs in the chapters on original intent and the seminal court decisions.

The Second Amendment consists of two clauses, joined by a comma: "A well-regulated Militia being necessary to the security of a free State, the right of the people to keep and bear Arms, shall not be infringed." A variety of scholars, republican and liberal, have interpreted this first clause as reflecting fears that a despotic government might use a standing army as an instrument of oppression. This interpretation of the first clause is not in dispute; Cromwell and his New Model Army were an example of the hazards of a standing army, and how easy it was for professional soldiers to impose a dictatorial reign on the population.[15]

As a consequence, we will not explore in any detail or make any attempt to prove that standing armies were regarded as, at best, a necessary evil by the Framers. We will not examine the ideals of an army composed of all able-bodied men, sharing equally in the obligations of collective defense. While fascinating for what they tell us about republican ideals in 1789, they are not in dispute; only the issue of

---

14 Albert Speer, transl. Richard & Clara Winston, *Inside The Third Reich*, (New York: Macmillan Co., 1970), 158.

15 Roy G. Weatherup, "Standing Armies And Armed Citizens: An Historical Analysis of The Second Amendment", *Hastings Constitutional Law Quarterly*, 2:1 [Winter 1975] reprinted in *The Right To Keep And Bear Arms*, 138.

whether an individual self-defense right was also included, remains controversial, and germane to this work.

That said, does it matter whether an individual self-defense right was included or not? Isn't individual ownership of arms protected, in either case? Does it matter whether the purpose is restraining the government, or restraining a common criminal? As we will see when we study the judicial history of the "right to keep and bear arms," a collective right could be regulated, or even, with enough stretching, forbidden to individuals, by arguing that the need no longer existed to restrain our own government. An individual self-defense right, on the other hand, creates considerably more complex problems of what constitutes legitimate regulation of arms.

An individual right to armed self-defense implies a right to carry arms appropriate to that purpose: a pistol, a knife, a sword, perhaps impact weapons. A right to arms for the purpose of resisting domestic tyranny, however, might allow the government considerable latitude in restricting the carrying of arms, and even prohibition of arms not appropriate to revolution. On the other hand, weapons specifically designed for short-range use against unarmed or lesser armed attackers (as might be appropriate for self-defense) are of no value for overthrowing a government.

What was the intent of the Second Amendment? In the process of researching the origins of the Second Amendment, many of the author's original assumptions were found to be without merit. The primary intent of the Second Amendment was to guarantee that the population retained the ability to resist domestic tyranny; maintaining a military force capable of defending the nation from invasion was a minor issue. By comparision, the various state analogs to the Second Amendment were (with a few exceptions) intended to guarantee a right to arms to protect against both domestic tyranny and private criminals. Underlying both federal and state guarantees, however, was the assumption that individual ownership of arms was a fundamental right of freemen.

Making sure that we understand the meaning of the words *arms, bear, militia,* and *well-regulated* is the first step towards understanding the Second Amendment. There is a natural tendency to do textual analysis of the Second Amendment using twentieth century denotations, and even worse, using twentieth century connotations. To be sure of correctly understanding original intent, we must find definitions contemporary with the Second Amendment and the Framers. Noah Webster's 1828 *An American Dictionary of the English Language* is an excellent starting point, not only because his was a dictionary of *American* usage, but also because Webster was one of the pamphleteers involved in the public debate surrounding ratification of the Constitution.

The *Oxford English Dictionary* (OED) is another excellent resource; not only does it provide a comprehensive list of definitions, but also examples of usage from earliest known use, through the Revolutionary period, and into modern times. This provides an opportunity to see how such usage has changed with time. Samuel Johnson's dictionary would also be a fine contemporary resource, except that none of the terms of interest are defined within it.[16]

Finally, we will use the best sources of all—the definitions of these terms contained within the ratification debates, and within the pamphlets of Federalists

16 E.L. McAdam, Jr. and George Milne, ed., *Johnson's Dictionary*, (New York: Pantheon Books, 1963).

and Antifederalists. When a definition is *clearly* established in such a source, and the definition is used consistently by all parties, this must take precedence over any dictionary definition.

Those three little words, "to bear arms," contain a controversy with which we must first deal. Levin, arguing for a republican meaning for the Second Amendment, asserts that at the time of the Revolution, the phrase "to *bear* arms" indicated an organized military force, while "to *have* arms" indicated an individual's possession of such arms.[17] What evidence exists to prove or disprove Levin's claim?

One of the most important sources to look to is William Blackstone, the noted eighteenth century English jurist, whose writings on English law formed the basis for legal schooling in the colonies throughout the Revolutionary period, and for many years into the nineteenth century. Blackstone asserted that personal security, liberty, and property were absolute rights, not dependent upon governmental grants, but "no other than either that *residuum* (remainder) of natural liberty, which is not required by the laws of the society to be sacrificed to public convenience: or else those civil privileges, which society hath engaged to provide, in lieu of the natural liberties so given up by individuals."[18]

Blackstone also defined the phrase "right to bear arms" as:

> The fifth and last auxiliary right of the subject, that I shall at present mention, is that of having arms for their defense, suitable to their condition and degree, and such as are allowed by law.... [I]t is indeed a public allowance, under due restrictions, of the natural right of resistance and self-preservation, when the sanctions of society and laws are found insufficient to restrain the violence of oppression.[19]

This is a statement of an *individual* right of a subject, and for "the natural right of resistance and self-preservation." The "right to bear arms," in Blackstone's mind, appears to have protected an individual right, not a collective right.

Blackstone also used the phrase, "right of having and using arms" in a collective revolutionary sense, when the "liberties of Englishmen" were subject to "tyranny and oppression," and appeals to the courts and Parliament were unsuccessful "and lastly, to the right of having and using arms for self-preservation and defense."[20]

Blackstone's use of these phrases is completely contrary to Levin's claimed meanings. It is possible that the rough and ready colonists on the American frontier were unaware of the fine distinction between "bear" and "have"; it strains one's credulity to believe that a British judge, the foremost law commentator of his day, would fail to make this distinction in his magnum opus.

Noah Webster's first edition of *An American Dictionary of the English Language*, published in 1828, showed several subtle variations on the verb "bear" in the sense of "carry" or "wear"; the closest sense to the one asserted by Levin is "to wear; to bear as a mark of authority or distinction; as, to bear a sword, a badge, a name; to bear arms in a coat."[21] But there is nothing specific to military service in that definition, even though one example—"a badge"—is official in nature.

---

17 Levin, 116. See also Steinberg, 26.

18 William Blackstone, *Commentaries on the Laws of England*, edited by William Carey Jones, (San Francisco: Bancroft-Whitney Co., 1916), §173, 219.

19 Blackstone, Jones ed., §199, 246.

20 Blackstone, Jones ed., §200, 247.

21 Noah Webster, *An American Dictionary of the English Language*, I, (1828; reprinted New York: Johnson Reprint Corp., 1970), *s.v.* "Bear".

The OED shows a definition of "bear" that might include a military sense: "To carry about with one, or wear, ensigns of office, weapons of offence or defence. *to bear arms against*: to be engaged in hostilities with." But only one definition is in any way specific to arms, and even there, only "*to bear arms against*" is specific to warfare or military service—the broader definition refers generally to weapons, not just in military service. These uses appear as early as *Beowulf,* in the ninth century, and as late as 1862. Under "arms," however, the OED defines "to bear arms" as a figurative term for "to serve as a soldier, do military service, fight."[22]

Further evidence that this distinction was not made in America is found in the constitutions adopted during the period 1776-1845. The constitutions of Connecticut (1818), Indiana (1816), Kentucky (1792 & 1799), Michigan (1835), Mississippi (1817), Missouri (1820), Ohio (1802), Pennsylvania (1776 & 1790), Republic of Texas (1838), State of Texas (1845), Vermont (1777, 1786, and 1793), all use the phrase "bear arms" and variants of the phrase, "in defence of themselves and the State." This use in reference to individual self-defense strongly suggests that "bear arms" was not exclusively of a military or republican nature.

Several state constitutions adopted during the same period of time specify the "right to bear arms for the common defence" or a variant of it: Maine (1819), Massachusetts (1780), North Carolina (1776), Tennessee (1796 & 1834). If "to bear arms" contained within it the idea of military duty, excluding private use, there would seem to be no need for the phrase "for the common defence" as a qualifier.

The Pennsylvania minority report on ratifying the Constitution (to be discussed in more detail on page 35), requested an amendment with the language: "That the people have a right to bear arms for the defence of themselves and their own state, or the United States, or for the purpose of killing game..."[23] While it could be argued that the use of "bear arms" here was with reference to "defence of... their own state," the references to self-defense and hunting provide evidence that the broader definition of "bear arms" was recognized.

Stephen Halbrook points to a Virginia game bill drafted by Thomas Jefferson, and proposed by James Madison that would have fined those "who hunted deer out of season, and if within a year '[the hunter] shall bear a gun out of his inclosed ground, unless while performing military duty,' he shall be in violation of his recognizance."[24] This use is evidence that to "bear a gun" included not only military duty, but also hunting.

In the many judicial opinions that we will explore starting in chapter five, there are statements and implications as to the meaning of the word "bear." While less relevant to original intent, since they are further removed from the era in which the language was adopted, it is significant that the decisions which recognize that the phrase "to bear arms" was not exclusively military far exceed those which draw this

22 J.A. Simpson & E.S.C. Weiner, ed., *Oxford English Dictionary,* 2nd ed., hereinafter cited as OED, (Oxford: Clarendon Press, 1989), 2:21, 1:634.

23 "The Address and Reasons of Dissent of the Minority of the Convention of the State of Pennsylvania to their Constitutents", in John P. Kaminski & Gaspare J. Saladino, ed., *The Documentary History of the Ratification of the Constitution: Commentaries on the Constitution,* (Madison, Wisc.: State Historical Society of Wisconsin, 1984), 3:19.

24 Stephen F. Halbrook, "What The Framers Intended: A Linguistic Analysis of the Right To 'Bear Arms'", in *Law and Contemporary Problems,* 49:1 [Winter 1986], 153.

distinction.[25] Even decisions that claimed to make such a distinction, such as *State v. Hill* (1874), were inconsistent: "the right to *bear* or *carry* arms," "if they may at pleasure be *borne* and used in the fields, and in the woods"[26] (emphasis added) showed that while the Georgia Supreme Court claimed that "bear" meant military carrying exclusively, their own usage showed otherwise.

While the OED provides some evidence to back up Levin's claim that "to bear arms" was military, the OED definitions are not exclusively military in nature, and the vast majority of the evidence—and the unanimous agreement of the evidence closest chronologically and geographically to the Framers—shows that it had a more general meaning of carrying arms, for *either* military or individual purposes.

Webster defined "arms" as: "In *law*, arms are any thing which a man takes in his hand in anger, to strike or assault another."[27] Such arms must be something that an individual can pick up and move. A sword, a dagger, a pistol, a gun, a grenade, and a Molotov cocktail, all qualify as "arms." An artillery piece, a helicopter gunship, or a nuclear missile launching submarine, would seem outside the definition, because they can not be taken "in his hand."

The OED definitions for "arms" is more specific than Webster's:

> 2. a. Instruments of offence used in war; weapons. *fire-arms*: those for which gunpowder is used, such as guns and pistols, as opposed to *swords, spears*, or *bows*. *small-arms*: those not requiring carriages, as opposed to *artillery*.

But all the examples cited in the OED of the usage of the word "arms," from 1300 to 1870, conform to the definition given by Webster—those which can be taken in the hand.[28]

On the question of whether only long guns were considered part of the militia equipment that each man was to "provide himself," rather than provided by the government, a section of the Militia Act of 1792 (introduced as HR-102, and debated by the First Congress) imposed the following requirement on every member of the militia serving as cavalry: "Each dragoon to furnish himself with... a pair of pistols, a sabre, and cartridge box to contain twelve cartridges for pistols."[29]

As we will see, starting in chapter five, the definition of arms protected by the Second Amendment and the state constitutional analogs has long been a subject of dispute, with different courts holding different opinions as to which weapons constitute "arms" within the sense of the Second Amendment. From the contemporary uses above, and from the dictionary definitions of the period, "arms" included not only military long guns, but handguns and other self-defense weapons as well.

The word *militia* is often assumed to mean "National Guard." But let us ask the Framers, "Who are the militia?" For a contemporary definition, we can look to George Mason's speech at the Virginia constitution ratification convention of 1788:

---

25 There are only a very few decisions which have held that "to bear arms" is specifically military in nature: *Aymette* v. *State*, 2 Hump. (21 Tenn.) 154, 155 (1840); *English* v. *State*, 35 Tex. 473, 475 (1872), *State* v. *Hill*, 53 Ga. 472 (1874).

26 *State* v. *Hill*, 53 Ga. 472, 475, 476 (1874).

27 Webster, *An American Dictionary of the English Language*, I, *s.v.*, "Arms".

28 OED, 1:634.

29 Charlene Bangs Bickford & Helen E. Veit, ed., *Documentary History of the First Federal Congress 1789-91*, (Baltimore: Johns Hopkins University Press, 1986), 5:1465.

MASON. Mr. Chairman, a worthy member has asked *who are the militia, if they be not the people of this country,* and if we are not protected from the fate of the Germans, Prussians, &c., by our representation? I ask, *Who are the militia? They consist now of the whole people, except a few public officers.* But I cannot say who will be the militia of the future day. If that paper on the table gets no alteration, the militia of the future day may not consist of all classes, high and low, and rich and poor; but they may be confined to the lower and middle classes of the people, granting exclusion to the higher classes of the people. If we should ever see that day, the most ignominious punishments and heavy fines may be expected. *Under the present government, all ranks of people are subject to militia duty.* Under such a full and equal representation as ours, there can be no ignominious punishment inflicted.[30] [emphasis added]

Earlier during the Virginia debates, Mason had equated "the people" and "the militia":

An instance within the memory of some of this house will show us how *our militia* may be destroyed. Forty years ago, when the resolution of enslaving America was formed by an artful man, who was governor of Pennsylvania, *to disarm the people;* that it was the best and most effectual way to enslave them; but that they should not do it openly, but weaken them, and let them sink gradually, *by totally disusing and neglecting the militia.*[31] [emphasis added]

Francis Corbin, arguing for the Constitution before the same body, held that the concerns about standing armies were overstated, and made the same equation:

The honorable gentleman then urges an objection respecting the militia, who, he tells us, will be made the instrument of tyranny to deprive us of our liberty. Your militia, says he, will fight against you. *Who are the militia? Are we not militia? Shall we fight ourselves?* No, sir; the idea is absurd. We are also terrified by the dread of a standing army. It cannot be denied that we ought to have the means of defence, and be able to repel an attack.[32] [emphasis added]

The following exchange at the Virginia ratifying convention in 1788 also demonstrates that "militia" was recognized as constituting the whole people:

Mr. CLAY wished to be informed why the Congress were to have power to provide for calling forth the militia, to put the laws of the Union into execution.

Mr. MADISON supposed the reasons of this power to be so obvious that they would occur to most gentlemen. If resistance should be made to the execution of the laws, he said, it ought to be overcome. *This could be done only in two ways—either by regular forces or by the people.* By one or the other it must unquestionably be done. If insurrections should arise, or invasions should take place, *the people ought unquestionably to be employed, to suppress and repel them, rather than a standing army.* The best way to do these things was *to put the militia on a good and sure footing,* and enable the government to make use of their services when necessary.

Mr. GEORGE MASON. Mr. Chairman, unless there be some restrictions on the power of calling forth the militia, to execute the laws of the Union, suppress insurrections, and repel invasions, we may very easily see that it will produce dreadful oppressions. It is extremely unsafe, without some alterations. It would be *to use the militia to a very bad purpose,* if any disturbance happened in New Hampshire, to call them from Georgia. *This would harass the people* so much that they would agree to abolish the use of the militia, and establish a standing army.[33] [emphasis added]

---

30 Elliot, 3:425-6.
31 Elliot, 3:380.
32 Elliot, 3:112-3.
33 Elliot, 3:378.

Gov. Randolph, also at the Virginia ratifying convention asserted:

In order to provide for our defence, and exclude the dangers of a standing army, *the general defence is left to those who are the objects of defence. It is left to the militia*, who will suffer if they become the instruments of tyranny.[34] [emphasis added]

Alexander Contee Hanson, a member of the Maryland ratification convention, also discussed the meaning of "militia." In his pamphlet in support of ratification of the Constitution, he argued that the concerns about standing armies were excessive, and that such standing armies were unavoidable. He concluded that the concerns are "a mere pretext for terrifying you," and that:

It may well be material here to remark, that although a well regulated militia has ever been considered as the true defense of a free republic, there are always honest purposes, which are not to be answered by a militia. If they were, the burthen of the militia would be so great, that a free people would, by no means, be willing to sustain it. If indeed it be possible in the nature of things, that congress shall, at any future period, alarm us by an improper augmentation of troops, *could we not, in that case, depend on the militia, which is ourselves.*[35] [emphasis added]

A committee of the Maryland ratifying convention, the same year as the Virginia convention, proposed ratification of the Constitution with a list of amendments, one of which is relevant to the Second Amendment.[36] Among these provisions: "That the militia shall not be subject to martial law, except in time of war, invasion, or rebellion." In explaining why this amendment was considered so important, the committee argued:

This provision to restrain the powers of Congress over the militia, although by no means so ample as that provided by Magna Charta, and the other great fundamental and constitutional laws of Great Britain, (it being contrary to Magna Charta to punish a freeman by martial law, in time of peace, and murder to execute him,) yet it may prove an inestimable check; for all other provisions in favor of the rights of men would be vain and nugatory, if the power of subjecting *all men, able to bear arms*, to martial law at any moment should remain vested in Congress.[37] [emphasis added]

The ratifying convention refused to support the full list of proposed amendments. In response, the committee requested the convention to ratify the Constitution with what it considered the most important three amendments. The committee explained further its concern:

The first of these objections, concerning the militia, they considered as essential; for, to march beyond the limits of a neighboring state *the general militia, which consists of so many poor people that can illy be spared from their families and domestic concerns*, by power of Congress, (who could know nothing of their circumstances,) without consent of their own legislature or executive, ought to be restrained.[38] [emphasis added]

The general militia, then, was recognized by the Maryland convention as the adult freemen of Maryland.

---

34 Elliot, 3:401.
35 Alexander Contee Hanson, *Remarks on the Proposed Plan of a Federal Government*, 21, in Paul Ford, ed., *Pamphlets On The Constitution of the United States*, (Brooklyn, N.Y.: 1888; reprinted New York: Da Capo Press, 1968), 234-5.
36 Elliot, 2:549.
37 Elliot, 2:552.
38 Elliot, 2:554.

Tench Coxe of Pennsylvania was a member of the Annapolis Convention in 1786 and the Continental Congress. His letters were among the first to appear in favor of ratification of the Constitution, and were widely reprinted in newspapers of the day.[39] Coxe admitted: "The apprehensions of the people have been excited, perhaps by persons with good intentions, about the powers of the new government to raise an army."

After stating that the Constitution contained adequate restrictions on the funding and control of standing armies, Coxe argued that:

> *The militia, who are in fact the effective part of the people at large*, will render many troops quite unnecessary. They will form a powerful check upon the regular troops, and will generally be sufficient to over-awe them—for our detached situation will seldom give occasion to raise an army, though a few scattered companies may often be necessary.[40] [emphasis added]

Richard Henry Lee was appointed to the Constitutional Convention, but declined to serve. His pamphlet against ratification of the Constitution was "one of the most popular" of the time.[41] His anxious description of what might happen if "one fifth or one eighth part of the men capable of bearing arms, be made a *select* militia," [emphasis added] suggests that the entire militia consisted of *all* men "capable of bearing arms."[42] Even a "select militia" consisted of a much larger part of the population than the modern National Guard.

Further evidence of the identity of the militia as "the people," and not just a select part of the population, can be found in James Madison's *Federalist* 46. Madison sought to alleviate concerns about Federal power, and to that end, he pointed out that: "The only refuge left for those who prophecy the downfall of the State Governments, is the visionary supposition that the Federal Government may previously accumulate a military force for the projects of ambition..." Madison next asserted the political unlikeliness of such an event, but:

> Extravagant as the supposition is, let it however be made. Let a regular army, fully equal to the resources of the country be formed; and let it be entirely at the devotion of the [Federal] Government; still it would not be going too far to say, that the State Governments with the people on their side would be able to repel the danger. The highest number to which, according to the best computation, a standing army can be carried in any country, does not exceed one hundredth part of the whole number of souls; or one twenty-fifth part of the number able to bear arms. This proportion would not yield in the United States an army of more than twenty-five or thirty thousand men. *To these would be opposed a militia amounting to near half a million of citizens with arms in their hands,* officered by men chosen from among themselves, fighting for their common liberties, and united and conducted by governments possessing their affections and confidence. It may well be doubted whether a militia thus circumstanced could ever be conquered by such a proportion of regular troops.[43] [emphasis added]

The "militia" was not a small professional military, but the entire male population of the country, "with arms in their hands."

39 Ford, *Pamphlets On The Constitution of the United States*, 133.
40 Tench Coxe, *An Examination of the Constitution for the United States of America*, 20-21, in Ford, *Pamphlets On The Constitution of the United States*, 150-1.
41 Ford, *Pamphlets On The Constitution of the United States*, 277.
42 Lee, 25, in Ford, *Pamphlets On The Constitution of the United States*, 305.
43 James Madison, "Federalist 46", in Jacob E. Cooke, ed., *The Federalist*, (Middletown, Conn.: Wesleyan University Press, 1961), in Cooke, 320-1.

A less clear-cut statement is found in Alexander Hamilton's *Federalist* 8. Like Madison, Hamilton also sought to alleviate fears of a tyrannical federal government, and to that end, compared the nature of military establishments "in a country, seldom exposed by its situation to internal invasions," such as the United States or Britain, and "one which is often subject to them, and always apprehensive of them," such as the continental powers of Europe:

> The smallness of the army renders the natural strength of the community an overmatch for it; and the citizens, not habituated to look up to the military power for protection, or to submit to its oppressions, neither love nor fear the soldiery: They view them with a spirit of jealous acquiescence in a necessary evil, and stand ready to resist a power which they suppose may be exerted to the prejudice of their rights. The army under such circumstances, may usefully aid the magistrate to suppress a small faction, or an occasional mob, or insurrection; but it will be unable to enforce encroachments against the united efforts of the great body of the people.[44]

This alone does not prove that Hamilton saw the militia as equivalent to the general population—but just before this comparison, he explained why the issue of standing armies had only recently become an issue of concern:

> The means of revenue, which have been so greatly multiplied by the [i]ncrease of gold and silver, and of the arts of industry, and the science of finance, which is the offspring of modern times, concurring with the habits of nations, have produced an [e]ntire revolution in the system of war, and have rendered disciplined armies, distinct from the body of the citizens, the inseparable companion of frequent hostility.[45]

There is other contemporaneous evidence that the Founding Fathers considered the militia to be equivalent to, if not, "the people," at least to a very large part of the people. The same Congress that debated the Bill of Rights, also debated HR-102, the Militia Bill which became, in the Second Congress, the Militia Act of 1792. Its language required:

> That each and every free able-bodied white male citizen of the respective States, resident therein, who is or shall be of the age of eighteen years, and under the age of forty-five years, (except as hereinafter excepted) shall severally, and respectively, be enrolled in the Militia by the Captain or commanding officer of the company, within whose bounds such citizens shall reside... That every citizen, so enrolled and notified, shall, within six months thereafter, provide himself with a good musket or firelock, a sufficient bayonet and belt, two spare flints, and a knapsack, a pouch with a box therein to contain not less than twenty-four cartridges, suited to the bore of his musket or firelock, each cartridge to contain a proper quantity of powder and ball; or with a good rifle, knapsack, shot-pouch and powder-horn, twenty balls suited to the bore of his rifle, and a quarter of a pound of powder; and shall appear so armed, accoutred, and provided, when called out to exercise or into service...[46]

This statute "remained in effect into the early years of the [twentieth] century as a legal requirement of gun ownership for most of the population of the United States."[47]

---

44 Alexander Hamilton, "Federalist 8", in Cooke, 47-48.

45 Alexander Hamilton, "Federalist 8", in Cooke, 47.

46 Joseph Gales, ed., *Debates and Proceedings in the Congress of United States*, (Washington: Gales & Seaton, 1834), hereinafter cited as *Annals of Congress*, 2 Cong., May 8, 1792, 1392.

47 Senate Subcommittee on The Constitution Staff, "History: Second Amendment Right To 'Keep and Bear Arms'", 7.

Debate on the Militia Bill, on December 16, 1790, shows general agreement that "all from eighteen to forty-five ought to be armed." Rep. Jackson stated "that he was of the opinion that the people of America would never consent to be deprived of the privilege of carrying arms. Though it may prove burdensome to some individuals to be obliged to arm themselves, yet it would not be so considered when the advantages were justly estimated." Jackson then followed up this statement with a series of examples of the advantages that had resulted in Switzerland, France, and Ireland, from "putting arms into the hands of their militia."

On the same day, a long discussion by members of the House centered on whether the government should provide arms for those too poor to purchase their own. Reps. Wadsworth and Sherman argued against such an action, because of the public expense involved, and "experience shows that public property of this kind, from the careless manner in which many persons use it, is soon lost." Further, Rep. Sherman felt sure that, "there are so few freemen in the United States who are not able to provide themselves with arms and accoutrements," that it was unnecessary and improper for the government to do so. Rep. Bloodworth argued that since the whole society benefited from arming the poorest members of the militia, that "those who were benefited by them should be at the expense of arming them."

When it was suggested that minors and apprentices should be armed at the public expense as well, Rep. Wadsworth argued against it on grounds that would seem incomprehensible to most people today:

> The motion at first appeared to be in favor of poor men, who are unable to purchase a firelock; but now, it seems, minors and apprentices are to be provided for. *Is there a man in this House who would wish to see so large a proportion of the community, perhaps one-third, armed by the United States, and liable to be disarmed by them?* Nothing would tend more to ex[c]ite suspicion, and rouse a jealousy dangerous to the Union. With respect to apprentices, every man knew that they were liable to the tax, and they were taken under the idea of being provided for by their masters; as to minors, their parents or guardians would prefer furnishing them with arms themselves, to depending on the United States when they knew they were liable to having them reclaimed.[48] [emphasis added]

Congress' fear was not that the population would have arms; but that if the government provided the arms, it would have the authority to ask for them back, and doing so would be dangerous to the Union.

On December 22, 1790, the First Congress debated whether it should define which persons would be exempted from militia duty, or if the state legislatures should do so. As part of that debate, Rep. Williamson observed:

> When we departed from the straight line of duty marked out for us by the first principles of the social compact, we found ourselves involved in difficulty. *The burden of the militia duty lies equally upon all persons*; and when we contemplate a departure from this principle, by making exemptions, it involves us in our present embarrassment.[49] [emphasis added]

Nor did this understanding of the militia as "all persons" disappear after the heady days of the new Constitution. On January 5, 1800, Rep. Randolph, in arguing for a reduction of the standing army, emphasized that standing armies were not only "useless and enormous expense," but contrary to the spirit of the Constitution:

---

48 *Annals of Congress*, 1 Cong., December 16, 1790, 1806-9.
49 Elliot, 4:423.

"A people who mean to continue free must be prepared to meet danger in person, not to rely upon the fallacious protection of mercenary armies."[50]

Presidential Inaugural Addresses in the first decades of the Republic provide additional evidence of the meaning of "militia." President James Madison's First Inaugural Address in 1809 continued the policy of articulating the hazards of standing armies, by asserting that the obligations of the President included "to keep within the requisite limits a standing military force, always remembering that an armed and trained militia is the firmest bulwark of republics—that without standing armies their liberty can be never be in danger, nor with large ones safe..."

This statement, of course, could be interpreted to refer to a select militia, or the general militia. That it still meant a general militia may be deduced from the First Inaugural Address of Madison's hand-picked successor, James Monroe, in 1817:

> But it ought always to be held prominently in view that *the safety of these States and of everything dear to a free people must depend in an eminent degree on the militia.* Invasions may be made too formidable to be resisted by any land and naval force which would comport either with the principles of our Government or the circumstances of the United States to maintain. *In such cases recourse must be made to the great body of the people,* and in a manner to produce the best effect. It is of the highest importance, therefore, that they be so organized and trained as to be prepared for any emergency. [emphasis added]

President Andrew Jackson continued this understanding of the role of the militia, and its contents, in his First Inaugural Address (1829):

> But the bulwark of our defense is the national militia, which in the present state of our intelligence and population must render us invincible. As long as our Government is administered for the good of the people, and is regulated by their will; as long as it secures to us the rights of person and of property, liberty of conscience and of the press, it will be worth defending; and so long as it is worth defending a patriotic militia will cover it with an impenetrable aegis. Partial injuries and occasional mortifications we may be subjected to, *but a million of armed freemen, possessed of the means of war,* can never be conquered by a foreign foe. [emphasis added]

That Jackson still had in mind the entire free male population of the country, and not a select militia, can be determined from the count; the total popular vote in the election in which Jackson was elected President was just over a million. That Jackson expected them to have their own arms for the purposes of warfare may be inferred from, "possessed of the means of war..." This phrase would be meaningless if the arms were issued by the government at the outbreak of hostilities.

President Franklin Pierce's Inaugural Address of 1853 continued this recognition that the militia were a body quite separate from a standing army: "The Army as organized must be the nucleus around which in every time of need the strength of your military power, the sure bulwark of your defense—a national militia—may be readily formed into a well-disciplined and efficient organization."[51]

Current U.S. law still recognizes this organic relationship between the people and the militia, describing, "The militia of the United States" as consisting of "all able-bodied males at least 17 years of age and... under 45 years of age who are, or who have made a declaration of intent to become, citizens of the United States and of

---

50 Elliot, 4:411-2.
51 Davis Newton Lott, *The Presidents Speak: The Inaugural Address of the American Presidents from Washington to Kennedy,* (New York: Holt, Rinehart & Winston, 1961), 26, 36, 56, 58, 106.

female citizens of the United States who are commissioned officers of the National Guard." The "organized militia... consists of the National Guard and the Naval Militia; and... the unorganized militia, which consists of the members of the militia who are not members of the National Guard or the Naval Militia."[52] The current National Guard was organized under Congress' power to "raise and support armies," and *not* under the "organizing, arming and disciplining the Militia" provision, since the militia "can be called forth only 'to execute the laws of the Union, suppress insurrections and repel invasions.'"[53]

In *Perpich* v. *Department of Defense* (1990), the U.S. Supreme Court provided a history of the process by which the National Guard was "federalized" in 1916, so as to eliminate questions of the constitutionality of sending National Guard units abroad. National Guardsmen are members of organized militias of the various states, and members of the U.S. Army, although not members of both at the same time. When the President orders a National Guard unit into federal service, they are no longer members of the organized militia, but members of the Regular Army.[54]

While not a definition of "militia," the U.S. Supreme Court in *U.S.* v. *Verdugo-Urquidez* (1990), recognized that "the people" referred to in the Second Amendment has the same meaning as it does in the rest of the Bill of Rights, and that the Second Amendment's protections are not limited to those who are active members of the militia:

> Contrary to the suggestion of *amici curiae*[55] that the Framers used this phrase "simply to avoid [an] awkward rhetorical redundancy," ... "the people" seems to have been a term of art employed in select parts of the Constitution. The Preamble declares that the Constitution is ordained and established by "the People of the United States." The Second Amendment protects "the right of the people to keep and bear Arms," and the Ninth and Tenth Amendments provide that certain rights and powers are retained by and reserved to "the people." See also U.S. Const., Amdt. 1, ("Congress shall make no law ... abridging ... *the right of the people* peaceably to assemble"); Art. I, §2, cl. 1 ("The House of Representatives shall be composed of Members chosen every second Year *by the People of the several States*") (emphasis added). While this textual exegesis is by no means conclusive, it suggests that "the people" protected by the Fourth Amendment, and by the First and Second Amendments, and to whom rights and powers are reserved in the Ninth and Tenth Amendments, refers to a class of persons who are part of a national community or who have otherwise developed sufficient connection with this country to be considered part of that community.[56]

Dictionaries give an answer consistent with the use of the word we have found in the quotations above. Both Webster's 1828 *Dictionary* and the OED contain definitions of "militia":

---

52 10 USC §311. Similar provisions exist in many state codes—see California Military & Veterans Code, §§120-123.

53 Senate Subcommittee on The Constitution Staff, "History: Second Amendment Right To 'Keep and Bear Arms'", 11.

54 *Perpich* v. *Department of Defense*, 110 S.Ct. 2418, 2423, 2424 (1990). The limitation that militia could not be forced to serve overseas was in effect as early as the fourteenth century, and was clearly still in effect as late as Henry VIII's reign. A.V.B. Norman and Don Pottinger, *English Weapons & Warfare: 449-1660*, (New York: Dorset Press, 1979), 178, 77-8.

55 "Friends of the court": legal briefs submitted by people and groups not a direct party to the suit.

56 *U.S.* v. *Verdugo-Urquidez*, 110 S.Ct. 1056, 1060, 1061 (1990).

The body of soldiers in a state enrolled for discipline, but not engaged in actual service except in emergencies; as distinguished from regular troops, whose sole occupation is war or military service. The militia of a country are the able bodied men organized into companies, regiments and brigades, with officers of all grades, and required by law to attend military exercises on certain days only, but at other times left to pursue their actual occupations.[57]

As expected, the OED provides a more complete set of definitions, of which only two refer to animate objects. Definition 3a: "A military force, esp. the body of soldiers in the service of a sovereign or a state; in later use employed in more restricted sense..., to denote a 'citizen army' as distinguished from a body of mercenaries or professional soldiers." Definition 4b is listed as a specifically American usage: 'The whole body of men declared by law amenable to military service, without enlistment, whether armed and drilled or not' (*Cent. Dict.* 1890)."[58]

Federalists and Antifederalists in state ratifying conventions, the language of the Militia Act of 1792, current federal and state laws, at least one U.S. Supreme Court decision (*Perpich*), and contemporary dictionaries, *all* agree that the militia was *not* a standing army, not a "select militia" like the National Guard, but the adult free male citizens of the country.

What does "well-regulated" mean? Webster's first definition of "well-regulated" refers to governmental regulation. But the second definition includes: "To put in good order; as, to *regulate* the disordered state of a nation or its finances."[59]

The OED's principal definitions of "well-regulated" include examples of governmental regulation, but also an example from 1812 where the sense is "properly adjusted," such as a clock or sundial. For the word "regulated," the second OED definition is, "Of troops: Properly disciplined," with the note that such use is rare, and only a 1690 example is given.[60]

Andrew Fletcher of Saltoun was one of the political philosophers of the Scottish Enlightenment, and was highly regarded by at least some of the American Revolutionaries.[61] Fletcher's "A Discourse of Government With Relation to Militias" uses the expressions "well-regulated militias" and "ill-regulated militia." The context does not provide a clear definition, but it appears that "properly disciplined" is what Fletcher meant by "well-regulated."[62]

Perhaps the best definition, from the standpoint of determining original intent, would be to find such a use of the phrase "well-regulated" from one of the Framers. We are not disappointed. Alexander Hamilton, in *Federalist* 29, pointed to the economic consequences of drilling the entire militia sufficiently to "[e]ntitle them to the character of a well regulated militia."[63] Certainly, the militia of that time were

---

57 Webster, *An American Dictionary of the English Language*, II, *s.v.* "Militia".
58 OED, 9:768.
59 Webster, *An American Dictionary of the English Language*, II, *s.v.* "Regulate".
60 OED, 13:524.
61 Edmund S. Morgan, "Slavery and Freedom: The American Paradox", *Journal of American History*, 59 [June 1972], 5-29, reprinted in Stanley N. Katz, John M. Murrin, and Douglas Greenberg, ed., *Colonial America: Essays in Politics and Social Development*, 4th ed., (New York: McGraw-Hill, Inc., 1993), 270.
62 Andrew Fletcher, *Selected Political Writings and Speeches*, edited by David Daiches, (Edinburgh: Scottish Academic Press, 1979), 16-17.
63 Alexander Hamilton, "Federalist 29", in Kaminski & Saladino, 3:320.

"regulated" in the sense of being governmentally controlled and directed; Hamilton's meaning would seem to be "properly trained." President James Polk's Inaugural Address of 1845 uses the phrase, "well-regulated self-government among men" in the sense of "properly adjusted."[64]   Indeed, even today, the process by which the barrels of a double-barreled shotgun are made to shoot to the same point is called "regulating a shotgun"—a distinctly non-governmental process, but one that results in a shotgun that can be properly used.

In modern debates about the constitutionality of restrictive gun laws, it is common for "well-regulated" to be thrown out as a red herring, in some way intended as proof that the Framers intended firearms instead of militias to be "well-regulated," in the sense of being strictly controlled.   The meaning of "well-regulated," at least in the context in which it is used in the Second Amendment, is ambiguous, but the bulk of the evidence suggests "well-disciplined."   This does not preclude the notion that the militia was to be under the direction and control of the government—until such time as that government needed to be overthrown—as we will shortly see.   Regardless of the meaning of "well-regulated militia," we will find, as we examine the history of judicial interpretation of the Second Amendment and its state analogs, only a very few courts have argued that "the right of the people" was limited to active members of a state "well-regulated militia...."

---

64 Lott, 90.

II. EUROPEAN ORIGINS

Stephen Halbrook argues that the tradition of a right to keep and bear arms has its roots in the classical world.[1] Because of space limitations, this work makes no attempt at evaluating the claims concerning classical civilization and the right to keep and bear arms.

Like many other civilizations founded on warfare, the Germanic tribes that overran and supplanted the Roman Empire considered that "arms bearing was a right and a duty of free men." Not surprisingly, the Anglo-Saxon culture that developed in Britain continued this tradition of bearing arms in military service.[2] However, the obligation of free men for military duty is not necessarily evidence of an individual right; many nations today have an obligation to military duty, without recognizing any individual right to possess arms. A nation may also provide for the widespread possession of arms as a military necessity, but without recognizing an individual right. An example of arms bearing as a narrowly granted privilege (not a right) can be found in the fourteenth century regulations of France, which prohibited the carrying of offensive weapons by the nobility, but allowed the carrying of defensive arms (if so licensed by the king). Mundy mentions an architect employed by the city of Orvieto who was given "a noble's right to bear arms," again suggesting the limited nature of this right.[3]

Perhaps the best example of this is Niccolo Machiavelli's writings on the need for an armed populace. Machiavelli held that arms in the hands of the citizens would act as a defense from external oppression, and from internal tyranny.[4] But Machiavelli's writings are pragmatic, not utopian. This statement is not necessarily evidence that Machiavelli considered widespread arms ownership an ideal, merely a statement of what *would* happen if a prince relied on military force to maintain his position.

---

1 Stephen P. Halbrook, *That Every Man Be Armed*, (University of New Mexico Press, 1984; reprinted Oakland, Calif.: The Independent Institute, 1984), 9-20.

2 Hardy, 45. Christopher Brooke, *Europe in the Central Middle Ages: 962-1154*, 2nd ed., (New York: Longman Group, 1987), 183. Richard W. Kaeuper, *War, Justice, and Public Order: England and France in the Later Middle Ages*, (Oxford: Clarendon Press, 1988), 17.

3 Kaeuper, 244-5. John H. Mundy, *Europe in the High Middle Ages: 1150-1309*, 2nd ed., (New York: Longman Group, 1991), 94.

4 Niccolo Machiavelli, *Discourses* 2:24, in *Machiavelli: The Chief Works And Others*, transl. Allan Gilbert, (Durham, N.C.: Duke University Press, 1965), 392-3.

Halbrook quotes Machiavelli's *The Prince* as asserting: "[I]t is not reasonable to suppose that one who is armed will obey willingly one who is unarmed; or that any unarmed man will remain safe among armed servants."[5] But Halbrook has quoted Machiavelli out of context. In the fourteenth chapter of *The Prince*, Machiavelli discusses "A Prince's Duty About Military Affairs." After discussing the importance of a prince being interested in military matters, Machiavelli tells us, "The Unmilitary Prince Is Despised":

> Between an armed and an unarmed man there is no reciprocity, and for an armed man gladly to obey one who is unarmed is unreasonable. An unarmed prince cannot be without fear among armed servants, because when the servant feels contempt and the master feels distrust, by no possibility can the two work well together.[6]

While Machiavelli's remarks concerning the nature of the relationship between the armed and unarmed may be extrapolated to the relationship between the people and their government, Machiavelli was concerned about the relationship between a prince and his army—not the citizens of a republic and the government. A better indication of the pragmatic approach that Machiavelli favored may be found by examining another passage from *The Prince*:

> Never has a new prince, then, disarmed his subjects; on the contrary, when he has found them unarmed, invariably he has armed them; because when they are armed those arms become yours; those who you fear become loyal; and those already loyal continue to be so and instead of mere subjects become your partisans. Because all your subjects cannot be armed, if those you do arm feel that they are favored, with the others you can deal more securely...[7]

But Machiavelli is here referring to a government armed and organized militia. On the subject of an "annexed province," Machiavelli is much clearer:

> But when a prince gains a new state that like a member is joined to his old one, then it is necessary to disarm that state, except those who have been your partisans in its conquest; and them as well, with time and opportunity, you must make soft and effeminate, and you must so arrange matters that the weapons of your entire state are in the hands of your own soldiers...[8]

Machiavelli considered an armed citizenry the best defense of the state against threats external and internal; but it is also clear that he did not consider this to be an individual right to keep and bear arms.

Professor Lawrence Cress argues that Machiavelli's republicanism, with its emphasis on civic virtue, strongly influenced James Harrington, and indirectly, Algernon Sidney, John Trenchard,[9] "and a host of other radical Whig essayists." But Cress argues that Harrington and the other radical Whigs did not consider possession of arms as an individual right: "The citizen bore arms not to deter personal assault or to protect the limits of his freehold; for Harrington, bearing arms, like voting, symbolized the political independence that allowed for and ensured a commitment to civic virtue." In Cress' understanding of 18th century Whiggish thought,

---

5 Machiavelli, (transl. L. Ricci, 1952), *The Prince*, 81, quoted in Halbrook, *That Every Man Be Armed*, 24.

6 Machiavelli, transl. Allan Gilbert, *The Prince*, 55.

7 Machiavelli, transl. Allan Gilbert, *The Prince*, 77.

8 Machiavelli, transl. Allan Gilbert, *The Prince*, 78.

9 These were seventeenth century political writers associated with the Whig Party, whose writings had a powerful influence on the ideas of the American Revolutionaries.

"liberty was preserved 'by making the Militia to consist of the same Persons as have the Property.'" Cress also quotes John Toland that arms should be "'in the hands of sober, industrious, and understanding [Freemen.' 'By Freemen,' wrote Toland, 'I understand Men of Property, or Persons that are able to live of themselves.'" Cress understands the republican militia of Harrington to be a system by which those of the leisure class, the elite, the propertied class, who therefore had the time and inclination to be concerned about the public good, would protect their interests, and thus become reliable "defenders of the public interest."[10]

By comparison, Professor Robert Shalhope sees Machiavellian republicanism very differently:

> For Machiavelli, the most dependable protection against corruption was the economic independence of the citizen and his ability and willingness to become a warrior. From this developed the sociology of liberty that rested upon the role of arms in society: political conditions must allow the arming of all citizens; moral conditions must be such that all citizens would willingly fight for the republic; and economic conditions must provide the citizen-soldier a home and occupation outside the army. This theme, relating arms and civic virtue, runs throughout Machiavelli, and from it emerged the belief that arms and a full array of civic rights were inseparable.[11]

Shalhope and Cress come to dramatically different understandings of Machiavellian ideas on arms, citizenship, and civic rights—and yet both cite the same work for their understanding of these ideas—J.G.A. Pocock's *The Machiavellian Moment: Florentine Political Thought and the Atlantic Republican Tradition*.

Considering Shalhope's understanding of Machiavelli, it is not surprising that Shalhope comes to a very different understanding of Harrington's beliefs concerning individual possession of arms:

> Harrington considered the bearing of arms to be the primary means by which individuals affirmed their social power and political participation as responsible moral agents. But now land ownership became the essential basis for the bearing of arms.[12]

Shalhope also quotes many other examples of this connection between popular ownership of arms and resistance to tyranny. Sir Walter Raleigh's "sophisms" of a tyrant included, "To unarm his people of weapons, money, and all means whereby they may resist his power," and the subtle tyrant's variant, "To unarm his people, and store up their weapons, under pretence of keeping them safe, and having them ready when service requireth, and then to arm them with such, and as many as he shall think meet, and to commit them to such as are sure men."[13]

Nor is this view without historical example. One recent history of medieval warfare argues that no European nation other than England adopted the longbow because to become competent with it, "a man needed constant practice, and therefore needed to have his own bow and arrows, not weapons issued from an arsenal in

10 Lawrence Delbert Cress, "An Armed Community: The Origins and Meaning of the Right to Bear Arms", *Journal of American History*, 71:1 [June 1984], 24-25.

11 Robert E. Shalhope, "The Ideological Origins of the Second Amendment", *Journal of American History*, 69:3 [December 1982], 601-2.

12 Shalhope, 603.

13 Walter Raleigh, *The Works of Sir Walter Raleigh, Kt., Now First Collected: To Which Are Prefixed The Lives of the Author, by Oldys and Birch* (Oxford, Eng.: 1829), VIII, 22, 25, quoted in Shalhope, 602.

times of crisis." Because of the gap between the nobles and the peasants, "the French ruling classes did not dare so arm the peasantry."[14]

James Burgh, an English libertarian with a significant influence on the American colonists, put the concept even more crisply:

> No kingdom can be secured otherwise than by arming the people. The possession of arms is the distinction between a freeman and a slave. He, who has nothing, and who himself belongs to another, must be defended by him, whose property he is, and needs no arms. But he, who thinks he is his own master, and has what he can call his own, ought to have arms to defend himself, and what he possesses; else he lives precariously, and at discretion.[15]

There are a number of other examples cited by Shalhope of seventeenth and eighteenth century English libertarian and Whiggish thought on the relationship between individual arms ownership and resisting tyranny, but none are so succinct as Raleigh and Burgh's observations.

Cress interprets Burgh, much as he interprets Harrington, in support of a more limited notion of citizens armed for militia service:

> "Men of property," Burgh insisted, "must be our only resource... A militia consisting of any others than the men of *property* in a country, is no militia; but a mungrel army." The importance of placing arms only in the hands of those "whose interest is involved in that of their country" was historically undeniable.[16]

While Cress sees Harrington's arms-bearing militia as an elite, Shalhope sees Harrington's ideas as "an intellectual foundation for subsequent writers,"[17] and in the New World, where land ownership rapidly became the norm, not the exception, it is easy to see how an elite of English country gentlemen quickly became the armed yeomanry repeatedly recognized as "the militia" in the previous chapter.

Professor Michael Downs, one of Harrington's biographers argues that:

> [T]he relationship between the gentry and the commons, or the people, in Harrington's terms, is the point at issue between Harrington and Machiavelli. Machiavelli believed that gentry and people were natural enemies. To him, every society was divided between those few who were ambitious and sought, first of all, to gain positions of dominance, and the many who wished only to pursue their own livelihood in an atmosphere of safety and security unhindered by the few. As a result of this division, the few, or gentry, and the many, the people, could never be at peace with one another. Harrington disagreed: in Switzerland, the gentry were admired by the people, and both classes cooperated in maintaining a healthy commonwealth... The attitude of gentry and people in regard to one another was determined, not by deeply seated unchanging and incompatible ambitions, but by the distribution of property. A gentry possessing the preponderance of property would be hostile; but, in a state in which the people held the preponderance and the gentry were an elite of talented men instead of powerful men, the gentry would be friendly.[18]

Examination of Pocock's *The Machiavellian Moment* shows that both Cress and Shalhope have correctly identified components of Harrington's beliefs. Pocock tells us that Harrington had added:

---

14 Terence Wise, *Medieval Warfare*, (New York: Hastings House, 1976), 116-7.

15 James Burgh, *Political Disquisitions: Or, an Enquiry into Public Errors, Defects, and Abuses*, (London: 1774-1775), II, 390, quoted in Shalhope, 604.

16 Cress, 27.

17 Shalhope, 603.

18 Downs, 28.

a further dimension—one which, as he put it, Machiavelli had very narrowly missed: the bearing of arms, once it was seen as a function of feudal tenure, proved to be based upon the possession of property. The crucial distinction was that between vassalage and freehold; it determined whether a man's sword was his lord's or his own and the commonwealth's; and the function of free proprietorship became the liberation of arms, and consequently of the personality, for free public action and civic virtue.[19]

Pocock believed that both Harrington and Machiavelli saw that "the bearing of arms is the essential medium through which the individual asserts both his social power and his participation in politics as a responsible moral being..."[20] While Pocock never directly addresses the issue of whether this idea implied an individual right to arms, separate from a citizen's duty to the state, he does recognize that the relationship of arms and citizenship played a role in the writing of the Bill of Rights:

> In a similar way, the Second Amendment to the Constitution, apparently drafted to reassure men's minds against the fact that the federal government would maintain something in the nature of a professional army, affirms the relation between a popular militia and popular freedom in language directly descended from that of Machiavelli, which remains a potent ritual utterance in the United States to this day.[21]

When we compare the distribution of property in Harrington's England, and Revolutionary America, and popular perceptions of the relative positions of the yeomanry and the elite that wrote the state and federal constitutions, it becomes clearer how Cress and Shalhope can both be correct about Harrington's notions of land ownership and militia membership—at different points in time. Cress has focused on Harrington's England, and sees Harrington as an elitist; Shalhope has focused on James Madison's America, and sees Harrington's ideas as supporting a broadly-based republic. But the method by which Harrington's idea of a militia of country gentlemen was transmuted into a militia of yeomen, can now be understood as a reflection of the dramatically widened distribution of property, with America's "natural aristocracy" replacing England's hereditary structure.

The arms technology and sociopolitical structures of 18th century America were dramatically different from classical civilization, and even Machiavelli's Italy; to trace a continuous thread from Plato to James Madison with respect to the Second Amendment requires a thread of great elasticity. In particular, the claim that Machiavellian republicanism is a source of the right to arms remains unpersuasive to this author. But if Machiavelli's ideas did indeed support such a view, once transplanted to English soil, they would have rapidly merged with English traditions of an armed citizenry.

The tradition of an armed citizenry in Britain, as part of the military obligation to the state, is of long standing. Henry II's Assize of Arms of 1181 required all freemen to arm themselves for the common defense, though the lower classes were prohibited from being better armed than was considered "appropriate" to their class. Henry III's Assize of Arms of 1242 again obligated freemen to possess arms, with "all those with incomes of between £2 and £5 to have bows." The Assize of

19 J.G.A. Pocock, *The Machiavellian Moment: Florentine Political Thought and the Atlantic Republican Tradition*, (Princeton, N.J.: Princeton University Press, 1975), 386.
20 Pocock, 390.
21 Pocock, 528.

Arms was reissued with minor changes as Edward I's Statute of Winchester (1285), which contained no restrictions on the sort of weapons the lower classes could possess. The failure of the population to obey the Statute of Winchester caused Henry VIII to reissue it in 1511, obligating every man between 16 and 60 to "possess a bow and know how to use it." The Statute of Winchester remained in effect until 1558.

Of more importance to a study of the liberal nature of the Second Amendment are the laws with respect to armed self-defense. "The Laws of Cnut (1020-1023) not only considered armed self-defense a right and duty," but provided for penalties for illegally disarming a man.[22] Edward III's Statute of Northampton (1328), "made it an offense to ride armed at night, or by day in fairs, markets, or in the presence of king's ministers."[23] However, these restrictions appear to have been aimed at private armies, who sought to intimidate judges and juries in cases involving their feudal lords.[24] Another goal was to discourage knights from engaging in tournaments and the often resulting private wars of the medieval period, though a more general concern about problems of law and order also played a part in these restrictions.[25] (The Statute of Northampton and its clarification by Hawkins will reappear throughout the judicial interpretation chapters of this book.)

Henry VIII's reign was marked by a series of laws that attempted to first restrict ownership of crossbows, then handguns. In 1511, a property qualification of £200 was required to own crossbows (apparently because crossbows were distracting the lower classes from their "proper" weapon, the longbow), followed by a law in 1514 that included firearms under the same property qualification. It became apparent that the law was not being obeyed, and in 1523, the property qualification was reduced to £100. In 1541, even this was relaxed, and the property qualification applied only to guns less than a yard long (the ancestors of the modern concealable firearm). Further, those meeting the property qualification were allowed to carry such weapons with them on the "King's highways and elsewhere."

Coke's *Institutes of the Laws of England*, published in 1671, defending the common law against the crown, held that, "the laws permit the taking up of arms against armed persons." During this same period of time, the Statute of Northampton, prohibiting the carrying of arms, was recognized as intended "to punish people who go armed *to terrify the King's subjects*." Similarly, William Hawkins' *Treatises of the Pleas of the Crown*, recognized the right of every person to arm himself for individual defensive purposes.[26]

As we have seen in the discussion of "to bear arms," Blackstone asserted an individual right to bear arms in self-defense against private criminals. Blackstone is not alone among English legal authorities in arguing for a right to self-defense; Coke also claimed self-defense as an absolute right.[27] The right to self-defense, admittedly, is not a right to arms. But the right to one without the other is akin to freedom of the press without the right to own printing equipment.

---

22 Norman and Pottinger, 39, 60, 147. Halbrook, *That Every Man Be Armed*, 38-40.
23 Weatherup, 134.
24 Wise, 16.
25 Kaeuper, 127, 202-4.
26 Halbrook, *That Every Man Be Armed*, 41-42, 49-50.
27 James J. Featherstone and Richard E. Gardiner, "The Second Amendment Guarantees an Individual Right To Keep and Bear Arms", in *The Right To Keep And Bear Arms*, 84.

Was Blackstone concerned only about *private* criminals? Apparently not. At the end of Chapter One, Book One, in which he articulates the "Absolute Rights of Individuals," Blackstone tells us:

> And, lastly, to vindicate these rights, when actually violated or attacked, the subjects of England are entitled, in the first place, to the regular administration and free course of justice in the courts of law; next, to the right of petitioning the king and parliament for redress of grievances; and lastly, to the right of having and using arms for self-preservation and defense.[28]

In short, arms in private hands were the *last* resort of the people, when peaceful methods had failed. "To arms," was the final court of appeal—as the American colonists demonstrated when they took up arms against the crown. The common law tradition appears to uphold the notion of a "right to bear arms" as an individual right, for the purposes of defending individuals from criminals both private and public.

It is sometimes asserted today that laws restricting firearms ownership have purposes other than the prevention of crime. Charles II's Hunting Act, prohibiting commoners from the possession of guns and bows, had the useful side effect of,

> preventing the "divers idle, disorderly and mean Persons" from securing sustenance and forcing them to continue in a position of serfdom for the benefit of the landlord class. Since it sought to disarm all but the landed aristocracy, the act was also aimed at the aspiring bourgeoisie, the burghers and professionals who supported progressive republicanism and opposed feudal domination. Passed not only to further economic exploitation, the act functioned also to enhance its necessary concomitant—political domination. As Blackstone observed, "prevention of popular insurrections and resistance to the government, by disarming the bulk of the people ... is a reason oftener meant, than avowed, by the makers of the forest and game laws."[29]

This use of arms control laws for reasons of economic exploitation will reappear when we explore the Black Codes and the *Presser* v. *Illinois* (1886) decision in later chapters. Similarly, statutes used to prevent certain classes from hunting have been used on occasion to disarm non-citizens in some American states.[30]

Could Blackstone have meant a collective right only? Is it within the realm of possibility that Blackstone referred only to a right to defend against external aggression, or against government run amok? With respect to invasion, the laws of England would have been quite irrelevant—only the rules of international warfare would have mattered. No victorious conqueror would have cared whether English law granted its population the right to collectively defend the nation. Such a right is completely irrelevant to a commentary on English laws.

That Blackstone was concerned about the dangers of criminal attack may be surmised from his assertion that "resistance and self-preservation" are allowed "when the sanctions of society and laws are found insufficient to restrain the violence of oppression." A tyrannical monarch or Parliament would have the laws on their side—his assertion makes no sense if the "violence of oppression" was governmental in nature.

---

28 Blackstone, Jones ed., §200, 247.

29 Halbrook, *That Every Man Be Armed*, 43.

30 *Patsone* v. *Pennsylvania* 232 U.S. 138, 34 S.Ct. 281 (1909); *People* v. *Zerillo*, 219 Mich. 635, 189 N.W. 927 (1922); and *People* v. *Nakamura*, 99 Colo. 262, 62 P.2d 246 (1936), all demonstrate the use of such laws, to be discussed in later chapters.

The English common law with respect to individual possession of arms was clearly recognized in the colonies. Writings from the period 1768-69, when British forces were increased in Boston to suppress dissent, assert the rights of British subjects to possess arms.[31] Similarly, when John Adams took on his defense of the British soldiers charged in the Boston Massacre of 1770, he cited Hawkins' *Treatises of the Pleas of the Crown*, and agreed that:

> Here every private person is authorized to arm himself, and on the strength of this authority, I do not deny the inhabitants had a right to arm themselves at that time, for their defense, not for offence, that distinction is material and must be attended to.[32]

Although Cress uses the request of the Continental Congress at the beginning of the Revolutionary War, "to disarm all such as will not associate to defend the American rights by arms" as evidence that the right to arms was not clearly recognized by the Revolutionaries,[33] the argument is weak; nations at war engage in denials of civil liberties that would not be acceptable in peacetime, and frequently are looked back upon a few years later with shame. Indeed, the passage of a bill of attainder by the State of Virginia during the Revolutionary War became a subject of some acrimonious discussion during the ratification debates, and even Patrick Henry attempted to justify the bill of attainder because of the war then in progress.[34]

The English common law tradition clearly recognized a right to arms for self-defense against private criminals, and for resistance against governments turned tyrannical. But this was not enough, when the struggle between Parliament and the Jacobean kings led to the English Civil War.

When the English Bill of Rights of 1689 was adopted, the abuses of Charles II and James II were fresh in Parliament's mind. Among these abuses were confiscations of arms, searches for hidden arms caches, a ban on firearms imports, licensing of firearms transport, and record keeping mandated for gunsmiths. In 1671, the Hunting Act was amended to severely restrict arms ownership. Gun and bow ownership was limited to those people with property worth more than £100.[35] It is not surprising that the English Bill of Rights (1689) complained that James II, "Did endeavor to subvert... the laws and liberties of this kingdom...." The specific complaints included "raising and keeping a standing army within this kingdom in time of peace, without consent of parliament, and quartering soldiers contrary to law," and "causing several good subjects, being protestants, to be disarmed, at the same time when papists were both armed and employed, contrary to law."[36]

The English Bill of Rights asserted that the nation was "vindicating and asserting their ancient rights and liberties," including the sixth and seventh articles:

> 6. That the raising or keeping a standing army within the kingdom in time of peace, unless it be with consent of parliament, is against law.

---

31 Halbrook, *That Every Man Be Armed*, 58.
32 L. Kinvin Wroth and Hiller B. Zobel, ed., *Legal Papers of John Adams*, (Cambridge, Mass.: Harvard University Press, 1965), 3:248.
33 Cress, 28.
34 Robert Allen Rutland, *The Birth of the Bill of Rights 1776-1791*, rev. ed., (Boston: Northeastern University Press, 1983), 168.
35 Hardy, 50-51.
36 Walter Laquer and Barry Rubin, ed., *The Human Rights Reader*, (New York: New American Library, 1979), 104.

7. That the subjects which are protestants, may have arms for their defence suitable to their conditions, and as allowed by law.[37]

At first glance, this seventh article sounds like an equivocal, limited right. First of all, the right is limited to Protestants, and in Cress' view, "the Bill of Rights laid down the right of a class of citizens, Protestants, to take part in the military affairs of the realm..." Cress also denies that this was intended as an individual right. But since only 1% of the population of England were openly Catholics at that time, this right would be so generally available, that the practical difference between this right for Protestants, and a general right, would be minor.

Cress makes a great deal of the phrase "suitable to their conditions and as allowed by law," arguing that the history of royal restrictions upon arms possession shows that this was not a "right." The "as provided by law" clause would seem easy to abuse, since gun ownership had been restricted by the 1671 amendment to the Hunting Act—except that this "was clarified by prompt amendment of the Hunting Act to remove the word 'guns' from items which even the poorest Englishman was not permitted to own."[38] While the authority still might exist to restrict arms ownership, that the same Parliament took steps to remove the legal restriction on arms ownership, suggests that "as provided by law" may have not been viewed in the same restrictive manner as Cress sees it.

Cress also holds that, "Nowhere was an individual's right to arm in self-defense guaranteed." It is apparent that Cress sees the phrase "may have arms for their defence" as a collective defensive right, not an individual one.[39] The debates in Parliament on this clause provide evidence in favor of the liberal perspective. The first draft of this right read: "It is necessary for the public safety, that the Subjects which are Protestants, should provide and keep Arms for Their common Defence: And that the Arms, which have been seized, and taken from them, be restored."[40] By removing the phrase, "for Their common Defence," Parliament clarified the individual nature of that right.

The final version of the sixth article expressed the understandable concerns about the dangers of a standing army. Equally clear is that the final version of the seventh article expressed concern about the dangers of *individuals* being disarmed, and this article sought to protect the rights of the overwhelming majority of Englishmen to possess arms. This right was individual, in that it sought to protect individuals from personal injury by criminals, and collective, since it sought to retain the power of individuals to own arms as a restraint on royal abuses.

The American Revolution is a child of the Enlightenment (and not always the child hoped for by the parents); if we wish to understand the well-educated men of the American Revolution, we need an understanding of Enlightenment ideas. In the area of criminal law, Cesare Beccaria's *On Crimes And Punishments*, published in 1764, provides the first organized Enlightenment theory of criminal justice:

Beccaria's book dealt with the state of criminal law. His opposition to arbitrary rule, to cruelty and intolerance, and his belief that no man had the right to take away the life of another human being constituted the moral basis on which his principles were built. His

---

37 Laquer & Rubin, 106.
38 Hardy, 50-51.
39 Cress, 26.
40 Halbrook, *That Every Man Be Armed*, 44.

ideas not only had an impact on all the cultivated people of Europe and America, but influenced the attitudes of statesmen and governments, and brought about needed reforms.

In his lifetime, Beccaria was greatly honored and admired: his cooperation was sought by Catherine the Great of Russia and Maria Theresa of Austria, and his writings were read and quoted by illustrious men of the time, from Voltaire to Thomas Jefferson, from Blackstone to John Adams.[41]

Beccaria's proposals included abolition of torture, and a dramatic reduction, if not abolition, of the death penalty. King Frederick II of Prussia started work on a new criminal code, consciously modelled on Beccaria's writings. While this new criminal code did not abolish the death penalty, it "limited its application to very few cases." The governments of Russia, Sweden, Tuscany, and France (both royal and revolutionary) adopted legal reforms patterned on Beccaria's ideas, the abolition of torture being a distinguishing characteristic. Not all European governments adopted Beccaria's reforms, nor was the revolution in criminal justice immediate, but Beccaria's book brought about not only the abolition of legally sanctioned torture throughout Western Europe, but also the elimination of the death penalty for theft, perjury, and blasphemy in Britain.

America was also influenced by the arguments advanced by Beccaria. When John Adams defended the British soldiers on trial for the Boston Massacre, he quoted Beccaria to the jury as his justification. At the time of the Revolution, Pennsylvania started reform of its criminal codes to bring them more into conformity with Beccaria's ideas. By 1786, these efforts had led to "an act which reserved the punishment of death for four crimes: murder, rape, arson, and treason."

Jefferson was another Revolutionary strongly influenced by Beccaria's ideas. "Jefferson's *Commonplace Book* ... contains ... no less than twenty-six extracts from Beccaria in Italian, all long passages cited in Jefferson's own handwriting,"[42] including Beccaria's comments (below) on carrying arms.[43] Jefferson's "Bill for Proportioning Crimes and Punishments in Cases heretofore Capital," introduced in the Virginia Legislature in 1778, repeatedly references Beccaria. When finally passed in 1796, it abolished the death penalty for all crimes except treason and murder.[44]

Beccaria's *On Crimes And Punishments* asserted:

False is the idea of utility that sacrifices a thousand real advantages for one imaginary or trifling inconvenience; that would take fire from men because it burns, and water because one may drown in it; that has no remedy for evils, except destruction. *The laws that forbid the carrying of arms are laws of such a nature. They disarm only those who are neither inclined nor determined to commit crimes.* Can it be supposed that those who have the courage to violate the most sacred laws of humanity, the most important of the code, will respect the less important and arbitrary ones, which can be violated with ease and impunity, and which, if strictly obeyed, would put an end to personal liberty—so dear to men, so dear to the enlightened legislator—and subject innocent persons to all the vexations that the guilty alone ought to suffer? *Such laws make things worse for the assaulted and better for the assailants; they serve rather to encourage than to prevent homicides, for an*

---

41 Marcello Maestro, *Cesare Beccaria and the Origins of Penal Reform,* (Philadelphia: Temple University Press, 1973), 3.
42 Maestro, 134-8, 141.
43 Halbrook, *That Every Man Be Armed,* 35, 209.
44 Maestro, 141-2.

unarmed man may be attacked with greater confidence than an armed man. They ought to be designated as laws not preventive but fearful of crimes, produced by the tumultuous impression of a few isolated facts, and not by thoughtful consideration of the inconveniences and advantages of a universal decree.[45] [emphasis added]

Beccaria certainly argued for an *individual* permission to carry weapons for self-defense. There was no notion of military duty or collective action expressed. It can not be established that Beccaria's argument for individuals carrying arms for self-defense led to the Second Amendment—but it does establish that European laws immediately before the American Revolution prohibited the bearing of arms, and Beccaria, a major influence on Revolutionary America's legal thought, strongly disapproved of them.

If the idea of allowing ordinary people to carry arms for self-defense was present in this widely read work of the time, and yet was not seriously debated in the context of the Second Amendment, we should wonder: was this widely known idea considered so strange that it was not seriously considered, or was it so widely accepted, that it was not seriously disputed? The reader is encouraged to consider the debates that might take place today considering the essential rights of Americans. Doubtless, "the right to keep and bear arms" would be argued at great length in any public meeting framing a new Bill of Rights; would anyone seriously debate the right of an individual to own a personal computer? The rights in dispute are always more thoroughly argued than the rights on which agreement is universal.

If, as we study the state constitutions and requests for a Bill of Rights, we find that the "right to keep and bear arms" was expressed as an *individual* right for self-defense, with no significant debate about the wisdom of such a right, the currency of Beccaria's ideas on this subject should give us reason to at least *suspect* that the individual right to keep and bear arms was not under serious dispute.

The notion of an individual right to arms is one of the significant differences between English and continental European traditions, but as we have seen, even under English law, this right was limited to certain classes, depending on the circumstances. In America, as with so many other rights, the idealism of the Revolution would take a guarantee hedged with exceptions, and turn it into a right shared by all.

---

45 Cesare Beccaria, trans. by Henry Palolucci, *On Crimes And Punishments*, (New York: Bobbs-Merrill Co., 1963), 87-88.

III. The Legislative History Of The Second Amendment

In determining the legislative intent of the Second Amendment, there are several areas appropriate for study: state constitutions of the period, the various states' requests for a Bill of Rights, the actions of the First Congress with respect to the Second Amendment, and contemporary commentaries on the meaning of the Second Amendment. In studying these documents, our goal is to examine their relationship to the ideas of resisting tyranny and self-defense.

Not surprisingly, many of the provisions contained in the Bill of Rights were present, in one form or another, in the constitutions adopted during the Revolutionary period. Those constitutions adopted before the Bill of Rights can tell us what sense "the right to keep and bear arms" had in the political vocabulary of the time.

Pennsylvania's 1776 Constitution declared: "That the people have a right to bear arms for the defence of themselves and the state...." Vermont's Constitution of 1777 similarly proclaimed: "That the people have a right to bear arms for the defence of themselves and the State..." The Vermont Constitution of 1786 retained the same individual rights wording.[1] If, as the republican school claims, the "right to keep and bear arms" reflected concerns about the enlarged powers of the central government, why do these state constitutions contain explicitly *individual* guarantees of the right to keep and bear arms? The evidence shows that at least some significant fraction of the newly independent states were worried not only about common defense, but also about personal self-defense. What motivated these concerns? Common defense is clear; the skirmishes at Lexington and Concord were the result of British attempts at seizing militia stores. Was self-defense and personal ownership of arms simply an expression of the common law right articulated by Blackstone?

South Carolina's 1776 Constitution, which combined elements of the American Declaration of Independence and a state charter, contained the telling claim:

> [H]ostilities having been commenced in the Massachusetts Bay, by the troops under command of General Gage, whereby a number of peaceable, helpless, and unarmed people were wantonly robbed and murdered... The colonists were therefore driven to the necessity of taking up arms, to repel force by force, and to defend themselves and their properties against lawless invasions and depredations.

---

1 Francis Newton Thorpe, ed., *The Federal and State Constitutions, Colonial Charters, and Other Organic Laws of the States, Territories, and Colonies,* (Washington: Government Printing Office, 1909), 5:3083, 6:3753-4, 6:3741.

There were a number of other state constitutions adopted during this period of time, however, that seem to argue for a republican reading of the intent of the Second Amendment. Massachusetts's 1780 Constitution asserted: "The people have a right to keep and bear arms for the common defence." Similarly, the North Carolina Constitution of 1776 restricted the people's "right to bear arms, for the defence of the State."[2]

This may be an indication that no general right to keep and bear arms was intended; it is hard to imagine why "for the common defence" would be present, unless it was intended to limit the breadth of that right—but as we will see in *Simpson* v. *State* (1833) and *State* v. *Huntly* (1843), "for the common defence" had an idiomatic meaning strikingly different from our twentieth century understanding. Other evidence that "for the common defence" has a meaning other than a collective one is that this clause was drafted by John Adams. As we have seen, Adams admitted an individual right to bear arms for self-defense at the Boston Massacre trial, and would later argue "arms in the hands of citizens [may] be used at individual discretion."[3] But there is also evidence for the collective understanding of "for the common defense." The town of Williamsburg expressed its disapproval of the 1780 Massachusetts Constitution's arms provision, insisting that, "[W]e esteem it an essential priviledge to keep Arms in Our houses for Our Own Defence and while we Continue honest and Lawful Subjects of Government we Ought never to be deprived of them."[4]

The New York Constitution of 1777 contains no guarantee of an individual right to keep and bear arms—but it does contain an interesting obligation:

> And whereas it is of the utmost importance to the safety of every State that it should always be in a condition of defence; and it is the duty of every man who enjoys the protection of society to be prepared and willing to defend it; this convention therefore, in the name and by the authority of the good people of this State, doth ordain, determine, and declare that *the militia of this State, at all times hereafter, as well in peace as in war, shall be armed and disciplined, and in readiness for service...*

> And that *a proper magazine of warlike stores, proportionate to the number of inhabitants,* be, forever hereafter, at the expense of this State, and by acts of the legislature, established, maintained, and continued *in every county in this State.*[5] [emphasis added]

A statutory Bill of Rights was adopted by the New York Legislature, including a provision identical to the Second Amendment (except for the words "cannot" replacing "shall not");[6] but, because it was not part of the Constitution, merely a statute passed by the legislature, it was not a limitation on later statutes passed by the legislature.[7]

The "duty of every man" included defense of the State, either in person, or for conscientious objectors, by the payment of in lieu fees. The "militia of this State, at

---

2 Thorpe, 6:3242, 3:1892, 5:2788.

3 Halbrook, *That Every Man Be Armed,* 65.

4 O. Handlin & M. Handlin, eds., *The Popular Sources of Political Authority: Documents on the Massachusetts Constitution of 1780,* (1966), 624, quoted in Robert E. Shalhope, "The Armed Citizen in the Early Republic", in *Law and Contemporary Problems,* 49:1 [Winter 1986], 135.

5 Thorpe, 5:2637.

6 *Moore* v. *Gallup,* N.Y.S.2d 63, 267 App. Div. 64, 67, 294 N.Y. 699 (1943).

7 *People ex rel. Darling* v. *Warden of City Prison,* 139 N.Y.S. 277, 154 App. Div. 413, 421, 29 N.Y.Cr. 74 (1913).

all times hereafter, ... shall be armed and disciplined, and in readiness for service..."
strongly suggests that New York intended a citizen's militia along the lines of the
Swiss Army. In light of the definition of "militia" provided by George Mason at
the Virginia ratifying convention, it would appear that in the words of Patrick
Henry, "The great object is, that every man be armed... Every one who is able may
have a gun."[8] Is this a "*right* to keep and bear arms," or an *obligation*? If the Second Amendment derives from such an obligation, the republican claim that no individual right was intended, can not be easily brushed aside. While every man
would be armed under such a system, except for the "religiously scrupulous," the
arms would be for the purpose of collective defense. An individual right might still
exist, separate from the collective obligations, but evidence would have to be produced to uphold that position.

Of perhaps the most importance to a history of the Second Amendment, is the
wording of the militia clause. While the statutory Bill of Rights is in nearly identical language to the Second Amendment, there is no commonality of language between the Second Amendment and the 1777 New York State Constitution's provision requiring the militia, "shall be armed and disciplined..." With respect to New
York, the adoption of a provision nearly identical to the Second Amendment, when
a constitutional provision clearly articulating the republican-collectivist understanding was already in place, suggests that the motivations behind the two provisions
were not identical. The militia clause created a militia; if the goal of the New York
analog to the Second Amendment was to protect the independence of the militia,
not an individual right, why bother reiterating it?

There are a number of indications of a more indirect nature concerning the right
to keep and bear arms. The New Hampshire Constitution of 1784 asserts, in Part I
§10:

> Government being instituted for the common benefit, protection, and security of the
> whole community, and not for the private interest or emolument of any one man, family
> or class of men; therefore, whenever the ends of government are perverted, and public
> liberty manifestly endangered, and all other means of redress are ineffectual, the people
> may, and of right ought, to reform the old, or establish a new government. The doctrine
> of non-resistance against arbitrary power, and oppression, is absurd, slavish, and destruc-
> tive of the good and happiness of mankind.[9]

This was not a guarantee of a right to keep and bear arms, of course, and there was
no such right contained within the New Hampshire Constitution—until 1982—
but it is hard to imagine how this right to revolution could be implemented, if not
by force of arms. This is not proof that the authors of the 1784 constitution pic-
tured an individual right—but in conjunction with the radical request that
"Congress shall never disarm any Citizen" made four years later by the New
Hampshire ratifying convention (to be discussed later in this chapter), it is hard to
imagine the men of New Hampshire arguing that such a right was *not* individual.

"Select militias" had been proposed on a number of occasions during the period
after the Revolution; these were, in a sense, the equivalent of today's National
Guard—groups of private citizens who would receive extra training, above and be-

8 Elliot, 3:386.
9 Thorpe, 4:2455.

yond the regular militia.[10] Select militias were evidently not popular at the time of
the Constitutional Convention in Philadelphia. On August 18, 1787, the Convention had debated the militia clause of the Constitution; specifically, what sort of
authority the federal government should have over the militia. Mr. Dickinson suggested that Congress' authority be limited to "one fourth part at a time, which, by
rotation, would discipline the whole militia." George Mason was concerned that
such a scheme would create "insuperable objections to the plan" and proposed that
Congress' authority be limited to only one tenth of the militia in any given year.
James Madison thought the authority over the militia was not "divisible between
two distinct authorities" and felt that federal authority over the entire militia was
acceptable. Mr. Ellsworth considered a select militia "impracticable; and if it were
not, it would be followed by a ruinous declension of the great body of the militia."[11]
    On August 23, 1787, debate on the militia clause of the Constitution resumed.
In debating the meaning of the phrase, "To make laws for organizing, arming, and
disciplining the militia...," Mr. King explained that,

> by *organizing*, the committee meant, proportioning the officers and men—by *arming*,
> specifying the kind, size, and calibre of arms—and by *disciplining*, prescribing the man-
> ual exercise, evolutions, &c.

Elbridge Gerry expressed his opposition to this clause because it would make

> the state drill-sergeants. He had as lief [would as readily] let the citizens of
> Massachusetts be disarmed, as to take the command from the states, and subject them to
> the general legislature. It would be regarded as a system of despotism.

> Mr. MADISON observed, that "*arming*," as explained, did not extend to furnishing
> arms; nor the term "*disciplining*," to penalties, and courts martial for enforcing them.

> Mr. KING added to his former explanation, that *arming* meant not only to provide for
> uniformity of arms, but included the authority to regulate the modes of furnishing,
> either by the militia themselves, the state governments, or the national treasury....[12]

Gerry expressed his disapproval of federal authority over state militias by comparing
it to disarming the citizens of Massachusetts—"a system of despotism." Whatever
the authority of the federal government with respect to command of the militia,
Gerry could be comfortable comparing it to disarming the "citizens of
Massachusetts" as a basis of ridicule, and be confident that the other Framers would
recognize it as such. The implication is that the Framers recognized a right of
citizens to individually possess arms.
    Many states made requests for amendments to the Constitution, reflecting the
concerns of both Federalists and Antifederalists in the various states. The requests
of only five state ratifying conventions were entered in the official journal of the
First Congress in 1789: Massachusetts, South Carolina, New Hampshire, Virginia,
and New York.[13] Some states neglected to make any requests for a Bill of Rights;
others, such as North Carolina and Rhode Island, did not ratify until after Madison's proposals had already been debated.

---

10 Lee, 25, in Paul Ford, *Pamphlets On The Constitution of the United States,* 305.
11 Elliot, 5:444.
12 Elliot, 5:465.
13 Bickford & Veit, 4:4, 4:12-26.

In Pennsylvania, the Federalist faction overwhelmed the Antifederalists at the state convention and approved the Constitution by a 46-23 vote. Attempts by the Antifederalists to add their request for a Bill of Rights were defeated by the same 46-23 margin. In response, 21 of the 23 Antifederalist delegates met after the convention,[14] and on December 18, 1787, published "The Address and Reasons of Dissent of the Minority of the Convention" in the *Pennsylvania Packet and Daily Advertiser*, which included their request for a Bill of Rights. While lacking the official status of the Pennsylvania ratifying convention, this can be considered to be a statement of the Antifederalist position, and should be studied alongside the official requests made by other state ratifying conventions.

The Pennsylvania Antifederalists' request included an amendment that can be clearly seen as a predecessor to the Second Amendment:

> That the people have a right to bear arms *for the defence of themselves* and their own state, or the United States, or for the purpose of killing game; and *no law shall be passed for disarming the people or any of them, unless for crimes committed, or real danger of public injury from individuals*; and as standing armies in the time of peace are dangerous to liberty, they ought not to be kept up; and that the military shall be kept under strict subordination to and be governed by the civil powers.[15] [emphasis added]

These phrases leave no doubt that the Antifederalists in Pennsylvania desired an *individual* right to keep and bear arms. The phrase "the people or any of them, unless for crimes committed" shows that only as punishment for a crime would individuals be disarmed. The phrase "or real danger of public injury from individuals" appears to be intended to handle those cases where no crime was alleged or proven, but where a clear-cut hazard by particular individuals could be established.

Professor Cress asserts that the Pennsylvania and New Hampshire requests show that they had not "moved far, if they had moved at all, beyond the eighteenth century notion that bearing arms meant militia service. That both states carefully qualified the individual's right to arms points the same conclusion."[16] But to call the Pennsylvania request "carefully qualified" is absurd—in fact, it "carefully qualified" the conditions under which the "individual's right to arms" could be restricted.

The request also showed a concern about standing armies, and the desire for "strict subordination" showed the concerns about military dictatorship. That this is expressed in the same paragraph as the "right to bear arms for the defense of themselves and their own state" suggests that a connection existed between personal armaments and the dangers of standing armies in the minds of the drafters—much as the English Parliament saw an obvious connection between private arms and standing armies.

Tench Coxe of Pennsylvania, attempting to reassure those who were concerned about standing armies, claimed that: "The militia... will form a powerful check upon the regular troops, and will generally be sufficient to over-awe them—for our detached situation will seldom give occasion to raise an army, though a few scat-

---

14 Rutland, rev. ed., 140-1.
15 "The Address and Reasons of Dissent of the Minority of the Convention of the State of Pennsylvania to their Constitutents", in Kaminski & Saladino, 3:19.
16 Cress, 34.

tered companies may often be necessary."[17] As discussed on page 11, Coxe asserted that revolution was the last resort of the people against aristocratic oppression; and assumed the ability of "friends to liberty" to possess arms for that purpose.

An Antifederalist essay published January 8, 1788, in the Philadelphia *Independent Gazetteer*, under the pseudonym "Centinel," warned of a possible conspiracy under way:

> The more I consider the manoeuvres that are practising, the more am I alarmed—forseeing that the juggle cannot long be concealed, and that the spirit of the people will not brook the imposition, they have guarded as they suppose against any danger arising from the opposition of the people, and rendered their struggles for liberty impotent and ridiculous. What otherwise is the meaning of disarming the militia, for the purpose as it is said, of repairing their musquets at such a particular period?... Are not these corps provided to suppress the first efforts of freedom, and to check the spirit of the people until a regular and sufficiently powerful military force shall be embodied to rivet the chains of slavery on a deluded nation.[18]

Another expression of the connection between private possession of arms, and restraints on tyranny can be found in Federalist delegate T. Sedgwick's remarks at the Massachusetts ratifying convention. When the subject of standing armies was raised, Sedgwick argued for ratification of the Constitution, and against the concerns about Federal power. He asserted that it was

> a chimerical idea to suppose that a country like this could ever be enslaved. How is an army for that purpose to be obtained from the freemen of the United States? They certainly, said he, will know to what object it is to be applied. Is it possible, he asked, that an army could be raised for the purpose of enslaving themselves and their brethren? or, if raised, whether they could subdue a nation of freemen, who know how to prize liberty, and who have arms in their hands?[19]

Sedgwick's argument was that the population was armed, and in such a manner that it would be impossible for a standing army to overwhelm the people. While this provides evidence for a republican view of the Second Amendment, it also shows that Sedgwick (and presumably those to whom the argument was aimed) recognized that arms would be widely distributed and available to "freemen of the United States."

At the Massachusetts ratifying convention, Theophilus Parsons explained why a Bill of Rights was not needed to protect the rights of individuals or the states:

> But there is another check, founded in the nature of the Union, superior to all the parchment checks that can be invented. If there should be a usurpation, it will not be on the farmer and merchant, employed and attentive only to their several occupations; it will be upon thirteen legislatures, completely organized, possessed of the confidence of the people, and having the means, as well as inclination, successfully to oppose it. Under these circumstances, none but madmen would attempt a usurpation. But, sir, the people themselves have it in their power effectually to resist usurpation, without being driven to an appeal of arms. An act of usurpation is not obligatory; it is not law; and any man may be justified in his resistance. Let him be considered as a criminal by the general government, yet only his fellow-citizens can convict him; they are his jury, and if they pro-

---

17 Coxe, 21, in Paul Ford, *Pamphlets On The Constitution of the United States,* 150-151.
18 "Centinel", "Centinel IX", in Kaminski & Saladino, 3:311.
19 Elliot, 1:97.

nounce him innocent, not all the powers of Congress can hurt him; and innocent they certainly will pronounce him, if the supposed law he resisted was an act of usurpation.[20]

Parsons assumed that individual citizens would not rise up alone against the federal government; yet clearly he recognized that "the people" were within their rights to "resist usurpation" by "an appeal of arms." Instead, he assumed that oppressive laws would be nullified by juries refusing to convict people accused of breaking unjust laws.

Massachusetts is one of the states whose request for a Bill of Rights, adopted February 6, 1788, did not include a predecessor to the Second Amendment—but came very close to doing so. Samuel Adams, John Adams' fiery but lesser known cousin, was a delegate to the Massachusetts ratifying convention. Adams proposed that a Bill of Rights be added to the state convention's ratification of the Constitution:

> And that the said Constitution be never construed to authorize Congress to infringe the just liberty of the press, or the rights of conscience; *or to prevent the people of the United States, who are peaceable citizens, from keeping their own arms;* or to raise standing armies, unless when necessary for the defence of the United States, or of some one or more of them; or to prevent the people from petitioning, in a peaceable and orderly manner, the federal legislature, for a redress of grievances; or to subject the people to unreasonable searches and seizures of their persons, papers or possessions.[21] [emphasis added]

In the ensuing machinations of Federalists and Antifederalists, Adams attempted to withdraw his own motion, at which point the Antifederalists revived it, and Adams voted against his own motion. It lost 187-168—a very narrow victory for the Federalists, and indicative of the widespread support that this list of rights had among Massachusetts delegates. It would be tempting to assume that Adams' list of rights was derived from the Pennsylvania minority report, but "The Address and Reasons of Dissent" did not reach Boston until after the Massachusetts convention had ratified the Constitution, without a request for a Bill of Rights.[22]

Professor Cress tells us that Adams "withdrew the proposal, however, probably after reflecting on the recent revolt by armed citizens in Massachusetts." His source appears to be Elliot's *Debates in the Several State Conventions*; review of the pages cited provides no evidence for Cress' conclusion. Cress also informs us: "Samuel Adams's recommendation allowed for the disarming of citizens falling outside the category of 'peaceable.' In other words, the order and security of society took precedence over the individual's right to arms."[23]

Criminal convictions, then as now, caused a loss of many of the rights that law-abiding citizens take for granted: freedom of movement, freedom of the press, protections from unreasonable search and seizure. To make the leap from disarming criminals, to disarming everyone, is equivalent to using the presence of jails as evidence that anyone could be incarcerated "for the order and security of society." It is *conceivable* that Samuel Adams' "peaceable citizens" was intended in a substantially narrower sense than we would use the expression today—but it is hard to imagine why Adams would have requested such a right, if it were intended to be limited to a tiny fraction of the society.

---

20 Elliot, 2:94.

21 *Debates of the Massachusetts Convention of 1788* (Boston: 1856), 86-87, quoted in Rutland, rev. ed., 147.

22 Rutland, rev. ed., 144, 147.

23 Cress, 34.

Once again, a request for a Bill of Rights had been made, recognizing the right of "peaceable citizens ... keeping their own arms," with no suggestion that such arms were specific to military duty or obligations. The phrase "keeping their *own* arms" shows that these were not governmentally owned weapons, which individuals kept in their homes, but were personally owned.

South Carolina's list of desired amendments to the Constitution, adopted May 23, 1788, is remarkably short, and contained no request for a right to keep and bear arms. South Carolina did request an amendment prohibiting a standing army in peacetime, except with the "consent of three fourths of the Members of each branch of Congress." The only amendment of the Bill of Rights clearly recognizable in South Carolina's request is the Tenth Amendment, reserving powers to the states.[24] South Carolina's proposed amendments contribute nothing meaningful to the liberal/republican dispute.

If the "right to keep and bear arms" was missing, but many other elements of the Bill of Rights were present, this could be interpreted as indicating a lack of interest or concern about "the right to keep and bear arms." But nearly all the other protections of our Bill of Rights were missing also, reflecting an uncomfortable situation for Charles Pinckney, a South Carolina delegate to the Constitutional Convention. Pinckney had made several proposals at the Constitutional Convention for what amounted to a Bill of Rights, but:

> Bills of rights usually began with a statement to the effect that all men are born free and equal. "Now," said Pinckney, the delegates realized that it would "make that declaration with a very bad grace, when a large part of our property consists of men who are actually born slaves."...
>
> Pinckney said that if the South insisted on slavery, it must be consistent and not talk about the natural freedom of all mankind.

The strength of such arguments appears to have put the Antifederalists that were arguing for a Bill of Rights at a disadvantage at the state convention. The Federalists controlled the convention, and the changes adopted were in response to "tedious but trifling opposition."[25]

New Hampshire's convention adopted a list of amendments on June 21, 1788. While longer than the requests of South Carolina and Massachusetts, the New Hampshire convention lacked the verbosity of the Virginia and New York conventions. New Hampshire's proposed amendments included two ancestors of the two different clauses of the Second Amendment. The tenth request was: "That no standing Army shall be Kept up in time of Peace unless with the consent of three fourths of the Members of each branch of Congress, nor shall Soldiers in Time of Peace be Quartered upon private Houses without the consent of the Owners...." The latter half of this proposal is clearly the ancestor of the Third Amendment; less direct is the connection to the first half of the Second Amendment. The same concerns about the dangers of a standing army that motivated the Pennsylvania and South Carolina requests and Samuel Adams' motion in the Massachusetts convention, appear to have motivated this New Hampshire request.

---

24 Bickford & Veit, 4:13-15.
25 Rutland, rev. ed., 113-4, 156-7.

The twelfth request was: "Congress shall never disarm any Citizen unless such as are or have been in Actual Rebellion."[26] This request is the most extreme form of "the right to keep and bear arms." The phrase "never disarm any Citizen" leaves little opportunity to argue that New Hampshire's request was for a collective right. The conditions under which New Hampshire was prepared to accept Congress disarming someone—"Actual Rebellion"—suggests that the right to arms was so basic that only the most serious of crimes could justify taking it away.

Even though New Hampshire's ratification had given the Constitution the nine states required for the new government to start operations, Virginia's ratification was still of great importance, because of its wealth and size.[27] Consequently, the battle between Federalist and Antifederalist was involved and trying. The danger of standing armies, and the risks of federal tyranny, formed a large part of the Virginia ratification debates, with Patrick Henry and George Mason being the principal opponents of ratification without a Bill of Rights.

Patrick Henry's eloquence was well used during the ratification debates. He articulated the essential problem that freedom is preserved only by the threat of revolution: "Guard with jealous attention the public liberty. Suspect every one who approaches that jewel. Unfortunately, nothing will preserve it but downright force. Whenever you give up that force, you are inevitably ruined."[28] While acknowledging that many of the concerns that motivated the new Constitution were legitimate, Henry reminded those present that there were other dangers present, besides the "anarchy" which the Constitution proposed to correct:

> We are cautioned by the honorable gentleman, who presides, against faction and turbulence. I acknowledge that licentiousness is dangerous, and that it ought to be provided against: I acknowledge, also, the new form of government may effectually prevent it: yet there is another thing it will as effectually do—it will oppress and ruin the people.[29]

Henry cautioned the delegates that protections for individual rights were lacking in the proposed Constitution, and that the militia was the only defense against tyranny—hence his concern about the powers over the militia being given to the Federal Government:

> In some parts of the plan before you, the great rights of freemen are endangered; in other parts, absolutely taken away. How does your trial by jury stand? In civil cases gone— not sufficiently secured in criminal—this best privilege is gone. But we are told that we need not fear; because those in power, being our representatives, will not abuse the powers we put in their hands. I am not well versed in history, but I will submit to your recollection, whether liberty has been destroyed most often by the licentiousness of the people, or by the tyranny of rulers. I imagine, sir, you will find the balance on the side of tyranny. Happy will you be if you miss the fate of those nations, who, omitting to resist their oppressors, or negligently suffering their liberty to be wrested from them, have groaned under intolerable despotism! Most of the human race are now in this deplorable condition; and those nations who have gone in search of grandeur, power, and splendor, have also fallen a sacrifice, and been the victims of their own folly. While they acquired those visionary blessings, they lost their freedom. My great objection to this government is, that it does not leave us the means of defending our rights, or of waging wars against tyrants. It is urged by some gentlemen, that this new plan will bring us an

---

26 Bickford & Veit, 4:14-15.
27 Rutland, rev. ed., 162.
28 Elliot, 3:45.
29 Elliot, 3:46.

acquisition of strength—an army, and the militia of the states. This is an idea extremely ridiculous: gentlemen cannot be earnest. This acquisition will trample on our fallen liberty. Let my beloved Americans guard against that fatal lethargy that has pervaded the universe. Have we the means of resisting disciplined armies, when our only defence, the militia, is put into the hands of Congress?[30]

In stinging language, Henry reminded those present—as he reminds us today—that against ambitious and tyrannical forces in charge of the federal government, only force would be an effective check:

The honorable gentleman who presides told us that, to prevent abuses in our government, we will assemble in Convention, recall our delegated powers, and punish our servants for abusing the trust reposed in them. O sir, we should have fine times, indeed, if, to punish tyrants, it were only sufficient to assemble the people! Your arms, wherewith you could defend yourselves, are gone.... Did you ever read of any revolution in a nation, brought about by the punishment of those in power, inflicted by those who had no power at all? You read of a riot act in a country which is called one of the freest in the world, where a few neighbors cannot assemble without the risk of being shot by a hired soldiery, the engines of despotism. We may see such an act in America.[31]

Henry's concerns about "a hired soldiery, the engines of despotism" in Britain were well-founded, as the Peterloo Massacre of 1819[32] and the incidents that led up to *Presser* v. *Illinois* (1886) demonstrate.

Next, Henry argued that if the Federal Government did not arm its citizens, they would be unable to arm themselves—an implausible position, in light of the widespread ownership of arms common at the time:

A standing army we shall have, also, to execute the execrable commands of tyranny; and how are you to punish them? Will you order them to be punished? Who shall obey these orders? Will your mace-bearer be a match for a disciplined regiment? In what situation are we to be? The clause before you gives a power of direct taxation, unbounded and unlimited, exclusive power of legislation, in all cases whatsoever, for ten miles square, and over all places purchased for the erection of forts, magazines, arsenals, dockyards, &c. What resistance could be made? The attempt would be madness. You will find all the strength of this country in the hands of your enemies; their garrisons will naturally be the strongest places in the country. Your militia is given up to Congress, also, in another part of this plan: they will therefore act as they think proper: all power will be in their own possession. You cannot force them to receive their punishment: of what service would militia be to you, when, most probably, you will not have a single musket in the state? For, as arms are to be provided by Congress, they may or may not furnish them.[33]

Here Henry argued that the Federal Government's authority over the state militias would be used in such a way as to render them useless—apparently arguing that without the government to arm and train them, the people would be incapable of rising up in revolution against tyranny.

Let me here call your attention to that part which gives the Congress power "to provide for organizing, arming, and disciplining the militia, and for governing such part of them as may be employed in the service of the United States—reserving to the states, respectively, the appointment of the officers, and the authority of training the militia according

30 Elliot, 3:47-48.
31 Elliot, 3:51-52.
32 John Carey, ed., *Eyewitness to History*, (Cambridge, Mass.: Harvard University Press, 1988), 299-301.
33 Elliot, 3:51-52.

to the discipline prescribed by Congress." By this, sir, you see that their control over our last and best defence is unlimited. If they neglect or refuse to discipline or arm our militia, they will be useless; the states can do neither—this power being exclusively given to Congress.... Will the oppressor let go the oppressed? Was there ever an instance? Can the annals of mankind exhibit one single example where rulers overcharged with power willingly let go the oppressed, though solicited and requested most earnestly?... Sometimes, the oppressed have got loose by one of those bloody struggles that desolate a country; but a willing relinquishment of power is one of those things which human nature never was, nor ever will be, capable of.[34]

Henry was accused by his opponents in the convention of using his rhetorical skills to propound contradictory arguments, and nowhere is this better illustrated than in the following speech:

Where are your checks in this government? Your strongholds will be in the hands of your enemies. It is on a supposition that your American governors shall be honest, that all the good qualities of this government are founded; but its defective and imperfect construction puts it in their power to perpetrate the worst of mischiefs, should they be bad men; and, sir, would not all the world, from the eastern to the western hemisphere, blame our distracted folly in resting our rights upon the contingency of our rulers being good or bad? Show me that age and country where the rights and liberties of the people were placed on the solid chance of their rulers being good men, without a consequent loss of liberty! I say that the loss of that dearest privilege has ever followed, with absolute certainty, every such mad attempt.

If your American chief be a man of ambition and abilities, how easy is it for him to render himself absolute! The army is in his hands, and if he be a man of address, it will be attached to him, and it will be the subject of long meditation with him to seize the first auspicious moment to accomplish his design; and, sir, will the American spirit solely relieve you when this happens?... [T]he President, in the field, at the head of his army, can prescribe the terms on which he shall reign master, so far that it will puzzle any American ever to get his neck from under the galling yoke. I cannot with patience think of this idea. If ever he violates the laws, one of two things will happen: he will come at the head of his army, to carry every thing before him; or he will give bail, or do what Mr. Chief Justice will order him. If he be guilty, will not the recollection of his crimes teach him to make one bold push for the American throne? Will not the immense difference between being master of every thing, and being ignominiously tried and punished, powerfully excite him to make this bold push? But, sir, where is the existing force to punish him? Can he not, at the head of his army, beat down every opposition? Away with your President! we shall have a king: the army will salute him monarch: your militia will leave you, and assist in making him king, and fight against you: and what have you to oppose this force? What will then become of you and your rights? Will not absolute despotism ensue?[35]

While his argument about the hazards of a President gone mad with monarchial ambitions is compelling—and in light of the experience of revolutionary governments throughout the world, especially these last two centuries, eerily prophetic— his contradictory assumption is that the militia, already well-established to be "the people," would obey the orders of such a President.

Henry appears to have used "people" as a rhetorical device to refer to the state governments—or so one must assume, after reading his declaration:

Congress, by the power of taxation, by that of raising an army, and by their control over the militia, have the sword in one hand, and the purse in the other. Shall we be safe

---

34 Elliot, 3:51-52.
35 Elliot, 3:59-60.

without either? Congress have an unlimited power over both: they are entirely given up
by us. Let him candidly tell me, where and when did freedom exist, when the sword
and purse were given up from the people? Unless a miracle in human affairs interposed,
no nation ever retained its liberty after the loss of the sword and purse.[36]

The power of taxation was, of course, already in the hands of the state governments,
and in the sense that Henry meant it, so was the power of the sword. Did Henry
mean that the state governments represented "the people" in a way that the distant
Federal Government would not? Probably, but the net significance of this speech
relative to a *right* to individual arms ownership is zero; it neither supports it, nor
denies it. Nonetheless, it would be hard to imagine a man who viewed armed
revolution as the only defense against tyranny, arguing against the widespread ownership of arms. We must also remember that it was men such as Patrick Henry that
James Madison sought to satisfy with a Bill of Rights.

In response to Madison's assertion that federal authority over the militia made
standing armies unnecessary, Henry responded:

> But, says the honorable member, Congress will keep the militia armed; or, in other
> words, they will do their duty. Pardon me if I am too jealous and suspicious to confide
> in this remote possibility. My honorable friend went on a supposition that the American
> rulers, like all others, will depart from their duty without bars and checks. No govern-
> ment can be safe without checks. Then he told us they had no temptation to violate
> their duty, and that it would be their interest to perform it. Does he think you are to
> trust men who cannot have separate interests from the people?...
>
> My honorable friend attacked the honorable gentleman with universal principles—that,
> in all nations and ages, rules have been actuated by motives of individual interest and
> private emoluments, and that in America it would be so also. I hope, before we part
> with this great bulwark, this noble palladium of safety, we shall have such checks inter-
> posed as will render us secure. The militia, sir, is our ultimate safety. We can have no
> security without it.[37]

In response to Henry's description of a monarchist coup, another delegate to the
convention, H. Lee (of Westmoreland) responded:

> But says he, "The President will enslave you: Congress will trample on your liberties; a
> few regiments will appear; Mr. Chief Justice must give way; our mace-bearer is no match
> for a regiment." It was inhuman to place an individual against a whole regiment. A *few*
> regiments will not avail; I trust the supporters of the government would get the better of
> *many* regiments. Were so mad an attempt made, the people would assemble in thou-
> sands, and drive thirty times the number of their few regiments. We would then do as
> we have already done with the regiments of that king whom he so often tells us of.[38]

Lee made the assertion that "the people would assemble in thousands" and
overwhelm a standing army that stood behind a tyrannical President. Organized
militia units? Or ordinary people? Lee's response to Henry can be read either way,
though the implication that "the people would assemble in thousands" suggests a
spontaneous uprising, rather than a state government organized resistance.

Earlier during the Virginia ratification debates, George Mason had expressed his
concerns about standing armies, and federal power over the militias:

---

36 Elliot, 3:169.
37 Elliot, 3:385.
38 Elliot, 3:181.

In times of real danger, the states will have the same enthusiasm in aiding the general government, and in granting its demands, which is seen in England, when the king is engaged in a war apparently for the interest of the nation. This power is necessary; but we ought to guard against danger. If ever they attempt to harass and abuse the militia, they may abolish them, and raise a standing army in their stead. There are various ways of destroying the militia. A standing army may be perpetually established in their stead. *I abominate and detest the idea of a government, where there is a standing army. The militia may be here destroyed by that method which has been practiced in other parts of the world before; that is, by rendering them useless—by disarming them.* Under various pretences, Congress may neglect to provide for arming and disciplining the militia; and the state governments cannot do it, for Congress has an exclusive right to arm them, &c... *Should the national government wish to render the militia useless, they may neglect them, and let them perish, in order to have a pretence of establishing a standing army.*

No man has a greater regard for the military gentlemen than I have. I admire their intrepidity, perseverance, and valor. *But when once a standing army is established in any country, the people lose their liberty. When, against a regular and disciplined army, yeomanry are the only defence,—yeomanry, unskilful and unarmed,—what chance is there for preserving freedom?* Give me leave to recur to the page of history, to warn you of the present danger. Recollect the history of most nations of the world. What havoc, desolation, and destruction, have been perpetrated by standing armies! An instance within the memory of some of this house will show us how our militia may be destroyed. *Forty years ago, when the resolution of enslaving America was formed in Great Britain, the British Parliament was advised by an artful man* [Sir William Keith, noted in Elliot] *who was governor of Pennsylvania, to disarm the people; that it was the best and most effectual way to enslave them; but that they should not do it openly, but weaken them, and let them sink gradually, by totally disusing and neglecting the militia....* This was a most iniquitous project. Why should we not provide against the danger of having our militia, our real and natural strength, destroyed? The general government ought, at the same time, to have some such power. But we need not give them power to abolish our militia. If they neglect to arm them, and prescribe proper discipline, they will be of no use... I wish that, in case the general government should neglect to arm and discipline the militia, there should be an express declaration that the state governments might arm and discipline them.[39] [emphasis added]

Especially in light of Henry's remarks, this could be interpreted as a statement that the state governments were the natural and only military defense of individual liberties against the Federal Government. Thus, the individual ownership of arms was for that purpose—or, that Mason considered "the people" as equivalent to "the militia," and therefore disarming the general population would have been anathema. But there is one more, very telling statement by Mason:

I consider and fear the natural propensity of rulers to oppress the people. I wish only to prevent them from doing evil. By these amendments I would give necessary powers, but no unnecessary power. If the clause stands as it is now, it will take from the state legislatures what divine Providence has given to every individual—the means of self-defence. Unless it be moderated to some degree, it will ruin us, and introduce a standing army.[40]

Mason thus drew an analogy between the right of the individual to "the means of self-defence" and the right of the state legislatures to defend themselves from the Federal Government. Mason implied that the state governments had the right to defend themselves from federal oppression, just as individuals had the right to arms

---

39 Elliot, 3:379-80.
40 Elliot, 3:381.

to defend themselves—presumably from private criminal attack, but perhaps from public criminals as well.

While widespread ownership of arms was commonly considered a restraint on ty-rannical tendencies in general, one delegate to the Virginia convention recognized a particular category of tyranny which was so restrained. Zachariah Johnson argued for ratification of the Constitution without a need for an amendment protecting freedom of religion:

> The diversity of opinions and variety of sects in the United States have justly been reck-oned a great security with respect to religious liberty. The difficulty of establishing a uniformity of religion in this country is immense. The extent of the country is very great. The multiplicity of sects is very great likewise. *The people are not to be disarmed of their weapons. They are left in full possession of them.* The government is administered by the representatives of the people, voluntarily and freely chosen.
>
> Under these circumstances, should any one attempt to establish their own system, in prejudice of the rest, they would be universally detested and opposed, and easily frus-trated. This is a principle which secures religious liberty most firmly.[41] [emphasis added]

To Johnson, the widespread ownership of arms was one component of the system which made it impossible to impose one sect's beliefs on the rest of the nation, be-cause *individuals* had in their hands the ability to stop any such effort.

Richard Henry Lee warned that Congress might not represent the interests of the common people in the levying of taxes and raising of standing armies; Lee argued:

> Powers to lay and collect taxes and to raise armies are of the greatest moment; for carry-ing them into effect, laws need not be frequently made, and the yeomanry, &c. of the country ought substantially to have a check upon the passing of these laws; this check ought to be placed in the legislatures, or at least, in the few men the common people of the country, will, probably, have in congress, in the true sense of the word, "from among themselves." It is true, *the yeomanry of the country possess the lands, the weight of property, possess arms, and are too strong a body of men to be openly offended*—and, therefore, it is urged, they will take care of themselves, that men who shall govern will not dare pay any disrespect to their opinions. [emphasis added]

But recognizing that slow change is frequently capable of lulling the population to sleep in a way that radical change will not:

> It is easily perceived, that if they have their proper negative upon passing laws in con-gress, or on the passage of laws relative to taxes and armies, they may in twenty or thirty years be by means imperceptible to them, totally deprived of that boasted weight and strength: This may be done in a great measure by congress, if disposed to do it, by modelling the militia. Should one fifth or one eighth part of the men capable of bearing arms, be made a select militia, as has been proposed, and those the young and ardent part of the community, possessed of but little or no property, and all the others put upon a plan that will render them of no importance, the former will answer all the purposes of an army, while the latter will be defenceless.[42]

Lee here recognized the hazards of what we would now call the National Guard—hazardous because the masses were not armed and trained to a comparable level.

After weeks of powerful oratory, the Virginia convention voted for ratification. Reflecting the Antifederalist concerns, their ratification consisted of a long philo-sophical discourse on natural rights, reminiscent of the Virginia Declaration of

---

41 Elliot, 3:645-6.
42 Lee, 25, in Ford, *Pamphlets On The Constitution of the United States,* 305.

Rights, and a concrete list of amendments desired in the new Constitution. Among the philosophical statements was:

> Seventeenth, That the people have a right to keep and bear arms; that a well regulated Militia composed of the body of the people trained to arms in the proper, natural and safe defence of a free State. That standing armies in time of peace are dangerous to liberty, and therefore ought to be avoided, as far as the circumstances and protection of the Community will admit; and that in all cases the military shall be under strict subordination to and governed by the Civil power.[43]

The concerns about standing armies previously mentioned, persisted. Again, the proximity to the people's "right to keep and bear arms" is evidence that there was some connection between this right and protection against the dangers of standing armies, but it does not preclude a liberal interpretation.

There is no proof that "the right to keep and bear arms" refers to an individual right. However, the phrase "the people" is used also in reference to the "right to peaceably assemble," and the "right to freedom of speech" in the 15th and 16th sections of this preamble. Attempts to fit "the people have a right to keep and bear arms" into a collective sense would require similar interpretations of the other sections of the Bill of Rights that refer to "the people." There is no evidence that a collective right alone was intended here; the use of "the people" in the Virginia request must therefore be considered evidence of an individual right.

Another clause defends the right of conscientious objectors to refuse militia duty: "Nineteenth, That any person religiously scrupulous of bearing arms ought to be exempted upon payment of an equivalent to employ another to bear arms in his stead." This clause appeared in Madison's draft of the Second Amendment, later to be deleted by First Congress.

While the preamble was an abstract statement of political philosophy, the requested amendments are considerably more precise. In the proposed amendments, there is no individual right to keep and bear arms requested. There is: "Ninth, That no standing army or regular troops shall be raised or kept up in time of peace, without the consent of two thirds of the members present in both houses."[44] While in accord with the concerns expressed previously by other state conventions as to the dangers of standing armies, there is no commonality of wording with Madison's first draft of the Second Amendment—unlike the 17th proposition in the preamble, which is clearly a direct ancestor of Madison's draft.

New York's ratification of the Constitution on July 26, 1788, was the last that requested a Bill of Rights before the new government began operation. Like Virginia's request, it included a preamble defining the nature of human rights, then launched into a lengthy description of the rights to be protected by a Bill of Rights. Among these rights:

---

43 Bickford & Veit, 4:17. This provision also appears in Levin, 114, but altered in a rather significant manner. As it appears in Levin, it starts out, "That a well-regulated militia, composed of the body of the people..." The capitalization of "That," without the use of brackets to show that the case has been changed, gives the reader the understanding that it is a free-standing clause, rather than showing him that something rather important—"That the people have a right to keep and bear arms;"—has been elided. Levin quoted from the same source as this work.

44 Bickford & Veit, 4:16-18.

That the People have a right to keep and bear Arms; that a well regulated Militia, in-cluding the body of the People *capable of bearing Arms*, is the proper, natural and safe defence of a free State; [emphasis in original]

That the Militia should not be subject to Martial Law, except in time of War, Rebellion or Insurrection.

That standing Armies in time of Peace are dangerous to Liberty, and ought not to be kept up, except in Cases of necessity; and that at all times, the Military should be under strict Subordination to the civil Power.[45]

Again, "the right to keep and bear Arms" is a right of "the People," and while mentioned in the same paragraph as a "well regulated Militia," the two are separate clauses, with no requirement that one be dependent on the other. The New York request's use of the phrase "the People" is clearly an individual right. There are a number of guarantees of individual rights which refer to "Person" in the singular, including the double jeopardy and *habeas corpus* clauses. But at the same time, "the People have a right peaceably to assemble" and "the People have an equal, natural and unalienable right, freely and peaceably to Exercise their Religion according to the dictates of Conscience."

Even if "the People" is read in a collective, governmental militia sense here, it requires a similar reading of "the People" with respect to the religion and peaceable assembly provisions—with absurd results. The freedom of religion clause then becomes freedom for a government recognized church, negating the second half of the paragraph, "and that no Religious Sect or Society ought to be favoured or established by law in preference of others." Similarly, "the People have a right peaceably to assemble" would only be valid for a governmentally sanctioned assembly, negating the "to consult for their common good, or to instruct their Representatives" provision of the same paragraph. It would be difficult to argue that New York's request was for a collective right only, without doing great damage to the clear intent of the other requests for a Bill of Rights.[46]

The Federalist Papers, written by Alexander Hamilton, James Madison, and John Jay, was a persuasive set of Federalist arguments in favor of ratification of the Constitution, and played a major part in winning popular support for the new government in New York. Not surprisingly, they address the issues of standing armies, the role of the militia, and the dangers of tyranny. Hamilton's *Federalist* 28 is devoted entirely to the concerns that had been expressed about a standing army, and its threat to liberty. While Hamilton argued that the best protection of the liberties of the people was their elected representatives, he recognized that there was a last, drastic solution to the problem of tyranny:

If the representatives of the people betray their constituents, there is then no resource left but in the exertion of that original right of self-defense which is paramount to all positive forms of government, and which against the usurpations of the national rulers, may be exerted with infinitely better prospect of success than against those of the rulers of an individual state. In a single state, if the persons [e]ntrusted with supreme power become usurpers, the different parcels, subdivisions, or districts of which it consists, having no distinct government in each, can take no regular measures for defense. *The citizens must rush tumultuously to arms, without concert, without system, without resource; except in their courage and despair.* The usurpers, clothed with the forms of legal authority, can too

---

45 Bickford & Veit, 4:20.
46 Bickford & Veit, 4:20-1.

often crush the opposition in embryo. The smaller the extent of the territory, the more difficult will it be for the people to form a regular or systematic plan of opposition, and the more easy will it be to defeat their early efforts. Intelligence can be more speedily obtained of their preparations and movements, and the military force in the possession of the usurpers can be more rapidly directed against the part where the opposition has begun. In this situation there must be a peculiar coincidence of circumstances to insure success to the popular resistance.

The obstacles to usurpation and the facilities of resistance increase with the increased extent of the state, provided the citizens understand their rights and are disposed to defend them. The natural strength of the people in a large community, in proportion to the artificial strength of the government, is greater than in a small, and of course more competent to a struggle with the attempts of the government to establish a tyranny. But in a confederacy the people, without exaggeration, may be said to be entirely the masters of their own fate. Power being almost always the rival of power, the general government will at all times stand ready to check the usurpations of the state governments, and these will have the same disposition towards the general government. *The people, by throwing themselves into either scale, will infallibly make it preponderate.* If their rights are invaded by either, they can make use of the other as the instrument of redress. How wise will it be in them by cherishing the union to preserve to themselves an advantage which can never be too highly prized![47] [emphasis added]

Hamilton perceived the state governments as the most effective protection of the rights of the people in the event that revolution became necessary; but it is equally clear that Hamilton recognized a right to revolution separate from the authority of the state, against both tyrannies of the state or federal governments. Hamilton's assertion that the people, "by throwing themselves into either scale," would guarantee victory, suggests that much of the weight in the scale would be the citizens' arms.

Hamilton's *Federalist* 29 continued in the same vein. Hamilton pointed to the economic consequences of drilling the entire militia sufficiently to "[e]ntitle them to the character of a well regulated militia," and suggested, instead, "Little more can reasonably be aimed at with respect to the people at large than to have them properly armed and equipped; and in order to see that this be not neglected, it will be necessary to assemble them once or twice in the course of a year."

After arguing that a "select corps" could be trained to a higher level of efficiency than a general militia, Hamilton acknowledged that a standing army might also under some conditions, be necessary:

[B]ut if circumstances should at any time oblige the government to form an army of any magnitude, that army can never be formidable to the liberties of the people, while there is a large body of citizens little if at all inferior to them in discipline and the use of arms, who stand ready to defend their own rights and those of their fellow citizens—This appears to me the only substitute that can be devised for a standing army; the best possible security against it, if it should exist.[48]

Hamilton argued for a select militia, but one "ready to defend their own rights," which implies that such a select militia would possess arms appropriate to military action against a standing army.

Further evidence of the identity of the militia as "the people," and not just a small part of the population, can be found in Madison's *Federalist* 46. Madison

---

47 Alexander Hamilton, "Federalist 28", in Cooke, 178-9.
48 Alexander Hamilton, "Federalist 29", in Kaminski & Saladino, 3:320.

sought to alleviate concerns about Federal power. To that end, he pointed out that, "The only refuge left for those who prophecy the downfall of the State Governments, is the visionary supposition that the Federal Government may previously accumulate a military force for the projects of ambition..." Madison asserted the political unlikeliness of such an event, but:

> Extravagant as the supposition is, let it however be made. Let a regular army, fully equal to the resources of the country be formed; and let it be entirely at the devotion of the [Federal] Government; still it would not be going too far to say, that the State Governments with the people on their side would be able to repel the danger. The highest number to which, according to the best computation, a standing army can be carried in any country, does not exceed one hundredth part of the whole number of souls; or one twenty-fifth part of the number able to bear arms. This proportion would not yield in the United States an army of more than twenty-five or thirty thousand men. To these would be opposed a militia amounting to near half a million of citizens with arms in their hands, officered by men chosen from among themselves, fighting for their common liberties, and united and conducted by governments possessing their affections and confidence. It may well be doubted whether a militia thus circumstanced could ever be conquered by such a proportion of regular troops.[49]

After observing that, "Besides the advantages of being armed, which the Americans possess over the people of almost every other nation," Madison pointed out the advantage that the citizens of the U.S. had in being attached to subsidiary governments. In Madison's estimation, this was a stronger advantage than the people being armed:

> Notwithstanding the military establishments in the several kingdoms of Europe, which are carried as far as the public resources will bear, the governments are afraid to trust the people with arms. And it is not certain that with this aid alone, they would not be able to shake off their yokes. But were the people to possess the additional advantages of local governments chosen by themselves, who could collect the national will, and direct the national force; and of officers appointed out of the militia, by these governments and attached both to them and to the militia, it may be affirmed with the greatest assurance, that the throne of every tyranny in Europe would be speedily overturned, in spite of the legions which surround it.[50]

Madison articulated a republican notion of the militia which is not necessarily supportive of, or opposed to, an individual right to keep and bear arms—but shows that widespread private arms ownership and training was part of the counterbalance required to restrain national governmental power. It is hard to imagine Madison countenancing laws that sought to restrict arms ownership by the general population.

Noah Webster was another prominent Federalist pamphleteer who supported ratification of the Constitution. There were widespread concerns about tyranny from the new government:

> But what is tyranny? Or how can a free people be deprived of their liberties? Tyranny is the exercise of some power over a man, which is not warranted by law, or necessary for

---

49 James Madison, "Federalist 46", in Cooke, 321.

50 James Madison, "Federalist 46", in Cooke, 322-3. The recent example of Boris Yeltsin's marshalling of the Russian Federation against the Soviet hard-liner coup, provides an example of the phenomenon that Madison described.

the public safety. A people can never been deprived of their liberties, while they retain in their own hands, a power sufficient to any other power in the state.[51]

After discussing the power of religion, and how "a singular concurrence of circumstances" (the wide diversity of religious beliefs) had made this "as a pillar of government ... totally precluded," Webster tells us:

Another source of power in government is a military force. But this, to be efficient, must be superior to any force that exists among the people, or which they can command; for otherwise this force would be annihilated, on the first exercise of acts of oppression. Before a standing army can rule, the people must be disarmed; as they are in almost every kingdom in Europe. The supreme power in America cannot enforce unjust laws by the sword; because the whole body of the people are armed, and constitute a force superior to any band of regular troops that can be, on any pretence, raised in the United States. A military force, at the command of Congress, can execute no laws, but such as the people perceive to be just and constitutional; for they will possess the *power*, and jealousy will instantly inspire the *inclination*, to resist the execution of a law which appears to them unjust and oppressive.[52] [emphasis in original]

While not a clear statement of an individual right to keep and bear arms for self-defense, it is clear that Webster would have vigorously opposed laws that attempted to disarm the general population. To Webster, widespread ownership of arms were part of the mechanism by which popular will could defeat standing armies turned tyrannical.

The Maryland ratifying convention met April 21-26, 1788; its debates and proposed amendments shed no light on the nature of the rights guaranteed by the Second Amendment,[53] though, as we saw on page 10, they do provide yet another piece of evidence that "the militia" was a large part of the population of the state. In a pamphlet in opposition to the Constitution, Luther Martin of Maryland, a member of the Philadelphia Convention, asserted:

By the principles of the American revolution, arbitrary power may, and ought to, be resisted even by arms, if necessary. The time may come when it shall be the duty of a state, in order to preserve itself from the oppression of the general government, to have recourse to the sword; in which case, the proposed form of government declares, that the state, and every one of its citizens who acts under its authority, are guilty of a direct act of treason...[54]

This can be interpreted as evidence that such revolutionary acts were the proper domain solely of the states, and therefore an individual right to arms was unnecessary; but just two months later, Martin warned:

But I appeal to the history of mankind for this truth, that when once power and authority are delegated to a government, it knows how to keep it, and is sufficiently and successfully fertile in expedients for that purpose. Nay more, the whole history of mankind proves that so far from parting with the powers actually delegated to it, government is constantly encroaching on the small pittance of rights reserved by the people to them-

---

51 Noah Webster, *An Examination into the Leading Principles of the Federal Constitution*, 42-43, in Ford, *Pamphlets On The Constitution of the United States*, 55.

52 Webster, 43, in Ford, *Pamphlets On The Constitution of the United States*, 56.

53 Elliot, 2:547-8.

54 Luther Martin, "Luther Martin's Letter of the Federal Convention of 1787", January 27, 1788, in Elliot, 1:382.

selves and gradually wresting them out of their hands until it either terminates in their slavery or forces them to arms, and brings about a revolution.[55]

Martin assumed the people would have access to arms for the purpose of revolution.

Rhode Island ratified the Constitution late—so late that discussions of setting up an international border at its boundaries may have influenced its decision. Its "Request For A Bill of Rights," adopted May 29, 1790 (after the First Congress had already completed deliberations on the Bill of Rights), was similar in form to those of Virginia and New York, containing a preamble of philosophical assumptions, and a series of concrete amendments to the Constitution.

The preamble asserts:

I. That there are certain natural rights of which men, when they form a social compact, cannot deprive or divest their posterity,—among which are the enjoyment of life and liberty, with the means of acquiring, possessing, and protecting of property, and pursuing and obtaining happiness and safety.

and:

XVII. That the people have a right to keep and bear arms; that a well-regulated militia, including the body of the people capable of bearing arms, is the proper, natural, and safe defence of a free state; that the militia shall not be subject to martial law, except in time of war, rebellion, or insurrection; that standing armies, in time of peace, are dangerous to liberty, and ought not to be kept up, except in cases of necessity; and that, at all times, the military shall be under strict subordination to the civil power; that, in time of peace, no soldier ought to be quartered in any house without the consent of the owner, and in time of war only by the civil magistrates, in such manner as the law directs.

XVIII. That any person religiously scrupulous of bearing arms ought to be exempted upon payment of an equivalent to employ another to bear arms in his stead.

The list of proposed amendments included:

XII. As standing armies, in time of peace, are dangerous to liberty, and ought not to be kept up, except in cases of necessity, and as, at all times, the military should be under strict subordination to the civil power, that, therefore, no standing army or regular troops shall be raised or kept up in time of peace.

Other proposed amendments referring to "the people" include, "That the people have a right peaceably to assemble together to consult for their common good, or to instruct their representatives," and "That the people have a right to freedom of speech, and of writing and publishing their sentiments."[56] The evidence strongly suggests that Rhode Island's request was for an *individual* right to keep and bear arms. Whether this right was for the purpose of checking domestic tyranny, or defense against private criminals, or both, is impossible to definitely determine from the available evidence.

On June 8, 1789, Rep. James Madison, a member of the First Congress of the new Federal Government, introduced a resolution: "That the following amendments ought to be proposed by Congress to the legislatures of the states, to become, if ratified by three fourths thereof, part of the constitution of the United States."[57]

---

55 Luther Martin, *Letters of Luther Martin, 5*, in *The Maryland Journal*, March 28, 1788, in Paul Ford, ed., *Essays on the Constitution of the United States*, (New York: Burt Franklin, 1892), 376.
56 Elliot, 1:334-6.
57 Bickford & Veit, 4:9.

Following this preamble were a series of separate articles, each of which sought to insert into the Constitution the rights requested by the various state conventions. The First Congress, on the whole, was in no hurry to adopt a Bill of Rights, and Madison was forced to remind them that a Bill of Rights had been promised. Some members of the new Congress were in actual opposition to "an explicit declaration of the great rights of mankind";[58] more typical may have been the attitude of Rep. Fisher Ames, a Massachusetts Federalist:

> Mr. Madison has introduced his long expected amendments. They are the fruit of much labor and research. He has hunted up all the grievances and complaints of newspapers, all the articles of convention, and the small talk of their debates. It contains a bill of rights, the right of enjoying property, of changing the government at pleasure, freedom of the press, of conscience, of juries, exemption from general warrants, gradual increase of representatives, till the whole number, at the rate of one to every thirty thousand, shall amount to _____, and allowing two to every State, at least. This is the substance. There is too much of it. Oh! I had forgot, the right of the people to bear arms.
>
> Risum teneatis amici? ["Friends, withhold your laughter?"]
>
> Upon the whole, it may do some good towards quieting men, who attend to sounds only, and may get the mover some popularity, which he wishes.[59]

Was Ames' remark, "*Risum teneatis amici?*" directed at the entire Bill of Rights, or just at the notion of the right of the people to bear arms? In either case, Ames' remarks suggest that Madison's intent for the Second Amendment was understood to be a "right of the people," not a right of the states.

Madison's fourth article included much of what is now the Bill of Rights, including:

> The right of the people to keep and bear arms shall not be infringed; a well armed, and well regulated militia being the best security of a free country; but no person religiously scrupulous of bearing arms, shall be compelled to render military service in person.[60]

Throughout Madison's resolution, "The rights of the people" and "The people" are consistently used to refer to what are today considered *individual* rights:

> The people shall not be deprived or abridged of their rights to speak, to write, or to publish their sentiments...

> The people shall not be restrained from peaceably assembling and consulting for their common good...

> The rights of the people to be secured in their persons, their houses, their papers, and their other property from all unreasonable searches and seizures, shall not be violated by warrants issued without probable cause...[61]

The word "person" is used in several places to refer to single individuals confronting the legal system—but there is no reason to think, based on the choice of

---

58 Rutland, rev. ed., 196-202.

59 Letter of Fisher Ames to Thomas Dwight, June 11, 1789, in William B. Allen, ed., *Works of Fisher Ames*, (Liberty Classics: Indianapolis, 1983), 1:642. It is not surprising that Ames, a Federalist, was apparently dismissive of the value of the Bill of Rights. More surprising is that Senator William Maclay, one of the early opponents of the Federalists, apparently made no mention of the Bill of Rights, or any of its components, in his rather extensive journal covering 1789-1791. William Maclay, *Journal of William Maclay*, (New York: Frederick Ungar Publishing Co., 1965).

60 Bickford & Veit, 4:10.

61 Bickford & Veit, 4:10-11.

"person" vs. "people," that Madison intended one word to be individual, and the other to be collective in nature—and as we saw on page 15 in *U.S.* v. *Verdugo-Urquidez* (1990), the Supreme Court agrees.

Madison originally proposed that these various amendments be inserted directly into the text of the Constitution. For "The right of the people to keep and bear arms," Madison proposed inserting it in Article I, §9 "alongside the other limitations on legislative power,"[62] between clauses three (prohibiting bills of attainder and *ex post facto* laws) and four (prohibiting "capitation, or other direct, Tax").[63] To Professor Shalhope, this is evidence that Madison saw these as individual rights, to be protected from Congress' legislative power.[64] To Professor Cress, the reason for the placement was "the widely held fear that Congress's access to the militia might be misused."[65]

What else is in Article I, §9? Some of the protections contained therein are clearly individual protections: the Writ of *Habeas Corpus*, "No bill of Attainder or ex post facto Law shall be passed," "No capitation, or other direct, Tax...," "No Title of Nobility shall be granted by the United States...." Others are restrictions on state power: prohibitions on export duties, no preferences given to "the Port of one State over those of another," prohibitions on states engaging in actions that would conflict with the powers of the new national government, including "No state shall, without the Consent of Congress, lay any duty of Tonnage, keep Troops, or Ships of War in time of Peace..." Not a single provision in that section protects state prerogatives from the national government, except to the extent that it puts all the states on an equal footing before the laws.

If there any evidence that might lead one to conclude that the proposed placement in Article I, §9 tells us something about the intent, it would be that it was intended as a defense of rights of individuals, from Congress' power. If, as Cress maintains, the goal was to protect the rights of the States to maintain militias, why didn't Madison propose to insert it in Article I, §8, where Congress' authority over the militia resided?

Other evidence of Madison's view of these as individual rights is found in his notes for the speech in support of the amendments, "They relate 1st. to private rights—"[66] In his consultation with Edmund Pendleton, "amendments may be employed to quiet the fears of many by supplying those further guards for private rights."[67] That Madison's concern were not limited to a President with monarchial ambitions, the fear most expressed by Patrick Henry, can be found later in his notes for that same speech:

62 Cress, 36.
63 Charles F. Hobson & Robert A. Rutland, ed., *The Papers of James Madison*, (Charlottesville, Va.: University Press of Virginia, 1977), 12:201.
64 Cress & Shalhope, "The Second Amendment and the Right to Bear Arms: An Exchange", 589.
65 Cress, 36.
66 Hobson & Rutland, 12:193.
67 Cress & Shalhope, "The Second Amendment and the Right to Bear Arms: An Exchange", 589.

Object of Bill of Rhts

To limit & qualify powr. by exceptg. from grant cases in wch. it shall not be exercised or exd. in a particular manner.

to guard   1. vs. Executive & in Engd. &c—
            2. Legislative as in Sts—
            3. the majority of people

---

ought to point to greatest danger which in Rep. is Prerogative of majority—[68]

Madison's Bill of Rights was intended as a protection against abuse of power by not only the executive branch, but against legislative abuse of power, even if it reflected "the majority of people." Indeed, the speech of June 8, 1789, when Madison introduced his proposal, showed this unambiguously:

> But whatever may be [the] form which the several states have adopted in making declarations in favor of particular rights, the great object in view is to limit and qualify the powers of government, by excepting out of the grant of power those cases in which the government ought not to act, or to act only in a particular mode. They point these exceptions sometimes against the abuse of the executive power, sometimes against the legislative, and, in some cases, against the community itself; or, in other words, against the majority in favor of the minority.[69]

This speech provides further evidence that he recognized these as protections of *individual* rights, not exclusively as states' rights, or some combination thereof: "It will be a desirable thing to extinguish from the bosom of every member of the community any apprehensions, that there are those among his countrymen who wish to deprive them of the liberty for which they valiantly fought and honorably died."[70] To argue that Madison considered the Bill of Rights as protection of *state* prerogatives, not individual rights, is a position wholly unsupported by, and contrary to, Madison's notes and speeches.

Evidence of how others perceived the right to arms is found in Samuel Nasson's letter to Rep. George Thatcher of July 9, 1789. Nasson had been a member of the Massachusetts ratifying convention, and had voted against the new Constitution.[71] Rep. Thatcher was a Federalist in the First Congress.[72] Nasson's letter (which serves to remind us that not every colonial wrote well) did not make it clear whether he was referring to the specific amendments introduced by Madison, or whether he had only heard that a Bill of Rights had been introduced:

> A Bill of rights well secured that we the people may know how far we may Proceade in Every Department then their will be no Dispute Between the people and rulers in that may be secured the right to keep arms for Common and Extraordinary Occasions such as to secure ourselves against the wild Beast and also to amuse us by fowling and for our Defence against a Common Enemy you know to learn the Use of arms is all that can Save us from a [foreign] foe that may attempt to subdue us for if we keep up the Use of arms and become well acquainted with them we Shall allway be able to look them in the

---

68 Hobson & Rutland, 12:194.
69 Hobson & Rutland, 12:204.
70 Hobson & Rutland, 12:198.
71 Helen Veit, Kenneth R. Bowling, & Charlene Bangs Bickford, ed., *Creating The Bill of Rights: The Documentary Record from the First Federal Congress*, (Baltimore: Johns Hopkins University Press, 1991), 309.
72 Veit, Bowling, & Bickford, 313.

face that arise up against us for it is impossible to Support a Standing armey large Enough to Guard our Lengthy Sea Coast and now Spare me on the subject of Standing armeys in a time of Peace they allway was first or last the downfall of all free Governments it was by their help Caesar made proud Rome Own a Tyrant and a Traytor for a Master.[73]

Nasson went on to discuss (with more run-on sentences, tortured spelling, and bewildering grammar) the dangers of standing armies and the necessity for a guar-antee of jury trial in all cases. Nasson certainly saw the need for arms in private hands as a way of avoiding the necessity of standing armies; but he also recognized the need for arms for individual defense (against wild animals), and for hunting.

Did Madison perhaps intend a little less sweeping protection than he wrote? Is it possible that the majesty of the sweeping language did not preclude whatever restrictions on arms ownership were necessary to public safety and order, however that might have been defined at the time? The correspondence of Thomas Jefferson and James Madison in the eleven months preceding Madison's introduction of the Bill of Rights provides some clues.

Madison's actions in drafting the Bill of Rights were not sudden; Thomas Jeffer-son, then ambassador to France, had carried on a lengthy correspondence with Madison about the need for a Bill of Rights since at least July of the previous year. Jefferson's letter of July 31, 1788 includes a list of rights that he felt should be in-cluded, including a prohibition on "standing armies in time of peace." In discuss-ing the need for a Bill of Rights, Jefferson recognized that a general principle was occasionally a mixed blessing: "The few cases wherein these things may do evil, cannot be weighed against the multitude where the want of them will do evil." Jefferson then discussed how the suspension of *habeas corpus* had been abused so often by the government of England that the few times it had

> done real good, that operation is now become habitual, & the minds of the nation al-most prepared to live under it's [*sic*] constant suspension... If no check can be found to keep the number of standing troops within safe bounds, wile they are tolerated as far as necessary, abandon them altogether, discipline well the militia, & guard the magazines with them... My idea then is, that tho' proper exceptions to these general rules are desir-able & probably practicable, yet if the exceptions cannot be agreed upon, the establish-ment of the rules in all cases will do ill in very few. I hope therefore a bill of rights will be formed to guard the people against the federal government, as they are already guarded against their state governments in most cases.[74]

In response to Jefferson's letter, Madison's letter of October 17, 1788, described his thoughts on how a Bill of Rights should be drafted:

> Supposing a bill of rights to be proper the articles which ought to compose it, admit of much discussion. I am inclined to think that *absolute* restrictions in cases that are doubtful, or where emergencies may overrule them, ought to be avoided. The restric-tions however strongly marked on paper will never be regarded when opposed to the decided sense of the public; and after repeated violations in extraordinary cases, they will lose even their ordinary efficacy. Should a Rebellion or insurrection alarm the people as well as the Government, and a suspension of the Hab. Corp. be dictated by the alarm, no written prohibitions on earth would prevent the measure. Should an army in time of peace be gradually established in our neighborhood by Britn: or Spain, declarations on

73 Veit, Bowling, & Bickford, 260-1.
74 Hobson & Rutland, 11:212-3.

paper would have as little effect in preventing a standing force for the public safety. The best security agst. these evils is to remove the pretext for them...[75]

Madison's perceptions of how republics work were more realistic than Jefferson's; the internment of Japanese-Americans during World War II shows that when the desire is strong, parchment protections give way. In a similar way, after the Civil War, at the end of the Roaring Twenties, and in the turbulent 1960s, the paper protections of the Second Amendment and its state analogs gave way.

Madison's reluctance to draw the sort of strict line that Jefferson proposed may be seen in the qualifying phrases, "but in a manner warranted by law" in the Third Amendment, and such broadly interpretable phrases as, "Excessive bail," "excessive fines," and "without probable cause." Yet other amendments proposed by Madison ring with Jeffersonian certainty:

> The civil rights of none shall be abridged on account of religious belief or worship, nor shall any national religion be established, nor shall the full and equal rights of conscience be in any manner, or on any pretext infringed.

> The people shall not be deprived or abridged of their right to speak, to write, or to publish their sentiments...

> The right of the people to keep and bear arms shall not be infringed;...[76]

Those who see the broad and sweeping language of the Second Amendment as reflecting a broader protection than was intended should consider this exchange between Madison and Jefferson. Madison expressed his desire to avoid unnecessarily broad declarations of rights; because they would be trespassed by the majority, such declarations would lose their importance in the public mind. Not surprisingly, we find that *some* of the rights that Madison sought to protect are sufficiently qualified and limited that they would not be a hopeless obstacle to the public desires; but some rights—including the individual rights section of the Second Amendment and the protections of the First Amendment—are written in the broadest possible language, leaving no room for the majority to restrict the individual rights.

Over the next few months, the Congress made a series of amendments to Madison's proposal. What became the Second Amendment was not exempted from these changes. Madison's proposal, along with the recommendations of the state ratifying conventions, was turned over to a House committee "composed of John Vining of Delaware, chairman, Madison, and Roger Sherman, a consistent opponent of a federal bill of rights" on July 21, 1789.[77] A week later, the committee report was completed, with the Second Amendment revised to:

> [6] "A well regulated militia, composed of the body of the people, being the best security of a free State, the right of the people to keep and bear arms shall not be infringed, but no person religiously scrupulous shall be compelled to bear arms."[78]

The phrase "the right of the people to keep and bear arms," was sandwiched between a philosophical assertion about the "best security of a free State," and a protection for conscientious objectors from compulsory military service.

---

75 Hobson & Rutland, 11:299.
76 Hobson & Rutland, 12:201.
77 Rutland, rev. ed., 207.
78 Bickford & Veit, 4:28.

The full House took up debate on the Bill of Rights in August of 1789. On August 17th, debate began on the committee report's revised "right to keep and bear arms" amendment. Rep. Elbridge Gerry of Massachusetts opened the debate by expressing the nature of the right to be protected, and how the "religiously scrupulous" clause could be abused to prevent individuals from bearing arms:

> This declaration of rights, I take it, is intended to secure the people against the maladministration of the government; if we could suppose that in all cases the rights of the people would be attended to, the occasion for guards of this kind would be removed. Now I am apprehensive, sir, that this clause would give an opportunity to the people in power to destroy the constitution itself. They can declare who are those religiously scrupulous, and prevent them from bearing arms.[79]

If the right protected only applied to military service under the control of the national government—as our current National Guard is—then Gerry's fear is baseless. Why would the Federal Government be prohibited from disarming soldiers under its command? Gerry's notion of "bearing arms" appears to have included having them under individual control.

Next, Gerry defined the purpose of a militia:

> What, sir, is the use of a militia? It is to prevent the establishment of a standing army, the bane of liberty. Now it must be evident, that under this provision, together with their other powers, congress could take such measures with respect to a militia, as make a standing army necessary. Whenever government mean to invade the rights and liberties of the people, they always attempt to destroy the militia, in order to raise an army upon their ruins... Now, if we give a discretionary power to exclude those from militia duty who have religious scruples, we may as well make no provision on this head; for this reason he wished the words to be altered so as to be confined to persons belonging to a religious sect, scrupulous of bearing arms.[80]

We do not know if this was the Senate's reason for removing this clause from the Second Amendment though it is reasonable to assume so, in the absence of other evidence. While Gerry's argument was essentially tied in with the notion of a militia duty that individuals owed to the state, his concern that the government might disarm the general population by declaring individuals "religiously scrupulous" again shows that Gerry would have opposed laws that disarmed the general population.

That same day, Rep. James Jackson of Georgia proposed adding "upon paying an equivalent to be established by law" at the end of the conscientious objector provision. Jackson then changed the phrase to, "No one, religiously scrupulous of bearing arms, shall be compelled to render military service in person, upon paying an equivalent." Finally, Egbert Benson's motion to strike out the entire conscientious objector clause was put to a vote, and lost, 24-22.

Aedanus Burke of South Carolina sought to add:

> A standing army of regular troops in time of peace, is dangerous to public liberty, and such shall not be raised or kept up in time of peace but from necessity, and for the security of the people, nor then without the consent of two-thirds of the members present of both houses, and in all cases the military shall be subordinate to the civil authority.

---

79 Veit, Bowling, & Bickford, 182.
80 Veit, Bowling, & Bickford, 182.

This measure also failed to win House approval. On August 20th, Rep. Scott objected to the "religiously scrupulous" clause:

> He observed that if this becomes part of the constitution, such persons can neither be called upon for their services, nor can an equivalent be demanded; it is also attended with still further difficulties, for a militia can never be depended upon. This would lead to the violation of another article in the constitution, which secures to the people the right of keeping arms, and in this case recourse must be had to a standing army. I conceive it, said he, to be a legislative right altogether.[81]

What was a "legislative right"? The right to establish a standing army? The right to decide who may be excused from militia duty? There is a strong implication that allowing people to refuse militia duty would be a violation of the "right of keeping arms," but unless the republican view was a binary choice—a standing army *or* popular arms ownership—it is hard to understand why a standing army necessarily excluded the people keeping arms.

Rep. Scott was more clear on why he was concerned about the religiously scrupulous clause:

> There are many sects I know, who are religiously scrupulous in this respect; I do not mean to deprive them of any indulgence the law affords; my design is to guard against those who are of no religion. It has been urged that religion is on the decline; if so, the argument is more strong in my favor, for when the time comes that religion shall be discarded, the generality of persons will have recourse to these pretexts to get excused from bearing arms.[82]

Rep. Boudinot argued for the necessity of this clause, because members of several pacifist groups had been compelled to fight during the Revolution, "Now, by striking out the clause, people may be led to believe that there is an intention in the General Government to compel all its citizens to bear arms."[83] The words "in person" were inserted at the end of the conscientious objector clause,[84] protecting the right of conscientious objectors, but not precluding laws to require them to hire a substitute.

Nowhere in the House debates does there seem to be any discussion of the clause which states, "the right of the people to keep and bear arms shall not be infringed." The language and intent were clear enough, and sufficiently agreed to, that no debate was necessary. At the same time, the lack of debate about "the right of the people" is strong evidence of agreement that an individual right was protected.

On August 24th, the House completed its deliberations on the Bill of Rights. As a result of renumbering and revisions, the "right to keep and bear arms" amendment was now "Article the Fifth":

> A well regulated militia, composed of the body of the People, being the best security of a free State, the right of the People to keep and bear arms, shall not be infringed, but no one religiously scrupulous of bearing arms, shall be compelled to render military service in person.[85]

---

81 *Annals of Congress*, 1 Cong., August 20, 1789, 796.
82 *Annals of Congress*, 1 Cong., August 20, 1789, 796.
83 *Annals of Congress*, 1 Cong., August 20, 1789, 796.
84 Bickford & Veit, 4:28.
85 Bickford & Veit, 4:36.

The Senate now took up the Bill of Rights. Unfortunately, our knowledge of the Senate's actions on the Bill of Rights is limited to the proposed amendments and motions; no record of debate survives because the Senate met in secret.[86] On September 4th, an attempt was made to append to the amendment:

> that standing armies, in time of peace, being dangerous to Liberty, should be avoided as far as the circumstances and protection of the community will admit; and that in all cases the military should be under strict subordination to, and governed by the civil Power. That no standing army or regular troops shall be raised in time of peace, without the consent of two thirds of the Members present in both Houses, and that no soldier shall be [e]nlisted for any longer term than the continuance of the war.

This phrase, clearly derived from the requests of the various state conventions, was voted down 9-6. However, on the same day, an amendment to strike the "religiously scrupulous" clause passed. While some scholars of the liberal school have postulated that the Senate did so to "preclude any constitutional authority of the government to 'compel' individuals (even those without religious scruples) to bear arms for any purpose,"[87] the evidence suggests quite the opposite. Rep. Williamson's argument (discussed in a previous chapter), that "The burden of the militia lies equally upon all persons,"[88] suggests that Congress' intent was that few freemen should be exempted from their responsibilities for militia duty. Rep. Gerry's speech of August 17th against the "religiously scrupulous" clause also suggests that the authority and intent of the government to compel militia service was wide-ranging. Professor Cress tells us, with reference to Gerry's speech, "His fear no doubt struck most in the hall as a bit farfetched," but Cress provides no basis for that assertion.[89]

Finally, on September 9th, the Senate replaced "the best" with "necessary to the," giving the Second Amendment its present language. On the same day, a motion to add "for the common defence" after "bear arms" failed. An opportunity to make the Second Amendment more clearly republican had been presented, and the Senate chose not to do so.

John Randolph, a student at Columbia College, was a ward of St. George Tucker and nephew of Rep. Theodorick Bland; he was politically well-connected. On September 11, 1789, Randolph wrote to St. George Tucker: "A majority of the Senate were for not allowing the militia arms & if two thirds had agreed it would have been an amendment to the Constitution. They are afraid that the Citizens will stop their full career to Tyranny & Oppression."[90]

Tucker was one of the Antifederalists,[91] and later, became a prominent legal commentator; it would appear that Randolph shared the Antifederalist fear that the new government had nefarious ambitions. Since the Senate debate was secret, we must assume that Randolph's statement was at least second-hand. The Senate, in any case, would not have been so bold as to directly state the goal that Randolph ascribed to them. Nonetheless, this is evidence that the Senate, or at least its

---

86 Veit, Bowling, & Bickford, xix.
87 Halbrook, *That Every Man Be Armed*, 81.
88 Elliot, 4:423.
89 Cress, 37.
90 Veit, Bowling, & Bickford, 310-1, 293.
91 Veit, Bowling, & Bickford, 313.

detractors, recognized that by adding "for the common defense" to the Second Amendment meant "not allowing the militia arms" and disarming "the Citizens."

On September 14, 1789, the Senate completed its deliberations on the Bill of Rights. A conference committee report on September 24th resolved differences between the House and Senate versions for the first, third, and eighth articles; no changes were required for the "right to keep and bear arms" article—now "Article the Fourth." On the same day, the House requested President Washington send the proposed amendments "to the executives of the several states which have ratified the Constitution," as well as North Carolina and Rhode Island, which had not yet ratified.[92]

In the same way that state constitutions adopted before the Bill of Rights told us something about the intent of the Second Amendment, the state constitutions containing a "right to keep and bear arms" clause adopted after ratification can tell us something about the meaning commonly ascribed to the Second Amendment.

I have chosen, somewhat arbitrarily, to examine those constitutions adopted in the period before 1845. Only a few adults alive at the time the Bill of Rights was ratified would have lived past this date. Thus, these early state constitutions can be considered to have been written by the generation that included and was directly influenced by the Framers.

In this formative period of American history, there are a total of fifteen constitutions, adopted by ten states, and one independent nation (the Republic of Texas) that contain a "right to bear arms in defense of himself and the State," or some slight variant.[93] These provisions specify "in defense of himself"; it is therefore unambiguous that the right protected in each case is individual. Each of these state supreme courts (with the exception of Mississippi) have held, on at least one occasion, that the right protected was an individual right; we will study each decision in detail in later chapters. These must be considered as evidence for the liberal school, because the language used is similar to, and doubtless borrowed from, the Second Amendment.

By comparison, there are only three constitutions in this period that specify "common defence:" the Maine Constitution of 1819, and the Tennessee Constitutions of 1796 and 1834. None of these specify an individual right, and so we might assume, without other evidence, that the intent was republican, and excluded a liberal interpretation.

But was the intent republican? Tennessee's "right to keep and bear arms" provision included an interesting distinction. The 1796 and 1834 constitutions contained the same language, with one minor difference that may tell us something about why "common defence" was present in some of the constitutions, but not others. Article XI, §26 of the 1796 Tennessee Constitution: "That the freemen of this State have a right to keep and to bear arms for their common defence." Article

---

92 Bickford & Veit, 4:45, 4:47-8.

93 State Constitutions: Indiana (1816), Thorpe, 2:1059; Connecticut (1818), Thorpe, 1:538; Kentucky (1792 & 1799), Thorpe, 3:1275, 3:1290; Michigan (1835), Thorpe, 4:1931; Missouri (1820), Thorpe, 4:2163; Mississippi (1817), Thorpe, 4:2034; Ohio (1802), Thorpe, 5:2911; Pennsylvania (1790), Thorpe, 5:3101; Texas (1845), Thorpe, 6:3548; Vermont (1793), Thorpe, 6:3741; and the Republic of Texas (1838), Thorpe, 6:3543. Although an independent nation, the Republic of Texas was settled and controlled by Americans, who wrote a constitution of similar sentiments to the U.S. Constitution.

I, §26 of the 1834 constitution: "That the free *white* men of this State have a right to keep and to bear arms for their common defence."[94] [emphasis added] This suggests that by 1834, a sufficient number of free blacks lived in the state that Tennessee's constitution-makers felt it was necessary to racially restrict the right of keeping and bearing arms. While not surprising—racism has frequently motivated gun control laws—it does suggest that this right had an individual component. If this clause had only protected a collective right of the state militia, Tennessee's constitution-writers could have achieved the same result (disarming free blacks) by simply refusing to allow free blacks into the state militia. Indeed, in the period before the Civil War: "Only North Carolina permitted free blacks to bear arms in the ranks of its militia..."[95] If "for their common defence" did not provide a sufficient basis for disarming individual free blacks, it suggests that individual ownership and carriage of arms was not dependent on being in militia service.

An additional problem of what constitutes "common defense" is pointed out by constitutional lawyer Don Kates:

> Although some early state constitutions guarantee a right to arms for "common defense," they are not necessarily guaranteeing a state's right nor are they differentiating individual self-defense against criminals from community defense by an organized military force. Rather, what they are expressing is the common law concept that an individual serves the entire community when he kills a felon who was attacking him, but only serves his private interests (and disserves those of the community generally) when he kills another citizen who has attacked him in the course of a private quarrel. This concept is the source of the common law distinction, which is so foreign to us, between "justifiable" homicide and "excusable" or *se defendendo* homicide (i.e., in the course of a private quarrel).[96]

This understanding is also asserted in *Simpson* v. *State* (1833),[97] and the partially concurring, partially dissenting opinion of Justices Nelson & Tunney in *Andrews* v. *State* (1871).[98] The more we study the meaning of "for the common defense," the more suggestive it becomes that an individual right was also included within it.

There are some state constitutions that are not clearly in either camp. The Rhode Island Constitution of 1842 (Rhode Island had continued to use its colonial charter after the Revolution) uses the second clause of the Second Amendment by itself: "The right of the people to keep and bear arms shall not be infringed." Since Rhode Island's Constitution also guaranteed "The right of the people to be secure in their persons, papers and possessions against unreasonable searches and seizures," and, "The people shall continue to enjoy and freely exercise all the rights of fishery, and the privileges of the shore," it is difficult to imagine "the people" referring only to a collective right. We may infer that "the people" was not a rhetorical device to refer to "persons" because §21, which restricts the "right in a peaceable manner to assemble for their common good, and to apply to those invested with the powers of government, for redress of grievances" uses the word "citizens."[99] The writers of the

---

94 Thorpe, 6:3424, 6:3428.
95 Bernard C. Nalty, *Strength For The Fight: A History of Black Americans in the Military*, (New York: Macmillan, 1989), 20.
96 Don B. Kates, Jr., "The Second Amendment: A Dialogue", in *Law and Contemporary Problems*, 49:1 [Winter 1986], 147, note 24.
97 *Simpson* v. *State*, 5 Yerg. (Tenn.) 356, 359, 360 (1833).
98 *Andrews* v. *State*, 3 Heisk. (50 Tenn.) 165, 193, 194 (1871).
99 Thorpe, 6:3224.

Rhode Island Constitution recognized and used the distinction between citizens and all persons.

The New York Constitution of 1821 carries over the language of the 1777 Constitution. It does not directly support either a republican or liberal interpretation of the Second Amendment but does provide some evidence to justify the republican argument that the intentions of the "well regulated militia" clause were for a collective defense.

We have seen substantial evidence that "common defence" was recognized at the time as protecting an individual right as well as a collective right. But let us give the benefit of the doubt to those who argue that only the republican understanding of the right to keep and bear arms was intended, and that no individual right to arms was thereby recognized. Even then, the very lop-sided split between the "common defence" provisions, and unmistakably individual rights clauses, indicates that the liberal understanding of the Second Amendment was predominant during this critical period of American history.

We have seen evidence that James Madison and the various state ratifying conventions intended the Second Amendment as a protection of an *individual* right to arms, primarily to keep the new federal government in check. The debates in the First Congress with respect to both the Second Amendment and the Militia Act of 1792, showed a fear not of an *armed* population, but of a *disarmed* population. The provisions of the various state constitutions in the early years of the Republic show overwhelming support for the understanding that "the right to keep and bear arms" was an individual right, for the purposes of restraining governmental power, and explicitly for individual self-defense.

The evidence of British common law, as articulated by both Blackstone and John Adams, also recognized an individual right to carry arms for self-defense. The widespread knowledge of Beccaria's *On Crimes And Punishments* by the Framers, including the celebrated passage in support of carrying defensive arms, and the apparent lack of debate about the wisdom of constitutional provisions that would have protected such actions, strongly suggests that the Framers intended not merely to protect the individual possession of arms, but the right to carry them for defensive purposes. The evidence on original intent is so overwhelmingly clear, that to argue against either the republican *or* liberal interpretation of the Second Amendment is a hopeless task—and so supporters of laws intended to disarm the general population today argue for the republican understanding exclusively, then deny that the circumstances that motivated the republican perspective are still applicable to a modern society.

If there were general agreement that the function of the judiciary was to interpret the Constitution based on original intent, the history of judicial interpretation of the right to keep and bear arms would be tremendously uninteresting. The evidence of the Framers' intentions is so overwhelming, that only a few laws restricting the keeping and carrying of man-portable arms could survive court challenge. But as we will see when we study the judicial interpretation of the Second Amendment and its analogs in the various state constitutions, the courts have not always held original intent as the primary determinant of constitutionality, nor have the courts always recognized the original intent. Worst of all, many times throughout the history of the Republic, when original intent was the stated rule for determining constitutionality of a law, the judiciary has simply ignored inconvenient original intent.

IV. PROBLEMS OF JUDICIAL INTERPRETATION

Judicial interpretation of the Second Amendment provides a wealth of information with which to prove either the republican or liberal position, depending on which decisions are cited, and how selectively the quotes are made. Courts frequently make decisions on the narrowest possible grounds, in response to particular points of law raised by one side or the other; it is therefore remarkably easy to quote individual sentences from a decision that completely contradict the overall meaning of the decision. This is especially true when lawyers—trained for advocacy, not objectivity—are writing history. The only way out of the morass of selectively quoted decisions is to read the originals, in their entirety.

In addition, we will be examining at least three different sets of rights in this part of the book, each of which reflects a progressively greater set of restrictions on the individual: the right to *concealed* carry of arms; the right to *open* carry of arms; and the right to possess arms on private property. There are many variations, and in the next few chapters we will examine court cases involving a variety of combinations of types of arms, carry modes, and places of possession.

Federal laws regulating private ownership, transfer, or carriage of firearms appear to be relatively recent, at least as applied to the non-Indian population of the United States. In a sense, federal laws restricting sales of firearms to Indians were export controls on hostile foreign powers, even though these foreign powers were within the boundaries of the United States. These federal restrictions on sales to Indians appear *at least* as early as 1873, and were not abolished until 1979.[1] State laws were also passed to restrict sales to Indians. While no attempt has been made to develop a comprehensive list of such statutes, Idaho, as one example, did not repeal a law prohibiting sales of firearms and ammunition to Indians until 1949.[2]

Even determining when the first federal laws appeared has been a frustrating experience. One source asserts that, "Federal involvement in firearms possession and transfer was not significant prior to 1934, when the National Firearms Act of

---

1 Halbrook, *That Every Man Be Armed*, 234-5. Carl P. Russell, *Guns On The Early Frontier*, (Berkeley: University of California Press, 1957), reprinted (Lincoln, Nebr.: University of Nebraska Press, 1980), 40-61, gives a detailed account of the arming of the Indians, first by the English, then by the American government through 1842, with no apparent attempt at limiting sales, except during the Revolution and the War of 1812.

2 Idaho Code Annotated §18-3309 (1987).

1934 was adopted."[3] Another source tells us that the first law was adopted in 1927, when Congress banned "the sending of handguns through the mails (18 USC 1715)."[4] As a result, the U.S. Supreme Court has made few rulings directly on the meaning of the Second Amendment but there *are* several decisions peripheral to the Second Amendment in which the Court has declared its meaning, with varying degrees of clarity.

There have been, however, many state court decisions based on the Second Amendment before and after the doctrine of incorporation was recognized by the federal courts,[5] and also a large number of state court decisions based on the various state analogs to it. These decisions concerning the state analogs are not proof of the Second Amendment's meaning, but the most detailed decisions have acknowledged it as the root of many of these analogs. Even without these acknowledgments, the similarities in language to the Second Amendment would be persuasive evidence of their ancestry.

There are difficulties in putting together a comprehensive list of state court decisions; many of the most detailed decisions were written before the Civil War, a period for which many law libraries are incomplete. This author has had the good fortune to have relatively easy access to the Hastings Law Library's extensive collection of nineteenth century state court decisions. The problems of indexing also make it a daunting task to find all the decisions which involve the Second Amendment and its state analogs, especially with the older decisions. The most effective strategy is to find the most recent decisions by the various state supreme courts, and follow back the citations recursively. Finally, the repeated errors of citation in state court decisions mean that some of these chains tracing the history of judicial interpretation are broken; whatever the citation *should* have been, that line of judicial reasoning is now lost.

Once the decisions are found, a more complex problem appears: which decisions represent new ground, and which are simply a restatement of existing precedents? In many decisions, old precedents were cited, with no apparent recognition that the old precedents held to a dramatically different interpretation of the constitutional protection under discussion. An additional problem is that when inconvenient, there is a disturbing tendency by the courts to label parts of previous decisions as dicta,[6] even when the statement is unambiguously the main point of the decision. The legal profession may comfortably label part of a decision as dicta, and then ignore it; when studying the history of the right to keep and bear arms, not only dicta, but minority opinions, can provide valuable information as to what beliefs were commonly held during that time. How "common" such beliefs were, of

---

3 Senate Subcommittee on The Constitution Staff, "Enforcement of Federal Firearms Laws From the Perspective of the Second Amendment", in *The Right To Keep And Bear Arms*, 19.

4 Carol D. Foster, Mark A. Siegel, Donna R. Plesser, Nancy R. Jacobs, *Gun Control: Restricting Rights or Protecting People*, (Plano, Tex.: Information Aids, Inc., 1987), 21.

5 Incorporation is the principle by which *most* of the guarantees of the first eight amendments of the Bill of Rights have been extended to protect individuals from not only laws passed by Congress, but also from laws passed by the state legislatures and local governments. While derived from the Fourteenth Amendment, we will find in our study of the Second Amendment that the Bill of Rights was recognized by some state supreme courts as a limitation on state power even before the Fourteenth Amendment.

6 A dictum, in law, is a judge's opinion which is not part of the main issue being decided. Dicta are seldom given the credence of the main point decided.

course, is open to debate, in the absence of other indications. An idea, however, that reappears throughout the judicial history is a fundamental part of American thought.

We will explore these judicial decisions chronologically, after first addressing the prohibited categories of "the people." Once we have examined these in detail, we will engage in a chronological examination of the right to keep and bear arms, where the right to carry arms, and the right to possess them on private property, are unsurprisingly interlinked. (It should be apparent that the right to carry arms includes the right to possess them at home. As a result, those decisions which recognized the right to carry arms seldom require re-examination with respect to private possession of arms.)

One surprisingly large class of decisions can be disposed of in this way: felons, prisoners, and drunks. As we saw on page 37, Professor Cress argues that because Samuel Adams, among others, recognized that citizens possessing arms must be "peaceable," the right to arms was not absolute, but dependent on the law-abiding behavior of the individual.[7] Perhaps reflective of the adversarial system of American justice, there are a great many decisions that have ruled on the subject of whether convicted felons and prisoners have a right to bear or possess arms;[8] there is a somewhat smaller body of decisions with respect to the right to bear arms while intoxicated, or in a bar.[9]

The earliest decisions found on this subject dated from the 1920s, during Prohibition. This may reflect an unwillingness of earlier appellate and supreme courts to hear appeals on such apparently absurd questions, since it defies any notion of common sense to allow prison inmates to possess firearms. While it is tempting to regard all the decisions involving prisoners as being frivolous—and

---

7 Cress, 34.

8 Felons not allowed to carry or possess arms: *People* v. *Camperlingo*, 69 Cal.App. 466, 231 P. 601 (1924); *People* v. *Gonzales*, 72 Cal.App. 626, 237 P. 812 (1925); *People* v. *McCloskey*, 76 Cal.App. 227, 244 P. 930 (1926); *State* v. *Tully*, 198 Wash. 603, 89 P.2d 517 (1939); *U.S.* v. *Tot*, 131 F.2d 261 (4th Cir. 1942); *Cases* v. *U.S.*, 131 F.2d 916 (1st Cir. 1942); *State* v. *Krantz*, 24 Wash.2d 350, 164 P.2d 453 (1945); *People* v. *Garcia*, 97 Cal.App.2d 733, 218 P.2d 837 (1950); *Jackson* v. *State*, 37 Ala. App. 335, 63 So.2d 850 (1953); *Mason* v. *State*, 103 So.2d 337 (Ala.App. 1956); *City of Akron* v. *Williams*, 113 Ohio App. 293 (1960); *State* v. *Noel*, 3 Ariz. App. 313, 414 P.2d 162 (1966); *State* v. *Cartwright*, 246 Or. 120, 418 P.2d 822 (1967); *Nelson* v. *State*, 195 So.2d 853 (Fla. 1967); *State* v. *Bolin*, 200 Kan. 369, 436 Pac.2d 978 (1968); *People* v. *McFadden*, 31 Mich. App. 512, 188 N.W.2d 141 (1971); *People* v. *Trujillo*, 178 Colo. 147, 497 P.2d 1 (1972); *Cody* v. *U.S.*, 460 F.2d 34 (8th Cir. 1972); *U.S.* v. *Weatherford*, 471 F.2d 47, 51 (7th Cir. 1972); *U.S.* v. *Johnson*, 497 F.2d 548 (4th Cir. 1974); *State* v. *Beorchia*, 530 P.2d 813 (Utah 1974); *People* v. *Blue*, 190 Colo. 95, 544 P.2d 385 (1975); *People* v. *Taylor*, 190 Colo. 144, 544 P.2d 392 (1975); *People* v. *Bergstrom*, 190 Colo. 105, 544 P.2d 396 (1975); *State* v. *Amos*, 343 So.2d 166 (La. 1977); *State* v. *Rupp*, 282 N.W.2d 125 (Iowa 1979); *Lewis* v. *U.S.*, 100 S.Ct. 915 (1980); *Carfield* v. *State*, 649 P.2d 865 (Wyo. 1982); *State* v. *Wacek*, 703 P.2d 296 (Utah 1985); *People* v. *Barger*, 732 P.2d 1225 (Colo.App. 1986); *State* v. *Friel*, 508 A.2d 123 (Me. 1986); *State* v. *Ricehill*, 415 N.W.2d 481 (N.D. 1987); *State* v. *Comeau*, 233 Neb. 910, 448 N.W.2d 598 (1989); *State* v. *Brown*, 571 A.2d 816 (Me. 1990). Prisoners denied a right to possess arms: *People* v. *Wells*, 68 Cal.App.2d 476 (1945).

The *State* v. *Beorchia* (Utah 1974) decision is also one of the few that included drug addicts and the mentally incompetent in the category of those that could be properly prohibited from possession of firearms under a state constitutional provision.

9 Decisions denying a right to bear arms while intoxicated or in a bar: *People* v. *Garcia*, 197 Colo. 550, 595 P.2d 228 (1979); *Second Amendment Foundation* v. *City of Renton*, 25 Wash. App. 583, 668 P.2d 596 (1983); *State* v. *Dees*, 100 N.M. 252, 669 P.2d 261 (App. 1983).

indeed, few of these decisions reached state supreme courts—this is not always the case. In *People* v. *Wells* (1945), Wesley Robert Wells, an inmate at California's Folsom prison, argued that he armed himself with a knife and used it in self-defense against another prisoner; substantial evidence was provided to the trial court that gave credence to his claim.[10]

The cases involving ex-felons are more complicated, especially in the last few decades, as the courts have increasingly restored the civil rights of felons upon completion of their sentences. In *People* v. *Blue* (1975), the defendant argued that a statute that prohibited ex-felons possessing "any dagger, dirk, knife, or stiletto... or any other dangerous instrument capable of inflicting cutting, stabbing, or tearing wounds..." would make it "criminal for an ex-felon to cut meat with a table knife, repair his car with a screwdriver..."[11] In *People* v. *Ford* (1977), the Colorado Supreme Court found that Colorado's right to keep arms in defense of "home, person and property" did allow ex-felons to possess pistols and rifles at home for self-defense, but put the burden on the defendant to establish that the weapons were for that purpose.[12]

Perhaps the most complete discussion of the topic is found in *People* v. *Camperlingo* (1924), where the Second Appellate Court of California wrote a decision that articulated the "reasonable regulation" viewpoint. Joseph Camperlingo, previously convicted of a felony, was charged with being a felon in possession of a concealable firearm.[13] The Appellate Court cited the *In re Rameriz* (1924) decision, in which the California Supreme Court had upheld a law prohibiting non-citizens from owning concealable firearms, and then went on to discuss the meaning of the right to bear arms:

> It therefore becomes apparent that the right of a citizen to bear arms is not acquired from any constitutional provision, and while it may be said that by the operation of the statute under consideration a citizen is deprived of one of his natural rights in that his ability to better defend himself from personal violence if offered will be somewhat lessened, such right is not greater than or different in character from any other natural right possessed by him. It is clear that in the exercise of police power of the state, that is, for the public safety or the public welfare generally, such rights may be either regulated or, in proper cases, entirely destroyed. Acting within the scope of such power, the legislature, by a proper classification of its citizens, has declared that persons heretofore convicted of a felony shall not possess firearms, and while such citizens are thus deprived of a natural right, in the judgment and discretion of the legislature such deprivation tends directly to the accomplishment of the desired end. As has been indicated by the authorities cited herein, a reasonable basis exists for the classification of citizens of the state in the manner provided by the statute, and there can be no question of the uniformity of its operation upon all persons within the designated class.[14]

By arguing that there were classes of people who were properly prohibited from keeping and bearing arms (*i.e.*, felons), the Appeals Court here *seems* to have found that this "natural right" could be completely destroyed by the legislature, if done under the excuse of public safety or public welfare.

---

10 *People* v. *Wells*, 68 Cal. App.2d 476, 479 (1945).
11 *People* v. *Blue*, 190 Colo. 95, 544 P.2d 385, 389 (1975).
12 *People* v. *Ford*, 193 Colo. 459, 568 P.2d 26, 27 (1977).
13 *People* v. *Camperlingo*, 69 Cal.App. 466, 469, 231 P. 601 (1924).
14 *People* v. *Camperlingo*, 69 Cal.App. 466, 473, 231 P. 601 (1924).

But the following paragraph gave a very small loophole that a future court might exploit: "The rule is unquestioned that in the absence of a clear abuse of legislative discretion, where the subject of the act relates to the exercise of the assumed powers, the courts are authorized to interfere with a construction unfavorable to constitutionality."[15] This decision left open an opportunity for a future court to overturn a gun control law that was "a clear abuse of legislative discretion." But it contains a dangerous notion—that a natural right could be completely destroyed in the interest of the greater good.

Since this issue will reappear throughout the remainder of this work, it is worthwhile to consider the paradoxical character of a "natural right" that may be "entirely destroyed." A Bill of Rights is a limitation on the power of the government. In a representative government, a Bill of Rights is therefore a limitation on the power of the majority. What purpose does the declaration of such a right serve, if it can be overridden by the majority's declaration that the "public safety or public welfare generally" requires it? Nearly any law, by a sufficiently tortuous path, can be found to be required for public health and safety. A law against flag-burning can be justified as a measure to prevent riot against the flag-burner; a law imposing religious obligations can be justified as promoting public morality, in the interests of public safety. Unless an extraordinary burden is imposed on the government to justify the regulation or destruction of a right, a Bill of Rights, under this "public health or safety" theory of rights, has no real authority to protect minority rights.

Unlike the prisoner and ex-felon cases, the laws prohibiting possession of a firearm while under the influence of alcohol are less obviously absurd. In *People* v. *Garcia* (1979), the Colorado Supreme Court ruled in favor of a statute that prohibited possession of a firearm while "under the influence of intoxicating liquor or of a narcotic drug or dangerous drug."[16] While at first glance an "obviously" correct decision, the argument presented by the defense includes several examples where someone might well be "under the influence," at least to some extent, but which could be considered "commonly accepted behavior... hunters drinking at their camps at night, policemen drinking when off duty, citizens drinking in their homes with firearms in the vicinity."[17]

In the *Second Amendment Foundation* v. *City of Renton* (1983) decision, the Second Amendment Foundation sought to overturn a local ordinance that prohibited the "possession of firearms where alcoholic beverages are dispensed by the drink." While the Renton, Washington, ordinance exempted restaurants that served alcohol, and the bartender (whose need for a firearm, at least in bars with a violent clientele, should be obvious),[18] the Second Amendment Foundation apparently sought to clarify to what extent the state constitutional provision pre-empted local regulation of firearms possession by those licensed to carry handguns. There was no requirement that a person be intoxicated, or even drinking alcohol, to be in violation of the law; mere presence in a bar was enough. The Washington Court of Appeals upheld the local ordinance as "reasonable regulation"—a position that relatively few people would argue, since there is a well-established connection between

---

15 *People* v. *Camperlingo*, 69 Cal.App. 466, 473, 231 P. 601 (1924).
16 *People* v. *Garcia*, 197 Colo. 550, 595 P.2d 228, 229 (1979).
17 *People* v. *Garcia*, 197 Colo. 550, 595 P.2d 228, 230, n.1 (1979).
18 *Second Amendment Foundation* v. *City of Renton*, 25 Wash. App. 583, 668 P.2d 596, 597 (1983).

alcohol and violence. In the *State* v. *Dees* (1983) decision a few days later, the New Mexico Court of Appeals upheld a similar statute.[19]

The cases in this category are interesting not only for the small number that reached state supreme courts, but also for their brevity and how little they have to say about the applicability of the federal and state constitutional protections with respect to others. While most of these decisions acknowledged that an individual right to keep and bear arms existed, sometimes based on the Second Amendment, sometimes based on the state constitution's analog, they are, as a class, remarkably silent on the nature of the rights which are protected for those who are law-abiding and sober. Perhaps reflective of the prevailing sentiments of the other twentieth century decisions that we will be examining in later chapters, the phrases "reasonable regulation" and "exercise of the police power" continually reappear, with no clear indication of how far such laws can continue to be considered "reasonable."

---

19 *State* v. *Dees*, 100 N.M. 252, 669 P.2d 261 (N.M.App. 1983).

V. "TO KEEP AND CARRY ARMS WHEREVER THEY WENT"

There are commentaries on the Second Amendment by a number of recognized legal scholars, many from the Revolutionary and Republican period, that shed light on the meaning of the right to keep and bear arms. Throughout the nineteenth century, and into the beginning of the twentieth century, Blackstone's *Commentaries on the Laws of England* was a popular starting point for legal scholars, who would annotate it for the purpose of explaining American law. As we have already seen, Blackstone's *Commentaries* made an explicit declaration of the right to keep and bear arms as an *individual* right. Consequently, we can get a sense of how the legal profession's understanding of this right changed by examining how each jurist's annotations of Blackstone explains the right to keep and bear arms. Examining these works also provides a yardstick to which to compare the early decisions of the courts.

Our first example is from St. George Tucker, Chief Justice of the Virginia Supreme Court at the beginning of the nineteenth century, and a friend and correspondent of Thomas Jefferson. St. George Tucker's 1803 edition of Blackstone's *Commentaries* cites the Second Amendment with reference to the right of subjects to bear arms, "And this without any qualification as to their condition or degree, as is the case in the British government." Tucker shared Blackstone's understanding that this was an individual right.

William Rawle is another one of the early commentators on the Constitution, and another friend and correspondent of Thomas Jefferson.[1] Rawle's background is a bit less distinguished; he was appointed U.S. Attorney for Pennsylvania by President Washington, and was one of the early abolitionists. Rawle's *A View of the Constitution* (1829), provides one of the first expositions of the meaning of the Second Amendment that argues that the second clause is not limited by the first, and that the prohibition extends to the states as well as the national government. Rawle tells us that:

> In the second article, it is declared, that *a well regulated militia is necessary to the security of a free state*; a proposition from which few will dissent. Although in actual war, the services of regular troops are confessedly more valuable; yet, while peace prevails, and in the commencement of a war before a regular force can be raised, the militia form the

---

1 William Blackstone, *Blackstone's Commentaries*, edited by St. George Tucker, (Philadelphia: William Young Birch & Abraham Small, 1803; reprinted Buffalo, N.Y.: Dennis & Co., 1965), 1:143 n. 40, 41. Senate Subcommittee on The Constitution Staff, "History: Second Amendment Right To 'Keep and Bear Arms'", 6-7.

palladium of the country. They are ready to repel invasion, to suppress insurrection, and preserve the good order and peace of government. That they should be well regulated, is judiciously added. A disorderly militia is disgraceful to itself, and dangerous not to the enemy, but to its own country. The duty of the state government is, to adopt such regulations as will tend to make good soldiers with the least interruptions of the ordinary and useful occupations of civil life. In this all the Union has a strong and visible interest.

The corollary, from the first position, is, that *the right of the people to keep and bear arms shall not be infringed.*

The prohibition is general. No clause in the Constitution could by any rule of construction be conceived to give to congress a power to disarm the people. Such a flagitious attempt could only be made under some general pretense by a state legislature. But if in any blind pursuit of inordinate power, either should attempt it, this amendment may be appealed to as a restraint on both....

This right ought not, however, in any government, to be abused to the disturbance of the peace.

An assemblage of persons with arms, for an unlawful purpose, is an indictable offence, and even the carrying of arms abroad by a single individual, attended with circumstances giving just reason to fear that he purposes to make an unlawful use of them, would be sufficient cause to require him to give surety of the peace. If he refused he would be liable to imprisonment.[2] [emphasis in original]

While "a single individual" might violate the law by carrying arms under circumstances that would cause "reason to fear ... an unlawful use of them," the carrying of arms alone was not a crime, and was protected by the Second Amendment as an individual right.

U.S. Supreme Court Justice Joseph Story's *Commentaries on the Constitution of the United States* (1833), not surprisingly, articulated the meaning of the various amendments in the Bill of Rights:

§1889. The next amendment is: "A well regulated militia being necessary to the security of a free state, the right of the people to keep and bear arms shall not be infringed."

§1890. the importance of this article will scarcely be doubted by any persons, who have duly reflected upon the subject. The militia is the natural defence of a free country against sudden foreign invasions, domestic insurrections, and domestic usurpations of power by rulers. It is against sound policy for a free people to keep up large military establishments and standing armies in time of peace, both from the enormous expenses, with which they are attended, and the facile means, which they afford to ambitious and unprincipled rulers, to subvert the government, or trample upon the rights of the people. *The right of the citizens to keep and bear arms has justly been considered, as the palladium of the liberties of the republic; since it offers a strong moral check against the usurpation and arbitrary power of rulers; and will generally, even if these are successful in the first instance, enable the people to resist and triumph over them.*[3] [emphasis added]

Again, the notion of popular resistance against the government is stated as one of the goals of an armed populace. "The right of the citizens" is clearly an *individual* right, not a right of the state governments, or of state militias. Next, Justice Story acknowledged:

And yet, though this truth would seem so clear, and the importance of a well regulated militia would seem undeniable, it cannot be disguised, that among the American people there is a growing indifference to any system of militia discipline, and a strong disposi-

---

2 William Rawle, *A View of the Constitution*, 2nd ed., (Philadelphia: n.p., 1829), 125-6.
3 Joseph Story, *Commentaries on the Constitution of the United States*, (Boston: n.p., 1833), 3:746-7.

tion, from a sense of its burthens, to be rid of all regulations. How it is practicable to keep the people duly armed without some organization, it is difficult to see. There is certainly no small danger, that indifference may lead to disgust, and disgust to contempt; and thus gradually undermine all the protection intended by this clause of our national bill of rights.

§1891. A similar provision in favour of protestants (for to them it is confined) it to be found in the bill of rights of 1688, it being declared, "that the subjects, which are protestants, may have arms for their defence suitable to their condition, and as allowed by law." But under various pretences the effect of this provision has been greatly narrowed; and it is at present in England more nominal than real, as a defensive privilege.[4]

Jonathan Elliot's *The Debates of the Several State Conventions on the Adoption of the Federal Constitution*, published in 1836, contained a "Digest of the Constitution," which indexes the various parts of the Constitution. Included in this index is: "*Rights of the citizen* declared to be —...To keep and bear arms..." Under the same heading are listed, "Liberty of conscience in matters of religion," "Freedom of speech and of the press," "To assemble and petition," "To be exempt from the quartering of soldiers in any house," "To be secure from unreasonable searches and seizures," and the rest of the rights traditionally recognized as individual. That the Second Amendment was intentionally included in this list, is further demonstrated by the fact that there is no entry for the Tenth Amendment, which protects *only* the rights of the states, but there is an entry for each of the first nine amendments.[5]

The first state supreme court decision on the meaning of "the right to bear arms" did not occur until more than thirty years after the Second Amendment's adoption—a long enough time for a younger generation of legislators to come into office, with no direct knowledge of the Revolution, but a short enough time that a number of the Framers were still alive.

Kentucky had passed a law that prohibited the carrying of concealed arms, including, "a pocket-pistol, dirk, large knife, or sword in a sword-cane, unless when traveling on a journey." In *Bliss* v. *Commonwealth* (1822), a man named Bliss was charged with concealing a sword in a cane, and was convicted in a jury trial. Bliss appealed his conviction, arguing that the law violated a state constitutional provision "that the right of the citizens to bear arms in defense of themselves and the state shall not be questioned." While the law in question did not completely ban the carrying of arms—only the concealed carry of arms, "unless when traveling"—the Kentucky Supreme Court held:

That the provisions of the act in question do not import an entire destruction of the right of the citizens to bear arms in defense of themselves and the state, will not be controverted by the court; for though the citizens are forbid wearing weapons, concealed in the manner described in the act, they may, nevertheless, bear arms in any other admissible form. But to be in conflict with the constitution, it is not essential that the act should contain a prohibition against bearing arms in every possible form; it is the right to bear arms in defense of the citizens and the state, that is secured by the constitution, and whatever restrains the full and complete exercise of that right, though not an entire destruction of it, is forbidden by the explicit language of the constitution. If, therefore, the act in question imposes any restraint on the right, immaterial what appellation may be given to the act, whether it be an act regulating the manner of bearing arms, or any

---

4 Story, 3:746-7.
5 Elliot, 1:xv.

other, the consequence, in reference to the constitution, is precisely the same, and its collision with that instrument equally obvious. And can there be entertained a reasonable doubt but the provision of the act import a restraint on the right of the citizens to bear arms? The court apprehends not. *The right existed at the adoption of the constitution;* it had then no limits short of the moral power of the citizens to exercise it, and it in fact consisted in nothing else but in the liberty of the citizens to bear arms... *For, in principle, there is no difference between a law prohibiting the wearing of concealed arms, and a law forbidding the wearing such as are exposed; and if the former be unconstitutional, the latter must be so likewise.*[6] [emphasis added]

Not only did "the right to bear arms" include *concealed* weapons, but this "right existed at the adoption of the [Kentucky] constitution"—which reinforces existing evidence that the carrying of concealed arms was an accepted and recognized practice in the early years of the Republic. In response to this decision, "the section was altered in the new constitution of that state, by the addition of the clause, 'but the general assembly may pass laws to prevent persons from carrying concealed arms.'"[7]

In 1831, Indiana passed a statute, "That every person, not being a traveller, who shall wear or carry any dirk, pistol, sword in a sword-cane, or other dangerous weapon concealed, shall upon conviction thereof, be fined in any sum not exceeding one hundred dollars."[8] In 1833, the Indiana Supreme Court upheld the constitutionality of this statute. From the frequency with which this decision is cited throughout the nineteenth and twentieth century decisions, in a variety of states, one might assume that it is a powerful opinion, containing a clear and unambiguous elucidation of why concealed carry laws are constitutional. In fact, the *entire* decision of the Indiana Supreme Court in this case is a single sentence: "It was *held* in this case, that the statute of 1831, prohibiting all persons, except travelers, from wearing or carrying concealed weapons, is not unconstitutional."[9]

The Indiana Supreme Court had upheld a lower court's decision, and found the question sufficiently uninteresting—or sufficiently difficult to justify—that they offered *no* explanation of the apparent conflict between Article I, §20 of the Indiana Constitution: "That the people have a right to bear arms for the defense of themselves and the State, and that the military shall be kept in strict subordination to the civil power,"[10] and a law prohibiting the carrying of concealed weapons. In light of the clear-cut contrary position taken in the only extant precedent, *Bliss* v. *Commonwealth* (1822), the position taken in St. George Tucker's 1803 edition of Blackstone, William Rawle's 1829 *A View of the Constitution*, and the clear language of the Indiana Constitution itself, the Indiana Supreme Court's apparent lack of need to explain its ruling is all the more puzzling.

Why then, is this slip of a decision so often cited? Probably because it was the only precedent to which later state courts could point, in order to uphold statutes that prohibited concealed carry of weapons. Such was the case in *State* v. *Reid* (1840), and *Aymette* v. *State* (1840), to be examined later in this chapter.

The next decision was in Tennessee:

---

6 *Bliss* v. *Commonwealth*, 2 Littell 90, 13 Am. Dec. 251, 252, 253 (1822).

7 A. C. Freeman, ed., *American Decisions*, (San Francisco: A.L. Bancroft & Co., 1879), 13:255.

8 *Laws of Indiana*, 1831 ed., 192, quoted in *State* v. *Reid*, 1 Ala. 620 (1840).

9 *State* v. *Mitchell*, 3 Blackford 229 (Ind. 1833). This decision was so brief that it was necessary to find even the language of the statute in question from a later decision, *State* v. *Reid* (1840).

10 Thorpe, 2:1059.

William Simpson, laborer, on the first day of April,... 1833, with force and arms,... being arrayed in a warlike manner, then and there in a certain public street and highway situate, unlawfully, and to the great terror and disturbance of divers good citizens of the said state, then and there being, an affray did make, in contempt of the laws of the land, to the evil example of all others in the like case offending, and against the peace and dignity of the state.[11]

Simpson was convicted, and fined $20. On appeal, the Tennessee Supreme Court concluded that the indictment leading to conviction was defective, because the crime of making an "affray" requires:

First. There must be fighting. Second. This fighting must be by or between two or more persons. And, Third. It must be in some public place to cause terror to the people. Hence it must follow, that if either of these requisites are wanting, to wit, fighting or actual violence, and the number of persons necessary for the constitution of it.[12]

After discussing Edward III's Statute of Northampton (1328) that prohibited the carrying of "dangerous and unusual arms," and Hawkins' interpretation of it as not prohibiting completely the carrying of arms, the Court went on to point out its inapplicability to this case:

But suppose it to be assumed on any ground, that our ancestors adopted and brought over with them this English statute, or portion of the common law, our constitution has completely abrogated it; it says, "that the freemen of this state have a right to keep and to bear arms for their common defence." Article 11, sec. 26. It is submitted, that this clause of our constitution fully meets and opposes the passage or clause in Hawkins, of "a man's arming himself with dangerous and unusual weapons," as being an independent ground of affray, so as of itself to constitute the offence cognizable by indictment. By this clause of the constitution, an express power is given and secured to all the free citizens of the state to keep and bear arms for their defence, without any qualification whatever as to their kind or nature; and it is conceived, that it would be going much too far, to impair by construction or abridgment a constitutional privilege which is so declared; neither, after so solemn an instrument hath said the people may carry arms, can we be permitted to impute to the acts thus licensed such a necessarily consequent operation as terror to the people to be incurred thereby; we must attribute to the framers of it the absence of such a view.[13]

The judgment against Simpson was reversed.

Justice Peck, in a dissenting opinion, was unwilling to reverse the judgement, but his reasoning similarly supports the majority opinion with respect to the applicability of the statute of Edward III and the carrying of arms:

One can commit an affray, as by arming himself, rushing into a public place and threatening to kill. Though the words do not make the affray, yet the acts coupled with them will, if fear ensue, amount to an affray... It is not true, as supposed, that to constitute an affray there must be a fighting of two in a public place. An assault by one in a public place will be an affray, though if in a private place, the same act would amount to nothing more than an assault.[14]

None of the justices on either side of this decision were prepared to hold the bearing of arms *by itself* as a violation of either common law or the Statute of Northampton, and the majority recognized Tennessee's "for the common defence"

---

11 *Simpson* v. *State*, 5 Yerg. 356, 357 (Tenn. 1833).
12 *Simpson* v. *State*, 5 Yerg. 356, 358 (Tenn. 1833).
13 *Simpson* v. *State*, 5 Yerg. 356, 359, 360 (Tenn. 1833).
14 *Simpson* v. *State*, 5 Yerg. 356, 363 (Tenn. 1833).

Constitutional provision as protecting an individual right to carry such arms. Since the justices were concerned with the carrying of arms in such a manner as would induce "terror to the people," it is hard to see how they could have justified a law that prohibited concealed carry. Arms that could not be seen could hardly produce terror.

But something interesting happened in 1834, the year after the *Simpson* decision—the Tennessee state constitution was revised. Article 11, §26, adopted in 1796, had originally said: "That the freemen of this State have a right to keep and to bear arms for their common defence." The 1834 revisions changed this section to: "That the free *white* men of this State have a right to keep and to bear arms for their common defence."[15] [emphasis added]

In 1833, it guaranteed the right to all "freemen," regardless of race. Did the *Simpson* v. *State* (1833) provision cause the 1834 revision to the Tennessee Constitution? Was Simpson a free black? Or did the awareness of the potential that free blacks could carry arms provoke the change?

There is another, more likely explanation for the Tennessee constitutional change, and the increasingly ambivalent attitude about the right to carry arms during this period in the South. Nat Turner's rebellion, in August 1831 had provoked great fear in the South:

> Despite the fact that after 1831 no more slave insurrections were seen in the South, it was precisely then that the South became most victimized by its own fears, being "racked at intervals," as Clement Easton writes, "by dark rumors and imagined plots." These periodic upheavals over suspected revolts—characterized by furious vigilante hunts and wild confusion, all based on mirage—constitute one of the more bizarre chapters in Southern history.[16]

and:

> Under the antebellum color-caste system, the status of free Negroes in Tennessee steadily deteriorated. The state legislature, in 1831, barred the immigration of free blacks into the state.... The constitutional convention of 1834 produced a further restriction by withdrawing the legal right to vote which free blacks previously had held in Tennessee.[17]

It appears that concern about the dangers of armed free blacks providing arms to slaves was already on the rise, even before Turner's particularly bloody uprising. Florida had enacted a license procedure for carrying of firearms by free blacks in 1828, but repealed it in February of 1831, disarming free blacks in public. It may be, however, that Turner's rebellion hastened a process already under way, for Maryland and Virginia both passed prohibitions of free blacks carrying arms in December 1831 and Georgia completely prohibited black possession of firearms in 1833. Similarly, Florida authorized "white citizen patrols to seize arms found in the homes of slaves and free blacks…" However, the statute provided at least the possibility that a good reason might prevent punishment.[18]

---

15 Thorpe, 6:3424, 6:3428.

16 Stanley M. Elkins, *Slavery*, (Chicago: University of Chicago Press, 1968), 209, 220.

17 Joseph H. Cartwright, *The Triumph of Jim Crow*, (Knoxville, Tenn.: University of Tennessee Press, 1976), 4.

18 Robert J. Cottrol and Raymond T. Diamond, "The Second Amendment: Toward An Afro-Americanist Reconsideration", in *Georgetown Law Journal*, 80:2 [December 1991], 337-8.

The next decision by the Tennessee Supreme Court was considerably different: *Aymette* v. *State* (1840). This is one of those cases with far-reaching impact, principally because it so narrowly defined the right to keep and bear arms. It was cited repeatedly during the nineteenth century as courts looked for precedents to uphold restrictions on the carrying of arms.

In 1837, the Tennessee Legislature had prohibited the carrying of concealed Bowie knifes; interestingly enough, no other weapons were similarly restricted. William Aymette, on June 26, 1839, at Pulaski, in Giles County,

> had fallen out with one Hamilton, and that about ten o'clock, p.m., he went in search of him to a hotel, swearing he would have his heart's blood. He had a bowie-knife concealed under his vest and suspended to the waistband of his breeches, which he took out occasionally and brandished in his hand. He was put out of the hotel, and proceeded from place to place in search of Hamilton, and occasionally exhibited his knife.

The jury, under the charge of the court, returned a verdict of guilty.

Aymette was fined $200, a stiff fine in 1840. On appeal, Aymette argued that the law was unconstitutional, based on article 11, §26 of the Tennessee Constitution. The Tennessee Supreme Court pointed to the laws of Charles II, prohibiting arms to those who had "not lands of the yearly value of £100," and argued that the English Bill of Rights (1689) protection of the right to arms:

> *does not mean for private defence, but, being armed, they may as a body rise up to defend their just rights, and compel their rulers to respect the laws.* This declaration of right is made in reference to the fact before complained of, that the people had been disarmed, and soldiers quartered among them contrary to law. The complaint was against the government. The grievances to which they were thus forced to submit were for the most part of a public character, and could have been redressed only by the people rising up for their common defence, to vindicate their rights.

> The section under consideration, in our bill of rights, was adopted in reference to these historical facts, and in this point of view the language is most appropriate and expressive. Its words are, "the free white men of this state have a right to keep and bear arms for their common defence." It, to be sure, asserts the right much more broadly than the statute of 1 William & Mary. For the right there asserted is subject to the disabilities contained in the act of Charles II. There, lords and esquires, and their sons, and persons whose yearly income from land amount to £100, were of suitable condition to keep arms. But, with us, every free white man is of suitable condition, and, therefore, every free white man may keep and bear arms. But to keep and bear arms for what? If the history of the subject had left in doubt the object for which the rights is secured, the words that are employed must completely remove that doubt. It is declared that they may keep and bear arms for their common defence... The object, then, for which the right of keeping and bearing arms is secured is the defence of the public. *The free white men may keep arms to protect the public liberty, to keep in awe those who are in power, and to maintain the supremacy of the laws and the constitution.*[19] [emphasis added]

The right to possess military arms as tools of revolution and resistance were guaranteed not simply to organized militias, but to individual free white men:

> The words "bear arms," too, have reference to their military use, and were not employed to mean wearing them about the person as part of the dress. As the object for which the right to keep and bear arms is secured is of a general and public nature, to be exercised by the people in a body, for their common defence, so the arms the right to keep which is secured are such as are usually employed in civilized warfare, and that constitute the

---

19 *Aymette* v. *State*, 2 Hump. (21 Tenn.) 154, 155, 156, 158 (1840).

ordinary military equipment. If the citizens have these arms in their hands, they are prepared in the best possible manner to repel any encroachments upon their rights by those in authority. They need not, for such a purpose, the use of those weapons which are usually employed in private broils, and which are efficient only in the hands of the robber and the assassin. These weapons would be useless in war. They could not be employed advantageously in the common defence of the citizens. The right to keep and bear them is not, therefore, secured by the constitution.[20]

The Tennessee Supreme Court gave an example of what today would be considered assault with a deadly weapon, or brandishing a weapon, which Aymette had certainly done:

> Suppose it were to suit the whim of a set of ruffians to enter the theatre in the midst of the performance, with drawn swords, guns, and fixed bayonets, or to enter the church in the same manner, during service, to the terror of the audience, and this were to become habitual; can it be that it would be beyond the power of the Legislature to pass laws to remedy such an evil? Surely not....

> It is true, it is somewhat difficult to draw the precise line where legislation must cease and where the political right begins, but it is not difficult to state a case where the right of legislation would exist. *The citizens have the unqualified right to keep the weapon, it being of the character before described as being intended by this provision.* But the right to bear arms is not of that unqualified character. The citizens may bear them for the common defence; but it does not follow that they may be borne by an individual, merely to terrify the people or for purposes of private assassinations.[21] [emphasis added]

The Tennessee Supreme Court acknowledged the decision of the Kentucky Supreme Court in *Bliss* v. *Commonwealth* (1822), but asserted that the Kentucky Supreme Court had misinterpreted the meaning of the Kentucky Constitution's arms provision. What should have carried more weight was the precedent set down seven years earlier by the Tennessee Supreme Court, in *Simpson* v. *State* (1833); but the Tennessee Supreme Court of 1840 dismissed it: "But in that case no question as to the meaning of this provision in the constitution arose, or was decided by the court, and the expression is only the incidental remark of the judge who delivered the opinion, and, therefore, is entitled to no weight."[22] Of course, as we have seen, this statement is simply *not* the case. What had changed the temper of the Tennessee Court so dramatically in those intervening seven years? Was it fear of free blacks with arms?

In *State* v. *Reid* (1840), the Alabama Supreme Court ruled on the constitutionality of an 1839 law that prohibited concealed carry of weapons. The defendant was convicted by a jury of carrying a concealed pistol—and the circumstances under which the defendant was carrying the pistol would seem the most blameless imaginable:

> On the trial it was proved, that the defendant carried concealed about his person, a pistol. That while making a settlement as sheriff, he had been attacked by an individual of a dangerous and desperate character, who afterwards threatened his person, and came to his office several times to look for him. It was also proved, that these threats were communicated to the defendant, and the pistol brought to him by a friend, who conceived his life was in danger.[23]

---

20 *Aymette* v. *State*, 2 Hump. (21 Tenn.) 154, 156, 158 (1840).
21 *Aymette* v. *State*, 2 Hump. (21 Tenn.) 154, 159, 160 (1840).
22 *Aymette* v. *State*, 2 Hump. (21 Tenn.) 154, 161 (1840).
23 *State* v. *Reid*, 1 Ala. 612, 613 (1840).

Apparently, the Alabama statute had no exemption for peace officers! On appeal:

> Mr. Goldthwaite for the defendant, insisted that the act of the Legislature on which the indictment was founded, abridges the right secured to the citizen by the 23d section of the 1st article of the constitution. There is no restriction on the exercise of the right, as the grant is in general terms, the Legislature cannot prescribe limits to it... Has not a subsequent Legislature (if the statute in question be constitutional) the right to prohibit the carrying of arms openly, and both acts being in force, the right of carrying arms at all, would be taken away. Such a state of things, all will admit, cannot exist without a violation of the constitution.[24]

The Alabama Supreme Court, in upholding the statute, agreed that the Alabama Constitutional provision, "Every citizen has a right to bear arms, in defence of himself and the State," was derived from the English Bill of Rights (1689), "doubtless induced by the high prerogative claims of the Stuarts," Charles II, and James II. The Court also acknowledged that the Constitutional protection was a limitation on state power, to the benefit of the individual, but:

> The question recurs, does the act, "To suppress the evil practice of carrying weapons secretly," trench upon the constitutional rights of the citizen? We think not. The constitution in declaring that, "Every citizen has the right to bear arms in defence of himself and the State," has neither expressly nor by implication, denied to the Legislature, the right to enact laws in regard to the manner in which arms shall be borne. The right guarantied to the citizen, is not to bear arms upon all occasions and in all places, but merely "in defence of himself and the State." The terms in which this provision is phrased seems to us, necessarily to leave with the Legislature the authority to adopt such regulations of police, as may be dictated by the safety of the people and the advancement of public morals.

The Alabama Supreme Court, however, acknowledged that there were limits to this power of the Legislature:

> We do not desire to be understood as maintaining, that in regulating the manner of bearing arms, the authority of the Legislature has no other limit than its own discretion. *A statute which, under the pretence of regulating, amounts to a destruction of the right, or which requires arms to be so borne as to render them wholly useless for the purpose of defence, would be clearly unconstitutional.* But a law which is intended merely to promote personal security, and to put down lawless aggression and violence, and to that end inhibits the wearing of certain weapons, in such a manner as is calculated to exert an unhappy influence upon the moral feelings of the wearer, by making him less regardful of the personal security of others, does not come in collision with the constitution.[25] [emphasis added]

Apparently, the Court felt that concealed carry of arms would cause the wearer to be less concerned about the safety of others—as if the secret possession of a weapon made the owner more willing to kill.

The Alabama Supreme Court cited the decisions in *Bliss* v. *Commonwealth* (1822) and *State* v. *Mitchell* (1833), but held that it was more comfortable with the reasoning of the Indiana Supreme Court in *Mitchell*—though as we have seen, there is no "reasoning" in that decision. The Alabama Supreme Court also claimed that

---

24 *State* v. *Reid*, 1 Ala. 612, 614 (1840).
25 *State* v. *Reid*, 1 Ala. 612, 615, 616, 617 (1840).

concealed carry provided no real advantage for self-defense, and therefore necessity[26] for self-protection was not a valid defense:

> In the case at bar, the defendant needed no arms for his protection, his official authority
> furnished him an ample shield. In this country a sheriff possesses all the powers, which
> pertained to his office at common law; except so far as they may have been divested by
> statute, or such as are incompatible with the nature of our institutions. He is the keeper
> of the peace within the county. He may apprehend, and commit to prison, all persons
> who break the peace, or attempt to break it; and may cause such persons to be bound in
> a recognizance to keep the peace. He may, and is bound ex officio, to pursue and take
> all traitors, murderers, felons, and rioters; he also hath the custody and safekeeping of the
> county jail; he is to defend the same against rioters, and for this purpose, as well as for
> taking rioters and others breaking the peace, he may call to his aid the posse comitatus,
> or power of the county, and the citizens are bound to obey his summons, on pain of fine
> and imprisonment.

> We will not undertake to say, that if in any case it should appear to be indispensable to
> the right of defense that arms should be carried concealed about the person, the act "to
> suppress the evil practice of carrying weapons secretly," should be so construed, as to op-
> erate a prohibition in such case. But in the present case, no such necessity seems to have
> existed; and we cannot conceive of its existence under any supposable circumstances.[27]

The Court acknowledged that open carry was protected by the Alabama Constitutional provision, but that concealed carry was not—even for a sheriff with a valid
reason to worry about his personal safety. The Court did leave the door open
where concealed carry "should appear to be indispensable to the right of defense,"
but even so, the Court saw concealed carry not as a right, but as a limited exemption from the law.

In *Owen* v. *State* (1858), the Alabama Supreme Court held that the concealed
carry of a weapon was not protected, even in private. The charge was carrying a
concealed weapon; the circumstances were that the defendant was in the room of a
friend, when, according to a man named Hutchinson: "[W]hile there, he asked the
defendant to give him a cap; and that the defendant put his hand into his vest
pocket, and took a small pistol out of his pocket, to get a cap; that the pistol was the
smallest he had ever seen, and he requested the defendant to let him look at it..."

The prosecution argued that even though there was no evidence that Owen had
left the room carrying a concealed weapon, that this was still a violation of §3274 of
Alabama's criminal code. The opinion, written by Chief Justice Rice, used the
precedent of *State* v. *Reid* (1840) to establish:

> That section was not designed to destroy the right, guarantied by the constitution to
> every citizen, "to bear arms in defense of himself and the State"; nor to require them to
> be so borne, as to render them useless for the purpose of defense. It is a mere regulation
> of the manner in which certain weapons are to be borne...

The Court upheld the conviction, on the grounds:

> The word "carries," in the section above cited, was used as the synonym of "bears"; and
> the word "concealed," as therein used, means, willfully or knowingly covered, or kept
> from sight. Locomotion is not essential to constitute a carrying within the meaning of
> that section.

---

26 The "necessity defense" recognizes that a violation of law may sometimes be necessary to prevent
loss of life or great bodily injury.

27 *State* v. *Reid*, 1 Ala. 612, 621, 622 (1840).

While the Alabama concealed weapon statute contained some exceptions for those who were "being threatened with, or having good reason to apprehend an attack, or travelling, or setting out on a journey,"[28] there is no evidence that the Court saw these as rights (which were not subject to discretionary repeal by the Legislature), but merely as state grants of privilege.

In 1842, the Arkansas Supreme Court heard *State* v. *Buzzard*, another case which will echo repeatedly as a precedent. The defendant, Buzzard, violated:

> [T]he 13th section of the first Article, Division VIII., Ch. 44, *Rev. St. Ark.,* p. 280, which declares, that "every person who shall wear any pistol, dirk, butcher, or large knife, or a sword in a sword-cane, concealed as a weapon, unless upon a journey, shall be adjudged [*sic*] guilty of a misdemeanor." The indictment was quashed, and the defendant ordered to be discharged by the Circuit Court; and the State has, by appeal, brought the case this Court, to revise said decision.[29]

This is among the longer antebellum "right to keep and bear arms" decisions. Both the Second Amendment and the similar provision of the Arkansas Constitution, were raised in opposition to the concealed weapons statute. The majority opinion, written by Chief Justice Ringo, contained a great many errors of fact concerning the origins of the Second Amendment and made very few citations of precedent or authority to justify its position; nonetheless, this decision raised interesting points about what constitutes an *absolute* right, and not just with respect to the right to keep and bear arms.

In attempting to justify the passage of the concealed weapons law, the majority opinion held:

> Among the objects for which all free governments are instituted, may be enumerated the increase of security afforded to the individual members thereof for the enjoyment of their private rights, the preservation of peace and domestic tranquility, the administration of justice by public authority, and the advancement of the general interests or welfare of the whole community. In addition to which, it is designed that adequate security shall be provided by law for the most perfect enjoyment of these blessings.[30]

The Arkansas Supreme Court then argued that as a consequence of this, many natural rights are given up to the state:

> For instance, the right of any individual to redress, according to the dictates of his own will or caprice, any injury inflicted upon his personal or private rights by another, is surrendered; and the right of determining not only what his rights are, but also whether they have been invaded, and the kind and measure of redress to which he is entitled, and are referred to the arbitrament of the law. Also, the natural right of speech must remain without restraint, if it were not surrendered and subjected to legal control upon the institution of government; yet every one is aware that such limitations as have been found necessary to protect the character and secure the rights of others, as well as to preserve good order and the public peace, have been imposed upon it by law, without any question as to the power of the government to enforce such restrictions. So the liberty of the press, which is based upon the right of speech, is to the like extent subject to legal control. So the right of migration and transmigration, or of every individual to pass from place to place, according to his own free will and pleasure, when and where he chose, acknowledged no restraint until surrendered upon the institution of government, when it became subject to such regulations as might be found necessary to prevents its exercise

28 *Owen* v. *State*, 31 Ala. 387, 388, 389 (1858).
29 *State* v. *Buzzard*, 4 Ark. 18 (1842).
30 *State* v. *Buzzard*, 4 Ark. 18, 19 (1842).

from operating prejudicially upon the private rights of others, or to the general interests of the community.[31]

The Court gave no example of what, exactly, they meant by the regulations that restricted "migration... from place to place," nor did they clarify if the limitations on free speech and the press were necessarily limited to civil penalties for slander or libel. The argument is an open-ended invitation to unlimited state power, especially since the Court failed to specify the limits of the interest-balancing act.

Next, however, the Arkansas Supreme Court raised an important issue about what is meant by a natural right:

Suppose the constitutional existence of such immunity in favor of the right to keep and bear arms as is urged by the appellee be admitted. By what legal right can a person accused of crime be disarmed? Does the simple accusation, while the law regards the accused as innocent, operate as a forfeiture of the right? If so, what law attaches to it this consequence? Persons accused of crime, upon their arrest, have constantly been divested of their arms, without the legality of the act having ever been questioned. Yet, upon the hypothesis assumed in the argument for the appellee, the act of disarming them must have been illegal, and those concerned in it trespassers, the constitution not limiting the right to such only as are free from such accusation. Nor could the argument of necessity or expediency justify one person in depriving another of the full enjoyment of a right reserved and secured to him by the constitution.[32]

The Court then argues that "arms" would include large quantities of gunpowder stored at home, even in quantities so large as to be a hazard to the neighbors—and hence, such a right to arms must not be absolute, but only relative to the rights of others. Of course, by the same reasoning used by the Court, because free speech can, under the right conditions, constitute treason, which is a criminal offense, then the right of free speech is not absolute; therefore, since the right of free speech is not absolute, the Legislature would be free to pass whatever regulatory laws it wished.

As to the purpose of the right to arms, the Court held that:

Is it to enable each member of the community to protect and defend by individual force his private rights against every illegal invasion, or to obtain redress in like manner for injuries thereto committed by persons acting contrary to law? Certainly not; because, according to the fundamental principles of government, such rights are created, limited, and defined by law, or retained subject to be regulated and controlled thereby; and the laws alone are and must be regarded as securing to every individual the quiet enjoyment of every right with which he is invested; thus affording to all persons, through the agency of the public authorities to whom their administration and execution are confided, ample redress for every violation thereof... Such legal remedies, however, can only be enforced by public authority...[33]

The Court found that the right to self-defense did not exist, because the government's job was redress of grievances. The Court also suggested self-defense was morally and legally equivalent to revenge.

So just what was the purpose of "the right to keep and bear arms"? The Court decided that the language of the Second Amendment protected the right of the militia to possess arms: "Besides which, the language used appears to indicate, distinctly, that this, and this alone, was the object for which the article under consid-

31 *State* v. *Buzzard*, 4 Ark. 18, 20, 21 (1842).
32 *State* v. *Buzzard*, 4 Ark. 18, 21 (1842).
33 *State* v. *Buzzard*, 4 Ark. 18, 22 (1842).

eration was adopted."[34] There is no authority cited to justify this position; indeed, not a single authority is cited for any of the Court's statements of intent for either the Second Amendment or the Arkansas Constitution's similar provision; only the existing state court precedents with respect to concealed weapons laws are given.

Justice Lacy, writing a dissenting opinion, had a better understanding of the common law, the motivations for the Second Amendment and Arkansas' similar constitutional protection. With reference to the question of whether the "well-regulated militia" clause circumscribed the "right of the people":

> Now, I take the expressions "a well regulated militia being necessary for the security of a free State," and the terms "common defence," to be the reasons assigned for the granting of the right, and not a restriction or limitation upon the right itself, or the perfect freedom of its exercise. The security of the State is the constitutional reason for the guaranty. But when was it contended before, that the reason given for the establishment of a right, or its uninterrupted enjoyment, not only limited the right itself, but restrained it to a single specific object? According to this construction, the right itself is not only abridged, but literally destroyed; and the security of a free State is made to depend exclusively and alone upon the force of the militia. And, in the opinion of one of my brother Judges, it is the militia alone who possess this right, in contradistinction from the mass of the people; and even they cannot use them for private defence or personal aggression, but must use them for public liberty, according to the discretion of the Legislature. *According to the rule laid down in their interpretation of this clause, I deem the right to be valueless, and not worth preserving; for the State unquestionably possesses the power, without the grant, to arm the militia, and direct how they shall be employed in cases of invasion or domestic insurrection. If this be the meaning of the Constitution, why give that which is no right in itself, and guaranties a privilege that is useless?*[35] [emphasis added]

Here Justice Lacy successfully demolished the argument that such state constitutional provisions were intended to guarantee the right of the state to organize its own militia. While an argument could be advanced that the Second Amendment was intended to protect the right of the state to maintain its own military force, such a constitutional guarantee makes no sense at all in a state constitution.

Justice Lacy then echoed the concerns about "sword and purse" that were heard during the Constitutional ratification debates:

> If the Legislature have the custody of the people's arms and the treasury of the State, what becomes of the separation and division of the political powers of the government? Are not these powers united in the same body of magistracy? And if this be the case, the balance of the Constitution is overthrown, and the State then possesses no real security for personal liberty. It is no answer to this argument, to say that the people may abuse the privilege or right of keeping and bearing arms. The Constitution thought and ordained it otherwise; and therefore it was deemed far safer to entrust the right to their own judgment and discretion, rather than to the will or ambition of the Legislature; and this right was excepted out of the general powers of the government, and declared inviolate.[36]

Justice Lacy pointed out that power to prohibit concealed carry is equivalent to the power to prohibit open carry:

> This principle I utterly repudiate. I deny that any just or free government upon earth has the power to disarm its citizens, and to take from them the only security and ultimate hope that they have for the defence of their liberties and their rights. I deny this,

---

34 *State* v. *Buzzard*, 4 Ark. 18, 24 (1842).
35 *State* v. *Buzzard*, 4 Ark. 18, 35 (1842).
36 *State* v. *Buzzard*, 4 Ark. 18, 36 (1842).

not only upon constitutional grounds, but upon the immutable principles of natural and equal justice, that all men have a right to, and which to deprive them of amounts to tyranny and oppression. Can it be doubted, that if the Legislature, in moments of high political excitement or of revolution, were to pass an act disarming the whole population of the State, that such an act would be utterly void, not only because it violated the spirit and tenor of the Constitution, but because it invaded the original rights of natural justice?[37]

Lacy also illustrated how the same reasoning used to justify laws prohibiting concealed carry could be extended in equally absurd ways to deprive the people of other rights protected by the Federal and state constitutions:

The people are secured in their persons, houses, papers, and effects, against unwarrantable searches and seizures; but on probable cause, supported by oath and affirmation. Now, if the Legislature possess the power claimed for it, it surely has the means of carrying it into effect. Can it, directly or indirectly, invade the sanctuaries of private life and of personal security, by authorizing a public inquisition to search for either open or concealed weapons? Besides, private property cannot be taken for public uses, without due compensation being first made according to law. A man's arms are his private property: how, then, can he be legally deprived of them? If they can forbid him, under the penalty of fine and imprisonment, to keep them concealed or exposed about his person, or on his own premises, although their unrestrained use may be necessary for all the purposes of his ordinary business and of personal defence, then certainly the right of keeping and bearing arms according to his own discretion, is infringed and violated, and his own free will in the management of this property abridged and destroyed.

Lacy pointed out a potential inequity from such an approach to this right:

[S]uppose a citizen of the State were indicted upon a charge of murder, and he could make out a clear case of justifiable homicide, the laws of nature, upon which the laws of society are presumed to be based, instead of punishing, commends for the act; of course, he stands acquitted of all blame; but, on the trial, the evidence shows that he was compelled to take life with a concealed weapon, and the State thinks proper to indict him for this new offence, which is forbidden by an act of the Legislature; and the proof being clear upon the point, of course he may be convicted and rendered infamous for life. What then becomes of the right of self-defence? Is it not swept away from him by legislative discretion, and the doctrine of self-preservation destroyed, which nature has implanted in the breast of every living creature, and which no laws, either human or divine, can abrogate or annul?[38]

The majority opinion in the *Buzzard* decision is by far the most extreme statement in opposition to an individual right to keep and bear arms in the period before the Civil War. It not only is contrary to the liberal view of the right to arms, but it also lacks the republican understanding that arms, to be effective in defense of public liberty, required widespread possession among the people.

The following year, the *State* v. *Huntly* (1843) decision was handed down by the North Carolina Supreme Court. The North Carolina Supreme Court's decision far more accurately describes both the republican and liberal schools of the Second Amendment. A Robert Huntly was convicted of, "The offence of riding or going armed with unusual and dangerous weapons to the terror of the people... an offence at common law...."

---

37 *State* v. *Buzzard*, 4 Ark. 18, 36, 37 (1842).
38 *State* v. *Buzzard*, 4 Ark. 18, 37, 38, 39 (1842).

While Huntly's attorney tried to claim that North Carolina's constitutional protection of the right to "bear arms for the defence of the State" overrode the Statute of Northampton (1328), the North Carolina Supreme Court did not agree:

> While it secures to him a *right* of which he cannot be deprived, it holds forth the *duty* in execution of which that right is to be exercised. If he employ those arms, which he ought to wield for the safety and protection of his country, to the annoyance and terror and danger of its citizens, he deserves but the severer condemnation for the abuse of the high privilege, with which he has been invested.

While acknowledging that the provision of the North Carolina Constitution was, as the text suggests, "for the defence of the State," this decision also recognized that an *individual* right was created by it.

For its justification of the conviction, the Court pointed to *Sir John Knight's case* in Hawkins' *Treatises of the Pleas of the Crown* to demonstrate that being armed for the purpose of terrorizing people was a violation of the common law, and that the Statute of Northampton merely codified and provided "only special penalties and modes of proceeding for its more effectual suppression." More important, North Carolina had specifically renounced the statutory law of England and Great Britain on January 1, 1838.

While agreeing that the actions for which Huntly was convicted were a violation of the common law, the North Carolina Supreme Court also held that:

> it is to be remembered that the carrying of a gun *per se* constitutes no offence. *For any lawful purpose—either of business or amusement—the citizen is at perfect liberty to carry his gun. It is the wicked purpose—and the mischievous result—which essentially constitute the crime.* He shall not carry about this or any other weapon of death to terrify and alarm, and in such manner as naturally will terrify and alarm, a peaceful people. [emphasis added]

The North Carolina Supreme Court acknowledged that the gun in question "a double-barrelled gun, or any other gun, cannot in this country come under the description of 'unusual weapons,' for there is scarcely a man in the community who does not own and occasionally use a gun of some sort."[39]

At no point did the North Carolina Supreme Court address the issue of concealed carry of arms. In light of their agreement with the common law prohibition on carrying weapons "to terrify and alarm," it might well be argued that concealed carry of arms was therefore more socially responsible.

The following year, the North Carolina Supreme Court made a decision whose full significance would not appear until after the Civil War and passage of the Fourteenth Amendment. An 1840 statute provided:

> That if any free negro, mulatto, or free person of color, shall wear or carry about his or her person, or keep in his or her house, any shot gun, musket, rifle, pistol, sword, dagger or bowie-knife, unless he or she shall have obtained a licence therefor from the Court of Pleas and Quarter Sessions of his or her county, within one year preceding the wearing, keeping or carrying therefor, he or she shall be guilty of a misdemeanor, and may be indicted therefor.

Elijah Newsom, "a free person of color," was indicted for carrying a shotgun without a license, in Cumberland County in June of 1843—at the very time the

---

39 *State* v. *Huntly*, 3 Iredell 418, 420, 421, 422, 423 (N.C. 1843). This case has been frequently miscited as *State* v. *Huntley*, perhaps because the name is spelled both ways in the decision.

North Carolina Supreme Court was deciding *Huntly*. Newsom was convicted by a jury; but "on motion of the defendant's counsel, the court arrested the judgement, and the Solicitor for the State appealed to the Supreme Court." Newsom's attorney argued that the statute requiring free blacks to obtain a license to "keep and bear arms" was "unconstitutional, being in violation of the 2d article of the amended constitution of the United States, and also of the 3d and 17th articles of the Bill of Rights of this State."

The North Carolina Supreme Court quickly disposed of the first claim, that the Second Amendment was a limitation on state laws: "It is therefore only restrictive of the powers of the Federal Government." The North Carolina Supreme Court then cited *Barron* v. *Baltimore* (1833) (though it was miscited as "*Barrow* v. *Baltimore*"), to buttress that position.

Next, the North Carolina Supreme Court tackled the state constitutional guarantees, which had been used in *State* v. *Huntly* (1843), the year before. The "3d article" referred to by Newsom's counsel, prohibited "the granting of exclusive privileges or separate emoluments." The North Carolina Supreme Court acknowledged that the 1840 statute imposed a restriction on free blacks, "from which the white men of the country are exempt." The Court then asked if racially discriminatory legislation was therefore unconstitutional, and gave the answer:

> If so, then is the whole of our legislation upon the subject of free negroes void. From the earliest period of our history, free people of color have been among us, as a separate and distinct class, requiring, from necessity, in many cases, separate and distinct legislation.[40]

What followed was a long list of laws that affected free blacks only, dating from 1777. The Court held that since society had long acquiesced in such distinctions, from the time that the North Carolina Constitution was written, therefore the third article was not intended as a guarantee against racially discriminatory laws.[41]

The 17th article of the 1776 North Carolina Constitution declared:

> That the people have a right to bear arms, for the defence of the State; and, as standing armies, in time of peace, are dangerous to liberty, they ought not to be kept up; and that the military should be kept under strict subordination to, and governed by, the civil power.[42]

The Court now addressed this constitutional protection, but in language subtly different from that used in *Huntly*: "We cannot see that the act of 1840 is in conflict with it... The defendant is not indicted for carrying arms in defence of the State, nor does the act of 1840 prohibit him from so doing."[43] But as seen in *Huntly*, the Court had acknowledged that the restrictive language "for the defence of the State" did not preclude an individual right.[44] The Court then attempted to justify the necessity of this law:

> Its only object is to preserve the peace and safety of the community from being disturbed by an indiscriminate use, on ordinary occasions, by free men of color, of fire arms or other arms of an offensive character. Self preservation is the first law of nations, as it is of individuals. And, while we acknowledge the solemn obligations to obey the constitu-

---

40 *State* v. *Newsom*, 5 Iredell 181, 27 N.C. 250, 251, 252 (1844).
41 *State* v. *Newsom*, 5 Iredell 181, 27 N.C. 250, 252, 253 (1844).
42 Thorpe, 5:2788.
43 *State* v. *Newsom*, 5 Iredell 181, 27 N.C. 250, 254 (1844).
44 *State* v. *Huntly*, 3 Iredell 418, 422 (N.C. 1843).

tion, as well in spirit as in letter, we at the same time hold, that nothing should be interpolated into that instrument, which the people did not will. We are not at liberty to give an artificial and constrained interpretation to the language used, beyond its ordinary, popular and obvious meaning. Before, and at the time our constitution was framed, there was among us this class of people, and they were subjected to various disabilities, from which the white population was exempt. It is impossible to suppose, that the framers of the Bill of Rights did not have an eye to the existing state of things, and did not act with a full knowledge of the mixed population, for whom they were legislating. They must have felt the absolute necessity of the existence of a power somewhere, to adopt such rules and regulations, as the safety of the community might, from time to time, require.[45]

The North Carolina Supreme Court also sought to repudiate the idea that free blacks were protected by the Bill of Rights by pointing out that the Constitution excluded free blacks from voting, and therefore free blacks were not citizens. Of course, article 17, unlike some other, more careful state arms provisions,[46] did not limit the right to bear arms to just *citizens*, but to *people*—and try as hard as they might, it would be difficult to argue that a "free person of color," in the words of the Court, was not one of "the people."

The North Carolina Supreme Court assumed that the framers of the North Carolina Constitution did not consider free blacks as being within the protections of the North Carolina Bill of Rights. Even at the first census in 1790, there were already 5,041 free blacks in North Carolina.[47] The other possibility—not considered by the Court—is that the framers of the North Carolina Constitution did not consider armed free blacks a worrisome matter.

To this point, all of these decisions have been based on the various state constitutional protections; none relied directly on the Second Amendment as the basis to overturn a law. But that changed with *Nunn* v. *State* (1846), when the Georgia Supreme Court became the first state supreme court to recognize the Second Amendment as a limitation on the states.

Georgia had passed a law in 1837 which prohibited the sale of "Bowie or any other kinds of knives, manufactured and sold for the purpose of wearing or carrying the same as arms of offence or defence; pistols, dirks, sword-canes, spears, &c., shall also be contemplated in this act, save such pistols as are known and used as horseman's pistols..."[48] Other language contained in the statute strongly suggests that the intent was to stop the sale of concealable deadly weapons, and to prohibit the carrying of small handguns. The Georgia Supreme Court overturned this law as violative of the Georgia Constitution and the Second Amendment of the U.S. Constitution:

> The language of the *second* amendment is broad enough to embrace both Federal and State governments—nor is there anything in its terms which restricts its meaning... Is this a right reserved to the *States* or to *themselves*? Is it not an unalienable right, which lies at the bottom of every free government? We do not believe that, because the people withheld this arbitrary power of disenfranchisement from Congress, they ever intended

45 *State* v. *Newsom*, 5 Iredell 181, 27 N.C. 250, 254 (1844).

46 Early constitutions limiting the right to bear arms to citizens: Connecticut (1818), Kentucky (1792 & 1799), Maine (1819), Mississippi (1817), Pennsylvania (1790)—but not the 1776 Pennsylvania Constitution, Republic of Texas (1838), State of Texas (1845).

47 Bureau of the Census, *Negro Population in the United States 1790-1915*, (Washington: Government Printing Office, 1918; reprinted New York: Arno Press, 1968), 57.

48 *Nunn* v. *State*, 1 Ga. 243, 246 (1846).

to confer it on the local legislatures. This right is too dear to be confided to a republican legislature.

It is commonly assumed that the doctrine of incorporation is a twentieth century interpretation of the Fourteenth Amendment; but here in *Nunn*, we are told, in relation to the Federal Bill of Rights:

> Questions under some of these amendments, it is true, can only arise under the laws and Constitution of the United States. But there are other provisions in them, which were never intended to be thus restricted, but were designed for the benefit of every citizen of the Union in all courts, and in all places; and the people of the several States, in ratifying them in their respective State conventions, have virtually adopted them as beacon-lights to guide and control the action of their own legislatures, as well as that of Congress.[49]

While the Fourteenth Amendment and the doctrine of incorporation caused some Southern state legislatures to recognize that the Second Amendment was a limitation on state power in the years immediately after the Civil War,[50] the Georgia Supreme Court in this decision recognized the Second Amendment as a restriction on the states well before the Civil War and the passage of the Fourteenth Amendment—even though the U.S. Supreme Court refused to recognize *any* of the Bill of Rights as limitations on state power. Nor was this interpretation of the Second Amendment's protection against both federal and state laws unique. William Rawle's *A View of the Constitution* (1829) also considered the Second Amendment to be a limitation on both federal and state power.

The breadth of members of the class with an individual right to bear weapons (albeit, for an ultimately collective purpose), in the Georgia Supreme Court's understanding, was extraordinary:

> The right of the whole people, old and young, men, women and boys, and not militia only, to keep and bear *arms* of every description, and not *such* merely as are used by the *militia*, shall not be *infringed*, curtailed, or broken in upon, in the smallest degree; and all of this for the important end to be attained: the rearing up and qualifying a well-regulated militia, so vitally necessary to the security of a free State. Our opinion is, that any law, State or Federal, is repugnant to the Constitution, and void, which contravenes this *right*, originally belonging to our forefathers, trampled under foot by Charles I. and his two wicked sons and successors, reestablished by the revolution of 1688, conveyed to this land of liberty by the colonists, and finally incorporated conspicuously in our own *Magna Charta!* And Lexington, Concord, Camden, River Raisin, Sandusky, and the laurel-crowned field of New Orleans, plead eloquently for this interpretation! [emphasis in the original]

Finally, after this paean to liberty—in a state where much of the population remained enslaved, forbidden by law to possess arms of any sort—the Court defined the valid limits of laws restricting the bearing of arms:

> We are of the opinion, then, that so far as the act of 1837 seeks to suppress the practice of carrying certain weapons *secretly*, that it is valid, inasmuch as it does not deprive the citizen of his *natural* right of self-defence, or of his constitutional right to keep and bear arms. But that so much of it, as contains a prohibition against bearing arms *openly*, is in conflict with the Constitution, and void...[51] [emphasis in the original]

---

49 *Nunn* v. *State*, 1 Ga. 243, 250, 251 (1846).
50 Halbrook, *That Every Man Be Armed*, 124-35.
51 *Nunn* v. *State*, 1 Ga. 243, 250, 251 (1846).

"Citizen"? Within a single page, the Court had gone from "right of the whole people, old and young, men, women and boys" to the much more restrictive right of a "citizen." It is one of the great ironies that, in much the same way that the North Carolina Supreme Court recognized a right to bear arms in 1843—then almost immediately declared that free blacks were not included—the Georgia Supreme Court did likewise.

The decision *Cooper and Worsham* v. *Savannah* (1848) is not, principally, a right to keep and bear arms case. In 1839, the city of Savannah, Georgia, in an admitted effort "to prevent the increase of free persons of color in our city," had established a one hundred dollar per year tax on free blacks moving into Savannah from other parts of Georgia. Samuel Cooper and Hamilton Worsham, two "free persons of color," were convicted of failing to pay the tax, and were jailed. On appeal, counsel for Cooper and Worsham argued that the ordinance establishing the tax was deficient in a number of technical areas; the assertion of most interest to us is, "In Georgia, free persons of color have constitutional rights..." Cooper and Worsham's counsel argued that these rights included writ of *habeas corpus*, right to own real estate, to be "subject to taxation," "[t]hey may sue and be sued," and cited a number of precedents under Georgia law in defense of their position.

Savannah's counsel countered with an argument that was correct, but did not directly address the issue raised:

> Free persons of color are not citizens, but residents: A citizen is entitled to all the privileges of the State. These persons are not... If citizens, they could represent us in the Legislature, for the constitution does not speak of free *white* citizens.

But Cooper and Worsham's counsel had carefully avoided the claim that free blacks were *citizens*—they had only argued that free blacks were protected by the state constitution.[52]

Justice Warner delivered the Court's opinion, of which one part showed the fundamental relationship between citizenship, arms, and elections:

> *Free persons of color have never been recognized here as citizens; they are not entitled to bear arms, vote for members of the legislature, or to hold any civil office.* They have always been considered as in a state of pupilage, and been regarded as our wards, and for that very reason we should be extremely careful to guard and protect all the rights secured to them by our municipal regulations. They have no *political* rights, but they have *personal* rights, one of which is personal liberty.[53] [emphasis added]

The Court finally held on the technical question of how the $100 per year tax could be collected, that the ordinance jailing Cooper and Worsham for non-payment was illegal, and ordered their release. But the comments of the Court made it clear that their brave words in *Nunn* v. *State* (1846) about "the right of the people," only meant *white* people.

In *Stockdale* v. *State* (1861), the Georgia Supreme Court heard a case which seems incomprehensible—whether open carry of a gun was actually concealed carry—but which reappears frequently in the period after the Civil War. Georgia's "Act of 19th January, 1852," provided that all pistols and other weapons were to be carried in such a manner that it would be obvious to all that the bearer of the weapon was armed. John J. Stockdale was indicted on September 8, 1858, for a

---

52 *Cooper and Worsham* v. *Savannah*, 4 Ga. 68, 69, 70, 71 (1848).
53 *Cooper and Worsham* v. *Savannah*, 4 Ga. 68, 72 (1848).

violation of that statute during the previous month. At trial, witnesses were produced that testified the pistol was "sticking in his breeches waistband, nearly in front, about the suspender button; that the butt and cock of the pistol could be plainly seen, the barrel being inserted beneath the pantaloons, and that the defendant had on no vest." The judge refused to instruct the jury that, if any part of the gun were visible, that the gun was therefore openly carried. Instead, he told them, "if any part of the barrel was stuck down beneath the pants, that it was a violation of law." The jury convicted Stockdale.[54]

On appeal, the Georgia Supreme Court cited *Nunn* v. *State* (1846), and held that "it is impossible for one to have and bear about his person a pistol or weapon of any kind, without having some part of the weapon concealed from view," and that, "To enforce the law, as the Court construed it to the jury, would be to prohibit the bearing of those arms altogether, and to bring the act within the decision in Nunn's case."[55] Not surprisingly, the Court reversed the conviction of Stockdale.

The Louisiana Supreme Court made a series of decisions recognizing the right to openly carry arms in 1850, 1856, and 1858. In the first case, *State* v. *Chandler* (1850), Chandler was tried and convicted of manslaughter. The details of the crime are not contained within the Louisiana Supreme Court's decision, but the weapon appears to have been a Bowie knife. While Chandler's appeal primarily raised self-defense issues, it was also based on his counsel's request that the jury be told "that to carry weapons, either concealed or openly, is not a crime in the State of Louisiana; that the Constitution which guarantees to the citizen the right to bear arms cannot be restricted by the action of the Legislature."

That this issue was raised on appeal suggests that Chandler's concealed carry of a weapon was used by the prosecution to suggest criminal intent, since a Louisiana statute of March 25, 1813, made it a misdemeanor to carry concealed weapons, including a "dirk, dagger, knife, pistol, or any other deadly weapon concealed in his bosom, coat, or any other place about him, that does not appear in plain view." In the Louisiana Supreme Court's opinion:

> This law became absolutely necessary to counteract a vicious state of society, growing out of the habit of carrying concealed weapons, and to prevent bloodshed and assassinations committed upon unsuspecting persons. It interfered with no man's right to carry arms (to use its own words), "in full open view," which places men upon an equality. This is the right guaranteed by the Constitution of the United States, and which is calculated to incite men to a manly and noble defence of themselves, if necessary, and of their country, without any tendency to secret advantages and unmanly assassination.[56]

Though the Court ordered a new trial for manslaughter, it did so based on errors related to the charge to the jury with respect to the law of self-defense.[57] More importantly to our current study, the Court recognized that the Second Amendment

---

54 *Stockdale* v. *State*, 32 Ga. 225, 226 (1861).
55 *Stockdale* v. *State*, 32 Ga. 225, 227 (1861). At first glance, it would seem strange that the *Nunn* decision, based at least partly on the Second Amendment, would still remain a valid precedent, since Georgia by this point had left the United States. However, the Confederacy had pointedly adopted a Constitution "almost word for word" identical to the United States Constitution. Forrest McDonald, *A Constitutional History of the United States*, (New York: F. Watts, 1982; reprinted Malabar, Fla.: Robert E. Krieger Publishing Co., 1986), 124.
56 *State* v. *Chandler*, 5 La. An. 489, 489, 490, 491 (1850).
57 *State* v. *Chandler*, 5 La. An. 489, 491 (1850).

was a restriction on state laws (many years before the Fourteenth Amendment), and that the right protected by the Second Amendment was an *individual* right to openly carry arms for self-defense.

Six years later, in *Smith* v. *State* (1856), the Louisiana Supreme Court backtracked from that bold statement. The defendant, J.T. Smith, was convicted of carrying a concealed weapon, even though the weapon was partially exposed. The defendant attempted to use the Second Amendment as a defense. The Louisiana Supreme Court's response was:

> The statute against carrying concealed weapons does not contravene the second article of the amendments of the Constitution of the United States. The arms there spoken of are such as are borne by a people in war, or at least carried openly. The article explains itself. It is in these words: "A well regulated militia being necessary to the security of a free State, the right of the people to keep and bear arms shall not be infringed." This was never intended to prevent the individual States from adopting such measures of police as might be necessary, in order to protect the orderly and well disposed citizens from the treacherous use of weapons not even designed for any purpose of public defence, and used most frequently by evil-disposed men who seek an advantage over their antagonists, in the disturbances and breaches of the peace which they are prone to provoke.[58]

The Louisiana Supreme Court presented a muddled argument; first, that the arms are "such as are borne by a people in war," is contrary to their ruling in *State* v. *Chandler* (1850), which recognized individual self-defense as well as common defense as a Constitutionally protected reason for carrying arms openly. The second half, "or at least carried openly," appears to be an attempt to extricate the Court from the assertion that only military weapons were protected. This decision recognized open carry as a Constitutionally protected mode in a much looser manner than *State* v. *Chandler* (1850)—though it still recognized that the Second Amendment was a limitation on state laws that prohibited the open carry of arms.

The third Louisiana decision is *State* v. *Jumel* (1858). Allen Jumel was indicted, and apparently convicted of carrying concealed weapons in violation of Louisiana's statute of March 14, 1855, §115. The defendant argued that the statute in question violated the Second Amendment of the U.S. Constitution. Again, the Louisiana Court argued: "The statute in question does not infringe the right of the people to keep or bear arms. It is a measure of police, prohibiting only a particular mode of bearing arms which is found dangerous to the peace of society."[59] The Louisiana Supreme Court then cited the *State* v. *Chandler* (1850) and *State* v. *Smith* (1856) decisions. The *Jumel* decision seemed to imply that *because* "only a particular mode of bearing arms" was restricted, it was not an infringement on the right protected by the Second Amendment.

The first federal decision to discuss the right to keep and bear arms is a well-known case—though it is not well-known for its relevance to the Second Amendment—*Dred Scott* v. *Sandford* (1857). The goal of the suit was to establish that slaves taken into free states were thus free. But the issue of whether free blacks were citizens, and could therefore sue in the Federal courts, had to be resolved first.[60] To that end, it sought to establish that free blacks were citizens of the United States. Justice Taney, writing for the majority, rejected this position:

58 *Smith* v. *State*, 11 La. An. 633, 634 (1856).
59 *State* v. *Jumel*, 13 La. An. 399, 400 (1858).
60 Smith, 425-6.

It would give to persons of the negro race, who were recognized as citizens in any one
State of the Union, the right to enter every other State whenever they pleased, singly or
in companies, without pass or passport, and without obstruction, to sojourn there as long
as they pleased, to go where they pleased at every hour of the day or night without mo-
lestation, unless they committed some violation of law for which a white man would be
punished; and it would give them the full liberty of speech in public and in private upon
all subjects upon which its own citizens might speak; to hold public meetings upon political affairs, *and to keep and carry arms wherever they went.* And all of this would be
done in the face of the subject race of the same color, both free and slaves, inevitably
producing discontent and insubordination among them, and endangering the peace and
safety of the State. [emphasis added]

Justice Taney then held that because of the disruption it would cause in slave states
for free blacks to be citizens of the United States, that "It is impossible ... that the
great men of the slaveholding States, who took so large a share in framing the Constitution of the United States ... could have been so forgetful or regardless of their
own safety," in intending that free blacks be citizens.[61]

Where did this right "to keep and carry arms" come from? Apparently from the
"privileges and immunities" section of the Constitution; but, if so, this right pre-
existed the Constitution, and could be included in the Ninth Amendment's protections, as well as the Second Amendment. Evidence that this right came from the
"privileges and immunities" clause[62] not the Second Amendment, is that Taney
called these rights of *citizens*—even though the language of the Bill of Rights protects these rights of the *people*.

The question of which rights were protected as "Privileges and Immunities" was a
continuing source of judicial dispute in the period before and immediately
following the Civil War. Several different theories existed, all of which suffered
from vagueness. Were these rights deduced from the nature of republican
government? Were they implied by federal laws, the Constitution, and the Bill of
Rights? Were they the common set of rights recognized by all the state
constitutions? Or were they merely a guarantee that if a citizen of New York
entered New Jersey, that he had all the same rights as a New Jersey citizen?[63]

Whether it was derived from its wide recognition by the various states, because it
was a pre-existing right (an issue that will reappear in the *U.S.* v. *Cruikshank* (1876)
decision), or because it was recognized and protected by the Second Amendment,
the *Dred Scott* decision recognized that there were limits not only on Federal
authority to restrict the carrying of arms by citizens, but also limits to state authority, even before the Fourteenth Amendment. Justice Taney's decision also recognized the *individual* nature of the right "to keep and carry arms wherever they
went."

Our next case, *Cockrum* v. *State* (1859), is the first of many Texas decisions. Article 610 of the penal code specified that manslaughter committed with a Bowie
knife or dagger would be considered to be murder, and punished accordingly. The
defendant, John Cockrum, was indicted in 1857 for murdering a William N. Self,

---

61 *Dred Scott* v. *Sandford*, 60 U.S. 393, 417 (1857).

62 Article IV, §2: "The citizens of each State shall be entitled to all Privileges and Immunities of
Citizens in the several States."

63 James H. Kettner, *The Development of American Citizenship, 1608-1870*, (Chapel Hill, N.C.:
University of North Carolina Press, 1978), 254-262, discusses the differing theories with respect to Art.
IV, §2. It is not at all clear which theory was used by Justice Taney in the *Dred Scott* decision.

in Freestone County. In 1858, Cockrum was convicted of murder, apparently based on article 610, and sentenced to life imprisonment in solitary confinement.

Cockrum appealed. The relevant part of his argument, as presented by his lawyer:

> It is contended, that Article 610 of the Penal Code, is in violation of both of the State and Federal Constitution, which contain substantially the same provision, securing the citizen from any infringement on the right to keep and bear arms. 1st. It is asserted, that any law prohibiting a citizen from keeping or bearing any knife, which is intended to be worn upon the person, which is capable of inflicting death, and not commonly known as a pocket-knife, would be unconstitutional. To prohibit absolutely the keeping and having of an ordinary weapon, is certainly to infringe on the right of keeping and bearing arms. A bowie-knife, or dagger, as defined in the Code, is an ordinary weapon, one of the cheapest character, accessible even to the poorest citizen. A common butcher-knife, which costs not more than half a dollar, comes within the description given of a bowie-knife or dagger, being very frequently worn on the person. To prohibit such a weapon, is substantially to take away the right of bearing arms, from him who has not money enough to buy a gun or a pistol.

Here, Cockrum's attorney, Robert S. Gould, crisply articulated the position that would be taken a century later, in opposition to laws banning so-called "Saturday Night Specials"—that such laws work principally to disarm the poor. But what is the relevance of a law enhancing the penalty for manslaughter, to the right to carry a "bowie-knife or dagger"?

Gould pointed to the court decisions on the right to keep and bear arms, in particular, *Nunn* v. *State* (1846), since it had overturned a law banning small pistols. He then argued that if it was unconstitutional to ban the carrying of an arm for a lawful purpose, such as self-defense; and discriminating against a particular arm by enhancing the penalty for criminal use would be an attempt to discourage law-abiding people from carrying such arms, for fear that a manslaughter might thus be punished as severely as murder.[64]

Most of the Texas Supreme Court's decision, written by Justice Roberts, addressed the issues of how the varying punishments available for a murder conviction could be determined by the jury, and are of no relevance to our interests. Of relevance to the Second Amendment and Texas' similar constitutional provision, especially in light of the post-war decisions by the Texas Court: "It is contended, that this article of the Code, is in violation of the Constitution of the United States, and of this State." After citing the Second Amendment and the 13th section of the Texas Bill of Rights: "Every citizen shall have the right to keep and bear arms, in the lawful defense of himself or the State," the Court explicated the purposes of the state and Federal Constitutional protections, with no apparent disagreement that both applied to a *state* law:

> The object of the first clause cited, has reference to the perpetuation of free government, and is based on the idea, that the people cannot be effectually oppressed and enslaved, who are not first disarmed. The clause cited in our Bill of Rights, has the same broad object in relation to the government, and in addition thereto, secures a personal right to the citizen. The right of a citizen to bear arms, in the lawful defence of himself or the State, is absolute. He does not derive it from the State government, but directly from the sovereign convention of the people that framed the State government. It is one of the "high powers" delegated directly to the citizen, and "is excepted out of the general

---

64 *Cockrum* v. *State*, 24 Tex. 394, 396, 397 (1859).

powers of government." A law cannot be passed to infringe upon or impair it, because it is above the law, and independent of the law-making power.

The Court then held that discrimination in sentencing based on the probable lethality of a weapon was legally justified, but:

> The right to carry a bowie-knife for lawful defence is secured, and must be admitted. It is an exceedingly destructive weapon. It is difficult to defend against it, by any degree of bravery, or any amount of skill. The gun or pistol may miss its aim, and when discharged, its dangerous character is lost, or diminished at least. The sword may be parried. With these weapons men fight for the sake of the combat, to satisfy the laws of honor, not necessarily with the intention to kill, or with a certainty of killing, when the intention exists. The bowie-knife differs from these in its device and design; it is the instrument of almost certain death. He who carries such a weapon, for lawful defence, as he may, makes himself more dangerous to the rights of others, considering the frailties of human nature, than if he carried a less dangerous weapon.[65]

Today's controversy over semiautomatic military style rifles (so-called "assault weapons") has strong parallels to the concern expressed here about the Bowie. In both cases, the weapon was perceived as an "instrument of almost certain death," and as a weapon against which there was no defense. Also like today's controversy, the distinction between a Bowie knife and a butcher knife is partly in the perception of the purposes of the weapon, not just their actual capabilities.[66]

The Court was prepared to uphold the law:

> May the State not say, through its law, to the citizen, "this right which you exercise, is very liable to be dangerous to the rights of others, you must school your mind to forbear the abuse of your right, by yielding to sudden passion; to secure this necessary schooling of your mind, an increased penalty must be affixed to the abuse of this right, so dangerous to others."[67]

Instead of banning this "instrument of almost certain death," which would have prohibited both criminals and law-abiding people from carrying it, the Texas Legislature chose to enhance the penalty for criminal use.

Why has such a complete explication of this decision been given? It in no way expands on the principles adopted in the *Nunn* v. *State* (1846) decision, and the three Louisiana decisions; it gives a clear-cut statement of the Texas Supreme Court's understanding of the protections afforded by the Federal and Texas Constitutional provisions—and so makes the post-war decisions by the Texas Supreme Court, to be discussed in the next chapter, all the more inexplicable.

In the period before the end of the Civil War, there are seventeen relevant decisions. In two of these decisions, *Aymette* v. *State* (1840) and *State* v. *Buzzard* (1842), the respective state supreme courts refused to recognize an individual right to carry arms, in any manner. One decision, *State* v. *Mitchell* (1833), refused to recognize a right to concealed carry, and open carry was not discussed. In eight decisions, the state supreme courts held that a right to openly carry arms was pro-

---

65 *Cockrum* v. *State*, 24 Tex. 394, 401, 402, 403 (1859).

66 As an example, California's Assault Weapons Control Act adopted in 1989 restricted most detachable magazine semiautomatic rifles firing .223 ammunition, including the Colt AR-15. Yet the Ruger Mini-14, a detachable magazine semiautomatic rifle, of comparable specifications and capabilities to a Colt AR-15, was not restricted. The Ruger Mini-14 had been sold primarily for use by varmint hunters, and has a brown wood stock. Either rifle would be a fearsome weapon in the hands of a criminal or a psychopath, but only one was restricted—the rifle with the more menacing appearance.

67 *Cockrum* v. *State*, 24 Tex. 394, 403 (1859).

tected by the respective state constitutions—though two of those decisions limited this protection to whites only. In three decisions by the Louisiana Supreme Court, the Second Amendment was recognized as a limitation on state laws, protecting an individual right to openly carry arms. In three decisions, all by the Georgia Supreme Court, the right of citizens to carry arms openly was recognized as protected by both state *and* federal provisions from state laws (though "citizens" would not include free blacks). In one decision by the U.S. Supreme Court, the right of *citizens* to carry arms, without state interference, was recognized, though whether openly or concealed is not explicit. Fourteen out of seventeen decisions during this period recognized the right of *citizens* to carry arms openly.

Less judicial agreement exists during this period about the concealed carry of weapons. Of the fourteen decisions that recognized a right to carry arms openly, six decisions held that carrying arms concealed was not constitutionally protected; one unambiguously recognized that concealed carry was constitutionally protected,[68] and three strongly suggested that such a right might exist.[69] Four decisions are silent on the issue.

In light of the clear-cut original intent of the Second Amendment and the absence of such laws in the early years of the Republic, what provoked these laws restricting the carrying of arms? There are a number of hypotheses: a scarcity of handguns on the frontier; technological advancement in handguns; an urbanizing population; fear of armed blacks; or a fear of armed abolitionists.

Don Kates sees the development of these laws as caused by the scarcity of handguns on the frontier. Kates asserts that the high cost of handguns before the Civil War meant that relatively few law-abiding people in the frontier states owned them. Therefore, restricting the carrying of handguns was perceived as only a restriction on criminals. Thus, the restrictions appeared first in the Wild West of the antebellum period. Kates also asserts that the only Eastern state to adopt any sort of concealed weapon law was Virginia, which had its own frontier, in West Virginia.[70]

There are significant problems with this hypothesis. A number of frontier states apparently adopted no weapons restrictions during this period (Ohio, Michigan, Wisconsin). Some of the states adopting restrictive arms laws during this period were no longer "frontier," when these laws were adopted (*e.g.*, 1837 Georgia).

Does technological change explain the sudden development of these laws? There is a strong tendency to focus on Samuel Colt's successful development of the revolver as the first "modern" handguns, allowing a single person to fire multiple rounds from a compact package.[71] Repeating firearms date back to at least the 1600s; concealable "pepperbox" handguns firing five to seven shots without reloading were in use by the end of the eighteenth century, and magazine-fed

---

68 *Bliss* v. *Commonwealth* (1822).

69 *Simpson* v. *State* (1833), *State* v. *Huntly* (1843), and *Nunn* v. *State* (1846).

70 Don B. Kates, Jr., "Toward a History of Handgun Prohibition in the United States", in Don B. Kates, Jr., ed., *Restricting Handguns: The Liberal Skeptics Speak Out*, 10-12.

71 Walter Prescott Webb, *The Great Plains*, (New York: Houghton Mifflin Co., 1936), 167-79, provides a history of the development of the revolver as a natural outgrowth of the expansion westward from woodlands into the grasslands, and the consequent emphasis on horseback combat. But this fails to explain the laws adopted before the introduction of Colt's revolver in 1838.

repeating guns were issued as early as 1658.[72] The development of the percussion system in 1816 encouraged further development of the pepperbox, by making revolving handguns more practical.

Colt's revolver appears to have been a very minor social factor when it was introduced. Less than 2000 revolvers were produced between 1838 and 1842, when the Paterson, New Jersey, factory went bankrupt, and many of the 2000 were sold to the Republic of Texas. To explain the rise of concealed weapons laws as an outgrowth of the development of Colt's revolver, we must confront the question of how such a tiny number of guns had so much influence. In addition, most of the revolvers made by Colt during this period were very large handguns with nine-inch barrels—scarcely concealable.[73]

Further, we have seen that most of these laws applied to traditional concealed weapons, and a few statutes applied only to Bowie knives, not to handguns. As the *Cockrum* v. *State* (1859) showed, the Bowie knife was the most feared of weapons, not the handgun. Indeed, throughout this period a variety of low-technology deadly weapons were subjects of concern with respect to concealed carry.

Does the appearance of gun control laws reflect an increasingly urban population in the United States? The modern police department—in the sense of a regular, full-time patrol force—developed during the period between 1830 and 1860. But while urban riots, reflecting ethnic tensions and struggles over slavery, were a factor in the rise of the modern city police department, urbanization by itself remains an inadequate answer. It is tempting to assume that laws restricting the carrying of arms were intended to protect the emerging police forces from those who might resist arrest; but police officers during this period were not issued firearms. Until the 1860s, American police were issued billy clubs, whistles, and handcuffs: "Even as late as 1880, the police of Brooklyn, New York, then a separate city of five hundred thousand persons, did not carry firearms."

Laws restricting the carrying of arms existed almost entirely in the South, yet the problems of urban rioting during this period occurred in Boston, St. Louis, New York, Cincinnati, Philadelphia, Chicago, and Baltimore. While Boston's day watch, established in 1838, and Philadelphia's experiments in the period 1833 through 1854 are significant precursors to urban police department, "Another main precursor was the slave-patrol system in the South."[74]

There is a common characteristic to the states adopting these restrictive arms laws: slavery. Every state law restricting the carrying of weapons with one interesting exception (Indiana), was a slave state. Indiana is interesting, because of its early leadership in adopting concealed weapon statutes, and because it is remarkable in its origins. It was largely settled by Southerners, and at the time of the Civil War, had "more people of Southern ancestry or Southern sympathies... than in any other free state."[75] Indeed, the 1850 constitution had prohibited both slavery and free blacks

---

72 Claude Blair, ed., *Pollard's History of Firearms*, (New York: Macmillan Co., 1983), 207, 214. Norman and Pottinger, 206-7.

73 Russell, 91-96.

74 Samuel Walker, *Popular Justice: A History of American Criminal Justice*, (New York: Oxford University Press, 1979), 57-59, 64. Cottrol and Diamond, 337, show that white citizen patrols were authorized as early as 1825 in Florida for this purpose.

75 Bruce Catton, *Glory Road*, (Garden City, N.J.: Doubleday & Co., 1952), 115.

from entering the state.[76] Perhaps the frontier was not the factor responsible for the new laws, as much as the issue of race? The evidence is strong, but not completely persuasive.

Cottrol and Diamond see the desire to keep blacks controlled as the reason, or at least one significant reason, for the development of Southern gun control laws during this period.[77] But while this explains the laws that licensed or prohibited blacks from carrying or owning arms, why would there be a need to similarly restrict whites? Slavery appears to be a factor in the passage of the laws disarming blacks, probably the most important factor, but it is not enough to explain the laws that restricted whites.

Another objection to this explanation is that restrictive gun control laws aimed at blacks, slave and free, were well-established throughout the English, French, and Spanish colonies in areas that became the United States.[78] At most, Turner's Rebellion increased the restrictions and level of fear towards *free* blacks. As an example, in the aftermath of Turner's Rebellion, the discovery that a free black family possessed lead shot for use as scale weights, without powder or weapon in which to fire it, was considered sufficient reason for a frenzied mob to discuss summary execution.[79]

One *possible* explanation, but one that seems implausible, even to this author, is that there was some genuine uncertainty about the race of many Southerners. William Lincoln, a student at Oberlin College in Ohio, made a series of journeys into the South, preaching abolitionism. On one such journey:

> Lincoln was asked to guess the race of the male parishioners as they entered the church. "I made 11 mistakes in 15 minutes," Lincoln acknowledged. Apparently, work outdoors in the sun and wind had tarnished the face and hands of the men. "One case, were I put on oath, I shd. still affirm to be colored," Lincoln said.[80]

If the police were not yet armed, and the laws restricting arms were not primarily directed at blacks, what was the purpose of these laws, and why did they appear first in the South? The answer may lie in the abolition movement:

> The struggle over slavery accentuated the lawlessness and violence. As early as the 1830s the antislavery movement aroused racial passions and provoked vigilante actions in both North and South. In Boston, Cincinnati, Philadelphia, and other cities, mobs attacked

---

76 Catton, 113. Catton refers to this as the 1851 Constitution, as do Cottrol and Diamond; it is usually considered the 1850 Constitution. Cottrol and Diamond, 339 n. 150, inform us that the 1850 Constitution superseded an existing statute (Ind. Rev. Laws 375) that required free blacks entering the state to post a bond. Significantly, Ind. Rev. Laws 375 was adopted in 1831, the same year as Indiana's concealed weapon statute.

77 Cottrol and Diamond, 335-6.

78 Thomas N. Ingersoll, "Free Blacks in a Slave Society: New Orleans, 1718-1812", *William and Marry Quarterly*, 48:2 [April, 1991], 178-9, 192-200. Daniel H. Usner, Jr., *Indians, Settlers, & Slaves in a Frontier Exchange Economy: The Lower Mississippi Valley Before 1783*, (Chapel Hill, N.C.: University of North Carolina Press, 1992), 139, 165, 187. Michael C. Meyer and William L. Sherman, *The Course of Mexican History*, 4th ed., (New York: Oxford University Press, 1991), 216. Benjamin Quarles, *The Negro in the Making of America*, 3rd ed., (New York: Macmillan Publishing, 1987), 81.

79 Harriet Jacobs [Linda Brant], *Incidents in the Life of a Slave Girl*, (Boston: 1861), in Henry Louis Gates, Jr., ed., *The Classic Slave Narratives*, (New York: Penguin Books, 1987), 395-6.

80 Nat Brandt, *The Town That Started The Civil War*, (Syracuse, N.Y.: Syracuse University Press, 1990), 9-11.

both white abolitionists and free black citizens. In the South, vigilantes suppressed all opposition to slavery...[81]

The problem of mob violence directed against abolitionists was sufficiently wide-spread during the 1830s, when the concealed weapons laws became increasingly common in the South, that President Martin Van Buren's Inaugural Address, delivered in March of 1837, addressed the problem twice.[82]

In the South, where slaveholders were overwhelmingly in control, laws to protect attacking mobs from the "unfair advantage" of abolitionists carrying concealed weapons would not be surprising. In the same church where William Lincoln had so poorly guessed the race of the men entering the church, he preached a sermon on the evils of slavery:

> As he spoke, Lincoln noticed that the attention of the congregation had been drawn to his side. "I turned and saw the sheriff & a deputy pointing 2 pistols at the pulpit & I said 'Ye seek to kill me, a man that hath told you the truth'..."

Indeed, before Lincoln left that valley, he narrowly missed being shot to death.

In the Northern states, where slaveholders had little direct influence on state governments, the need to keep abolitionists in fear might have been less obvious. One celebrated example of the abolitionist use of arms in the North is the Oberlin rescue of runaway slave John Price in September 1858. The slavecatchers and U.S. marshals were besieged by hundreds of armed abolitionists, black and white, thus effecting the non-violent release of Price.[83] The connection between arms ownership and revolution was expressed during the trial of the Oberlin Rescuers in a letter to the *Portage County Democrat*, "We must no longer submit to the despotism of the Federal government. Our wrongs we must right if we can through the Ballot Box, and if this fail us, through the Cartridge Box."[84]

The most obvious connection to prohibition of concealed carry of arms in the South is that most of these laws were adopted in the years immediately following Nat Turner's 1831 rebellion. While free blacks were banned from carrying weapons (openly or concealed) in statutes different from those that banned concealed carry, the curious grouping in geography and time of these laws suggests that fear of slave revolt, or of armed abolitionists, or both, provoked these laws. A detailed history of each state's concealed weapons statutes is beyond the scope of this work, but is necessary to resolve the question of why these laws appeared almost exclusively in slave states during the antebellum period.

---

81 Walker, 58.
82 Lott, 68, 70.
83 Brandt, 11-12, 68-111.
84 *Cleveland Plain Dealer*, May 11, 1859, quoted in Brandt, 201.

VI. "No Negro... Shall Be Allowed To Carry Fire-Arms"

After the Civil War, the modern understanding of the right to bear arms began to take shape, almost entirely in the former states of the Confederacy, and the border states where slavery had existed before the war—and this understanding accepted new, more restrictive laws on the open carry of arms. At least part of the impetus for these laws was related to the newly freed slaves.

At the end of the Civil War, the newly restored Southern legislatures adopted a series of laws known as the Black Codes; the purpose of these laws was to create restrictions on free blacks that would maintain the dominant position of Southern whites. Many of these restrictions were aimed at reducing the freedmen to a position of economic dependence; others seem designed to make them unable to defend themselves. (A case can be made that the two situations were connected.) An example is the Mississippi black code, which required "that no freedman, free Negro, or mulatto not in the military service of the United States government, and not licensed so to do by the board of police of his or her county, shall keep or carry firearms of any kind, or any ammunition, dirk, or Bowie knife..." Similarly, St. Landry Parish, Louisiana, passed a series of "Police Regulations" that included: "No negro who is not in the military service shall be allowed to carry fire-arms, or any kind of weapons, within the parish, without the special written permission of his employers, approved and [e]ndorsed by the nearest and most convenient chief of patrol..."[1] Alabama's variant did not even include a process by which a "freedman, free negro or mulatto" might obtain a permit.[2]

Of course, white Southerners had a different perspective on why such laws were needed, with even respected Southern historians arguing, half a century later, "The restrictions in respect to bearing arms, testifying in court, and keeping labor contracts were justified by well-established traits and habits of the negroes...."[3] Before the Civil War, free blacks had not been allowed to possess arms in many (perhaps all) of the slave states, so it is difficult to see how there could be "well-established traits and habits" with respect to bearing arms immediately on the end

---

1 "Mississippi Black Code", in *Annals of America*, (Chicago: Encyclopedia Britannica, Inc., 1976), 9:634. Michael Les Benedict, *The Fruits of Victory: Alternatives in Restoring the Union, 1865-1877*, (New York: J.B. Lippincott Co., 1975), 87. Cottrol and Diamond, 344, quote a very similar Louisiana statute adopted in 1865.

2 Cottrol and Diamond, 345.

3 William A. Dunning, *Reconstruction, Political and Economic*, (New York: Harper, 1907), quoted in Francis L. Broderick, *Reconstruction and the American Negro, 1865-1900*, (London: Macmillan Co., 1969), 21.

of the war.[4] Maryland, a slave state that had remained within the Union, had prohibited slaves from carrying guns without "a license from his said master" before the war, and free blacks were completely forbidden possession of either firearms or ammunition.[5] These arms prohibitions prohibited free blacks from owning *dogs* without a license, and authorized any white to kill an unlicensed dog owned by a free black, out of fear that blacks would use dogs as weapons. Mississippi went further, and prohibited *any* ownership of a dog by a black person.[6]

Maryland abolished slavery in 1864, and the slave codes were repealed the following year. In 1867, Maryland held a constitutional convention; at that convention, an attempt was made to add "and every citizen has the right to bear arms in defence of himself and the State" to the new constitution. Some delegates, including champions of compensation to slaveowners, argued against it, on the grounds that, "Every citizen of the State means every white citizen, and none other." Apparently, there was fear that the language would entitle blacks to carry arms. An attempt to add a considerably more narrow form of the right, "and the citizen shall not be deprived of the right to keep arms on his premises," was also rejected. Halbrook tells us: "Barnes's amendment may have been rejected so that former slaves in Maryland could not keep arms in their homes."[7] However, Halbrook provides no persuasive evidence to support his conjecture.

It had been widely recognized in the period before the Civil War that there was an inverse relationship between arms possession and slavery:

[B]oth proponents and opponents of slavery were cognizant that an armed black population meant the abolition of slavery, although some blacks were trusted with arms to guard property, for self defense, and for hunting. This sociological fact explained not only the legal disarming of blacks, but also the advocacy of a weapons culture by abolitionists. Having employed the instruments for self-defense against his pro-slavery attackers, abolitionist and Republican Party founder Cassius Marcellus Clay wrote that "'the pistol and the Bowie knife' are to us as sacred as the gown and pulpit."[8]

An example of the terror that Southerners held of armed blacks may be found in a decision of the Confederate Congress, May 1, 1863. Black Union soldiers bearing arms would be treated as insurrectionary slaves under the laws of the state where they were captured—which almost certainly would result in the death penalty. The same decree "approved the death penalty for white officers captured while leading black units," and indeed, this had already been the practice in Arkansas in 1862.

---

4 Stephen P. Halbrook, *A Right To Bear Arms*, (Westport, Conn.: Greenwood Press, 1989), 94, 111. While slaves were allowed to possess firearms in Georgia, it was only with permission of his master for specified purposes, and the arms were to be stored in the master's house. Also, see Featherstone & Gardiner, 102.

5 Halbrook, *A Right To Bear Arms*, 111-3. Halbrook, "The Fourteenth Amendment and the Right to Keep and Bear Arms: The Intent of the Founders", in *The Right To Keep And Bear Arms*, 70. Featherstone and Gardiner, 102.

6 Theodore Brantner Wilson, *The Black Codes of the South*, (University of Alabama Press, 1965), 26-30.

7 Halbrook, *A Right To Bear Arms*, 111-3.

8 Featherstone & Gardiner, 101. Featherstone and Gardiner cite the quote from Cassius Marcellus Clay as H. Greeley, ed., 7 *The Writings of Cassius Marcellus Clay*, 257 (1848).

Black Union soldiers were massacred by Confederate troops while trying to surrender at Fort Pillow, Tennessee, in April 1864.[9]

During the closing days of the Civil War, the Virginia Legislature passed a bill providing for the use of black soldiers; an opponent argued: "What would be the character of the returned negro soldiers, made familiar with the use of fire-arms, and taught by us, that freedom was worth fighting for?"[10] The South was not alone in its fear of armed blacks. Representative Thaddeus Stevens observed: "When it was first proposed to free the slaves, and arm the blacks, did not half the nation tremble? The prim conservatives, the snobs, and the male waiting-maids in Congress, were in hysterics."[11]

After the war, the fear of armed blacks remained strong. Senator Willard Saulsbury, a Delaware Democrat, expressed his opposition to the presence of black soldiers in the post-war Regular Army: "'What would be the effect,' he asked his fellow senators, 'if you were to send negro regiments into the community in which I live to brandish their swords and exhibit their pistols and their guns?'"[12] When the Civil Rights Act of 1866 was being debated, Senator Saulsbury spoke against it, on the grounds that if passed, it would invalidate the Delaware law that required "that free negroes shall not have the possession of firearms or ammunition."[13]

Myrta Lockett Avary's *Dixie After The War* contains a chapter on "Secret Societies" which articulates white fears of bloodthirsty freedmen, out to murder white men, in order to rape the white women. Many of the hearsay accounts involve armed blacks, engaging in wanton murders, and negligent discharges of firearms.[14]

Fear of black retribution provoked tremendous stress among white Georgians in the summer of 1865: "Everywhere there were vivid secondhand accounts of armed blacks drilling in nightly conclaves, waiting only for the signal that would trigger a coordinated massacre sometime during the Christmas holidays." Similar fears soon appeared in the Carolinas. While no evidence was found that such uprisings were actually planned, by November the panic had spread to more than sixty counties throughout the former Confederacy—largely in the states with the largest black populations. These fears increasingly centered on organized black rifle companies, and not surprisingly, many whites began to see disarming the freedmen as necessary for their safety (or at least found it necessary to use this as a cover for some other purpose):

> In the late summer of 1865 a Summerton, South Carolina, vigilance committee agreed to disarm the freedmen of the area because of the danger of insurrection. At the vigilance meeting, however, conservative planter Warren Manning challenged the plan to disarm the blacks. He recalled that some of his slaves carried weapons for the protection of the plantation before the war, and now these men had been "made free and therefore had a right to carry arms."

9 William S. McFeely, *Frederick Douglass*, (New York: W.W. Norton & Co., 1991), 227-8. Nalty, 44.

10 Halbrook, "The Fourteenth Amendment...", 69.

11 Kenneth M. Stampp, *The Era of Reconstruction, 1865-1877*, (New York: Vintage Books, 1965), 104.

12 Nalty, 51.

13 Cong. Globe, 39th Cong., 1st Sess., pt. 1, 474 (Jan. 29, 1866), quoted in Featherstone and Gardiner, 102.

It also appears that a wildly distorted description of an insurrection at Morant Bay, Jamaica, in October of 1865 may have added fuel to the fire of fear.

White-dominated state governments that formed at this point rapidly began to form militias; their concern was that the federal troops which occupied the region would be insufficient, or perhaps unwilling, to protect whites from the feared insurrection of the freedmen. In many cases, militias formed without formal state recognition, and began searching black homes, confiscating the freedmen's firearms. In Eufala, Alabama, a militia company was joined by federal troops in confiscating arms from free blacks.[15]

Some white southern conservatives did recognize that the old laws would have to change, and that the old "criminal and police regulations" would have to be made color-blind, even before the Fourteenth Amendment had been proposed.[16] Many of the antivagrancy laws adopted in the South after the Civil Rights Act of 1866 "made no reference to race, to avoid the appearance of discrimination... But it was well understood... that 'the vagrant contemplated was the plantation negro.'"[17] As we examine the ostensibly color-blind laws completely prohibiting the carrying of weapons, suddenly adopted by the slave states after the Civil War, we should consider that color-blindness is as much in the application of the law, as the written statute itself.

It would be convenient if we could find clear-cut evidence that the post-war laws prohibiting the carrying of arms were passed for the purposes of selective enforcement. Certainly, with a great deal of work, it might be possible to ascertain the race of the defendants in some of the post-war cases, and to the extent that available records allow it, more detailed, state-by-state studies should attempt it.[18] But *if* these laws were passed for the purpose of selective enforcement, appeals through the courts might have been selective as well; it is interesting to find that many of the decisions from this period in the Southern states manage to uphold the laws, and release the defendants.

That arms were used frequently by the freedmen for self-defense, should come as no surprise:

> Blacks sought to arouse the conscience of the nation, but they also availed themselves of the right of self-defense. They were defending not only their individual lives but the lawful state and local governments established by Reconstruction... The night riders who set out on a lynching expedition often found in their targeted victim a fighter who would offer the greatest possible resistance. Collectively, groups of blacks fought back

---

14 Myrta Lockett Avary, *Dixie After The War*, (New York: Doubleday, Page & Co., 1906; reprinted New York: Da Capo Press, 1970), 263-278.

15 Dan T. Carter, *When The War Was Over: The Failure of Self-Reconstruction in the South, 1865-1867*, (Baton Rouge: Louisiana State University Press, 1985), 192-4, 199-201, 219-21.

16 Carter, 190.

17 Eric Foner, *Reconstruction*, (New York: Harper & Row, 1988), 200-1.

18 While county of original trial is present for nearly all cases, this may not always be the county of residence of the defendant; last names only are used in most of these decisions; unless the defendant was of long residence in the county in question, the chances of finding them in the previous or following decennial censuses are remote.

against the terror and, where offered the opportunity, blacks eagerly volunteered to serve in the militias organized by the Radical state governments.[19]

Eric Foner's *Reconstruction* gives many examples of white violence directed against former slaves, many for imagined crimes, and many because the former slaves failed to give the expected level of deference to their former masters. Violence directed against blacks engaged in political agitation was widespread, and blacks engaging in armed self-defense provoked "waves of fear among Southern whites."[20] In the words of one Louisiana black: "As one of the disfranchised race... I would say to every colored soldier, 'Bring your gun home'."[21]

In response to the murder of a black militiaman in 1876 in South Carolina, a protest meeting of 1000 blacks and 500 whites adopted a resolution that made it clear that such outrages carried a high risk:

> We tell you that it will not do to go too far in this thing. Remember that there are 80,000 black men in this State who can bear Winchester rifles and know how to use them, and that there are 200,000 women who can light a torch and use the knife, and that there are 100,000 boys and girls who have not known the lash of a white master, who have tasted freedom, once and forever, and that there is a deep determination never, so help them God, to submit to be shot down by lawless regulators for no crimes committed against society and law.[22]

Both sides took up arms in the pursuit of their political goals, although the goal of conservatives in doing so was to reduce the freedmen to submission. A proposal by which South Carolina Democrats sought to recover control from the freedmen included:

> 3. That the Democratic Military Clubs are to be armed with rifles and pistols and such other arms as they may command...

> Democrats must go in as large numbers as they can get together, and well armed...

> 16. Never threaten a man individually. If he deserves to be threatened, the necessities of the times require that he should die...[23]

The first post-war decision, *Smith* v. *Ishenhour* (1866), took place in Tennessee. The Confederate state government had passed an ordinance ordering all arms to be taken from the citizens of each county, apparently for the purpose of arming Tennessee soldiers. Conrad Ishenhour was appointed by Governor Harris to effect this action in Cocke County; after the war, one A.E. Smith filed suit for the value of a gun seized from him, and won a judgement against Ishenhour. Ishenhour then appealed to the Tennessee Supreme Court.

While the decision in this case principally revolved around the postwar actions of the state government in declaring all acts of the Confederate state government, "null and void from the beginning," the Tennessee Supreme Court expressed its horror at such an effort:

> In the passage of this Act, the 26th section of the Bill of Rights, which provides, "that the free white men of this State have a right to keep and bear arms for the common de-

19 Herbert Shapiro, *White Violence and Black Response*, (Amherst, Mass.: University of Massachusetts Press, 1988), 21.
20 Foner, 119-123.
21 Foner, 120.
22 Shapiro, 21.
23 Benedict, 142.

fense," was utterly disregarded. This is the first attempt, in the history of the Anglo-Saxon race, of which we are apprised, to disarm the people by legislation.[24]

Tennessee had returned to Conservative control in the 1869 state elections[25] because of factional rivalries within the Republican Party. The new Conservative majority in the legislature arranged for a constitutional convention in 1870 to revise the Tennessee Constitution. If there had been any doubt as to the goals of the new Conservative legislative majority, they were quickly dispelled as the legislature repealed laws designed to protect blacks from the Ku Klux Klan, rejected the Fifteenth Amendment (black voting rights), abolished the state school system established by the Republicans, and repealed a statute that guaranteed non-discrimination in railroad accommodations.

The 1870 constitutional convention made a number of changes, clearly intended to preserve white dominance: segregation of the public schools was mandated, and interracial marriage or cohabitation was prohibited.[26] Another provision allowed the Legislature to regulate the carrying of arms. The Legislature then passed "The Act of 1870, c. 13," which prohibited the carrying of "a dirk, sword-cane, Spanish stiletto, belt or pocket pistol or revolver," either openly or concealed.[27] (It appears that the law in question did not prohibit the open carrying of large pistols.) In 1871, the Tennessee Supreme Court heard three similar appeals, and gave a single ruling on all three: *Andrews* v. *State* (1871), *State* v. *O'Toole* (1871), and *State* v. *Custer* (1871).

In *Andrews* v. *State* (1871), Andrews was convicted of violating the new law, and appealed his conviction. In *State* v. *O'Toole* (1871), O'Toole was indicted, but the judge quashed the indictment on the grounds that the law in question was unconstitutional, and because the indictment was defective in not charging that the pistol O'Toole carried was a "belt pistol, or pocket pistol." The district attorney then appealed the judge's decision in quashing the indictment. In the third case, *State* v. *Custer* (1871), Custer appears to have pleaded guilty to the charge, was sentenced to prison, but the District Attorney asked that Custer be "required to give sureties to keep the peace, which being refused, he appealed for the State."[28]

The same attorney represented both Andrews and O'Toole; attorneys for all three defendants argued that, "by Article 2 of the amendments to the Constitution of the United States, the right to bear arms was protected." Andrews and O'Toole's attorney also argued that the 1870 Constitution's authority

> to regulate did not involve the power to prohibit, and that this act was a prohibition. That in Aymette's case the arms carried were not arms of warfare, the wearing of which the Legislature had the power to prohibit; that this is the only point decided in that case—all else is *dictum*. He insisted that the words relied upon by Judge Green [the judge in the *Aymette* decision] as restrictive, *i.e.*, "for the common defense," could not be of any effect, as the right was guaranteed without any such restriction in the Constitution of the United States; that the necessity was not only to keep them at all times, to be inured to their use by constantly bearing them about with them; that the power in the

24 *State* v. *Ishenhour*, 43 Tenn. (3 Coldwell) 214, 215, 216, 217 (1866).
25 Richard H. Abbott, *The Republican Party and the South, 1855-1877*, (Chapel Hill, N.C.: University of North Carolina Press, 1986), 207-8.
26 Cartwright, 13-14, 18.
27 *Andrews* v. *State*, 3 Heisk. (50 Tenn.) 165, 171 (1871).
28 *Andrews* v. *State*, 3 Heisk. (50 Tenn.) 165, 166 (1871).

Constitution of 1870 to regulate the wearing of arms, implies a right to wear as well as to bear arms, and that this right was subject only to be regulated, not destroyed.[29]

Similarly, Custer's attorney, "insisted upon the protection of the Constitution of the United States, and of the State, and that the Legislature had no power over the arms of civilized warfare, but might prohibit the carrying of other arms."[30]

The Tennessee Supreme Court's decision cited *Barron* v. *Baltimore* (1833) as evidence that the Second Amendment like the rest of the Bill of Rights, did not apply to the states.[31] It appears that neither defense attorney argued that the recently ratified Fourteenth Amendment incorporated the protections of the Bill of Rights.

The Court went on to argue that because of similarities between the Second Amendment and Tennessee's 1834 constitutional protection that "the free white men of this State have a right to keep and bear arms for their common defense," that the same reasoning should be applied to both—even though the U.S. Senate specifically rejected "for the common defense." Next, the Court concluded that because both provisions were found in proximity to discussions of the militia, that the right in question was only for the purpose of collective defense, "when called into actual service for the security of the State"—although the principal concern of the Framers was not the security of the State, but the security of the civil liberties of the people.

The Court acknowledged that the right of keeping arms:

necessarily involves the right to purchase and use them in such a way as is usual, or to keep them for the ordinary purposes to which they are adapted; and as they are to be kept, evidently with a view that the citizens making up the yeomanry of the land, the body of the militia, shall become familiar with their use in times of peace, that they may the more efficiently use them in times of war: then the right to keep arms for this purpose involves the right to practice their use, in order to attain to this efficiency. The right and use are guaranteed to the citizen, to be exercised and enjoyed in time of peace, in subordination to the general ends of civil society; but, as a right, to be maintained in all fulness....

The right to keep arms, necessarily involves the right to purchase them, to keep them in a state of efficiency for use, and to purchase and provide ammunition suitable for such arms, and to keep them in repair. And clearly for this purpose, a man would have the right to carry them to and from his home, and no one could claim that the Legislature had the right to punish him for it, without violating this clause of the Constitution.

But farther than this, it must be held, that the right to keep arms involves, necessarily, the right to use such arms for all the ordinary purposes, and in all the ordinary modes usual in the country, and to which arms are adapted, limited by the duties of a good citizen in times of peace; that in such use, he shall not use them for violation of the rights of others, or the paramount rights of the community in which he makes a part.[32]

This reasoning, with respect to "ordinary modes usual in the country" creates an interesting question: was the carrying of "pocket pistols" a mode "usual in the country"? From the speed with which three different cases came to trial after the Tennessee Legislature made carrying pocket pistols illegal, and from the comments in Kentucky's *Hopkins* v. *Commonwealth* (1868) decision, it would appear that, in-

---

29 *Andrews* v. *State*, 3 Heisk. (50 Tenn.) 165, 167 (1871).
30 *Andrews* v. *State*, 3 Heisk. (50 Tenn.) 165, 167, 168 (1871).
31 *Andrews* v. *State*, 3 Heisk. (50 Tenn.) 165, 172, 173 (1871).
32 *Andrews* v. *State*, 3 Heisk. (50 Tenn.) 165, 177, 178, 179 (1871).

deed, it was a common practice, and could therefore be considered protected by this line of argument.

That there were limits to the authority of the Legislature to restrict the carrying of arms, at least arms of a military nature, may be found in the Court's statement:

The Convention of 1870, knowing that there had been differences of opinion on this question, have conferred on the Legislature in this added clause, the right to regulate the wearing of arms, with a view to prevent crime.

It is insisted by the Attorney General, as we understand his argument, that this clause confers power on the Legislature to prohibit absolutely the wearing of all and every kind of arms, under all circumstances. To this we can not give our assent. The power to regulate, does not fairly mean the power to prohibit; on the contrary, to regulate, necessarily involves the existence of the thing or act to be regulated... Adopt the view of the Attorney General, and the Legislature may, if it chooses, arbitrarily prohibit the carrying of all manner of arms, and then, there be no act of the citizen to regulate.[33]

The Court continued with its explanation of the nature of the right to bear arms:

It is insisted by the Attorney General, that the right to keep and bear arms is a political, not a civil right. In this we think he fails to distinguish between the nature of the right to keep, and its necessary incidents, and the right to bear arms for the common defense. Bearing arms for the common defense may well be held to be a political right, or for protection and maintenance of such rights, intended to be guaranteed; *but the right to keep them, with all that is implied fairly as an incident to this right, is a private individual right, guaranteed to the citizen, not the soldier.* [emphasis added]

It is said by the Attorney General that the Legislature may prohibit the use of arms common in warfare, but not the use of them in warfare; but the idea of the Constitution is, the keeping and use of such arms as are useful either in warfare, or in preparing the citizen for their use in warfare, by training him as a citizen, to their use in times of peace.

The Court next quoted Joseph Story's remarks about the meaning of the Second Amendment that we examined on page 70, and observed:

We cite this passage as throwing light upon what was intended to be guaranteed to the people of the States, against the power of the Federal Legislature, and at the same time, as showing clearly what is the meaning of our own Constitution on this subject, as it is evident the State Constitution was intended to guard the same right, and with the same ends in view. So that, the meaning of the one, will give us an understanding of the purpose of the other.

The passage from Story, shows clearly that this right was intended, as we have maintained in this opinion, and was guaranteed to, and to be exercised and enjoyed by the citizen as such, and not by him as a soldier, or in defense solely of his political rights....

We may for a moment, pause to reflect on the fact, that what was once deemed a stable and essential bulwark of freedom, "a well regulated militia," though the clause still remains in our Constitutions, both State and Federal, has, as an organization, passed away in almost every State of the Union, and only remains to us as a memory of the past, probably never to be revived.[34]

---

33 *Andrews* v. *State*, 3 Heisk. (50 Tenn.) 165, 180, 181 (1871). The Tennessee Attorney General, Joseph B. Heiskell, was also the reporter for Tennessee Supreme Court decisions; Heiskell took advantage of this opportunity to get the last word by footnoting this portion and asserting that this was *not* his argument.

34 *Andrews* v. *State*, 3 Heisk. (50 Tenn.) 165, 182, 183, 184, 185 (1871). Perhaps this was the case in former states of the Confederacy, but it is by no means clear that the militia was fading away elsewhere in the United States. California, for example, appears to have maintained an active state militia;

The Court next used the *Aymette* v. *State* (1840) precedent, and quoted it that, "the object for which the right to keep and bear arms is secured is of a general nature, to be exercised by the people in a body for their common defense, so the arms—the right to keep which is secured—are such as are usually employed in civilized warfare, and constitute the ordinary military equipment." Further, "The Legislature, therefore, have a right to prohibit the wearing or keeping weapons dangerous to the peace and safety of the citizens, and which are not usual in civilized warfare, or would not contribute to the common defense."[35]

The Court acknowledged that there was an individual right to possess military arms on private property. But on the subject of carrying arms off of private property, the Court held to a narrower definition of this right:

> The principle on which all right to regulate the use in public of these articles of property, is, that no man can so use his own as to violate the rights of others, or of the community of which he is a member.

> So we may say, *with reference to such arms, as we have held, he may keep and use in the ordinary mode known to the country, no law can punish him for so doing, while he uses such arms at home or on his own premises; he may do with his own as he will, while doing no wrong to others.* Yet, when he carries his property abroad, goes among the people to public assemblages where others are to be affected by his conduct, then brings himself within the pale of public regulation, and must submit to such restrictions on the mode of using or carrying his property as the people through their Legislature, shall see fit to impose for the general good.[36] [emphasis added]

The Tennessee Court's opinion was not unanimous. Justice Sneed "dissented from so much of the opinion as questioned the right of the Legislature to prohibit the wearing of arms of any description, or sought to limit the operation of the act of 1870." Justices Nelson and Turney concurred in much of the majority decision, and agreed that the intent of the Legislature was "to promote the public peace," but:

> I am, nevertheless constrained by a sense of duty to observe, that, in my opinion, that statute is in violation of one of the most sacred rights known to the Constitution. Ever since the opinions were promulgated, it has been my deliberate conviction that the exposition of the Constitution by Judge Robert Whyte, in Simpson v. The State... was much more correct than that of Judge Green in Aymette v. The State.... The expression in the case last named, that the citizens do not need for the purpose of repelling encroachment upon their rights, "the use of those weapons which are generally employed in private broils, and are efficient only in the hands of the robber and assassin," is, in my view, an unwarrantable aspersion upon the conduct of many honorable men were well justified in using them in self-defense.... The provision contained in the declaration of rights in the Constitution of 1834, that "that the free white men of this State have a right to keep and bear arms for their common defense," is not restricted to public defense.... Had such been the intention, the definite article "the," would would [sic] have been employed, instead of the personal pronoun "their," which is used in a personal sense, and was intended to convey the idea of a right belonging equally to more than one, general in its nature, and universally applicable to all the citizens. The word "bear" was not used alone in the military sense of carrying arms, but in the popular sense of

---

this author has seen a certificate from 1879, issued by the Adjutant General of California, acknowledging seven years of good service in the state militia, which exempted the militiaman from jury duty.

35 *Andrews* v. *State*, 3 Heisk. (50 Tenn.) 165, 184, 185 (1871).

36 *Andrews* v. *State*, 3 Heisk. (50 Tenn.) 165, 185, 186 (1871).

wearing them in war or in peace. The word "arms," means "instruments or weapons of offense or defense," and is not restricted, by any means, to public warfare.[37]

Justice Nelson went on to explain how the carrying of pistols had been commonplace during the Civil War, and that after the war ended, the practice had continued, with "dangerous wounds, as well as frequent homicides" being the result, and that giving authority to the Legislature to regulate the carrying of deadly weapons was recognized by the 1870 Constitutional Convention as not completely prohibiting the carrying of weapons, but that:

> if worn upon the person, they shall be worn in a public manner. The act of 1870, instead of regulating, prohibits the wearing of arms, and is, therefore, in my opinion, unconstitutional and void...

> Regretting, as I do, that the nobler objects of bearing and wearing arms are too often and too horribly perverted, I can not approve legislation which seems to foster and encourage a craven spirit on the part of those who are disposed to obey the laws, and leaves them to the tender mercies of those who set all law at defiance.[38]

In the majority decision, the Court came to the conclusion that regulation of the *manner* in which arms could be carried on public property was, for some classes of weapons, within the purview of the Legislature, but that ownership was not; and furthermore, that the distinction between those weapons that could be restricted, and those that could not, was dependent upon whether or not the weapons were weapons of war—this being an especially protected class.

Determining the history of the 1870 Convention, the motives of the various parties involved, and the nature of the brawls which so frightened the Tennessee Court would be a worthwhile pursuit, though unfortunately outside the scope of this work. Nonetheless, it would appear that Tennessee's law reflected the will of the resurgent white majority of Tennessee. Throughout the 1870s, KKK violence operated to the detriment of Tennessee blacks.[39] It seems unlikely that the arms laws were intended as a restraint on the KKK.

Later that year, the Tennessee Supreme Court heard an appeal that led to a simpler decision—and one that has been widely cited in support of restrictive arms carrying laws, in spite of its inappropriateness. The defendant, Thomas Page, was convicted of carrying a revolver, "about eight inches long, but that it was not such weapon as is used as a weapon of war," and threatening to use it against an apparently non-aggressive person. The Court clarified that while the carrying of a weapon was not necessarily criminal, the case before them was definitely one of those criminal misuses of the right to bear arms:

> In the case before us, the intent with which Page was carrying his pistol was fully developed. He was carrying it that he might be armed, as was shown by his threatened assault upon [Page's victim]. It would probably be difficult to enumerate all the instances in which one of these weapons could be carried innocently, and without criminality. It is sufficient here to say, that, without the intent or purpose of being or going armed, the offense described in this statute can not be committed.[40]

37 *Andrews* v. *State*, 3 Heisk. (50 Tenn.) 165, 193, 194 (1871).
38 *Andrews* v. *State*, 3 Heisk. (50 Tenn.) 165, 194, 195, 201 (1871).
39 Cartwright, 19.
40 *Page* v. *State*, 3 Heisk. (50 Tenn.) 198, 200, 201 (1871).

In 1871, in response to the *Andrews* v. *State* (1871) decision, the Tennessee Legislature revised the law prohibiting the carrying of pistols, such that it was illegal to carry a

> belt or pocket pistol, or revolver, other than an army pistol, or such as are commonly carried and used in the United States army, and in no case shall it be lawful for any person to carry such army pistol publicly or privately about his person in any other manner than openly in his hands...[41]

By exempting "army pistols" carried "openly in his hands," the Legislature hoped to write a law that would still prohibit the carrying of most deadly weapons, by allowing only one mode of carry—the mode which is the most aggressive and dangerous manner imaginable.

Robert Wilburn was charged with violating this new statute. The first count charged him with carrying "a belt and pocket pistol and revolver pistol, the same being an arm such as is not commonly carried and used in the United States army." The second count charged that Wilburn did "unlawfully and willfully carry an army pistol privately and concealed, and not openly in his hands..." which contradicts the claim in the first charge, since the Act of 1871 had defined an "army pistol" to be something other than "a belt or pocket pistol." The judge quashed the second count of the indictment, and at trial, Wilburn was acquitted on the first count. The State appealed the judge's decision quashing the second count of the indictment.[42] Since the Legislature had rewritten the law specifically to meet the requirements handed down by the Court in the earlier cases, the Court found the law, as written, constitutional.[43]

As part of the continuing effort to discourage concealable handguns, on March 17, 1879, Tennessee passed a law prohibiting the sale of "belt or pocket pistols, or revolvers, or any other kind of pistol except army or navy pistols." Persons already licensed to sell pistols were allowed to continue to sell them until their license expired, at which point no future sales were allowed.

Some time after the expiration of his license, Burgoyne was indicted for having illegally sold pistols prohibited under the ordinance. In this case, the Second Amendment was apparently not raised by the defendant, and the case was decided on the narrow grounds of whether it was within the authority of a state government to prohibit the sale of a good in the interests of public welfare—which the Court held that the state government possessed.[44]

While not strictly a "right to keep and bear arms" case, the Tennessee Supreme Court's decision in this case presents a disturbing question: can a right continue to exist if the mechanisms for the exercise of that right are no longer available for purchase? Would a law banning the sale of printing presses necessarily violate the First Amendment protections of free speech?

In *Carroll* v. *State* (1872), the Arkansas Supreme Court upheld the precedent in *State* v. *Buzzard* (1842). The defendant Carroll argued that he had carried a concealed pistol because he was in danger of "receiving great bodily violence," did so only within his own home, and asked the judge to charge the jury accordingly. The

---

41 *State* v. *Wilburn*, 7 Bax. 57, 61 (Tenn. 1872).
42 *State* v. *Wilburn*, 7 Bax. 57, 58 (Tenn. 1872).
43 *State* v. *Wilburn*, 7 Bax. 57, 62, 63 (Tenn. 1872).
44 *State* v. *Burgoyne*, 7 Lea 172, 173, 179, 40 Am. Rep. 60 (Tenn. 1881).

trial judge refused to do so.   The Arkansas Supreme Court recapitulated the
Buzzard decision:

> a constitutional right to bear arms in defense of person and property does not prohibit
> the legislature from making such police regulations as may be necessary for the good of
> society, as to the manner in which such arms shall be borne.   Neither natural nor consti-
> tutional right authorizes a citizen to use his own property or bear his own arms in such
> way as to injure the property or endanger the life of his fellow citizen, and these regula-
> tions must be left to the wisdom of the legislature, so long as their discretion be kept
> within reasonable bounds.   And it is not unreasonable for the legislature to enact that
> deadly weapons shall not be worn concealed, that those associating with the bearer may
> guard against injury by accident or otherwise.[45]

"Reasonable bounds," of course, is a highly elastic phrase—one that reappears
throughout the judicial history of the right to keep and bear arms—and with substantially different meanings in different eras.   The Court upheld the right of the
Legislature to ban concealed carry, because that was "reasonable," but hinted that
there were limits beyond which such laws were not "reasonable," and that banning
open carry might well be beyond those limits.   But over the next few years, the Arkansas Supreme Court gave a series of contradictory decisions about the meaning of
this right—changing direction so readily as to make it questionable whether there
was any overriding theory behind these decisions.

In 1874, the Republicans lost control of the Arkansas Legislature.[46]   In 1875, Arkansas passed a law making it a misdemeanor to "wear or carry any pistol of any
kind whatever, or any dirk, butcher or Bowie knife, or sword or spear in a cane,
brass or metal knucks, or razor, as a weapon..." with the usual exceptions for police
officers, travellers carrying such weapons "with their baggage," or any person directed by a police officer "to assist in the execution of any legal process."   Not only
concealed carry, but also open carry had been outlawed.   Later that year, in *Fife* v.
State (1876), Alfred Fife was indicted for violating this law in Pine Bluff, Arkansas.
Perhaps of some relevance to the decision of the court, Fife threatened a person
who was apparently not a threat to him.

The Arkansas Supreme Court used Joseph Story's *Commentaries on the Constitution of the United States* and Thomas Cooley's *Constitutional Limitations* to decide
that arms were protected by the Second Amendment as a restraint on "usurpation
and arbitrary power of rulers," and that "the arms which it guarantees American
citizens the right to keep and to bear, are such as are needful to, and ordinarily used
by a well-regulated militia, and such as are necessary and suitable to a free people,
to enable them to resist oppression, prevent usurpation, repel invasion, etc., etc.,"
but that the Second Amendment was "a restraint upon Federal, and not upon State
legislation."[47]

The Arkansas Constitution contained a "right to keep and bear arms for their
common defense" clause, which according to the Arkansas Supreme Court, was
carried over from the 1836 state constitution; but the Court used "for their common defense," and quoted the Tennessee Court's decision in *Andrews* v. *State*
(1871) to decide that only weapons

---

45 *Carroll* v. *State*, 28 Ark. 99, 100, 101 (1872).
46 Birdsall S. Viault, *American History Since 1865*, (New York: McGraw-Hill, 1989), 17-18.
47 *Fife* v. *State*, 31 Ark. 455, 25 Am. Rep. 556, 557, 558 (1876).

adapted to the ends indicated above, that is, the efficiency of the citizen as a soldier, when called on to make good the defense of a free people; and these arms he may use as a citizen, in all the usual modes to which they are adapted, and common to the country. What then, is he protected in the right to keep and thus to use? Not every thing that may be useful for offense or defense, *but what may properly be included or understood under the title of "arms," taken in connection with the fact that the citizen is to keep them, as a citizen.* Such, then, as are found to make up the usual arms of the citizen of the country, and the use of which will properly train and render him efficient in defense of his own liberties, as well as of the State. *Under this head, with a knowledge of the habits of our people, and of the arms in the use of which a soldier should be trained, we hold that the rifle, of all descriptions, the shot gun, the musket and repeater, are such arms, and that, under the Constitution, the right to keep such arms cannot be infringed or forbidden by the legislature.*[48] [emphasis added]

While recognizing that large military handguns (what the Court called a "repeater") were protected, the Arkansas Court held that this "did not mean pocket revolver."[49] Without acknowledging that the Arkansas law had made it illegal to "wear or carry any pistol of any kind whatever," the Court held "that the plaintiff in error was carrying a pistol of that class or character intended to be prohibited by the legislature, and which we think may be prohibited, in the exercise of the police power of the State, without any infringement of the constitutional right of the citizens of the State to keep and bear arms for their common defense."[50] If we accept that pocket pistols were not arms of a soldier, and that the Second Amendment was not restrictive of state legislative authority, this decision, based on the "common defense" clause, was perfectly logical.

It is tempting to see the *Fife* decision as part of an increasingly restrictive attitude by the Arkansas Supreme Court towards the right to keep and bear arms. But two years later, in *Wilson* v. *State of Arkansas* (1878), the Court once again changed course. Chancy Wilson was indicted on the grounds that he did "unlawfully carry a pistol as a weapon, contrary to the statute such case made and provided, and against the peace and dignity of the State..." Wilson had borrowed "a large army size six shooter, a revolving pistol, 44 caliber, eight inches in the barrel, such as is commonly used in warfare" for the purpose of pig hunting. Upon reaching his destination, Wilson spoke with his host, "pulled the pistol out of his boot, cocked it a few times to see if it would revolve, and then put it around under his coat, and went into dinner." It is not clear if the revolver was concealed in his boot, but it certainly was concealed under his coat. The trial court refused to allow a statement either by the owner of the pistol or Wilson as to the purpose of having the revolver, and refused to charge the jury that "an army size pistol" was not subject to the restriction of the Arkansas law.

The Arkansas Supreme Court, citing *Fife*, agreed that regulation was acceptable, but:

No doubt in time of peace, persons might be prohibited from wearing war arms to places of public worship, or elections, etc. *Andrews* v. *State*, 3 *Heiskell*, 182.

But to prohibit the citizen from wearing or carrying a war arm, except upon his own premises or when on a journey traveling through the country with baggage, or when

---

48 *Fife* v. *State*, 31 Ark. 455, 25 Am. Rep. 556, 560 (1876).
49 *Fife* v. *State*, 31 Ark. 455, 25 Am. Rep. 556, 560 (1876).
50 *Fife* v. *State*, 31 Ark. 455, 25 Am. Rep. 556, 561 (1876).

acting as or in aid of an officer, is an unwarranted restriction upon his constitutional right to keep and bear arms.

If cowardly and dishonorable men sometimes shoot unarmed men with army pistols or guns, the evil must be prevented by the penitentiary and gallows, and not by a general deprivation of a constitutional privilege.[51]

In the same session, the Arkansas Supreme Court decided another weapons case, *Holland* v. *State* (1878):

James Holland was indicted in the Circuit Court of Yell county, for carrying a pistol as a weapon.

On the trial but one witness was examined. He stated, in substance, that the first time he ever saw defendant, was on the 1st of October, 1875, in Yell county. He had two large sized six shooting pistols, one of them a Remington, navy size and loaded, and the other a Colt's army pistol. The pistols were such as are commonly used in the United States military and naval service. Defendant was carrying them in his saddle-bags, and stated he was from Texas. Witness did not know whether he was on a journey or not.

Not surprisingly, Holland

asked the court to charge the jury that if they found from the evidence that the pistols, proven to have been carried, were army sized pistols, and were such as are commonly used in the United States military and naval service, they must acquit defendant.

The court refused this instruction, defendant was convicted, a new trial refused him, he took a bill of exceptions and appealed.[52]

Chief Justice English again delivered the opinion of the Arkansas Supreme Court: "The court erred in refusing to instruct the jury as moved by appellant." After citing *Fife* v. *State* (1876) and *Wilson* v. *State of Arkansas* (1878), the Arkansas Supreme Court reversed the conviction, and ordered a new trial. The pistols in question were apparently concealed "in his saddle-bags," but the defense of the pistols being standard U.S. military models was sufficient to justify their concealed carriage.

The Arkansas Legislature responded to the *Wilson* and *Holland* decisions by passing a new weapons law. The Act of April 1, 1881, prohibited "the carrying of army pistols except uncovered and in the hand." In *Haile* v. *State* (1882), the first two sections of this act (which regulated carrying of handguns) were challenged. The defendant, Haile, was convicted in Pope County of carrying "uncovered, and buckled around his waist... a large revolving pistol, known as the Colts army pistol, and such as is used in the army and navy of the United States..."

The Arkansas Supreme Court decided:

The question is, can the Legislature regulate the mode of carrying any arms which the citizens have the constitutional right to keep and bear for their common defense? We have decided that it may, to some extent, which means that it may, in a reasonable manner, so as, in effect, not to nullify the right, nor materially embarrass its exercise.

At this point, the Court had taken a position which could be considered the "reasonable" regulation school—the manner could be regulated, but the right could not be destroyed.

---

51 *Wilson* v. *State of Arkansas*, 33 Ark. 557, 558, 559, 560 (1878).
52 *Holland* v. *State*, 33 Ark. 560, 561 (1878).

Next, the Court articulated its republican view of the nature of the right protected by the Arkansas Constitution:

The constitutional provision sprang from the former tyrannical practice, on the part of governments, of disarming the subjects, so as to render them powerless against oppression. It is not intended to afford citizens the means of prosecuting, more successfully, their private broils in a free government. It would be a perversion of its object, to make it a protection to the citizen, in going, with convenience to himself, and after his own fashion, prepared at all times to inflict death upon his fellow-citizens, upon the occasion of any real or imaginary wrong. The "common defense" of the citizens does not require that. The consequent terror to timid citizens, with the counter violence which would be incited amongst the more fearless, would be worse than the evil intended to be remedied. [emphasis added]

This paragraph, too, can be regarded as an honest statement of belief. But next, the Court explains its reasoning in upholding the 1881 statute:

The Legislature, by the law in question, has sought to steer between such a condition of things, and an infringement of constitutional rights, by conceding the right to keep such arms, and to bear or use them at will, upon one's own premises, and restricting the right to wear them elsewhere in public, unless they be carried uncovered in the hand. It must be confessed that this is a very inconvenient mode of carrying them habitually, but the habitual carrying of them does not seem essential to "common defense." The inconvenience is a slight matter compared with the danger to the whole community, which would result from the common practice of going about with pistols in a belt, ready to be used on every outbreak of ungovernable passion. It is a police regulation, adjusted as wisely as the Legislature thought possible, with all essential constitutional rights.[53]

If "timid citizens" were terrorized by the wearing of holstered guns, how would requiring those guns to be carried in the hand reduce the fear? The purpose of the law was to make the carrying of guns for defensive purposes so inconvenient, and so likely to provoke an accidental shooting, as to make it impractical to carry a gun.

The Court did not abandon the notion of a right to keep arms, however:

The constitutional right is a very valuable one. We would not disparage it. A condition of things within the experience of men, still very young, illustrates the importance of keeping alive in the mind, and well defined, these old land-marks of Saxon liberty. "*Semper paratus,*" [always ready] is a good motto. Yet if every citizen may keep arms in readiness upon his place, may render himself skillful in their use by practice, and carry them upon a journey without let or hindrance, it seems to us, the essential objects of this particular clause of the bill of rights will be preserved, although the citizen be required to carry them uncovered, and in the hand, off his own premises, if should deem it necessary to carry them at all.[54]

The Arkansas Supreme Court referred to the Tennessee Bill of Rights, with its very similar protection of the right to keep and bear arms, and how the Tennessee Supreme Court had found a very similar law constitutional in *State* v. *Wilburn* (1872). Alas, the Court had transformed the name into *State* v. *Welburne*, which is not a particularly persuasive piece of evidence that they had actually read the decision.

The final paragraph of the *Haile* decision, however, contains a statement that was a reminder that there were limits to the authority of the state to regulate the possession of military weapons: "There need be no fear, from any thing in these

---

53 *Haile* v. *State*, 38 Ark. 564, 565, 566 (1882).
54 *Haile* v. *State*, 38 Ark. 564, 566, 567 (1882).

sections, that the citizen may not always have arms, and be skilled in their proper use, whenever the common defense may require him to take them up."[55]

In *Dabbs* v. *State* (1882), the Arkansas Supreme Court upheld the third section of the Act of April 1, 1881, which prohibited the sale of any pistol other than those "used in the army or navy of the United States and known as the navy pistol." Dabbs pled guilty in Pulaski County, Arkansas, of selling such a pistol. On appeal, Dabbs' attorney cited a number of provisions of the U.S. Constitution with respect to regulation of interstate commerce, sought to use the Fourteenth Amendment and the "privileges and immunities" clause of the Constitution, as a basis for overturning the ban. Dabbs' attorney also pointed to the Georgia decision *Nunn* v. *State* (1846) which overthrew a similar law. He also claimed that *Fife* v. *State* was "no authority in this case. No act of this description ever sustained by any court. Not even this court has gone so far, although it has gone to considerable length..." Dabbs' attorney then cited *State* v. *Buzzard* (1842), and *Wilson* v. *State of Arkansas* (1878).

Attorney-General Moore, arguing for the law, claimed "The right to 'keep and bear arms' may be absolutely prohibited," and pointed to *State* v. *Buzzard* (1842) and *Fife* v. *State* (1876) as precedents.[56] While this is certainly an accurate description of the *Buzzard* decision, the *Fife* v. *State* (1876) decision, as we have seen, did not go so far as to completely deny such a right.

Justice Smith wrote the opinion of the Arkansas Supreme Court. First, he disposed of the interstate commerce provision, citing such well-known precedents as *Gibbons* v. *Ogden* (1824), to find that since the state had authority to regulate, "and even to suppress, the traffic in intoxicating liquors within its borders," it certainly had the authority to regulate or prohibit gun sales, at least with respect to the issue of interstate commerce.[57]

Next, Justice Smith dispensed with the Fourteenth Amendment since it was "to secure to negroes all the civil rights that white citizens enjoy, and to prevent discriminations against them as a class, or on account of their race." While Justice Smith did not say so explicitly, the implication was that because it was intended to protect blacks against racial discrimination, it could therefore *not* be relevant to the rights of citizens who were not subject to racial discrimination—a position that would certainly provoke a hearty laugh from the legal community today, when the Fourteenth Amendment has become the heart of lawsuits protecting all sorts of classes.

With respect to the "privileges and immunities" argument:

> Nor does it conflict with *sec. 2 of art. 4*, of the Constitution of the United States, which provides that the citizens of each State shall be entitled to all the privileges and immunities of citizens of the several States; for all are placed upon an equality by the act. The citizen of Tennessee can not sell the forbidden articles upon the territory of Arkansas any more than one of our citizens.[58]

---

55 *Haile* v. *State*, 38 Ark. 564, 567 (1882).

56 *Dabbs* v. *State*, 39 Ark. 353, 354, 355, 43 Am. Rep. 275 (1882).

57 The *Gibbons* decision had struck down a New York State granted monopoly on steamship operations, on the grounds that any commerce between two states was within the power of the Congress to regulate, and while a state could regulate internal commerce, it could not regulate interstate commerce. McDonald, 80-82.

58 *Dabbs* v. *State*, 39 Ark. 353, 356, 43 Am. Rep. 275 (1882).

But of course, such an argument ignores the natural rights view that the right of bearing arms for self-defense, recognized by the common law of England, was one of the "privileges and immunities" shared by citizens "of the several States," discussed in *Dred Scott* v. *Sandford* (1857).

Finally, the heart of the dispute is addressed in the last paragraph of the decision:

> The law was enacted as a measure of precaution for the prevention of crimes and calamities. It is leveled at the pernicious habit of wearing such dangerous or deadly weapons as are easily concealed about the person. It does not abridge the constitutional right of citizens to keep and bear arms for the common defense; for it in no wise restrains the use or sale of such arms as are useful in warfare. *Fife v. State*, 31 Ark., 455.[59]

Don Kates argues that such statutes were passed to disarm blacks, by making the only affordable handguns unavailable.[60] The parallel to efforts in the 1960s and 1970s to ban so-called "Saturday Night Specials"—guns on average smaller, cheaper, and more concealable than military & police sidearms—should be obvious. If, in fact, the motivations for such laws were racial in nature, we should not be surprised that these statutes were all passed in former slave states.

It is asserted that the name, "Saturday Night Special" is derived from the phrase, "niggertown Saturday night,"[61] an uncomplimentary assertion about the level of violence among blacks. Attempts to verify this origin for the term "Saturday Night Special" were inconclusive. The OED defines it as, "a cheap, low-calibre pistol or revolver such as might be used by a petty criminal," with its first use in a *New York Times* article of 1968. "Saturday Night," used as an attribution, is defined as, "some form of revelry."[62] The leap from "revelry" to a petty criminal's gun, is mystifying. A search of several dictionaries of slang found no definition of "niggertown Saturday night," but did reveal a definition of "Saturday Night Special" as "a small handgun, often used in the many fracas that occur over Saturday night in a big US city."[63] A North Carolinian acquaintance reports having heard the terms "Niggertown" and "Saturday night" used in 1968 in a form that suggested that the combination of Saturday night, alcohol, and blacks, inevitably led to violence.[64] The leap from murder as a form of black revelry, to any cheap handgun being a "niggertown Saturday Night Special," to the cleaned-up "Saturday Night Special," is a logical one. However, this does not necessarily mean that it is etymologically correct, and this topic is in need of further research.

Texas, unlike the other states of the Confederacy, remained a frontier society. The close of the Civil War appears to have led to a dramatic increase in violence—though from the sketchy available evidence, in quite the opposite direction feared by the whites of the deep South. The Texas Constitutional Convention of 1868-69 compiled a report on lawlessness and violence from a variety of sources; while there is reason to suspect the accuracy and completeness of the data, even a historian with a strong bias against the report has agreed that violence had reached unprecedented levels during this period.

---

59 *Dabbs* v. *State*, 39 Ark. 353, 356, 357, 43 Am. Rep. 275 (1882).
60 Kates, "Toward A History of Handgun Prohibition...", 11, 13-14.
61 Kates, "Toward a History of Handgun Prohibition...", 25.
62 OED, 14:509.
63 Jonathan Green, *The Dictionary of Contemporary Slang*, (New York: Stein & Day, 1984), 241.
64 Joseph Knapp, Personal communication to the author, November 12, 1991.

From the close of the war to June of 1868 the report found 1,035 murders had been committed: 509 of the victims were white, and 409 victims were freedman. The Convention's report may have overemphasized political and racial motivations for these murders, but murder was a serious and increasing problem.   The combination of disenfranchised whites, newly freed blacks about to get the vote, and a variety of adjustment problems as former slaves and masters worked out new economic relationships, would seem to have been factors in this problem.[65]   The 1860 population of Texas was 604,000; by 1870, the population was 819,000.[66] If we accept the population during the period 1865-1868 as 700,000, this would give an annual murder rate of 49 per 100,000 population—more than four times the highest murder rate for the entire United States in the twentieth century.[67]

Circumstances leading to the 1869 state elections were highly irregular; General Reynolds, the military governor of Texas, appointed Edmund J. Davis as Provisional Governor.   Actual control of the state government remained in the hands of General Reynolds until April 16, 1870.   Governor Davis and the Radical Republican-dominated legislature passed a series of laws designed to deal with the problems of lawlessness: organizing a state militia; creating, for the first time, a state police force of 250 men, under the direct control of the governor; and a law to "put restrictions on the indiscriminate carrying of dangerous weapons."[68]   It appears that the State Police succeeded in suppressing the Klan's violence, "providing freedmen with a real measure of protection in a state notorious for widespread violence."[69]

The act of April 12, 1871 made it illegal to carry arms openly.   It was quickly challenged, and in 1872, the Texas Supreme Court wrote a single decision which covered three very different cases: *William English* v. *State* (1872), *State* v. *G. W. Carter*, and *State* v. *William Daniel*, appealed from the district courts of Marion, Kaufman, and Van Zandt counties, respectively.   All involved a violation of the new law, which prohibited the carrying of pistols, Bowie knives, sword-canes, spears, brass knuckles,[70] "unless he has reasonable grounds for fearing an unlawful attack on his person, and that such ground of attack shall be immediate and pressing," with the usual exemptions for peace officers, active members of the militia, and in one's own home or business.[71]

Each of the cases was somewhat different, and yet a single decision was rendered for all:

> In English's case the offensive weapon was a pistol, and it was proved that he was in a state of intoxication while wearing it about in the city of Jefferson. He proved, in de-fense, that the pistol was not loaded at the times it was seen by the witnesses against him;

---

65 Charles William Ramsdell, *Reconstruction in Texas*, (New York: Columbia University Press, 1910; reprinted Gloucester, Mass.: Peter Smith, 1964), 219-24. Also, see Foner, 119-23, for evidence that this problem of violence directed against freedmen was not confined to Texas.

66 *Historical Statistics of the United States, Colonial Times to 1970*, (Washington: Government Printing Office, 1975), 35.

67 Bureau of Justice Statistics, *Report to the Nation on Crime and Justice*, 2nd ed., (Washington: Government Printing Office, 1988), 15.

68 Ramsdell, 285-6, 289, 291-2, 295-8.

69 Foner, 440.

70 *English* v. *State*, 35 Tex. 473 (1872). In a later case—*State* v. *Duke*, 42 Tex. 455 (1875)—the Texas Supreme Court quoted the entire law in question, but cites it as the act of April *11*, 1871, not April *12*.

71 *State* v. *Duke*, 42 Tex. 455, 456, 457 (1875).

and further, that it was out of repair, and he had taken it along with him to have it mended, as he expected soon to go to a neighboring county after his mother, and wished to carry the pistol with him....

The charge against Daniels was going "into a religious assembly, having about his person a butcher knife." The state's witnesses proved that they saw the defendant in church on the occasion in question, and that the handle of a butcher knife was sticking out above the waistband of his breeches, and between the skirts of his frock coat. They saw nothing but the handle. The court below charged that the handle raised a presumption of a blade.

No transcript in Carter's case has come to the hands of the reporter, nor any brief in his behalf, or in behalf of Daniels.[72]

Of course, this is not surprising; from the form of the case names involving Carter and Daniel, it would appear that Carter and Daniel succeeded in persuading the district court judge that the cases against them were without merit, and that these were appeals by the prosecutor. In the case of Carter, the Texas Supreme Court reversed the district court's decision.

In the case of Daniel, or Daniels (for the Court referred to this defendant by both names, and to the case as both *State* v. *Daniel* and *Daniels* v. *State*), the Court affirmed the decision of the district court.[73] Was Daniels convicted by the district court, or released? The lack of brief on behalf of Daniels suggests that he was already a free man, and had no reason to appeal the district court's decision—a problem that repeatedly occurs in cases involving the right to keep and bear arms. Not surprisingly, without an advocate opposing such laws, the court would be primarily influenced by the brief filed by the attorney general.

The Court quoted Bishop's *Criminal Law* to the effect that the Second Amendment was a restriction not only on the federal government, but on the states as well, in language very similar to Rawle's statements in *A View of the Constitution*. The Court quoted Bishop's straightforward admission that there was no authority for the narrow view of "arms" given in *Aymette* v. *State* (1840):

As to its interpretation, if we look to this question in the light of judicial reason, *without the aid of specific authority*, we shall be led to the conclusion that the provision protects only the right to 'keep' such 'arms' as are used for purposes of war, in distinction from those which are employed in quarrels and broils, and fights between maddened individuals, since such only are properly known by the name of 'arms,' and such only are adapted to promote 'the security of a free state.' In like manner the right to 'bear' arms refers merely to the military way of using them, not to their use in bravado and affray. [emphasis added]

The Court also quoted Bishop with respect to the Georgia decision *Nunn* v. *State* (1846), the antebellum Louisiana decisions, and Alabama's *Owen* v. *State* (1858). The Texas Supreme Court then cited Bishop as asserting that "the doctrine generally approved by the American authorities" is the one taken in *Aymette* v. *State* (1840), *State* v. *Reid* (1840), *State* v. *Mitchell* (1833), and *State* v. *Newsom* (1844)—and then tells us this doctrine was accepted by Blackstone: "[T]he offense of riding or going around armed with dangerous or unusual weapons is a crime against the public peace, by terrifying the good people of the land."[74]

---

72 *English* v. *State*, 35 Tex. 473, 474 (1872).
73 *English* v. *State*, 35 Tex. 473, 481 (1872).
74 *English* v. *State*, 35 Tex. 473, 475, 476 (1872).

But of course, the decisions taken in *Aymette* and *Reid* are very different—only *concealed* carry was held to be unprotected in *Reid*, while open carry was clearly protected; in *Aymette*, the issue of open carry was not directly addressed, though it was implied that open carry was not protected. The Court next addressed the issue of what arms are protected:

> To refer the deadly devices and instruments called in the statute "deadly weapons," to the proper or necessary arms of a "well-regulated militia," is simply ridiculous. No kind of travesty, however subtle or ingenious, could so misconstrue this provision of the constitution of the United States, as to make it cover and protect that pernicious vice, from which so many murders, assassinations, and deadly assaults have sprung, and which it was doubtless the intention of the legislature to punish and prohibit. *The word "arms" in the connection we find it in the constitution of the United States, refers to the arms of a militiaman or soldier, and the word is used in its military sense.* The arms of the infantry soldier are the musket and the bayonet; of cavalry and dragoons, the sabre, holster pistols and carbine; of the artillery, the field piece, siege gun, and mortar, with side arms. [emphasis added]
>
> The terms dirks, daggers, slungshots, sword-canes, brass knuckles and bowie knives, do not belong to military vocabulary. Were a soldier on duty found with any of these things about his person, he would be punished for an offense against discipline.[75]

The Court made a distinction between a bayonet, a piece of military equipment which every member of the militia was required to own under the Militia Act of 1792,[76] and a "dagger" or "bowie knife." (If such a distinction was valid in 1872, it has evaporated today, when bayonets have become equivalent to a nineteenth century Bowie knife in size, and combat knives are issued to soldiers.) But those arms that were unambiguously military weapons were completely protected. The discrepancy between this decision and *Cockrum* v. *State* (1859) is a yawning chasm.

Yet the Court did agree that there were circumstances under which the carrying of deadly weapons for personal defense was appropriate, if not constitutionally protected:

> The act referred to makes all necessary exceptions, and points out the place, the time and the manner in which certain deadly weapons may be carried as means of self-defense, and these exceptional cases, in our judgment, fully cover all the wants of society. There is no abridgement of the personal rights, such as may be regarded as inherent and inalienable to man, nor do we think his political rights are in the least infringed by any part of this law.[77]

The Court then echoed the language of *Aymette* v. *State* (1840) about the evils of revenge:

> It will doubtless work a great improvement in the moral and social condition of men, when every man shall come fully to understand that, in the great social compact under and by which states and communities are bound and held together, each individual has compromised the right to avenge his own wrongs, and must look to the state for redress. We must not go back to that state of barbarism in which each claims the right to administer the law in his own case; that law being simply the domination of the strong and the violent over the weak and submissive.

---

75 *English* v. *State*, 35 Tex. 473, 476, 477 (1872).
76 *Annals of Congress*, 2 Cong., May 8, 1792, 1394.
77 *English* v. *State*, 35 Tex. 473, 477 (1872).

But as with *Aymette*, the Court blurred the distinction between revenge and self-defense—holding that having the ability to defend oneself was equivalent to taking away the state's authority to try and punish a criminal.

The Court's feelings on personal liberty are also explicated:

> It is useless to talk about personal liberty being infringed by laws such as that under consideration. The world has seen too much licentiousness cloaked under the name of natural or personal liberty; natural and personal liberty are exchanged, under the social compact of states, for civil liberty.[78]

With respect to the more narrowly worded Texas Constitutional provision:

> It is further claimed that this is a law in violation of the thirteenth section, first article, of our own constitution, which reads thus: "Every person shall have the right to keep and bear arms in the lawful defense of himself or the state, under such regulations as the legislature may prescribe." We understand the word "arms," when used in this connection, as having the same import and meaning which it has when used in the amendment of the federal constitution.[79]

But where the Court held that the Second Amendment did not protect an individual right for self-defense, the language of the Texas Constitution was explicitly individual ("Every person shall have the right to keep and bear arms") and explicitly for self-defense ("in the lawful defense of himself").

Without question, the Texas Constitutional provision gave the Legislature authority to regulate the keeping and bearing of arms. But unlike many other courts, which recognized that it was possible to regulate a right into non-existence, the Texas Supreme Court held that the legislature had regulated it by this law, without taking the right away.

That the Court intended some nineteenth century "social engineering" can be found in the closing paragraphs of its decision:

> But a law is not be to be set aside because it may be repugnant to the wishes, or distasteful to a class of the community, for it is generally to that class that the law is more especially addressed. Were such a rule to obtain in civilized states, it would operate a revocation of all legislative functions; the mob would assume to declare what should be law, and what should not. There could be no reformation of evils in society. Communities and states would degenerate just in proportion as their laws were wise and wholesome, or foolish and immoral.

Careful reading of these sentences leads to some disturbing questions: what "class of the community" was this law supposed to reform? What "mob" was the Court concerned about? Somehow, the language of this decision makes it hard to picture a small number of criminals as the class the Court felt compelled to restrain and chastise.

Even more astonishing is the wishful thinking and elitist sentiment expressed in the next paragraph:

> The law under consideration has been attacked upon the ground that it was contrary to public policy, and deprived the people of the necessary means of self-defense; that it was an innovation upon the customs and habits of the people, to which they would not peaceably submit. We do not think the people of Texas are so bad as this, and we do think that the latter half of the nineteenth century is not too soon for Christian and civilized states to legislate against any and every species of crime. Every system of public

---

78 *English* v. *State*, 35 Tex. 473, 477 (1872).
79 *English* v. *State*, 35 Tex. 473, 478 (1872).

laws should be, in itself, the purest and best system of public morality. We will not say to what extent the early customs and habits of the people of this state should be respected and accommodated, where they may come in conflict with the ideas of intelligent and well-meaning legislators.

We now reach the part of this decision that suggests the "class" at whom this law may have been aimed, or at whom the Texas Supreme Court felt that it should be aimed:

> A portion of our system of laws, as well as our public morality, is derived from a people the most peculiar perhaps of any other in the history and derivation of its own system. Spain, at different periods of the world, was dominated over by the Carthagenians, the Romans, the Vandals, the Snovi, the Allani, the Visigoths, and Arabs; and to this day there are found in the Spanish codes traces of the laws and customs of each of these nations blended together in a system by no means to be compared with the sound philosophy and pure morality of the common law.[80] [emphasis added]

Are we to interpret this as indicating that the statute was aimed at the Hispanic population of Texas? None of the defendants have Hispanic names; yet this may indicate only the quality of justice, and possibility for appeal, available to Hispanics who violated this law. And, as we have also seen, the common law *did* recognize a right to self-defense, and a right to carry arms.

Three years passed, and in the intervening period, the Republicans lost control of Texas,[81] though not before Democrats and a black militia came close to armed warfare in the statehouse. The Democrats, once again in control of the legislature, rapidly repealed many of Governor Davis' measures, including the state police,[82] but not the weapons restrictions.

In the next case, *State* v. *Duke* (1875), George Duke was indicted for violation of this act; it was charged that Duke did "unlawfully carry on his person one pistol, known as a six-shooter." The trial judge in Caldwell County set aside Duke's indictment on the grounds that a violation of law had not been charged, because the carrying of a pistol, by itself, was not a violation of the law.[83] The technical nature of the indictment's inadequacy occupied much of the Court's decision in this case, and is uninteresting from the standpoint of the right to keep and bear arms.

However, the issue of what constitutes "protected arms" was addressed by the Texas Supreme Court, as was the extent of state and Federal Constitutional protections. The Court first excluded the Second Amendment from consideration, because, in the Court's opinion, the Bill of Rights was not a limitation on state laws. Next, the Court considered the Texas constitutional provision.[84]

While the Court in *State* v. *Duke* (1875) upheld the precedent of *English* v. *State* (1872), that the law limiting the carrying of weapons did not conflict with this constitutional provision, they did take issue with the *English* decision's definition of "arms":

> We... do not adopt the opinion expressed that the word "arms," in the Bill of Rights, refers only to the arms of a militiaman or soldier. Similar clauses in the Constitution of other

---

80 *English* v. *State*, 35 Tex. 473, 478, 479, 480 (1872).
81 Viault, 17-18.
82 Ramsdell, 313, 316-7.
83 *State* v. *Duke*, 42 Tex. 455, 456, 459, 460 (1875).
84 *State* v. *Duke*, 42 Tex. 455, 457, 458 (1875).

States have generally been construed by the courts as using the word *arms* in a more comprehensive sense....[85] [emphasis added]

The arms which every person is secured the right to keep and bear (in the defense of himself or the State, subject to legislative regulation), must be such arms as are commonly kept, according to the customs of the people, and are appropriate for open and manly use in self-defense, as well as such as are proper for the defense of the State. *If this does not include the double-barreled shot-gun, the huntsman's rifle, and such pistols at least as are not adapted to being carried concealed, then the only arms which the great mass of the people of the State have, are not under constitutional protection. But beyond question, the dragoon or holster pistol is part of the arms of a soldier in that branch of the service.* (Coldwell *v.* The State, 3 Heiskell, 166,[86] and English *v.* The State, 35 Texas, 476). Regarding, then, some kinds of pistols as within the meaning of the word, we are of the opinion that the Act in question is nothing more than a legitimate and highly proper regulation of their use. We are not called on to lay down general rules, prescribing how far legislative regulation may be extended, without trespassing on the constitutional rights of the citizen. The question for our decision is the constitutionality of the Act under which this indictment was proved. It undertakes to regulate the place where, and circumstances under which a pistol may be carried; and in doing so, it appears to have respected the right to carry a pistol openly when needed for self-defense or in the public service, and the right to have one at the home or place of business. We hold that the statute under consideration is valid, and that to carry a pistol under circumstances where it is forbidden by the statute, is a violation of the criminal law of the State.[87] [emphasis added]

And so the action of the district judge in overturning the indictment was upheld, but the statute was again upheld as constitutional.[88]

Immediately after the *Duke* decision, the Texas Supreme Court decided a number of other appeals in conjunction with the same law. While interesting in their own right, no constitutional issues were raised or discussed in *Young* v. *State* (1875), *Smith* v. *State* (1875), or *Williams* v. *State* (1875).[89]

The Georgia Court's prewar recognition of a right to keep and bear arms began to crumble after the Civil War. Most of the details of *State* v. *Hill* (1874) have not made it into the decision. Unfortunately, all that the headnotes tell us about the case is that the plaintiff was named Miles Hill, and that he was indicted "under section 4528 of the Code, prohibiting the carrying of pistols... to any court of justice...." The decision itself tells us nothing else about the circumstances under which Mr. Hill violated the law.

Justice McCay, writing the opinion of the Georgia Supreme Court, quickly disposed of the Second Amendment as well as natural law:

It is now well settled that [the Bill of Rights] are all restriction, not upon the states, but upon the United States. And this would seem to be the inevitable conclusion from the history of these amendments as well as from their nature and even their terms. I do not myself assent to that other limitation of the legislative powers of our general assembly

---

85 But, as has been the case in many of these decisions, there are some disturbing errors in the cited cases: *Bliss* v. *Commonwealth* became *Bliss* v. *Cane* in the list of citations that followed.

86 *State* v. *Duke*, 42 Tex. 455, 458 (1875). *Coldwell* v. *The State* is incorrect; the location cited is *Andrews* v. *State*, 3 Heisk. (50 Tenn.) 165, 8 Am. Rep. 8 (1871).

87 *State* v. *Duke*, 42 Tex. 455, 458, 459 (1875).

88 *State* v. *Duke*, 42 Tex. 455, 462 (1875).

89 *Young* v. *State*, 42 Tex. 462 (1875); *Smith* v. *State*, 42 Tex. 464 (1875); *Williams* v. *State*, 42 Tex. 466 (1875).

insisted upon in the argument, and sometimes announced by courts, to-wit: the "higher law," which is appealed to as above even the constitution.

But Hill also argued that the Georgia constitutional provision protected his right to bear arms—and in light of the decision of the Georgia Supreme Court in *Nunn* v. *State* (1846), it was a reasonable argument to advance. But there had been changes in the Georgia Constitution, and the changes created an loophole:

> At last, therefore, if this act be unconstitutional it must be because it is conflict with the state constitution. Article I., section 14, of the constitution of 1868 is as follows: "A well regulated militia being necessary to the security of a free state, the right of the people to keep and bear arms shall not be infringed; but the general assembly shall have power to prescribe by law the manner in which arms may be borne." The act of October, 1870, upon which this indictment is based, is in these words: "No person in said state shall be permitted or allowed to carry about his or her person any dirk, Bowie-knife, pistol or revolver, or any kind of deadly weapon, to any court of justice or any election ground or precinct, or any place of public worship, or any other public gathering in this state, except militia muster grounds."[90]

What was the purpose of this law? Violence had successfully intimidated blacks into not voting in Georgia in the 1868 elections, giving control of the Legislature to the Democrats.[91] The 1865 Georgia Constitution adopted the entire U.S. Bill of Rights, including the Second Amendment. The 1868 constitutional convention used the Second Amendment with the addition of "but the General Assembly shall have the power to prescribe by law the manner in which arms may be borne."[92] The exact reason for this addition is not clear, but at least one black Republican newspaper had advised its readers in 1866 that the Second Amendment protected their right to arms: "All men, without distinction of color, have the right to keep and bear arms to defend their homes, families or themselves."[93]

In October 1870 the Georgia Legislature was under Republican control because of military intervention by the occupying Union army, and new elections were scheduled for December of that year. It would seem likely that the Republicans sought to protect blacks from intimidation in the courts and polling places. By 1874, when this decision was decided, Georgia was back in the control of the Democrats.[94]

The Georgia Supreme Court devoted more than a page to expressing Justice McCay's opinion that, "Were this question entirely a new one, I should not hesitate to hold" that the state and Federal provisions guaranteed "only the right to keep and bear the 'arms' necessary for a militiaman," and proceeded to explain:

> I have always been at a loss to follow the line of thought that extends the guarantee to the right to carry pistols, dirks, Bowie-knives, and those other weapons of like character, which, as all admit, are the greatest nuisances of our day. It is in my judgment a perversion of the meaning of the word arms, as used in the phrase "the right to keep and bear arms," to treat it as including weapons of this character. *The word "arms," evidently means the arms of a militiaman, the weapons ordinarily used in battle, to-wit: guns of every*

---

90 *State* v. *Hill*, 53 Ga. 472, 473, 474 (1874).
91 Abbott, 201.
92 Halbrook, *A Right To Bear Arms*, 116.
93 *The Loyal Georgian* (Augusta), Feb. 3, 1866, 3, col. 4, quoted in Halbrook, *A Right To Bear Arms*, 115-6.
94 Abbott, 209. Viault, 17-18.

kind, swords, bayonets, horseman's pistols, etc. The very words, "bear arms," had then and now have, a technical meaning.[95] [emphasis added]

Justice McCay then went on to articulate his reasons for believing that "to bear arms" was specifically military, based on the use of this construction in a number of contexts which are military. No historical or lexicographical authority was cited for his understanding of this meaning of "bear arms," or his narrow definition of "arms." As we have already seen, contemporary use and dictionaries demonstrate that Justice McCay was incorrect about the Framers' meanings.

Justice McCay then admits that his own personal beliefs on the subject are insufficient justification:

> But assuming that the guarantee of our state constitution was intended to include weapons of this character, (which, considering that it was made a part of the constitution after the decision of *Nunn vs. The State*, in 1 *Kelly*, is not improbable,) we still are of the opinion that the act of October, 1870, is not unconstitutional. The practice of carrying arms at courts, elections and places of worship, etc., is a thing so improper in itself, so shocking to all sense of propriety, so wholly useless and full of evil, that it would be strange if the framers of the constitution have used words broad enough to give it a constitutional guarantee. Take the clause in its largest sense; let the word "arms" include weapons of every kind; we think its guarantee would not cover so absurd, useless, defiant, and disorderly a practice as this act of 1870 forbids.[96]

Justice McCay then argued that the clause concerning a "well regulated militia" declared the purpose of the "the right of the people," and therefore the Constitutional provision restricted the purpose of the right:

> The constitution declares that as such a militia is necessary to the existence of a free state, the right of the people to keep and bear arms shall not be infringed. To effect this end, the right to have arms would seem to be absolute, since without this right, it would not be possible to attain the end contemplated, to-wit: an armed militia, organized and ready for the public exigencies. But it is obvious that the right to bear or carry arms about the persons at all times and places and under all circumstances, is not a necessity for the declared object of the guarantee; nay, that it does not even tend to secure the great purpose sought for, to-wit: that the people shall be familiar with the use of arms and capable from their habits of life, of becoming efficient militiamen. If the general right to carry and to use them exist; if they may at pleasure be borne and used in the fields, and in the woods, on the highways and byeways, at home and abroad, the whole declared purpose of the provision is fulfilled.[97]

At this point, the differences between this decision, and *Nunn v. State* (1846), are undramatic. Justice McCay acknowledged a right to possess arms out on the highways, but then held that this guarantee

> is in no fair sense a guarantee that the owners of these arms may bear them at concerts, and prayer-meetings, and elections. At such places, the bearing of arms of any sort, is an eye-sore to good citizens, offensive to peaceable people, an indication of a want of proper respect for the majesty of the laws, and a marked breach of good manners. If borne at all under the law, they must be borne openly and plainly exposed to view, and under the circumstances we allude to, the very act is not only a provocation to a breach of the peace, but dangerous to human life.[98]

---

95 *State* v. *Hill*, 53 Ga. 472, 474 (1874).
96 *State* v. *Hill*, 53 Ga. 472, 474, 475 (1874).
97 *State* v. *Hill*, 53 Ga. 472, 475, 476 (1874).
98 *State* v. *Hill*, 53 Ga. 472, 476 (1874).

On the one hand, they are "offensive" and a "provocation" if exposed to view, but may only be "borne openly." Justice McCay's notion of a right could easily be squeezed out between the requirement for open carry and the requirement to not offend or provoke.

To justify the idea that there were proper limitations on the power of the government that did not destroy that right, Justice McCay next cited a section of the Georgia bill of rights that requires, "The right of the people to appeal to the courts... shall not be impaired," and drew an analogy between that right and the right to bear arms:

> If the legislature restrict the appeal to certain times and places, and under certain reasonable conditions necessary for the public good; if it pass a statute of limitations, or regulate the rules of evidence or provide that one judgment of the court shall be conclusive, all these are limitations upon the right to appeal to the courts... One guarantee is not to swallow up all others, but each is to be construed reasonably in reference to its plain intent, and other rights guaranteed to the people. The right to go into a court-house and peacefully and safely seek its privileges, is just as sacred as the right to carry arms, and if the temple of justice is turned into a barracks, and a visitor to it is compelled to mingle in a crowd of men loaded down with pistols and Bowie-knives, or bristling with guns and bayonets, his right of free access to the courts is just as much restricted as is the right to bear arms infringed by prohibiting the practice before courts of justice.[99]

After arguing that the clause of the Georgia constitutional provision which provides, "the legislature may prescribe the manner in which arms may be borne," was broader than an allowance for the legislature to prohibit concealed carry," McCay seemed to back down, and admit that such regulations must be "reasonable":

> The right to "tote" them, as our colored people say, would be a bootless privilege, fitting one, perhaps, for playing soldier upon a drill ground, but offering no aid in that knowledge which makes an effective, to-wit: a shooting soldier. To acquire this skill and this familiarity, the words "bear arms" must include the right to load them and shoot them and use them as such things are ordinarily used, so that the "people" will be fitted for defending the state when its needs demand; and *when the constitution grants to the general assembly the right to prescribe the manner in which arms may be borne, it grants the power to regulate the whole subject of using arms, provided the regulation does not infringe that use of them which is necessary to fit the owner of them for a ready and skillful use of them as a militiaman. Any restriction which interferes with this is void, whether it relates to the carrying of them about the person, or to the place or time of bearing them.*

> The manner of bearing arms includes not only the particular way they may be carried upon the person, that is openly or secretly, on the shoulder or in the hand, loaded or unloaded, cocked or uncocked, capped or uncapped, but it includes, also, the time when, and the place where, they may be borne. It is no reply to this view of the subject to say that if the legislature may do this, they may, in effect, prohibit the carrying them altogether. The same reply may be made to the admitted right to prescribe the manner of carrying arms upon the person. *If the legislature were to say arms shall not be borne on the shoulder, nor in the hands, or on the arms, but they shall only be borne strapped or fastened upon the back, this would be prescribing only the manner, and yet, it would, in effect, be a denial of the right to bear arms altogether.* The main clause and the limitation to it are both to be construed reasonably, and in view of the declared object of the provision.[100] [emphasis added]

---

99 *State* v. *Hill*, 53 Ga. 472, 477, 478 (1874).
100 *State* v. *Hill*, 53 Ga. 472, 479, 480, 481 (1874).

What, exactly, does this mean? This decision is like a drunken driver, weaving from side to side, and narrowly missing clear statements of what is protected. The right does not exist in a church, a courtroom, or a concert, but it does exist on the highways, and apparently, in a number of other public places. The legislature may prohibit open carry, or concealed carry, or nearly any aspect of how a weapon is to be carried, except that such a restriction must not deny the right to bear arms altogether.

The history of the 1877 state constitutional convention suggests that the Georgia Supreme Court's willingness to uphold restrictions on open carry had an impact on the populace. The language of the 1868 constitution was again adopted, with only the deletion of the words "by law." When this clause was being debated, the arguments advanced suggest that the purpose was to allow the legislature to prohibit concealed carry; a proposal to allow the legislature to "prescribe the manner *and place* in which arms may be borne" was voted down. Concealed carry was not protected, but by implication, open carry, nearly anywhere, was protected.[101]

By the end of Reconstruction, the notion of a right to carry concealed arms had been so thoroughly denied by the courts of the former Confederacy that defense attorneys were no longer arguing it before Southern state supreme courts. Typical of a number of cases during this period is *Chatteaux* v. *State* (1875). Chatteaux, a fruit and vegetable dealer in Mobile, Alabama, carried a concealed pistol in the early hours of the morning, as he passed through a dangerous section of town on his way to the marketplace. Later that same evening, Chatteaux went to the post office, no longer concerned about his safety, but still carrying the pistol in his pocket, where it had been since morning. He removed the pistol from his pocket, though the decision does not tell us why he did so.

Citing the *Eslava* decision, in which the constitutional right to carry arms was neither asserted nor denied,[102] the Alabama Supreme Court held "that the right to carry a pistol, or other weapon concealed, for any of the reasons mentioned in the statute, was co-extensive only with the necessity or occasion on which the right depended." Chatteaux's conviction was upheld.[103] Neither the Second Amendment, nor the Alabama Constitution's protection of a right to keep and bear arms, was raised by the defense.

The *Dred Scott* decision had recognized that the rights of "citizens of the United States" were protected against state action; this should have been sufficient basis for Congress to pass federal laws protecting freedmen from state action. But since the *Dred Scott* decision had successfully drawn a line between "citizens" and "people," it is not surprising that a more explicit extension of the Bill of Rights to restrict state laws was desired. While rhetoric of the time was built around protecting the rights of the freedmen, crasser political motivations have been postulated as well. (Improving the conditions of free blacks in the South would tend to reduce migration of them to the North—where they were no more welcome than in the South.) As part of that effort, the Civil Rights Act of 1866 and the Fourteenth Amendment were passed, intended to guarantee that the "privileges and

---

101 Halbrook, *A Right To Bear Arms*, 116.
102 *Eslava* v. *State*, 49 Ala. 355 (1873).
103 *Chatteaux* v. *State*, 52 Ala. 388, 391 (1875).

immunities" of citizens of the United States would be protected from abusive state laws.

In the debates surrounding the Civil Rights Act of 1866, both opponents and supporters agreed that passage of it would restrict the authority of the states to disarm blacks. Opponents argued that it would prohibit racially discriminatory gun control laws, while supporters insisted it would protect the rights of blacks to have arms—a subject of some importance, as many of the Southern states and municipalities attempted to restrict or prohibit possession or carrying of arms by blacks.[104]

Considerable dispute still surrounds the intentions of the Fourteenth Amendment, but recent scholarship is increasingly willing to recognize that the Fourteenth Amendment was intended to extend *all* of the Bill of Rights to the states. When the Fourteenth Amendment was introduced in Congress in 1866, "a chief exponent referred to 'the personal rights guaranteed and secured by the first eight amendments of the Constitution; such as freedom of speech and of the press; ... the right to keep and bear arms...'"[105]

The noted Reconstruction historian Eric Foner recently wrote:

The states, declared Michigan Sen. Jacob Howard, who guided the Amendment to passage in the Senate, could no longer infringe on the liberties the Bill of Rights had secured against federal violation; henceforth, they must respect "the personal rights guaranteed and secured by the first eight Amendments." [Rep. John] Bingham said much the same thing in the House. Some portions of the Bill of Rights were of little moment in 1866.... *But it is abundantly clear that Republicans wished to give constitutional sanction to states' obligation to respect such key provisions as freedom of speech, the right to bear arms,* trial by impartial jury, and protection against cruel and unusual punishment and unreasonable search and seizure. The Freedmen's Bureau had already taken steps to protect these rights, and the Amendment was deemed necessary, in part, precisely because every one of them was being systematically violated in the South in 1866.[106] [emphasis added]

Other supporters argued for the amendment because it was needed to overturn laws that prohibited "colored men to carry weapons without a license."[107] Two years later, when the anti-Klu Klux Klan bill was debated in Congress, Bingham, the principal draftsman of the Fourteenth Amendment, repeated what the "rights and privileges" secured by it included:

Mr. Speaker, that the scope and meaning of the limitations imposed by the first section, fourteenth amendment of the Constitution may be more fully understood, permit me to say that the privileges and immunities of citizens of a State, are chiefly defined in the first eight amendments to the constitution of the United States.[108]

In *U.S.* v. *Cruikshank* (1876), the Supreme Court had an opportunity to express its opinion about the Second Amendment and its relation to the Fourteenth

104 Halbrook, "The Fourteenth Amendment...", 70-71. Halbrook is a proponent of the view that the Fourteenth Amendment was intended, at least partly, to protect freedmen from state gun control laws; evidence corroborating Halbrook's understanding of the philosophy of the Radical Republicans from a less partisan source can be found in Avery Craven, *Reconstruction: The Ending of the Civil War,* (New York: Holt, Rinehart, and Winston, 1969), 168-71, 174-5.

105 Congressional Globe, 39th Congress, 1st Sess., pt. 3, 2765 (May 23, 1866), quoted in Halbrook, "The Fourteenth Amendment...", 72.

106 Foner, 258-9.

107 Halbrook, "The Fourteenth Amendment...", 72.

108 Congressional Globe, 42nd Congress, 1st Sess., pt. 2, Appendix, 84 (March 31, 1871), quoted in Halbrook, "The Fourteenth Amendment...", 75.

Amendment. The Supreme Court decision described this case as a mob of whites, including one William Cruikshank, who had broken up a freedmen's political meeting, deprived them of their arms, and prevented them from voting in a state election. In fact, more than one hundred black men were prevented from voting by being murdered by Cruikshank's mob.[109] Under the Enforcement Act of 1870, the whites involved were indicted, tried, and convicted in the federal courts.[110] On appeal, the Supreme Court overturned their convictions in an ingenious manner, completely subverting Congressional intent with respect to the Fourteenth Amendment and the Enforcement Act of 1870. While only some parts of the decision are relevant to the Second Amendment, the Court used the same arguments with respect to the First and Second Amendments.

Acknowledging that the Fourteenth Amendment had extended the rights of national citizenship to be protected from state abuse, the Court adopted a novel concept: such rights were protected *only* to the extent that they were related to the *national* government. The Court contended that, "The right of the people peaceably to assemble for the purpose of petitioning Congress for a redress of grievances, or for anything else connected with the powers or duties of the National Government, is an attribute of national citizenship and, as such, under the protection of and guarantied by, the United States." Similarly, the First Amendment "was not intended to limit the powers of the state governments in respect to their own citizens, but to operate upon the National Government alone." It is within this narrowly defined view of the Bill of Rights that the Court found:

> The right of bearing arms for a lawful purpose is not a right granted by the Constitution; neither is it any manner dependent upon that instrument for its existence. The Second Amendment declares that it shall not be infringed, but this means no more than that it shall not be infringed by Congress.[111]

The *Cruikshank* decision, in essence, held that the Bill of Rights was *not* incorporated by the Fourteenth Amendment, except as such rights related to the national government. Republican commentary on the *Cruikshank* decision is astonishing for the conclusions reached:

> Supreme Court decisions on the "right to bear arms" have repeatedly stated that the Second Amendment was conceived of as a restraint on the power of the federal government over the state militias. In *U.S. v. Cruickshank*, 95 U.S. 542 (1874), the Court held that while there may be an individual right to possess arms, it existed independently of the Second Amendment.[112]

In fact, there is no such statement of intent in the *Cruikshank* decision, contrary to the assertion in the first sentence quoted above, and no reference to "state militias." With respect to the second sentence above, the Court ruled that the right existed before the Constitution, and that the meaning of the Second Amendment was "that it shall not be infringed by Congress." Later in the decision, the Court declared:

---

109 Lucy E. Salyer, "Cruikshank, United States v.," in Kermit L. Hall, ed., *The Oxford Companion to the Supreme Court of the United States*, (New York: Oxford University Press, 1992), 209.

110 *U.S. v. Cruikshank*, 92 U.S. 542, 548, 555 (1876).

111 *U.S. v. Cruikshank*, 92 U.S. 542, 552 (1876).

112 Michael K. Beard and Samuel S. Fields, "National Coalition to Ban Handguns Statement on the Second Amendment", in *The Right To Keep And Bear Arms*, 92. Note that the spelling and citation of this case are incorrect. Since the spelling is incorrect throughout Beard & Fields' paper, it can't be a typo.

The Second Amendment declares that it shall not be infringed; but this, as has been seen, means no more than that it shall not be infringed by Congress. This is one of the amendments that has no other effect than to restrict the powers of the National Government, leaving the people to look for their protection against any violation by their fellow-citizens of the rights it recognizes, to what is called, in City of N.Y. v. Miln, 11 Pet. 129, the "powers which relate to merely municipal legislation, or what was perhaps, more properly called internal police," "not surrendered or restrained" by the Constitution of the United States.[113]

Levin, another member of the republican school, tells us:

> U.S. v. Cruickshank, implied that there was a *personal* right to bear arms upon which Congress could not infringe. The central point of the opinion, however, was to state that the second amendment did not apply to state governments, and such governments could pass whatever legislation they desired without fear of federal sanction.[114]

But of course, this is *not* the central point of the opinion. The Court decided that the Fourteenth Amendment did *not* include all the protections of the Bill of Rights, and then set about determining which rights were incorporated. Beard, Fields, and Levin never tell us that the *Cruikshank* decision held that *only* the right to vote and assemble had come under the authority of the Federal Government, and then, only if voting for federal offices or assembling to petition Congress.[115]

Further, the Court made an interesting assertion with respect to the nature of the rights protected by the Bill of Rights. In discussing the right to peaceably assemble:

> The particular Amendment now under consideration assumes the existence of the right of the people to assemble for lawful purposes, and protects it against encroachment by Congress. The right was not created by the Amendment; neither was its continuance guarantied, except as against congressional interference. For their protection in its enjoyment, therefore, the people must look to the States.[116]

The same logic and phrasing was used by the Court with respect to the Second Amendment:

> The second and tenth counts are equally defective. The right there specified is that of "bearing arms for a lawful purpose." This is not a right granted by the Constitution. Neither is it in any manner dependent upon that instrument for its existence.[117]

The Court asserted that these rights were not *granted* by the Constitution, but were pre-existing. The Amendments *recognized* those rights, and protected them against Congress' infringement. It is possible to quote "The right was not created by the Amendment..." in such a manner as to imply that the Court believed that no such right existed; within the larger context of the discussion, it is clear that the Court was resisting the incorporation doctrine clearly stated by the principal author, proponents, and opponents of the Fourteenth Amendment, but was not denying that these rights existed, at least in a moral sense.

---

113 *U.S. v. Cruikshank*, 92 U.S. 542, 553 (1876). *New York* v. *Miln* (1837) upheld a New York State law that required ship captains landing immigrants to post a bond against them becoming public charges. McDonald, 82-83.

114 Levin, 124-5. At least Levin cites the case location correctly; only the name is misspelled, but that error is made consistently. It appears that Beard, Fields, and Levin are all relying on a common (and erroneous) secondary source for their information about this case.

115 *U.S. v. Cruikshank*, 92 U.S. 542 (1876).

116 *U.S. v. Cruikshank*, 92 U.S. 542, 552 (1876).

117 *U.S. v. Cruikshank*, 92 U.S. 542, 553 (1876).

In the twentieth century, this doctrine of incorporation has been recognized as extending nearly all of the Bill of Rights to protect citizens against state laws. To use *Cruikshank* as evidence that the Second Amendment does not protect an individual right is valid only if we accept *Cruikshank*'s reasoning with respect to free speech, freedom of assembly, and all the rest of the protections of the Bill of Rights that are now incorporated.

Nearly all the decisions during this period took place in former slave states; our next two decisions are remarkable in that they took place in states not experiencing the social dislocations of emancipation. *Wright* v. *Commonwealth* (1875), took place in Pennsylvania. A Jonathan Wright was indicted in April 1871 in Schuylkill County, charging that: "he 'did unlawfully and maliciously carry on and about (his) person, a certain concealed deadly weapon, commonly called a pistol, with intent, with the pistol aforesaid, unlawfully and maliciously, to do bodily harm to some other person, to the inquest unknown, &c.'"

While the jury found Wright innocent, they did order him to pay court costs. The defendant appealed the order to pay court costs, arguing that the May 5, 1864 county ordinance which prohibited the carrying of concealed weapons was a violation of the 21st section of Pennsylvania's Bill of Rights. Since his indictment was for an action which was not a crime, Wright felt that he should not be obligated to pay.

The Pennsylvania Supreme Court's ruling is short, without citation of either precedent or authority for their decision about the constitutionality of the law in question: "Such an unlawful act and malicious intent as this has no protection under the 21st section of the Bill of Rights, saving the right of the citizens to bear arms in defence of themselves and the state." The Court further held that the jury must have had a good reason for imposing court costs on the defendant, even if they found him innocent. While the headnotes for this decision assert that "prohibiting the carrying of concealed weapons, is not obnoxious to the Bill of Rights, sect. 21," the decision itself specifies both "an unlawful act and malicious intent,"[118] suggesting that the combination of the two elements was required to constitute a crime. But did the court consider the carrying of concealed weapons to be part of the malicious intent, or was some other evidence of criminal intent required?

An additional interesting question is what part, if any, the 1873 Pennsylvania Constitutional Convention played. The 1790 Pennsylvania Constitution, Article IX, §21, contained the guarantee: "That the right of citizens to bear arms, in defence of themselves and the State, shall not be questioned."[119] At the 1873 convention, an attempt was made to add the word "openly" after the word "citizens": "Thomas Struthers, the proponent of the change, argued that persons charged with carrying arms secretly 'fall back on the Constitution, which they say authorizes the bearing of arms, and therefore the act of Assembly is unconstitutional.'"

His opponents responded that this would require them "to walk the streets of this city at night without any protection whatever from ruffians"; another argued that the law in Pennsylvania "required showing of evil intent" in conjunction with concealed carrying of weapons, and was thus a constitutional law. The proposed

---

118 *Wright* v. *Commonwealth*, 77 Pa. St. 470, 471 (1875).
119 Thorpe, 5:3101.

amendment lost, 54-23.[120] It is not clear if the Pennsylvania Supreme Court took into account the actions of the constitutional convention two years before, or independently reflected the same sentiments held by the majority of the delegates.

Another Northern decision during this period was *Wiley* v. *Indiana* (1876). The defendant Wiley was convicted of carrying a concealed weapon. No attempt was made to challenge the law on constitutional grounds; the only dispute was whether the prosecution was required to prove that Wiley was *not* a traveller, and thus subject to the law, or whether the defense had an obligation to demonstrate that Wiley *was* a traveller, and thus exempt from the law. The Indiana Supreme Court held that the obligation was on the defense to prove that he was a traveller, not on the prosecution to prove that he wasn't.[121] This strongly suggests that the carrying of concealed arms was not recognized as a right by the Indiana Court, consistent with the decision in *State* v. *Mitchell* (1833).

Labor violence played a part in two decisions from Illinois during this period. One of these decisions is *Presser* v. *Illinois* (1886), one of the U.S. Supreme Court's often misquoted statements about the meaning of the Second Amendment. By examining the circumstances under which this decision was handed down, we can better understand—and be horrified—by the logic of the Court.

One of the original theses upon which research for this work was started was that fear of labor violence, and the desire to oppress workers, played a major role in the narrow republican interpretations of the right to arms that have appeared throughout the history of the Republic. But while there is some evidence to support this position, the bulk of the evidence suggests that labor unions were only a small part of this judicial misinterpretation of the Second Amendment and its state analogs.

There are a number of decisions in which the Second Amendment is merely an innocent bystander. These decisions reflect the increasingly severe violence associated with the development of large industrial combinations in late nineteenth century America, and the growth of labor unions in response. While sometimes cited as evidence by the republican school that no individual right is protected by the Second Amendment, a more detailed examination of the decisions suggests otherwise. Also of interest is what the circumstances that led to these decisions tell us about the loss of the ideal of a people's militia. The National Guard, by the period after the Civil War, began to play an increasingly important role in intimidating labor unions. In Chicago, a group of immigrant German socialists formed an armed club to defend themselves and their families against criminal attacks by the National Guard.[122]

The first decision in this vein is primarily *not* a "right to keep and bear arms" case. But exactly what it is, from the syllabus and decision, is a bit of a mystery. What should have been a straightforward case of refusing jury duty, turned into a decision eighteen pages long, with three pages of syllabus, and a baffling array of secondary issues. For those researching the issues of militia duties, and the relationship between the National Guard, standing armies, and military duty, *Dunne* v. *People* (1879) is a gold-mine of citations and issues.

---

120 Halbrook, *A Right To Bear Arms*, 116-7.

121 *Wiley* v. *Indiana*, 52 Ind. 516, 517, 518 (1876).

122 Sanford Levinson, "The Embarrassing Second Amendment", *Yale Law Journal*, 99 [December 1989], 637, 652-3.

Peter J. Dunne had been summoned to jury duty in Cook County, in September 1879. He attempted to excuse himself from jury duty by arguing that "he was an enlisted, active member of the 'Illinois National Guard'," and was therefore exempt under the statute of May 28, 1879. The court refused to accept his excuse, and fined him $50. There was apparently some question about the validity of this statute (at least in part), and both parties requested that the Illinois Supreme Court hear the case. They did hear it, in November of that same year.[123]

Mr. Dunne challenged, it appears, nearly every aspect of the law in question; of interest to us is the authority of the state government to regulate the private bearing of arms. The Illinois Supreme Court upheld the authority of the state to regulate private organizations parading with arms:

> The right of the citizen to "bear arms" for the defence of his person and property is not involved, even remotely, in this discussion. This section has no bearing whatever on that right, whatever it may be, and we will enter upon no discussion of that question. Whether bodies of men, with military organizations or otherwise, under no discipline or command by the United States or the State, shall be permitted to "parade with arms" in populous communities, is a matter within the regulation and subject to the police power of the state.[124]

The Illinois Supreme Court appears to have acknowledged that a "right of the citizen to 'bear arms' for the defence of his person and property" did exist, but then the Court backtracked and referred to it as, "that right, whatever it may be," and refused to discuss it further. Was this just clumsy writing, or were more sinister motives involved?

Immediately following this statement was an assertion far removed from both Revolutionary and modern notions of the proper limits of governmental power:

> In matters pertaining to the internal peace and well-being of the State, its police powers are plenary and inalienable. It is a power co-extensive with self-protection, and is sometimes termed, and not inaptly, the "law of overruling necessity." Every necessary act for the protection, safety and best interests of the people of the State may be done under this power. Persons and property may be subjected to all reasonable restraints and burdens for the common good. Where mere property interests are involved, this power, like other powers of government, is subject to constitutional limitations; but where the internal peace and health of the people of the State are concerned, the limitations that are said to be upon the exercise of this power are, that such "regulations must have reference to the comfort, safety and welfare of society." It is within the power of the General Assembly to enact laws for the suppression of that which may endanger the public peace, and impose penalties for the infraction of such laws. What will endanger the public security must, as a general rule, be left to the wisdom of the legislative department of the government.[125]

As will become apparent in the next case, opposition to the Illinois statute regulating private militias did not end with *Dunne*; the month after this decision, the issue of private militias ceased to be an abstraction. *Presser* v. *Illinois* (1886) presents an example of how the U.S. Supreme Court narrowly upheld the right to keep and bear arms, apparently as an individual right, based on a republican view of military obligation—while upholding a law that violated the spirit of the Second Amendment.

---

123 *Dunne* v. *People*, 94 Ill. 120, 123 (1879).
124 *Dunne* v. *People*, 94 Ill. 120, 140, 141 (1879).
125 *Dunne* v. *People*, 94 Ill. 120, 141 (1879).

In response to the previously mentioned abuses of workers by the Illinois National Guard, a workers' militia was established.[126] Herman Presser led a march of this workers' militia, called the *Lehr und Wehr Verein* ("teaching and defense union"), through the streets of Chicago, with Presser on horseback carrying a sword in his hand, and the workers carrying rifles behind him. Presser was indicted under the 1879 Illinois militia statute, which prohibited any militia from organizing, drilling, or parading "without the license of the governor."

On appeal from the Illinois Supreme Court, the U.S. Supreme Court upheld the validity of the statute forbidding private militias. At the same time, in response to Presser's claim that his Second Amendment rights were being denied, the court ruled that: "A state cannot prohibit the people therein from keeping and bearing arms to an extent that would deprive the United States of the protection afforded by them as a reserve military force."[127] While the Court upheld the restrictions on unofficial militias, it argued that:

> We think it clear that the sections under consideration, which only forbid bodies of men to associate together as military organizations, or to drill or parade with arms in cities and towns unless authorized by law, do not infringe the right of the people to keep and bear arms. But a conclusive answer to the contention that this amendment prohibits the legislation in question lies in the fact that the amendment is a limitation only upon the power of congress and the national government, and not upon that of the state.[128]

The Second Amendment was only a limitation on the power of the Federal Government—not the states. But the "right of the people to keep and bear arms," was in the Court's opinion, protected from federal interference. While Presser had invoked the "privileges and immunities" clause of the Fourteenth Amendment in asserting his protection from Illinois law,[129] the Court's acceptance of the Fourteenth Amendment incorporation doctrine was still many years in the future.

The Court also acknowledged:

> It is undoubtedly true that all citizens capable of bearing arms constitute the reserved military force or reserve militia of the United States as well as of the states, and, in view of this prerogative of the general government, as well as of its general powers, the states cannot, even laying the constitutional provision in question out of view, prohibit the people from keeping and bearing arms, so as to deprive the United States of their rightful resource for maintaining the public security, and disable the people from performing their duty to the general government.[130]

Even if the Second Amendment was ignored, the states could not prohibit the people from keeping and bearing arms. While maintaining the republican view of arms ownership, the Court implied that the widespread ownership of military arms in private hands, "for maintaining the public security," was a right guaranteed against state interference. Those who cite *Presser* as evidence that the Second Amendment is not a restraint on state laws, appear to have missed this other part of the decision.

What makes this decision so disturbing is that by acknowledging the validity of the Illinois statute that established a "select militia"—effectively a state army used to

126 Levinson, 99:652-3.
127 *Presser* v. *Illinois*, 116 U.S. 252, 254, 255 (1886).
128 *Presser* v. *Illinois*, 116 U.S. 252, 265, 266 (1886).
129 *Presser* v. *Illinois*, 116 U.S. 252, 262 (1886).
130 *Presser* v. *Illinois*, 116 U.S. 252, 266 (1886).

suppress labor unionists, while denying the right of workers to defend themselves collectively—the Court had completely subverted the intent of the "no standing armies" requests. Is this what Madison had in mind in *Federalist* 46, when he suggested a standing army of 30,000 men would be opposed by a militia consisting of the whole people? The intent of the Framers had been perverted in the interests of maintaining the status quo of nineteenth century industrialism.

Ten years later, the Massachusetts Supreme Judicial Court heard *Commonwealth* v. *Murphy* (1896), a case quite similar to *Presser* v. *Illinois* (1886). Murphy and a number of associates had styled themselves as the "Sarsfield Guards," and marched together with inoperative rifles, in violation of: "St. 1893, c. 367, §124, which prohibits all but certain bodies of men from drilling or parading with firearms..." Murphy argued that the statute that he was convicted of violating was: "in contravention of the seventeenth article of the Massachusetts Declaration of Rights, which declares that 'the people have a right to keep and bear arms for the common defence.'"[131]

The Court did not agree:

> This view cannot be supported. The right to keep and bear arms for the common defence does not include the right to associate together as a military organization, or to drill and parade with arms in cities and towns, unless authorized to do so by law. This is a matter affecting the public security, quiet, and good order, and it is within the police powers of the Legislature to regulate the bearing of arms so as to forbid such unauthorized drills and parades. *Presser* v. *Illinois*, 116 U.S. 252, 264, 265. *Dunne* v. *People*, 94 Ill. 120.

Up to this point, the decision was correct: armed bands marching through the streets certainly could be construed as an attempt at intimidating others—although intimidating the government might be argued as the purpose suggested in *Federalist* 46. Certainly, the *Dunne* and *Presser* decisions are correctly cited as precedent. But next:

> The protection of a similar constitutional protection has often been sought by persons charged with carrying concealed weapons, and it has been almost universally held that the Legislature may regulate and limit the mode of carrying arms... The early decision to the contrary of *Bliss* v. *Commonwealth*, 2 Litt. 90, has not been generally approved.[132]

It is certainly true that the right *of individuals* to carry arms, either openly or concealed, had been argued repeatedly before various state supreme courts. But the Court appears to have been unaware that *Bliss* v. *Commonwealth* (1822) was only one of several decisions that had recognized a right to carry concealed. Further, a more accurate comparison would have been to those cases where equivalent state constitutional provisions had been argued successfully, to protect the right of individuals to carry arms openly—for indeed, the rifles in question were carried openly by the "Sarsfield Guards." The Massachusetts Supreme Judicial Court made no statement about whether the right of *individuals* to openly carry arms, or to keep arms, was within the protections of the state constitutional protection, and the Second Amendment was apparently not raised by the defendant.

---

131 *Commonwealth* v. *Murphy*, 166 Mass. 171, 172 (1896). Unfortunately, the decision of the Court gives us no information for determining to what purpose this private army was established.
132 *Commonwealth* v. *Murphy*, 166 Mass. 171, 172, 173 (1896).

Without question, industrial strife was a major concern of the period between the Civil War and World War I. The 1873 panic, induced by the bankruptcy of Jay Cooke and Co., provoked a depression of unprecedented length.[133] Contemporary accounts of the series of strikes which took place during 1877 show that armed violence and the threat of armed violence by labor unionists played a significant role in strengthening the union position relative to employers. Many incidents related in Joseph Dacus' *Annals of the Great Strikes* involved unionists preventing the carrying out of business with the threat of armed violence.[134] When confronting regular army units, the workers were, in at least one instance, markedly better armed than the soldiers; the workers "were supplied with Henry and Winchester repeating rifles, and from this circumstance were able to overawe any train-guard likely to be sent out." The Army still had not made the step up to repeating rifles, and were consequently less effectively armed than the civilian population.[135]

National Guard units in some instances refused to fight against unionists, apparently because they were insufficient in arms and numbers to be effective; and in a few instances, they joined the strikers in horror at the needless bloodshed caused by other National Guard units.[136] Francis Corbin's, "Are we not the militia? Shall we fight ourselves? No, sir; the idea is absurd,"[137] was found to be at least occasionally effective as a restraint on needless bloodshed. That the population took advantage of their right to keep and bear arms under such circumstances may be found in a description of a massacre in Reading, Pennsylvania, where the National Guard opened fire on an unresisting and peaceful crowd, in response to rock throwing by an related group of strikers. A number of people under attack by the Guardsmen responded with handguns, leading to injuries among the Guardsmen, some serious. Similarly, an overreaction by Guardsmen in Pittsburgh led to open armed warfare with not only strikers, but with ordinary citizens, sickened by the senseless killings. The widespread ownership of handguns and rifles made the Guardsmen's Gatling guns of limited value, as urban guerrilla warfare erupted.[138]

Arms were employed by factions other than strikers and National Guardsmen, however. In some cities, strikes did not remain peaceful, and not always because of Guardsmen shooting down unarmed and unresisting civilians. In Pittsburgh, rioting quickly extended beyond the property of the railroads:

> The militia having fled the city, and there being no United States regulars at hand, the citizens of Pittsburgh were at the mercy of a mob, without the least possibility of resisting its demands. Such was the situation late Sunday evening, when... a vigilance committee was raised for the purpose of preventing a further waste of property. The

133 Jeremy Brecher, *Strike!*, (San Francisco: Straight Arrow Books, 1972), xiv.

134 Joseph A. Dacus, *Annals of the Great Strikes*, (Chicago: L.T. Palmer & Co., 1877; reprinted New York: Arno Press, 1969), 33, 59, 212-213. Dacus was a journalist, and *Annals of the Great Strikes*, while containing a vivid and detailed contemporary account of the events, suffers the deficiencies one might expect from a journalist: no sources, and no clear distinctions between eyewitness accounts, second-hand sources, and simple rumor. Dacus makes it clear that his sympathies, and that of many other Americans, were at least partially with the strikers. Dacus clearly distinguishes between the strikers, and mobs of hooligans, and "idlers," that Dacus called "Internationalists" and "Communists."

135 Dacus, 59. Robert V. Bruce, *1877: Year of Violence*, (Indianapolis: Bobbs-Merrill Co., 1959; reprinted Chicago: Quadrangle Books, Inc., 1970), 94, 96.

136 Dacus, 42, 212-3, 216, 156. Bruce, 194.

137 Elliot, 3:112-3.

138 Dacus, 208. Bruce, 165-7, 191-3.

committee was rapidly recruited and its members were first supplied with base-ball bats, but these were afterwards exchanged for guns.... As soon as the force was organized they marched to Seventh avenue, where hundreds of spectators who had been waiting for some one to lead, joined with them in preventing further incendiarism.[139]

Concerned that the strikers might turn riotous in Buffalo, New York, the police department and sheriff swore in hundreds of ordinary citizens as temporary police-men to deal with the threat in July 1877; similar events took place in Indianapolis, Indiana, Chicago, St. Louis, and San Francisco at the same time.[140] Similarly, Governor Thomas Young of Ohio issued a proclamation on July 25, 1877:

To avert all danger, and in order to successfully meet all resistance to thorough execution of the law, I hereby call on all law-abiding men in all our cities, towns and villages to tender their services to their respective civil authorities, and under their direction and control organize themselves into a volunteer police force sufficiently strong to overawe the lawless elements.[141]

In essence, *this* was the sort of militia envisioned by the Founding Fathers—though in this case, concerned about the problems of anarchy, not tyranny. Not all the strikes turned violent and, in some cases, arms in the hands of the strikers actually protected railroad property from drunken rioters, and prevented loss of life.

While contemporary accounts of murders committed with concealed weapons during the 1877 disturbances are scarce, the horrified tone of these accounts suggests that the murderous use of concealed weapons was considered especially execrable.[142] Concealed weapons in the hands of strikers also played a significant role in the eruption of violence at the Homestead Steel Works in 1892.[143]

Throughout the 1890s, the arms carried by strikers were a fundamental part of the process by which unions sought to counterbalance both company private armies and National Guard units. The disturbances in Anderson County, Tennessee, provoked by the use of convict labor as strikebreakers, provide an example:

[M]iners from the surrounding counties, including some from Kentucky, armed with shotguns, Winchester rifles, and Colt pistols, began pouring into Briceville and Coal Creek, on trains and mules and even on foot. They formed a line and marched on the offending mine, spreading out into the mountain ranges and taking cover behind rocks and trees as they drew close. They sent a committee forward to demand the expulsion of prisoners. When a militia Colonel moved as if to capture the committee, one of its members waved a handkerchief as a signal to the miners, who sprang from cover. The 2,000 armed miners had little difficulty persuading the militia and guards to accompany them to the railroad station with the convicts, and return again to Knoxville.[144]

Another strike, in Pennsylvania, caused the following message to be delivered by the strikers to the strikebreakers and deputies who were protecting them from union intimidation: "We are heavily armed and will return bullet for bullet if the deputies fire on us."[145]

---

139 Dacus, 141.
140 Dacus, 156-7, 296, 313, 385, 418. Bruce, 178-80, 200-1, 240-1. The San Francisco riots had the added element of anti-Chinese violence and arson.
141 Dacus, 274.
142 Dacus, 297, 300, 336-7.
143 Brecher, 57.
144 Brecher, 67.
145 *New York Times*, May 25, 1894, quoted in Brecher, 72.

An example of conditions that should have caused the courts to retreat from the right to keep arms (if any labor violence could have done so), were associated with the Illinois Central Railroad strike of 1911. In Illinois and Mississippi, handguns and rifles were widely used by strikers in murderous attacks on strikebreakers, and "led to a complete breakdown of civil government in parts of Mississippi." Martial law was finally declared when ten National Guard regiments failed to restore order.[146]

One historian of the 1892 Homestead strike argues:

> The decisive effect of militiamen cannot be overemphasized; one searches United States labor history in vain for a single case where the introduction of troops operated to the strikers' advantage. In virtually all conflicts before and after 1892 the state guard acted, in effect, as a strikebreaking agency...[147]

It is in this context that we must consider the increasing unwillingness to admit that the "militia" referred to something wider than just the National Guard.

Somewhat after the close of Reconstruction is *State* v. *Wilforth* (1881). The defendant, Wilforth, was indicted and convicted for "going into a church house in said county where people were assembled for literary purposes, viz: for the purposes of a school exhibition, the same defendant having about his person fire-arms..." Apparently, Wilforth was carrying a pistol concealed, in violation of an 1875 state law that made it a misdemeanor to have "any kind of fire-arms, bowie-knife, dirk, dagger, slung-shot, or other deadly weapon" upon one's person in "any church or place where people have assembled for religious worship."

While Wilforth attempted to argue that he was unaware of the law, the Missouri Court responded with "*Ignorantia legis excusat neminem*"—ignorance of the law is no excuse. Wilforth also argued that the law in question violated the Second Amendment. The Court acknowledged that some state courts had recognized that their state constitutions protected concealed carry of arms, including *Bliss* v. *Commonwealth* (1822), but erroneously included Tennessee in that category. The Missouri Court went on to cite the more common cases, including *Nunn* v. *State* (1846), *State* v. *Reid* (1840), and *State* v. *Jumel* (1858) to bolster their position that concealed carry was *not* protected by state constitution arms provisions.[148] However, *Jumel* was decided based on the Second Amendment, and *Nunn* was decided based on both the Georgia Constitution and the Second Amendment.

Finally, the Missouri Court expressed its opinion about the Missouri law being challenged:

> Whether such statutes are or not in conflict with the federal constitution, is an open question so far as the federal courts are concerned, the question never having been passed upon by any of them, as far as we know. Following the weight of authority as indicated by the state courts, and in the light of section 17, article 2 of the constitution of this State, which declares "that the right of no citizen to keep and bear arms in defense of his home, person or property, or in aid of the civil power, when thereto legally summoned, shall be called in question; but nothing herein contained is intended to justify the prac-

---

146 Graham Adams, *Age of Industrial Violence 1910-15*, (New York: Columbia University Press, 1966), 132-5.

147 Leon Wolff, *Lockout, The Story of the Homestead Strike of 1892: A Study of Violence, Unionism and the Carnegie Steel Empire* (New York: Harper & Row, 1965), 228, quoted in Brecher, 236.

148 *State* v. *Wilforth*, 74 Mo. 528, 529, 530, 531 (1881).

tice of wearing concealed weapons," we must hold the act in question to be valid and binding, and as intended only to interdict the carrying weapons concealed.[149]

In so doing, the Missouri Supreme Court had recognized that the right to carry arms openly was protected by the state constitutional protection of the right "to keep and bear arms"—only concealed carry was within the Legislature's power to prohibit.

In 1883, Missouri passed yet another law regulating the carriage of deadly weapons; the new law prohibited "the carrying of concealed, dangerous, and deadly weapons upon the person, and the exhibition of the same, and the carrying of deadly weapons when intoxicated..." The defendant in *State* v. *Shelby* (1886) had withdrawn a revolver from his pocket in a saloon, while intoxicated. The Missouri Supreme Court reaffirmed its position that the Legislature had the authority to prohibit the concealed carrying of deadly weapons, and similarly held that the provision prohibiting possession of a deadly weapon while intoxicated was within the proper regulatory authority of the government. The only significant change from the *State* v. *Wilforth* (1881) decision was that the Missouri Court was now aware of the *U.S.* v. *Cruikshank* (1876) decision: "The second amendment to the constitution of the United States is a restriction upon the powers of the national government only, and is not a restriction upon state legislation."[150] But since the Missouri Court's decision in *Wilforth* had been based on the Missouri Constitution, this did not affect the precedent from the *Wilforth* decision.[151]

The first post-Civil War North Carolina case was *State* v. *Speller* (1882). L.R. Speller and a man named Jenkins had been engaged in a progressively more severe argument; according to Speller, Jenkins made an attempt to cut Speller on Saturday with a razor, and made death threats against Speller. Jenkins and Speller subsequently swore out complaints against each other, and when a police officer serving the warrant against Speller on Monday found a concealed pistol on him, Speller was arrested, indicted, and convicted of carrying a concealed weapon, in violation of an 1879 North Carolina law. It is easy to be sympathetic to Speller's fears; Jenkins lived half a mile from Speller, while the nearest peace officer was a mile and a half away. In an age before telephones and patrol cars, the chances of Speller successfully surviving an armed attack by Jenkins would have been remote.

On appeal, Speller's attorney argued that the jury should have been charged that the extenuating circumstances behind his carrying of a concealed weapon took precedence over the concealed weapon law.[152] Speller's attorney also raised the issue of the constitutionality of the concealed weapons law.

The North Carolina Supreme Court refused to overturn the lower court's decision, and in discussing the constitutional issues:

> We concede the full force of the ingenious argument made by counsel upon this point, but cannot admit its application to the statute in question. The distinction between the *"right to keep and bear arms,"* and *"the practice of carrying concealed weapons"* is plainly

149 *State* v. *Wilforth*, 74 Mo. 528, 531 (1881).
150 *State* v. *Shelby*, 90 Mo. 302, 304, 305, 306, 2 S.W. 460 (1886).
151 The Missouri Court also cited *"Anderson* v. *State*, 3 Heiskell (Tenn.) 172" as evidence for the non-applicability of the Second Amendment to state laws — but of course, the case wasn't *Anderson*, but *Andrews*.
152 *State* v. *Speller*, 86 N.C. 697, 698 (1882).

observed in the Constitution of this State. The first, it is declared, shall not be infringed, while the latter may be prohibited. Art. I, sec. 24.

As the surest inhibition that could be put upon this *practice* deemed so hurtful as to be the subject of express mention in the organic law of the State, the Legislature has seen fit to enact that at no time, and under no circumstances, except upon his own premises, shall any person carry a deadly weapon *concealed* about his person, and it is the strict duty of the courts, whenever an occasion offers, to uphold a law thus sanctioned and approved. But without any constitutional provision whatever on the subject, can it be doubted that the Legislature might by law *regulate* this right to bear arms—as they do all other rights whether inherent or otherwise—and require it to be exercised in a manner conducive to the peace and safety of the public? This is as far as the statute assumes to go. It does not say that a citizen when beset with danger shall not provide for his security by wearing such arms as may be essential to that end; but simply that if he does do so, he must wear them openly, and so as to be seen by those with whom he may come in contact. The right to wear *secret weapons* is no more essential to the *protection* of one man than another, and surely it cannot be supposed that the law intends that an unwary advantage should be taken even of an enemy.[153] [emphasis in original]

Open carry was protected; concealed carry was not—even in life-threatening circumstances.

In *State* v. *Pigford* (1895), Sam Pigford was arrested outside his home for "failure to work the public road." He was convicted, and sentenced to three days in jail, at which point, the jailer found that he was carrying a concealed pistol. While Pigford was serving his sentence, he was charged with the concealed weapons charge, and convicted. On appeal, the issue of the North Carolina Constitution's provision appears not to have been raised, but the North Carolina Supreme Court held:

> The defendant was not prohibited from carrying the pistol on his own premises, and if it had been made to appear that when arrested he had asked to be allowed to leave it at home and the officer had refused, here would have been some semblance of a defense, but even in that event it would still have been incumbent on the defendant to explain satisfactorily why he did not carry the pistol openly as he had a right to do, after leaving his premises, and not concealed about his person.[154]

The Court did not articulate where this right to carry openly came from; nor did they hold that there was a right to carry a pistol concealed at one's own premises—merely that it was not prohibited. Nonetheless, the decision in *Pigford* is consistent with the rest of the post-war North Carolina decisions—open carry was a "right," while concealed carry was not.

While Southern supreme courts were busy hearing cases involving the carrying of arms, and in many cases, denying that any individual right to bear arms was protected by either the Federal or state constitutions, the legal commentators up North seem not to have noticed. Broom & Hadley's edition of Blackstone's *Commentaries*, published in 1875, carries an annotation on Blackstone's statement of "The fifth and last auxiliary right of the subject... is that of having arms for defence" that quoted the Second Amendment. The same note then tells us: "The constitutions of several of the states contain a similar clause. The right of carrying arms for self-protection was discussed in *Bliss* v. *Commonwealth*..."[155]

---

153 *State* v. *Speller*, 86 N.C. 697, 700 (1882).
154 *State* v. *Pigford*, 117 N.C. 748, 749 (1895).
155 William Blackstone, *Commentaries on the Laws of England*, edited by Herbert Broom & Edward A. Hadley, (Albany, N.Y.: John D. Parsons, 1875), 1:121, note 64.

It would appear that the decisions of the Southern courts made little or no impact on Broom and Hadley, who clearly saw the Second Amendment and the state analogs as protecting a right to carry arms—even in that most extreme of decisions, *Bliss* v. *Commonwealth* (1822). This suggests that the South was, once again, pursuing a set of policies not generally shared with the rest of the United States.

The Reconstruction governments were ephemeral; Republican rule collapsed in Virginia, North Carolina, and Georgia in 1871; in Texas in 1873, Alabama and Arkansas in 1874, Mississippi in 1876. The last of the Republican-dominated state governments fell in South Carolina, Louisiana, and Florida with the removal of federal troops in 1877.[156] But the loss of the rights of blacks was usually a gradual process, not completed until the 1890s. Consequently, we should not expect, if firearms laws were racially motivated, that they would be passed immediately and completely on the collapse of the Republican governments.[157] Furthermore, the Reconstruction governments in many cases were coalitions of white Republicans (both Northern "carpetbaggers" and Southern "scalawags"), other whites who had remained loyal to the Union, and freedmen. The conventions that wrote new constitutions

> were, with only one and possibly two exceptions, predominantly white... [T]he new governments, as now formed, were never Negro-dominated, as was once thought. Only in South Carolina, and at times in Louisiana, was the Negro in a majority in any branch of government, and then it was in the lower house.[158]

As tempting as it might be to see these Republican state governments of freedmen and whites pursuing the social equality that Radical Republicans such as Thaddeus Stevens promoted, the evidence is otherwise. In many cases, the freedman's white allies saw blacks as members of an inferior, child-like race. In Mississippi, for example, Whigs were most of the whites who participated in the reformed Union government, and operated as a conservative influence. Similarly in Virginia and Tennessee, white Unionists were unenthusiastic about giving the freedmen the vote and full equality in the courts.[159] Even Northern Republicans began to look askance at the apparent lack of combativeness of Southern blacks in responding to the violence of the KKK: "'The capacity of a people for self-government,' a Northern friend lectured Judge Tourgee, 'is proved, first of all, by its inclination and capacity for self-protection... If people are killed by the Ku-Klux, why do they not kill the Ku-Klux?'"[160]

As we have already seen in the summary of the Texas decisions, the Republican Party was in control of the Texas Legislature when the statute prohibiting the bearing of arms was passed; similarly, Georgia was under Republican control at the time its restrictive law was passed. It is, however, important to remember that relations between white and black Republicans during Reconstruction were sometimes strained,[161] and Texas, where blacks were less essential to white Republicans than elsewhere, was no exception.[162]

---

156 Viault, 17-18.
157 Elkins, 12.
158 Craven, 229.
159 Craven, 235-6. Stampp, 162-3.
160 Foner, 435-6.
161 Abbott, 185-6, discusses how public accommodations and integrated schools bills split the Republican Party in Louisiana along racial lines. Abbott, 228-9, discusses how the actions of Southern

Tennessee and Arkansas passed laws severely restricting open carry shortly after the loss of Republican Party control, and the resurgence of white conservatives in the legislatures. It is tempting to conclude from the combination of post-war fear of armed freedmen, and the dates of adoption of many of these statutes, that the purpose of these laws prohibiting or severely limiting open carry, was to make it impossible for blacks to carry arms for either defense or offense.

Other evidence that tends to support this hypothesis is that the Texas statute contained so many exceptions, and these exemptions were phrased with such a lack of clarity (what constitutes "travelling"?) that it provided many opportunities for the prosecution to not charge a violation, and for juries to find the defendant innocent. That so many of the Texas decisions upheld the constitutionality of the law, while finding the defendants innocent, also lends credibility to this argument. The language of the Texas Supreme Court, comparing the "sound philosophy and pure morality of the common law" to the Spanish, "a people the most peculiar perhaps of any other" in *English* v. *State* (1872), certainly gives a credible basis for suspecting that the law restricting open carry may have been intended for "a class of the community"[163] (*i.e.*, Hispanics), other than criminals.

Don Kates, perhaps reflective of his years as a civil rights attorney in the South, sees a correlation between the availability of cheap handguns in the late 1860s, the struggle for political dominance in Reconstruction governments, and the sudden burst of laws severely restricting open carry, as part of an effort by the Klan to crush the freedmen into subservience, by limiting their right to defend themselves. In particular, the prohibition of the Tennessee Legislature on the carrying of any handguns but "the Army and Navy model," was an attempt, in Kates' opinion, to make all but the most expensive type of handgun unusable for self-defense away from home.

Kates argues that handguns did not become "financially accessible... until the end of the Civil War brought the sale of large stocks of military surplus weapons," and that until extremely cheap handguns, called "suicide specials," appeared on the market in the late 1860s, handguns were not common in the West or South. Further, that the practice of carrying concealed weapons was so widespread in the East that: "By the 1870s the practice of Eastern manufacturers of men's ready-to-wear trousers was to sew a holster into the right hip pocket of every pair made, to allow the concealed gun-carrying which was still legal in the East."[164]

Indeed, an examination of the decisions during the period after the Civil War shows that nearly all took place in states of the former Confederacy, or the former slave states that had stayed with the Union. Until 1890, when the West Virginia decisions started, the only Northern states where concealed weapons statutes were brought before state supreme courts were Indiana and Pennsylvania. In the case of

---

Republican legislatures injured the prospects of the Republican Party in the North, leading to increasingly hostile statements towards blacks by Horace Greeley, Carl Schurz, and James Shepherd Pike.

162 J. Mason Brewer, *Negro Legislators of Texas*, (Dallas, Tex.: Mathis Publishing Co., 1935; reprinted San Francisco: R&E Research Associates, n.d.), 26-27, contains examples of the needless hostility of white Republicans towards black Republicans in the Texas Legislature, to the detriment of common political goals.

163 *English* v. *State*, 35 Tex. 473, 479 (1872).

164 Kates, "Toward A History of Handgun Prohibition...", 11, 13-14.

Pennsylvania, we saw evidence that concealed carry *by itself* was not a crime in the eyes of the Pennsylvania Supreme Court.

Kates sees the flood of cheap handguns as motivating these restrictions; a strong case can be made that the other event coincidental with the end of the Civil War—a huge increase in the percentage of free blacks in the former slave states—may be the real cause of this burst of activity in prohibiting *concealed* carry of arms.

What about the laws restricting *open* carry? Kates' position with respect to the suddenly lowered prices of revolvers after the Civil War might be a good explanation for the sudden emergence of open carry laws, as the "riffraff" could suddenly carry an effective arm of either defense or offense. But it fails to explain why such laws prohibiting open carry of cheap weapons, such as the much feared Bowie knife, did not appear before the Civil War everywhere, and also fails to explain why laws prohibiting open carry of arms did not appear in the North until the end of the nineteenth century or later.[165] Once again, the only obvious common denominator of the states that passed prohibitions on open carry is that they were former slave states.

Even in the absence of cheap revolvers, there is some evidence that cheap handguns of other types were common before the war. Henry Deringer's well-known design appeared originally in 1850, selling for three dollars.[166] To explain the laws regulating or restricting open carry—nearly all of which appear to have been passed in former slave states—we must look to the unsettled conditions and unsettling white fears that resulted from the Civil War, emancipation, Reconstruction, and the restoration of white hegemony (albeit, a nervous one) over the black population. Was there a real problem of public safety, or were these laws passed with the intention that only blacks would be subject to them?

What caused the Texas laws against open carry? The obvious answer—that there was a serious problem of murder in post-war Texas—may well be the correct one. The question that remains to be addressed is why the Democrats, who with great industry repealed many of the Republican laws,[167] did not repeal this one as well, since the available evidence suggests that the murder victims were disproportionately blacks, not whites.

Reconstruction remains a controversial period; historians continue to argue about the extent to which partisan political concerns, racism, and genuine Southern grievances determined the policies and actions of the various participants. While there is strong evidence that racism motivated this burst of laws restricting open carry, the evidence is not conclusive, and to some extent, this reflects the lack of scholarship which has been devoted to studying the motivations of the Reconstruction and "redeemed" Southern Democrat state governments on this issue. A more complete

---

165 It is also a valid question whether handguns were rare before the Civil War; this author's great-great-great-grandfather expropriated a Colt's revolver from a captured Confederate soldier after the Battle of Fishing Creek. Clayton E. Cramer, ed., *By The Dim And Flaring Lamps: The Civil War Diary of Samuel McIlvaine*, (Monroe, N.Y.: Library Research Associates, 1990), 15.

166 Michael Newton, *Armed and Dangerous: A Writer's Guide to Weapons*, (Cincinnati, Ohio: Writer's Digest Books, 1990), 31-32. Newton's work is intended as an tutorial on guns for fiction writers; in spite of an impressive bibliography, few of the facts contained in it are footnoted, and it should be regarded with caution. It does provide, however, a painless introduction to the technology of firearms.

167 Brewer, 66-67.

answer requires in-depth studies of gun control in each of the former slaveholding states.

VII. "CARRYING CONCEALED WEAPONS IS A GRIEVOUS EVIL"

After the close of the Reconstruction era, and until the end of World War I, decisions about the meaning of the right to bear arms began to fall into a more consistent pattern, perhaps because there were now a great many precedents from which to choose, once the justices had decided whether to uphold or overturn a state law. Signs of a certain ambiguity as to whether such laws should apply to everyone, or just to certain classes of people, were still apparent.

Our first West Virginia decision, is another example of the sort of weapons law passed by Texas in 1871, with enough loopholes to allow judges and juries to almost arbitrarily convict or free those accused of violating the law. In *State* v. *Workman* (1891), Erastus Workman was convicted of violating West Virginia's weapons law, which prohibited carrying "any revolver or other pistol, dirk, bowie-knife, razor, slung-shot, billy, metallic or other false brass knuckles, or any other dangerous or deadly weapon of like kind or character," but with the interesting exception that,

> if upon the trial... the defendant shall prove to the satisfaction of the jury that he is a quiet and peaceable citizen, of good character and standing in the community in which he lives, and at the time he was found with such pistol, dirk, razor, or bowie-knife... he had good cause to believe, and did believe, that he was, in danger of death or great bodily harm at the hands of another person, and that he was, in good faith, carrying such weapon for self-defense and for no other purpose, the jury shall find him not guilty.[1]

The jury was thus given a way to find "the right sort" of person innocent if the defendant successfully proved his good character and motives. In Workman's case, he successfully demonstrated that his life was being threatened by calling a number of witnesses—including the wife of the man threatening his life—but evidently neglected to provide evidence to the jury that he was a "quiet and peaceable citizen, of good character and standing in the community."

Workman appealed on the basis that the requirement to prove oneself of good character was a violation of the "privileges and immunities" clause of the Fourteenth Amendment, since he was, in essence, required to prove himself of good character, or be convicted,[2] and also that the law in question violated the Second Amendment of the U.S. Constitution. The West Virginia Supreme Court held that:

---

1 *State* v. *Workman*, 35 W.Va. 367 (1891).
2 *State* v. *Workman*, 35 W.Va. 367, 369, 370 (1891).

The presumption which the law establishes, that every man who goes armed in the midst of a peaceable community is of vile character, and a criminal, is in consonance with the common law, and is a perfectly just and proper presumption, and one which ought to prevail in every community which aspires to be called civilized.[3]

The West Virginia Supreme Court went on to discuss the question of the Second Amendment's applicability to the states, and agreed that this was "a question upon which authorities differ," mentioned Edward III's Statute of Northampton (1328) prohibiting all persons "to go or ride armed by night or by day," and the common law against "going around with unusual or dangerous weapons to the terror of the people" as evidence that the laws of England had never allowed the carrying of arms.[4] As we have already seen in the discussion concerning English law, both of these claims are demonstrably incorrect understandings of the laws of England.

Finally, the Court argued that,

in regard to the kind of arms referred to in the amendment, it must be held to refer to the weapons of warfare to be used by the militia, such as swords, guns, rifles, and muskets—arms to be used in defending the State and civil liberty—and not to pistols, bowie-knives, brass knuckles, billies, and such other weapons as are usually employed in brawls, street-fights, duels, and affrays, and are only habitually carried by bullies, blackguards, and desperadoes, to the terror of the community and the injury of the State.[5]

Even this narrow and factually inaccurate reading of the origins of the Second Amendment acknowledged the right of individuals to possess weapons of a military character, to be used in protecting "civil liberty" from governmental tyranny.

In *Miller* v. *Texas* (1894), the question of the Fourteenth Amendment and incorporation of the Bill of Rights was again taken to the U.S. Supreme Court. Franklin P. Miller was tried for murder in Dallas County, Texas, after shooting a man to death. When the case was given to the jury, they were informed that Miller had violated Texas law by carrying weapons. Miller was convicted and sentenced to death. Miller appealed to the U.S. Supreme Court, arguing that the Texas law prohibiting the carrying of weapons was in violation of the Second Amendment; he apparently felt that the jury had been prejudiced in his murder trial by his violation of Texas law. Further, he asserted that Texas law allowing the arrest without warrant of any person carrying arms, was a violation of his Fourth Amendment rights.[6]

The Court's ruling, while continuing the position of *U.S.* v. *Cruikshank* (1876) and *Presser* v. *Illinois* (1886)—that the Bill of Rights was not incorporated by the Fourteenth Amendment—also found a more serious problem with Miller's appeal: "And if the fourteenth amendment limited the power of the states as to such rights, as pertaining to citizens of the United States, we think it was fatal to this claim that it was not set up in the trial court."[7]

The Court asserted that not only were the First, Second, Fourth, and Fifth Amendment protections not extended by the Fourteenth Amendment to protect against state actions, but that even if they did, Miller had failed to use this defense at his original trial—and therefore the Court weren't going to take seriously the claim on appeal.

3 *State* v. *Workman*, 35 W.Va. 367, 371 (1891).
4 *State* v. *Workman*, 35 W.Va. 367, 372 (1891).
5 *State* v. *Workman*, 35 W.Va. 367, 373 (1891).
6 *Miller* v. *Texas*, 153 U.S. 535, 536 (1894).
7 *Miller* v. *Texas*, 153 U.S. 535, 538 (1894).

In *Robertson* v. *Baldwin* (1897), the U.S. Supreme Court heard a case in which a group of merchant sailors who had jumped ship, asserted that the Bill of Rights protected them against being seized and returned to their ship without due process. The Court summarized its understanding of the intent of the Bill of Rights in this way:

3. The first 10 amendments to the constitution of the United States, commonly known as the "Bill of Rights," were not intended to lay down any novel principles of government, but simply embodied certain guaranties and immunities which we had inherited from our English ancestors, and which had, from time immemorial, been subject to certain well-recognized exceptions, arising from the necessities of the case. In incorporating these principles into the constitution, there was no intention of disregarding the exceptions, which have continued to be recognized as if formally expressed. Thus, the freedom of speech and of the press (article 1) does not permit the publication of libels, blasphemous or indecent articles, or other publications injurious to public morals or private reputation; *the right of the people to keep and bear arms (article 2) is not infringed by laws prohibiting the carrying of concealed weapons*; the provision that no person shall be twice put in jeopardy (article 5) does not prevent a second trial, if upon the first trial the jury failed to agree, or if the verdict was set aside upon the defendant's motion....[8] [emphasis added]

Here the Court placed the Second Amendment (in which the Court considered "right of the people to keep and bear arms" to be a free-standing right) in the same category as freedom of speech, press, and the procedural safeguards of the Fifth Amendment—all individual rights. While agreeing that "laws prohibiting the carrying of concealed weapons" were Constitutional, this statement implied that carry of arms in *some* manner was Constitutionally protected. Since no Federal laws yet existed prohibiting concealed carry of arms, and the Court had held the Second Amendment was a restriction on the Federal Government only, there was no statute to which such reasoning could be applied.

Patsone v. *Pennsylvania* (1914), provides a fascinating example of the prejudices which were considered acceptable by the U.S. Supreme Court, and Justice Holmes, who wrote the majority opinion. The state of Pennsylvania had made it illegal for unnaturalized foreign-born residents "to kill any wild bird or animal except in defense of person or property," and with that goal, prohibited non-citizens from owning a rifle or shotgun. Joseph Patsone, an Italian citizen, resident in the United States, was found guilty of illegally possessing a shotgun. Patsone appealed, asserting that his Fourteenth Amendment rights were violated.[9] The Court found that the purpose—protecting wildlife—was a lawful object, and to that end, members of a class prohibited from hunting could be similarly prohibited from owning a rifle or shotgun, although, "The prohibition does not extend to weapons such as pistols that may be supposed to be needed occasionally for self-defense."[10]

While *Patsone* made no reference to the Second Amendment, and is therefore not immediately relevant to the problem of its meaning, it is an interesting decision in what is implied. One possible reading of *Patsone* is that pistols, having an individual defensive use, are outside the bounds of legitimate restriction by the states. Another possible reading is that since the Pennsylvania law had as its ostensible pur-

---

8 *Robertson* v. *Baldwin,* 165 U.S. 275, 281, 282, 17 S.Ct. 826, 829 (1897).

9 Unlike many other states, the Pennsylvania Constitution of 1790 limited the right to keep and bear arms to citizens.

10 *Patsone* v. *Pennsylvania,* 232 U.S. 138, 143, 144 (1914).

pose the preservation of wildlife, pistols were necessarily outside the realm of weapons that could be legitimately prohibited *on that basis*, but a law more broadly worded might not be subject to that same limitation.

There was an increasing trend in the period after the Civil War for both state and federal courts to deny that the Bill of Rights was a limitation on state laws; the Idaho Supreme Court bucked the trend, returning to the principles articulated by the Georgia Supreme Court in *Nunn* v. *State* (1846). The case *In Re Brickey* (1902)[11] involved a man named Brickey who was convicted of carrying a loaded revolver within the city limits of Lewiston, Idaho. On appeal, the Idaho Supreme Court raised federal and state constitutional provisions:

> The second amendment to the federal constitution is in the following language: "A well-regulated militia, being necessary to the security of a free state, the right of the people to keep and bear arms shall not be infringed." The language of section 11, article 1 of the constitution of Idaho is as follows: "the people have the right to bear arms for their security and defense, but the legislature shall regulate the exercise of this right of law." Under these constitutional provisions, the legislature has no power to prohibit a citizen from bearing arms in any portion of the state of Idaho, whether within or without the corporate limits of cities, towns, and villages. The legislature may, as expressly provided in our state constitution, regulate the exercise of this right, but may not prohibit it. A statute prohibiting the carrying of concealed deadly weapons would be a proper exercise of the police power of the state. But the statute in question does not prohibit the carrying of weapons concealed, which is of itself a pernicious practice, but prohibits the carrying of them in any manner in cities, towns, and villages. We are compelled to hold this statute void.[12]

Brickey was ordered released. The Idaho Supreme Court had partly taken the position expressed in *Bliss* v. *Commonwealth* (1822)—that the right to bear arms could not be so limited as to be eliminated, as well as the position of *Nunn* v. *State* (1846)—that the Second Amendment was a limitation on state *and* Federal authority, contrary to the U.S. Supreme Court's position in *Presser* v. *Illinois* (1886).

In *Wilson* v. *State* (1903), a Jim Wilson was convicted in Alcorn County of carrying a pistol concealed in his pants pocket at home. Wilson argued that because of a series of incidents over the preceding nights, Wilson had been worried about his own safety, and had carried the pistol concealed for that reason. On appeal, Wilson sought the protection of §12 of the Mississippi Constitution: "that the right of every citizen to keep and bear arms in defense of his home, person, or property shall not be called in question, but the legislature may forbid carrying concealed weapons."

The Mississippi Supreme Court held that the law against carrying concealed weapons "is unquestionably constitutional." The only issue that remained to be decided was whether the circumstances alleged by Wilson at trial was an adequate basis for violating the concealed weapons law. The Court refused to accept this as a defense, nor did they articulate that open carry was protected, either by the absence of statute, or by constitutional protection. On the other hand, they did not dispute

---

11 The expression *in re* is one of those pieces of legal lingo that means, "In the matter of" or "pertaining to the person of."

12 *In Re Brickey*, 8 Ida. 597, 70 Pac. 609, 101 Am. St. Rep. 215, 216 (1902).

that the language of the Mississippi Constitutional provision protected an individual right—simply that it did not extend to concealed carry of a weapon.[13]

In *City of Salina* v. *Blaksley* (1905), the Kansas Supreme Court gave a dramatic new interpretation of "the people." The General Statutes of 1901 gave Kansas cities authority to "prohibit and punish the carrying of firearms or other deadly weapons, concealed or otherwise, and may arrest and imprison, fine or set at work all vagrants and person found in said city without visible means of support, or some legitimate business." James Blaksley was convicted "of carrying a revolving pistol within the city while under the influence of intoxicating liquor." Blaksley appealed based on §4 of the Kansas Bill of Rights: "The people have the right to bear arms for their defense and security; but standing armies, in time of peace, are dangerous to liberty, and shall not be tolerated, and the military shall be in strict subordination to the civil power."[14]

The Court held:

> The power of the legislature to prohibit or regulate the carrying of deadly weapons has been the subject of much dispute in the courts. The views expressed in the decisions are not uniform, and the reasonings of the different courts vary. It has, however, been generally held that the legislatures can regulate the mode of carrying deadly weapons, provided they are not such as are ordinarily used in civilized warfare.

> To this view there is a notable exception in the early case of Bliss v. Commonwealth... where it was held, under a constitutional provision similar to ours, that the act of the legislature prohibiting the carrying of concealed deadly weapons was void; that the right of the citizen to own and carry arms was protected by the constitution and could not be taken away or regulated. While this decision has frequently been referred to by the courts of other states, it has never been followed. The same principle was announced in Re Brickey... but no reference was made to Bliss v. Commonwealth... nor to any other authority in support of the decision.[15]

The Kansas Supreme Court's errors started almost immediately. *In Re Brickey* (1902) did *not* use the same principle as *Bliss* v. *Commonwealth* (1822)—that no regulation of the bearing of arms was valid—but that a law which prohibited *all* carriage of arms was unconstitutional; a similar position was taken in *State* v. *Huntly* (1843), *State* v. *Chandler* (1850), *State* v. *Jumel* (1858), *Andrews* v. *State* (1871), *State* v. *Wilforth* (1881), *State* v. *Speller* (1882), *State* v. *Shelby* (1886), *State* v. *Reams* (1897), *State* v. *Boone* (1903), and arguably, *State* v. *Smith* (1856), and *State* v. *Wilburn* (1872). *Bliss* was *not* the only such decision—*Nunn* v. *State* (1846) was quite similar in its breadth of protection of bearing arms. Where *Bliss* was based on the Kentucky Constitution's protections only, *Nunn* and *In Re Brickey* were based on both state and U.S. Constitutional protections.

Next, the Kansas Supreme Court contended:

> The provision in section 4 of the Bill of Rights that "the people have the right to bear arms for their defense and security" refers to the people as a collective body. It was the safety and security of society that were being considered when this provision was being put into our constitution. It is followed immediately by the declaration that standing armies in time of peace are dangerous to liberty and should not be tolerated, and that "the military shall be in strict subordination to the civil power." It deals exclusively with the military; individual rights are not considered in this section. The manner in which

---

13 *Wilson* v. *State*, 81 Miss. 404, 33 South. 171, 172 (1903).

14 *City of Salina* v. *Blaksley*, 72 Kan. 230, 83 Pac. 619, 115 Am. St. Rep. 196 (1905).

15 *City of Salina* v. *Blaksley*, 72 Kan. 230, 83 Pac. 619, 115 Am. St. Rep. 196, 197 (1905).

the people shall exercise this right of bearing arms for the defense and security of the people is found in article 8 of the constitution, which authorizes the organizing, equipping and disciplining the militia, which shall be composed of "all able-bodied male citizens between the ages of twenty-one and forty-five years." The militia is essentially the people's army, and their defense and security in time of peace. In the absence of constitutional or legislative authority no person has the right to assume such duty.[16]

Here we have an authoritative statement that in the Kansas Bill of Rights, "[t]he people have the right to bear arms for their defense and security" was *not* an individual right—but no reference to any authority was made for that claim. The Court argued that the proximity of this right to a discussion of standing armies implies this right "deals exclusively with the military," despite the fact that Madison's rough draft of the Second Amendment, the requests for a Bill of Rights, and the various state constitutions adopted in the early years of the Republic, used similar construction and language for what are generally recognized as *individual* rights. Even *Aymette* v. *State* (1840), while refusing to recognize a right to arms for individual self-defense, had admitted that: "The free white men may keep arms to protect the public liberty, to keep in awe those who are in power, and to maintain the supremacy of the laws and the constitution."[17]

The Arkansas Supreme Court in *Aymette* had insisted that the right was for the benefit of the society as a whole, as a restraint on tyranny, but that to be an effective check on the government, arms must be widely distributed. The Kansas Supreme Court was not prepared to admit even this limited, republican understanding of the right.

Finally, the Court acknowledged that in some states,

> it has been held... that the citizen has the right... to carry such arms as are ordinarily used in civilized warfare, it is placed on the ground that it was intended that the people would thereby become accustomed to handling and using such arms, so that in case of an emergency they would be more or less prepared for the duties of a soldier. The weakness of this argument lies in the fact that in nearly every state in the Union there are provisions for organizing and drilling state militia in sufficient numbers to meet any such emergency.[18]

But the "state militia" to which the Court here referred, was by 1905, the modern National Guard. It was not the all encompassing militia envisioned in the Militia Act of 1792, or that militia lamented in Story's description of the early nineteenth century. The state militias "in sufficient numbers to meet any such emergency" referred to by the Kansas Supreme Court were the ones that were engaged in ostensibly even-handed enforcement of laws during labor disputes.

The Court ended its decision by claiming that the right of the people may only be exercised "as a member of a well-regulated militia, or some other military organization as provided for by law." To justify their position, the Court cited *Commonwealth* v. *Murphy* (1896) and *Presser* v. *Illinois* (1886),[19] both of which applied only to organized bodies of armed men. *City of Salina* v. *Blaksley* (1905) represents a radical departure from previous judicial interpretation of the right to keep and bear

---

16 *City of Salina* v. *Blaksley*, 72 Kan. 230, 83 Pac. 619, 115 Am. St. Rep. 196 (1905).

17 *Aymette* v. *State*, 2 Hump. (21 Tenn.) 154, 156, 158 (1840).

18 *City of Salina* v. *Blaksley*, 72 Kan. 230, 83 Pac. 619, 115 Am. St. Rep. 196, 197, 198 (1905).

19 *City of Salina* v. *Blaksley*, 72 Kan. 230, 83 Pac. 619, 115 Am. St. Rep. 196, 198, 199 (1905).

arms. For the first time, a state supreme court had held that the right was a collective right *only*, and *only* within a governmentally approved body.

The first Oklahoma decision, *Walburn* v. *Territory* (1899), took place while Oklahoma was still a territory. A John Walburn was convicted in Garfield County of carrying arms in violation of "article 45, c. 25, St. 1893." Most of the decision concerned itself with the admission of evidence of other criminal misconduct by the defendant that Walburn claimed had prejudiced the jury against him. Only one paragraph of the Oklahoma Supreme Court's decision is relevant to a right to bear arms:

> The first contention is that the law under which he was convicted is in conflict with the constitution of the United States. No authorities are cited in support of this position, nor is the proposition very earnestly urged. As at present advised, we are of the opinion that the statute violates none of the inhibitions of the constitution of the United States, and that its provisions are within the police power of the territory.[20]

The Court cited no authorities in support of its position. The evidence suggests that Walburn's attorney recognized that the precedent established in *Presser* v. *Illinois* (1886) left him without a leg to stand on. More interesting is that the prosecutor felt it necessary to bring up evidence of other misconduct by Walburn; indeed, the Court's opinion cites a number of Texas and Alabama Supreme Court decisions involving prejudicial evidence introduced in concealed weapons trials.[21]

The Court considered evidence of Walburn's other misconduct irrelevant to the question of whether the concealed weapons law had been broken and ordered a new trial; this shows that criminal intent was not considered a necessary component of violating the law. But that prosecutors felt it necessary, apparently in a number of cases, to introduce such prejudicial evidence, suggests that proof of a concealed weapons violation, in and of itself, was not enough to persuade a jury to convict. It is outside the scope of this work to study how often juries refused to convict on this charge, but if convictions were difficult to obtain, it might provide some evidence of whether concealed weapons laws enjoyed popular support, or were simply a tool for convicting those "troublemakers" who neglected to break any more serious laws.

When Oklahoma became a state in 1907, the Oklahoma Constitution, article 2, §26, provided:

> The right of a citizen to keep and bear arms in defense of his home, person, or property, or in aid of the civil power, when thereunto legally summoned, shall never be prohibited; but nothing herein contained shall prevent the Legislature from regulating the carrying of weapons.[22]

Two statutes adopted while Oklahoma was still a territory regulated the carrying of arms; §2502 prohibited concealed carry "or about his person, saddle, or saddle bags, any pistol, revolver, bowie knife, dirk, dagger, slung-shot, sword, sword-cane, spear, metal knuckles, or any other kind of knife or instrument manufactured or sold for the purpose of defense except as in this article provided." In addition, §2503 prohibited carrying "about his person, any pistol, revolver, bowie knife, dirk,

---

20 *Walburn* v. *Territory*, 9 Okl. 23, 59 Pac. 972, 973 (1899).
21 *Walburn* v. *Territory*, 9 Okl. 23, 59 Pac. 972, 974 (1899).
22 *Ex Parte Thomas*, 21 Okl. 770, 1 Okl. Cr. 210, 97 Pac. 260, 261 (1908).

knife, loaded cane, billy, metal knuckles, or any other offensive or defensive weapon, except as in this article provided."[23]

By subtraction of the enumerated weapons in §2503 from those in §2502, it might appear that a sword-cane or billy could be carried openly, but not concealed—except that §2502 prohibited all defensive weapons (which might include the billy and the sword-cane) from being carrying concealed, and §2503 prohibited all offensive and defensive weapons (which would cover everything) from being carried openly. In the Oklahoma Legislature's view of things, self-defense was evidently something to be done bare handed. While the Oklahoma Constitution undoubtedly allowed regulation of carrying weapons, did it allow the Legislature to prohibit all modes of carrying arms?

In *Ex Parte*[24] *Thomas* (1908), Richard Thomas was charged and convicted in Payne County of carrying a concealed pistol. On appeal to the Oklahoma Supreme Court, Thomas' counsel argued that the Oklahoma Constitution protected the right to bear arms; agreed that §2502, which prohibited concealed carry, was constitutional; argued that §2503 effectively repealed §2502, since almost all violations of §2502 were also violations of §2503; but since §2503 was unconstitutional, there was no law prohibiting concealed carry. This would seem an echo of the logic used in *Bliss* v. *Commonwealth* (1822), *Nunn* v. *State* (1846), and *In Re Brickey* (1902)—that a law which prohibited all carry was unconstitutional, and so at least one mode of carry must be lawful.

The Oklahoma Supreme Court acknowledged, "Counsel for petitioner makes a very ingenious argument on the subject, but in our judgment it is more ingenious than sound." The Oklahoma Supreme Court held that the two sections did not conflict, and that §2503 did not repeal or nullify §2502. The Court also pointed to a long line of state supreme court decisions that upheld concealed carry laws as not violative of the right to keep and bear arms: *Nunn* v. *State* (1846), *State* v. *Mitchell* (1833), *State* v. *Reid* (1840), *State* v. *Jumel* (1858), *State* v. *Wilburn* (1872), *Cockrum* v. *State* (1859), and *State* v. *Buzzard* (1842). (But *Cockrum* made no decision about whether concealed carry was constitutionally protected or not—only that the right to bear arms was "absolute.")

> The question now arises: Is a pistol the character of arms in contemplation of the constitutional convention and of the people of the state when they declared that the right of a citizen "to carry and bear arms," etc. "shall never be prohibited." We hold that it is not, and most of the states where it has been passed upon support us in this conclusion.[25]

The Court next cited *Andrews* v. *State* (1871), *Fife* v. *State* (1876), *English* v. *State* (1872), *Aymette* v. *State* (1840), *Hill* v. *State* (1874), and *City of Salina* v. *Blaksley* (1905) as evidence for this claim. But the Court was in error; the *Andrews* decision, and the related decisions in *Page* v. *State* (1871) and *State* v. *Wilburn* (1872), had recognized a right to open carry of large military pistols, even though pocket pistols were not similarly protected. Arkansas Supreme Court decisions subsequent to *Fife*, including *Wilson* v. *State of Arkansas* (1878) and *Haile* v. *State*

---

23 *Ex Parte Thomas*, 21 Okl. 770, 1 Okl. Cr. 210, 97 Pac. 260, 261 (1908).

24 *Ex Parte* is a legal term for a hearing in which only one party is present—in this case, Thomas, who had apparently already been imprisoned.

25 *Ex Parte Thomas*, 21 Okl. 770, 1 Okl. Cr. 210, 97 Pac. 260, 261, 262 (1908).

(1882), had recognized a right to open carry of military pistols, though subject to creative hamstringing of the right. The *Hill* decision recognized a right to carry pistols in many, but not all public places.

Another problem is that in the first list of decisions cited by the Oklahoma Supreme Court to justify prohibiting *concealed* carry, four of the eight decisions unambiguously recognized a right to *open* carry of arms, and the *Nunn* decision held that a prohibition on *concealed carry* necessarily required that *open carry* be protected. The Court was using contradictory precedents to justify its actions.

Of the 56 state and Federal decisions up to this point, 37 explicitly or implicitly recognized a constitutional right to open carry, and the Arkansas and Tennessee decisions had recognized that military pistols could be carried, although in a very restricted manner; only twelve explicitly or implicitly denied a right to open carry. It might be argued that the Oklahoma Supreme Court was unaware of many of these earlier decisions, except that the Court's list of citations that upheld concealed carry laws included many of the decisions that protected open carry. Clearly, the Court decided what it wanted to find, but preferred a long list of citations (even though wrong or contradictory), over a short list that supported their position correctly.

The remainder of the Court's decision consists of long, one-sided quotations from *Aymette, Andrews, Hill, English, Fife,* and *City of Salina.*[26] The Oklahoma decision may be considered a derivative decision, and one difficult to take seriously, in light of their selective and incorrect use of precedents to justify both a concealed carry law, and an open carry law. Nonetheless, the Court was reluctant to go as far as the Kansas Supreme Court in the *Salina* decision; while asserting that the right protected was for the benefit of the militia, the Court did not deny that an individual right to possess and bear arms existed. Instead, the Court acknowledged that "there is no room for doubt that the arms defendant had a right to bear, and which right could never be prohibited to him, relates solely to such arms as are recognized in civilized warfare and not those used by the ruffian, brawler, or the assassin..."[27] What were these arms?

> Not everything that may be useful for offense or defense; but what may, properly be included or understood under the title of 'arms,' taken in connect with the fact that the citizen is to keep them as a citizen. Such, then, as are found to make up the usual arms of the citizen of the country, and the use of which will properly train and render him efficient in defense of his own liberties, as well as of the state. *Under this head, with a knowledge of the habits of our people, and of the arms in the use of which a soldier should be trained, we would hold that the rifle of all descriptions, the shotgun, the musket, and repeater are all such arms; and that under the Constitution the right to keep such arms cannot be infringed or forbidden by the Legislature...*[28] [emphasis added]

In 1903, the Vermont Supreme Court made a ruling that ran completely contrary to the post-war trend on concealed weapons. An Andrew Rosenthal was convicted in Rutland City Court of violating city ordinance No. 10, "prohibiting a person from carrying within the city any brass knuckles, pistol, slung shot, or weapon of similar character, or any weapon concealed on his person, without permission of the mayor or chief of police," though in what way, and with what

---

26 *Ex Parte Thomas*, 21 Okl. 770, 1 Okl. Cr. 210, 97 Pac. 260, 262, 263, 264 (1908).
27 *Ex Parte Thomas*, 21 Okl. 770, 1 Okl. Cr. 210, 97 Pac. 260, 264, 265 (1908).
28 *Ex Parte Thomas*, 21 Okla. 770 97 P. 260, 263 (1908).

arms, is not told by the headnotes or the decision. The Vermont Supreme Court struck down the ordinance based on Vermont Constitution "art. 16, [which] declares that the people have a right to bear arms for the defense of themselves and the state," and that the ordinance in question "so far as it relates to the carrying of a pistol under any circumstances without such consent, is repugnant to the Constitution, and to that extent void."

While Vermont Statutes §4922 prohibited the carrying of arms, "with the intent or avowed purpose of injuring a fellow man":

> Under the general laws, therefore, a person not a member of a school may carry a dangerous or deadly weapon, openly or concealed, unless he does it with the intent or avowed purpose of injuring another; and a person who is a member of a school, but not in attendance upon it, is at liberty, in a similar way, to carry such weapons.[29]

The Court pointed out that the Rutland ordinance banned any carrying of a weapon concealed, whether a criminal intent was present or not, and was therefore contrary to the "Constitution and the general laws of the state." The Court emphasized that while other parts of the Rutland ordinance might be also invalid, these were "questions not now before the court."[30]

Significantly, the Vermont Supreme Court cited not a single authority, and only the precedent of *State* v. *Carlton* (1876), which did not address the Vermont Constitution's arms provision at all.[31] The language of the Vermont Constitution was enough. To this day, Vermont alone of the 50 states, remains without a statute limiting or regulating concealed carry, except "with the intent or avowed purpose of injuring another."

There was still no state law prohibiting concealed carry of arms in California but there were ordinances in some counties. The first case, *Ex parte Cheney* (1891), dealt with a conviction under San Francisco county ordinance 1603, which prohibited concealed carry of "any pistol, dirk, or other dangerous or deadly weapon." Punishment included a fine of not less than $250, and imprisonment of not less than three months. The usual exceptions for "travellers" and police officers were present, and permits were available from the police commissioners, but the language of the ordinance made the issuance of permits discretionary on their part. Cheney had been convicted under this ordinance.

On appeal to the California Supreme Court, his attorney primarily argued that the ordinance's punishments were so severe as to exceed the authority of a local ordinance, but he also asserted that the ordinance was unconstitutional. The California Supreme Court disagreed: "Counsel for petitioner has not pointed out to us any specific provisions of the statutes or constitution of this state with which the ordinance is directly repugnant or in conflict..."

It is perhaps a sign of how widespread the view expressed in *Presser* had become that Cheney's counsel made no effort to use the Second Amendment as a basis for overturning a local ordinance. The California Supreme Court acknowledged that police regulations were subject to some limitations, and must be reasonable, except when such ordinances "are intended for the prevention of crime and the preserva-

---

29 *State* v. *Rosenthal*, 75 Vt. 295, 55 Atl. 610, 611 (1903).
30 *State* v. *Rosenthal*, 75 Vt. 295, 55 Atl. 610, 611 (1903).
31 *State* v. *Carlton*, 48 Vt. 636 (1876).

tion of the public peace, and in reference to which the legislative body of the city is vested with a discretion that is not reviewable by the courts."[32]

Yet there was recognition that *concealed* carrying of arms was the problem:

It is a well-recognized fact that the unrestricted habit of carrying concealed weapons is the source of much crime, and frequently leads to causeless homicides, as well as to breaches of the peace, that would not otherwise occur. The majority of citizens have no occasion or inclination to carry such weapons, and it is often the case that the innocent by-stander is made to suffer from the unintended act of another, who, in the heat of passion, attempts to instantly resent some fancied insult or trivial injury. It is to protect the law-abiding citizen, as well as to prevent a breach of the peace or the commission of crime, that the ordinance in question has been passed. By its terms, ample provision is made for those whose necessities of life or of occupation require protection from carrying such weapons, and as the prohibition does not extend to those who come within the exceptions, there is no invasion of the rights of the citizen.[33]

In the case *Ex Parte Luening* (1906), San Bernardino County's Ordinance No. 102, which prohibited concealed carry of deadly weapons without a permit from the sheriff, was challenged by a William J. Luening, Jr. Luening was "found in a public place with a loaded revolver, a deadly weapon, concealed upon his person...." Luening pleaded guilty, but appealed to the Second California Court of Appeals on the grounds that the county ordinance was unconstitutional:

Petitioner contends, further, that the ordinance is unreasonable, oppressive and dis-criminating, that it leaves to the arbitrary will of the sheriff the right to determine who may enjoy the privileges thereunder, and this upon the theory that the right to bear arms is a natural right which may not be prohibited. Whatever may be the source of the right to bear arms, in the general acceptation of such term, it does not follow as a natural consequence that such right extends to every conceivable manner in which arms may be borne.[34]

It would be interesting to know on which constitution Luening based his claim, since the California Constitution did not (and does not today) contain a right to keep and bear arms provision, and the *Presser* precedent could have been cited by the California Court of Appeals; yet the language of the decision suggests that they recognized that such a right existed, even if subject to regulation:

The habit of carrying concealed weapons is one of the most fruitful sources of crime, and, in our opinion, may be entirely prohibited by the proper authorities. It is true there may be instances and circumstances under which the bearing of arms in that manner may be justified. This ordinance by its terms makes ample provision in relation to such exigencies... It is clear that no general rule could be established beforehand that would meet the emergencies of individual cases; therefore, the power to give relief in particular instances is conferred on certain officers, and it is not to be presumed that they will exercise it wantonly, or for purposes of profit or oppression.... If, therefore, the carrying of deadly weapons concealed about the person, in public places, is a menace to public safety, injurious to the public welfare, no right so to do exists; and if the legislative body has seen fit to confer authority upon certain persons under certain circumstances so to act, it is not taking away a right to do the thing from others, because they have no such right.... Legislation in this regard is referable to the police power, and the body to whom such legislation has been intrusted is to determine the reasonableness of such regulations as applying to the localities to which they apply. Nothing appearing which

---

32 *Ex parte Cheney*, 90 Cal. 617, 619, 620, 621 (1891).
33 *Ex parte Cheney*, 90 Cal. 617, 621 (1891).
34 *Ex Parte Luening*, 3 Cal.App. 76, 77, 78 (1906).

would indicate an abuse of discretion in this instance, none will be presumed, and this ordinance must be taken as a reasonable exercise of police power upon the part of the supervisors of San Bernardino county. In our opinion, the ordinance here involved is valid, and the petitioner should be remanded.[35]

In *State* v. *Gohl* (1907), the Washington Supreme Court heard an appeal from Chehalis County. The defendant Gohl was convicted of "organizing, maintaining and employing an armed body of men," in violation of P.C. §1967. On appeal, Gohl argued that the statute in question was in violation of article I, §24 of the Washington Constitution: "The right of the individual citizen to bear arms in defense of himself or the state shall not be impaired." However, as the Court pointed out, this section is immediately followed by the statement that this right was not to be "construed as authorizing individuals or corporations to organize, maintain or employ an armed body of men," which is exactly what Gohl was charged with doing. This should have been enough to resolve the question, but the Court went on to argue:

> A constitutional guaranty of certain rights to the individual citizen does not place such rights entirely beyond the police power of the state. The freedom of speech and of the press guaranteed by the constitution of the United States and the constitutions of the several states has never been construed to carry with it an unbridled license to libel and defame. Nearly all the states have enacted laws prohibiting the carrying of concealed weapons, and the validity of such laws has often been assailed because denying to the citizen the right to bear arms, but we are not aware that such a contention has ever prevailed, except in the courts of the state of Kentucky.[36]

That libel is to freedom of the press, as carrying a concealed weapon is to the right to bear arms, is a tortured analogy; but more importantly, the Washington Supreme Court's statement was wrong. Not only *Bliss* v. *Commonwealth* (1822), but also *State* v. *Rosenthal* (1903) had recognized such a right; the *Simpson* v. *State* (1833) strongly implied that such a right was protected, as did *Wright* v. *Commonwealth* (1875). The decisions *Nunn* v. *State* (1846) and *In Re Brickey* (1902) had recognized that concealed carry could only be prohibited if open carry was allowed. At the time of this decision, *at least* three states had no prohibition on concealed carry: California,[37] Vermont, and New Jersey.[38] This strongly suggests that the Court had failed to do adequate research on the existing statutes.

The next year, in *McIntyre* v. *State* (1908), the second Indiana Supreme Court decision on the meaning of its constitutional guarantee occurred. An Edwin E. McIntyre was convicted of carrying a concealed revolver, apparently in Indianapolis, though he was convicted by a Marion County court, where McIntyre resided. The sequence of events is unclear from the decision, but it appears that McIntyre was a deputy constable in Marion County at the time of his arrest—though it appears that he was not acting in that capacity at the time of the offense in Indianapolis. On appeal, McIntyre argued that the state constitutional protection gave him the right to carry concealed weapons.

---

35 *Ex Parte Luening*, 3 Cal.App. 76, 78, 79 (1906).

36 *State* v. *Gohl*, 48 Wash. 408, 409, 410, 90 P. 259 (1907).

37 Assembly Office of Research, *Smoking Gun: The Case For Concealed Weapon Permit Reform*, (Sacramento: State of California, 1986), 5.

38 Kates, "Toward a History of Handgun Prohibition...", 12. Halbrook, *A Right To Bear Arms*, 88.

In the period between the *State* v. *Mitchell* (1833) decision, and *McIntyre* v. *State* (1908), Indiana had adopted a new constitution, but had left intact the provision contained in the 1816 Constitution: "That the people have a right to bear arms for the defense of themselves, and the State; and that the military shall be kept in strict subordination to the civil power." The Indiana Supreme Court therefore held that, "when a clause or provision of a constitution or statute has been readopted after the same has been construed by the courts of such state, it will be concluded that it was adopted with the interpretation and construction which said courts had enunciated."[39] Based on this, the Court pointed to *State* v. *Mitchell* (1833)—the shortest, least complete "opinion" imaginable, which was just a refusal to hear an appeal from a lower court—and held that the statute banning concealed carry was legal.

In 1910, Georgia took another step towards regulation of the carrying of arms, and the Georgia Supreme Court in *Strickland* v. *State* (1911) upheld that next step. The right to open carry had been whittled away in *Hill* v. *State* (1874); now the right to open carry was licensed. Much like the decision in *Ex Parte Thomas* (1908), this decision is a masterpiece of sophistry and contradictory citations.

The 1910 statute required a license to carry a handgun. The license fee was 50¢, and a $100 bond was required of those who wished a license to carry. A J.L. Strickland was convicted of carrying a handgun without a license. He appealed to the Court of Appeals, and from there to the Georgia Supreme Court, arguing that his rights under the Georgia Constitution and the Second Amendment were violated by the statute.

Justice Lumpkin wrote the majority decision, in which the Statute of Northampton (1328) was again cited as evidence that the protections of the Second Amendment were not intended to protect an individual right to self-defense. While the Court acknowledged that the language of the state constitutional provisions were not uniform, they seemed to have ignored the differences when discussing the decisions of the various state supreme courts as to the limits of state regulation of the bearing of arms.

The *Bliss* v. *Commonwealth* (1822) decision that concealed carry was protected was cited by the Court, but, "This ruling has not been followed, but severely criticized. The decisions are practically unanimous to the contrary." As evidence for this, the Court cited *Aymette* v. *State* (1840), *State* v. *Wilforth* (1881), *State* v. *Reid* (1840), *State* v. *Speller* (1882), *State* v. *Mitchell* (1833), *Wright* v. *Commonwealth* (1875), *State* v. *Jumel* (1858), *State* v. *Buzzard* (1842), *In re Brickey* (1902), and *Ex parte Thomas* (1908). As we have previously seen, the decision in *Wright* v. *Commonwealth* (1875) was somewhat ambiguous, and many of these other decisions, such as *In re Brickey* (1902), *State* v. *Reid* (1840), and *State* v. *Jumel* (1858), recognized a right to open carry, especially if concealed carry was prohibited.

From there, the Georgia Court cited *Andrews* v. *State* (1871), *Page* v. *State* (1871), and *Fife* v. *State* (1876), as evidence that regulation of open carry was constitutional. *State* v. *Wilburn* (1872) and *Haile* v. *State* (1882) were also cited as evidence that this regulation could be carried to the extreme of prohibiting carrying of pistols, "except uncovered and in the hand." *State* v. *Workman* (1891) and *Ex parte Thomas* (1908) were used to demonstrate that the carrying of handguns could

---

39 *McIntyre* v. *State*, 170 Ind. 163, 164, 165, 83 N.E. 1005 (1908).

be banned completely, and *City of Salina* v. *Blaksley* (1905) was approvingly spoken of by the Georgia Court, even though it denied that "the right of the people" included any individual right.

The Court attempted to resolve the dramatic differences between these different decisions. Of the three major exceptions, *Bliss* was characterized as out of the mainstream because it acknowledged a right to carry concealed;[40] the decision of the Idaho Supreme Court in *Brickey* which acknowledged the limitations of the Second Amendment was called, "the result of oversight"; and *Nunn* was written off as: "At that time it was still a somewhat mooted question whether the second amendment to the Constitution of the United States was a limitation on the power of Congress only, or also affected that of the state Legislatures," though the Court admitted that *Barron* v. *Baltimore*, the U.S. Supreme Court decision that limited the Bill of Rights to actions of the federal government, "had already been decided" when *Nunn* was handed down.[41]

The Georgia Supreme Court apparently did not even consider the possibility that the *Nunn* Court, closer in time to the Framers, might have had a better understanding of the intent of the Bill of Rights than the *Cruikshank* Court. But more troubling is the manner in which the Court harmonized the tremendous variety of decisions they had cited:

> An examination of the various decisions, whether dealing with laws against carrying concealed weapons, or with regulations as to the prohibition against carrying weapons of a particular character, will show that two general lines of reasoning have been employed in upholding such statutes: First, that such provisions are to be construed in the light of the origin of the constitutional declarations, or their connection with words declaratory of the necessity for an efficient militia or for the common defense, or the like, where they are used, and in view of the general public purpose which such provisions were intended to subserve; and, second, that the right to bear arms, like other rights of person and property, is to be construed in direct connection with the constitutional declaration as to the right.

But what about all those decisions where the state constitutional provision was unambiguously individual, for the purposes of individual self-defense? How would the Georgia Supreme Court handle this?

> But even where such expressions do not occur, it has been held that the different provisions of the Constitution must be construed together, and that the declaration or preservation of certain rights is not to be segregated and treated as arbitrary, but in connection with the general police power of the state, unless the language of the instrument itself should exclude such a construction. Thus, if the right to bear arms includes deadly weapons of every character, and is absolute and arbitrary in its nature, it might well be argued, as it was in earlier days, that the citizen was guaranteed the right to carry weapons or arms, in the broadest meaning of that term, whenever, wherever, and however he pleased, and that any regulation, unless expressly provided for in the Constitution, was an infringement of that right.[42]

But that is *exactly* why some of the constitutions adopted after the Civil War, including the Georgia Constitution of 1877, had included clauses granting the right

---

40 *Strickland* v. *State*, 137 Ga. 1, 72 S.E. 260, 261, 262 (1911).
41 *Strickland* v. *State*, 137 Ga. 1, 72 S.E. 260, 263 (1911).
42 *Strickland* v. *State*, 137 Ga. 1, 72 S.E. 260, 262, 263 (1911).

to regulate the manner of carrying arms, as Justice Atkinson pointed out in his lone dissent.[43]

The reasoning of *Hill* v. *State* (1874) was quoted at great length to justify the position that the constitution must be "construed together." Where the Georgia Supreme Court in the *Hill* decision had given the example of a law that prohibited criminals brandishing firearms as an example of constitutional regulation, the *Strickland* Court went one step beyond, in setting up a straw man argument: "Surely no one will contend that children have a constitutional right to go to school with revolvers strapped around them..." Because there was clearly *some* appropriate level of regulation of the bearing of arms, the Court found that almost any level of regulation was therefore constitutional.

On the subject of the $100 bond required as a condition of obtaining a permit, the justices asserted that because bonds were required for a number of activities, such as holding public office, and seeking a writ of attachment, that there was no constitutional problem with requiring such a bond. That such a bond requirement would tend to work to the interest of the wealthy, and to the detriment of the poor, was not discussed as an issue of concern. Finally, the Court, in both the majority and minority opinions, agreed that the Second Amendment, like the rest of the Bill of Rights, was not a limitation on state laws.[44]

Florida had adopted statutes requiring a license to carry handguns as early as 1893,[45] which was revised in 1901 and 1906. It appears to have been a general prohibition on carry of handguns and repeating rifles, openly or concealed, with exceptions for peace officers and those licensed by the county commissioners.[46] What prompted this statute? We have the good fortune to have a completely honest statement of its original purpose. In 1941, the Florida Supreme Court refused to find that a pistol in an automobile glove compartment was "carrying" within the meaning of the statute. A concurring opinion by Justice Buford asserted:

I know something of the history of this legislation. The original Act of 1893 was passed when there was a great influx of negro laborers in this State drawn here for the purpose of working in turpentine and lumber camps. The same condition existed when the Act was amended in 1901 and the Act was passed for the purpose of disarming the negro laborers and to thereby reduce the unlawful homicides that were prevalent in turpentine and saw-mill camps and to give the white citizens in sparsely settled areas a better feeling of security. *The statute was never intended to be applied to the white population and in practice has never been so applied.* We have no statistics available, but it is a safe guess that more than 80% of the white men living rural sections of Florida have violated this statute. It is also a safe guess to say that not more than 5% of the men in Florida who own pistols and repeating rifles have ever applied to the Board of County Commissioners for a permit to have the same in their possession and there has never been, within my knowledge, any effort to enforce the provisions of this statute as to white people, because it has been generally conceded to be in contravention of the Constitution and non-enforceable if contested.[47] [emphasis added]

43 *Strickland* v. *State*, 137 Ga. 1, 72 S.E. 260, 268 (1911).
44 *Strickland* v. *State*, 137 Ga. 1, 72 S.E. 260, 264, 265, 268, 269 (1911).
45 *Watson* v. *Stone*, 4 So.2d 700, 703 (Fla. 1941).
46 *State ex rel. Russo* v. *Parker*, 49 So. 124, 125 (Fla. 1909) and *Carlton* v. *State*, 63 Fla. 1, 58 So. 486, 488 (1912).
47 *Watson* v. *Stone*, 4 So.2d 700, 703 (Fla. 1941).

No more damning statement can be imagined as to the purpose of the Florida law. It also fits well with our hypothesis about the nominally color-blind laws of the Reconstruction period.

Florida's first right to keep and bear arms case appears to be *State ex rel. Russo* v. *Parker* (1909). A Giocomo Russo had applied for a permit to carry a pistol, and he was refused. Significantly, the character references rejected by the county commissioners as "unknown" to them had names every bit as "foreign" as Russo's. Russo then sought a writ of mandamus compelling issuance of a permit to carry a pistol, as required under the Act of 1906. The Florida Supreme Court cleverly sidestepped Russo's claim that the Florida Constitution's guarantee of the right to bear arms was violated by this law. The Court claimed that if the statute requiring a permit to carry a pistol was unconstitutional, then Russo's request for a mandamus to require issuance of a permit was void, because "there would remain no authority in the county commissioners to issue a permit to any one in such cases..."[48]

Shortly thereafter, the Florida Supreme Court did venture an opinion about the meaning of the Florida Constitutional provision in *Carlton* v. *State* (1912). The principal crime involved was first degree murder of a peace officer in St. Johns County, by three brothers named Carlton. Relative to the murder conviction the three brothers were appealing, the weapons violations would seem like a small matter, and perhaps for this reason, the Florida Supreme Court put relatively little effort into the discussion of this issue.

The Carlton brothers sought to overturn the concealed weapons statute based primarily on §20 of the Florida Bill of Rights, which granted to the people the right "to bear arms in defense of themselves and the lawful authority of the state." In response, the Florida Supreme Court held: "This section was intended to give the people the means of protecting themselves against oppression and public outrage, and was not designed as a shield for the individual man, who is prone to load his stomach with liquor and his pockets with revolvers or dynamite, and to make of himself a dangerous nuisance to society."[49]

The only precedents cited in defense of this position were *State* v. *Workman* (1891) and *Presser* v. *Illinois* (1886). *Workman* had certainly taken the position that the carrying of handguns was not protected by the Second Amendment, and *Presser* had found the Second Amendment to be a limitation on the powers of Congress only. Neither precedent directly addressed the issue of whether a state constitutional provision was applicable to this issue. In light of the more major issues decided in *Carlton*, it is not surprising that so little attention was given to this matter—and as we shall see, this back of the envelope approach to the issue would be used in the 1960s by the Florida Supreme Court, looking for a precedent to justify laws that restricted not just concealed carry, but open carry as well.

In *People* v. *Persce* (1912), New York's highest court[50] heard a challenge to Penal Law §1897, which prohibited the possession or carrying of a "slungshot, billy, sand

---

48 *State ex rel. Russo* v. *Parker*, 49 So. 124, 125 (Fla. 1909).

49 *Carlton* v. *State*, 63 Fla. 1, 58 So. 486, 488 (1912).

50 Unfortunately, the various states are not uniform in their terminology for their courts. The New York Supreme Court is merely one of the appeals courts, with one "Supreme Court" for each county. Above each county's Supreme Court is the Appellate Division of the Supreme Court, and the apex of the New York court system, the New York Court of Appeals. John P. Lomenzo, *Manual for the Use of the Legislature of the State of New York: 1969*, (Albany, N.Y.: n.p., 1969), 1048-55. For those states

club or metal knuckles." The statute in question is certainly one of the less clearly written laws of this type; it might well be argued that it was unclear if possession in one's home, or carrying with criminal intent, or simply carrying in public, was prohibited.[51]

Giuseppe Persce was arrested by a detective at two o'clock in the morning, in a room with two other men. A slungshot was found in his pocket, and he was charged and convicted under §1897 in New York County. On appeal, Persce's attorneys argued that the statute made "mere possession of a slungshot or a billy, no matter how innocent, a felony," and therefore unconstitutional. Persce's attorneys cited the Eighth and Fourteenth Amendments to the U.S. Constitution, but not the Second Amendment. They also cited provisions of the New York State constitution, but apparently, no provisions relating to the right to keep and bear arms contained in the state Bill of Rights. Nonetheless, New York's high court addressed these provisions in their decision.

The Court refused to overturn the statute in question, and held that it was within the authority of the legislature to prohibit simple possession of an object, even where no criminal intent was associated with it. While it did Persce no good, the Court did clarify that the statute did not necessarily prohibit all possession, and would not prohibit "legal ownership of a weapon in a collection of curious and interesting objects or which might result temporarily and incidentally from the performance of some lawful act, as disarming a wrongful possessor."

The purpose of this statute was discussed, and the weapons to which it applied, were characterized as "dangerous and foul weapons seldom used for justifiable purposes but ordinarily the effective and illegitimate implements of thugs and brutes in carrying out their unlawful purposes."[52]

Finally, the Court addressed the right to bear arms:

> Neither is there any constitutional provision securing the right to bear arms which prohibits legislation with reference to such weapons as are specifically before us for consideration. The provision in the Constitution of the United States that "the right of the people to keep and bear arms shall not be infringed" is not designed to control legislation by the state. (*Presser* v. *Illinois*, 116 U.S. 252.) There is no provision in the State Constitution at least directly bearing on this subject, but only in the statutory Bill of Rights. But beyond this, as has already been suggested, the act in question relates to instruments which are ordinarily used for criminal and improper purposes and which are not amongst those ordinary legitimate weapons of defense and protection which are contemplated by the Constitution and the Bill of Rights.[53]

The New York high court refused to recognize a right to carry a slungshot; refused to recognize the Second Amendment as a restriction on state laws; but did imply that the Second Amendment was a restriction on federal authority to limit "legitimate weapons of defense and protection." Unfortunately, the Court did not define those "legitimate weapons," except to the extent that those weapons listed in §1897 were defined to be illegitimate.

---

with unusual names for their highest court of appeal, I have used the terms "high court" or "highest court," to prevent confusion.

51 *People* v. *Persce*, 204 N.Y. 397, 398 (1912).
52 *People* v. *Persce*, 204 N.Y. 397, 398, 399, 400, 403 (1912).
53 *People* v. *Persce*, 204 N.Y. 397, 403 (1912).

The Sullivan Law, passed in 1911, licensed not simply carrying of handguns, but also their ownership. Still, there was a pretense that the Sullivan Law was merely a regulation of handgun ownership, not a prohibition. The distinction between "prohibition" and "regulation" was made in *People Ex Rel. Darling* v. *Warden of City Prison* (1913), a New York case where the state appellate court upheld a conviction for unlicensed possession of a handgun at home. This was apparently a "test case," since:

> The relator notified the police that he had a pistol in his house without a permit. Thereupon a captain of police went to his house and found a loaded revolver and some loaded shells in a small cabinet in the bedroom adjoining the parlor. He asked the defendant why he kept the revolver there and defendant said he preferred not to answer the question. The captain asked if defendant had a permit, to which he replied no. Whereupon the captain placed the relator under arrest and took him before a city magistrate, charging him with a violation of section 1897....

The State of New York had passed a series of progressively more restrictive laws on the carrying of arms, and it would appear that having failed to solve the problem ("the problem," as we have discussed in a previous chapter, may not have been crime), elected to license private possession of handguns. Darling argued against the statute based on

> the inherent and inalienable right to keep and bear arms, declared by the English Bill of Rights, inherited by the Colonies, recognized by the Bill of Rights as adopted in this State, and in the Constitutions of many other States, and alluded to in the second amendment to the Constitution of the United States...[54]

Not surprisingly, the appellate court found that the U.S. Bill of Rights was not a limitation on state actions—a perfectly valid assertion, in 1913. (Nor had Darling argued otherwise, except as a form of moral example.) To that end, the court cited all the usual precedents, but also *Robertson* v. *Baldwin* (1897), and quoted it that: "the right of the people to keep and bear arms... is not infringed by laws prohibiting the carrying of concealed weapons."[55] But of course, the Sullivan Law was not about *carrying* of concealed weapons, but of *owning* concealable weapons.

Concerning the New York Civil Rights Law (also known as the New York Bill of Rights), the Court pointed out that it was not a part of the New York Constitution, and being statutory, was simply another law which could be overturned by a subsequent act of the state legislature, but:

> Nevertheless we fully recognize the proposition that the rights enumerated in the Bill of Rights were not created by such declaration. They are of such character as necessarily pertains to free men in a free State. But in order to appeal thereto for the purpose of declaring null and void an act of the Legislature, possessing all the law-making power of the people, it is necessary, before the act is declared null and void, that it should clearly be made to appear that it is in flat violation of some fundamental right of which the citizen may not be deprived by any power.

> The right to keep and bear arms is coupled with the statement why the right is preserved and protected, viz., that "a well regulated militia being necessary to the security of a free

---

54 *People Ex Rel. Darling* v. *Warden of City Prison*, 139 N.Y.S. 277, 154 App. Div. 413, 414, 415, 419, 29 N.Y.Cr. 74 (1913).

55 *People Ex Rel. Darling* v. *Warden of City Prison*, 139 N.Y.S. 277, 154 App. Div. 413, 419, 420, 29 N.Y.Cr. 74 (1913).

State." (Civil Rights Law, §4). If the Legislature had prohibited the keeping of arms, it would have been clearly beyond its power.[56]

The Court went on to quote *Presser* v. *Illinois* (1886) and *English* v. *State* (1872), for the purpose of demonstrating that only "the arms of a militiaman or soldier" were protected. Yet the *English* decision, even the section quoted by the Court, acknowledged that "holster pistols" were such militia arms, though they were similarly restricted by the Sullivan Law.[57]

To justify their decision, the Court concluded:

> In the statute at bar the Legislature has not prohibited the keeping of arms. For the safety of the public, for the preservation of the public peace, in the exercise of the police power, the means employed being within its discretion and not in that of the courts, unless flagrantly in violation of constitutional provisions, the Legislature has passed a regulative, not a prohibitory, act. Legislation which has for its object the promotion of the public welfare and safety falls within the scope of the police power and must be submitted to even though it imposes restraints and burdens on the individual. The rights of the individual are subordinate to the welfare of the State. The only question that can then arise is whether the means employed are appropriate and reasonably necessary for the accomplishment of the purpose in view and are not unduly oppressive....
>
> There has been for many years upon the statute books a law against the carriage of concealed weapons. No court in this country, so far as I know, has ever declared such a law in violation of the Constitution or the Bill of Rights. It did not seem effective in preventing crimes of violence in this State. Of the same kind and character, but proceeding a step further with the regulatory legislation, the Legislature has now picked out one particular kind of arm, the handy, the usual and the favorite weapon of the turbulent criminal class, and has said that in our organized communities, our cities, towns and villages where the public peace is protected by the officers of organized government, the citizen may not have that particular kind of weapon without a permit, as it had already said that he might not carry it on his person without a permit. If he has it in his possession, he can readily stick it in his pocket when he goes abroad.[58]

The decision of the Court was split 3-2; Justice Scott wrote the dissenting opinion, in which he pointed out:

> [T]hat every statute shall be given a reasonable construction, where its language is susceptible of more than one construction, and in determining what is a reasonable construction, regard is to be had not only to the language but also to the evil sought to be guarded against and to the nature of the remedy provided. This is especially true of statutes like the one now under consideration which is highly penal, creates a crime out of that which was formerly lawful and relies for its authority upon the existence of that somewhat vague and shadowy right known as the police power.[59]

Much as a vagrancy statute in Kansas led to a right to keep and bear arms decision, so Ohio's similar problems and concerns led to the decision *State* v. *Hogan* (1900)—but with a very different result. Ohio had passed a statute known as the "Tramp Law," §6995, Rev. St., which along with prohibiting begging (except by

---

56 *People Ex Rel. Darling* v. *Warden of City Prison*, 139 N.Y.S. 277, 154 App. Div. 413, 420, 421, 29 N.Y.Cr. 74 (1913).

57 *People Ex Rel. Darling* v. *Warden of City Prison*, 139 N.Y.S. 277, 154 App. Div. 413, 422, 29 N.Y.Cr. 74 (1913).

58 *People Ex Rel. Darling* v. *Warden of City Prison*, 139 N.Y.S. 277, 154 App. Div. 413, 422, 423, 29 N.Y.Cr. 74 (1913).

59 *People Ex Rel. Darling* v. *Warden of City Prison*, 139 N.Y.S. 277, 154 App. Div. 413, 425, 29 N.Y.Cr. 74 (1913).

women and the blind), included a provision that made it a criminal offense for a tramp to bear arms. While the defendant, Timothy Hogan, was not accused of carrying any sort of arms, the Ohio Supreme Court chose to discuss this issue as well, when it upheld the constitutionality of the Tramp Law:

> But it is insisted that the bill of rights is infringed, because the act forbids the tramp to bear arms. The question was not involved in this prosecution, but we see no real difficulty in it. The constitutional right to bear arms is intended to guaranty to the people, in support of just government, such right, and to afford the citizen means for defense of self and property. While this secures to him a right of which he cannot be deprived, it enjoins a duty in execution of which that right is to be exercised. If he employs those arms which he ought to wield for the safety and protection of his country, his person, and his property, to the annoyance and terror and danger of its citizens, his acts find no vindication in the bill of rights. That guaranty was never intended as a warrant for vicious persons to carry weapons with which to terrorize others. Going armed with unusual and dangerous weapons, to the terror of the people, is an offense at common law. A man may carry a gun for any lawful purpose, for business or amusement, but he cannot go about with that or any other dangerous weapon to terrify and alarm a peaceful people.[60]

The Court then cited *Sir John Knight's Case*, and the North Carolina decisions, *State* v. *Huntly* (1843) and *State* v. *Roten* (1882).

This is a unambiguous statement that there existed an individual right to carry arms for self-defense, and collective defense, as long as one was not a "vicious person" and the purpose was not "to terrorize others." Neither the headnotes nor the Court's decision tell us whether this right came from the state constitution or from the Second Amendment, but it is a fair assumption, in light of the decisions which were being made at that time, that this refers to the Ohio Constitutional provision.

What "vicious persons" was the Ohio Supreme Court concerned about? The rest of the *Hogan* decision is, by modern standards, amazing:

> Speaking of the class, the genus tramp, in this country, is a public enemy. He is numerous, and he is dangerous. He is a nomad, a wanderer on the face of the earth, with his hand against every honest man, woman, and child, in so far as they do not promptly and fully supply his demands. He is a thief, a robber, often a murderer, and always a nuisance. He does not belong to the working classes, but is an idler. He does not work, because he despises work. It is a fixed principle with him that, come what may, he will not work. He is so low in the scale of humanity that he is without that not uncommon virtue among the low, of honor among thieves. He will steal from a fellow tramp, if in need of what that fellow has, and will resort to violence when that is necessary. So numerous has the class become that the members may be said to overrun the improved parts of the country, especially the more thickly-settled portions.[61]

And this passionate, angry denunciation continues, for many more paragraphs. Clearly, there was tremendous fear of "tramps," and it was considered desirable to have some confidence that when tramps came begging, that "decent people" would not fear them drawing a weapon. Yet, instead of denying the right of the general population to carry weapons, the Ohio Supreme Court decided simply that tramps were outside the protections of the right to bear arms.

---

60 *State* v. *Hogan*, 63 Ohio St. 202, 81 Am. St. Rep. 626, 58 N.E. 572, 575 (1900). The careful reader will notice the very strong similarity of the language to the *State* v. *Huntly* (1843) decision.
61 *State* v. *Hogan*, 63 Ohio St. 202, 81 Am. St. Rep. 626, 58 N.E. 572, 574 (1900).

The last of the decisions before the end of World War I was *State* v. *Keet* (1916). Minon Keet was convicted in Greene Criminal Court of carrying a concealed revolver, and appealed that decision to the Missouri Supreme Court. On appeal, Keet's attorney argued that the trial judge, by excluding testimony concerning an immediately preceding attack on Keet that justified his actions, had violated the natural rights, common law rights, and rights guaranteed by, article II, §17 of the Missouri Constitution, which declared: "that the right of no citizen to keep and bear arms in defense of his home, person and property... shall be called in question."

While acknowledging that the rest of this section, "but nothing contained herein is intended to justify the practice of wearing concealed weapons" limited this right, Keet's counsel argued that it was:

> not intended to be a limitation upon the right to bear arms in self-defense—each man being either justified or condemned by the facts in each particular case. The negation is designed merely to prevent the abuse of a natural right; is designed to prevent the practice of wearing concealed weapons or such practice under the guise of defense of the person.

Keet's counsel next argued that more explicit, "plainer, clearer language" would have been used, if the framers of the Missouri Constitution had intended "such a radical, repressive measure against the laws of nature." Keet's counsel also pointed to §1863 which provided that it was: "good defense... if the defendant shall show that he has been threatened with great bodily harm, or has good reason to carry the same in the necessary defense of his person."[62]

The Missouri Supreme Court used the *State* v. *Shelby* (1886) and *Presser* v. *Illinois* (1886) precedents to hold that the Second Amendment was not a limitation on state laws. On the subject of the Missouri Constitution's protection, the Court refused to accept the argument of Keet's attorney that distinguished the "practice of carrying concealed" from occasional carrying of concealed arms for self-defense. The Court pointed out that there were only two cases of which they were aware that found concealed carry to be constitutionally protected, one being *State* v. *Rosenthal* (1903), based on Vermont's state constitutional provision, which made no reference to concealed carry at all; and the other being *Bliss* v. *Commonwealth* (1822): "That case has never been cited with approval, but has often been disapproved."

The Missouri Supreme Court then pointed to the discussion in Bishop's *Statutory Crimes*, and proceeded to analyze (quite correctly, in this author's understanding) the deficiencies in the cases cited there that Bishop purported were in harmony with *Bliss*.[63] The Court also cited the decisions of the Idaho Supreme Court in *In Re Brickey* (1902), the Arkansas Supreme Court in *State* v. *Buzzard* (1842), the Georgia Supreme Court in *Nunn* v. *State* (1846), and the Missouri Supreme Court in *State* v. *Wilforth* (1881), all of which recognized that concealed carry was not con-

---

62 *State* v. *Keet*, 269 Mo. 206, 207, 190 S.W. 573 (1916).

63 *State* v. *Keet*, 269 Mo. 206, 208, 210, 211, 212, 190 S.W. 573 (1916). One of the cases cited, while not an arms case, is quite interesting: the Kentucky Supreme Court, before the Civil War, found that free blacks were protected by at least some of the protections of the state constitution, and were, at least to some extent, "parties to the political compact." *Ely* v. *Thompson*, 3 A.K. Marshall (Ky.) 70, 75 (1820).

stitutionally protected, by either the Second Amendment or the state constitutional provisions.

On the history of concealed weapons laws in Missouri:

> Our constitutional provision on the subject originated in 1875. The words, "the practice of wearing concealed weapons," are, as we have seen, the language of the courts of our sister states; and there is no reason for thinking that those words are used in the Constitution in a sense other than the one given them in the reported cases....

> The provision exempting those who carried a weapon in self-defense from the penalty of the law originated in the Revised Statutes of 1879, section 1275. This provision was expressly repealed by the Act of April 28, 1909 (Laws 1909, p. 452) and has never been re-enacted...

> Less than a century ago the arms of the pioneer were carried openly, his rifle on his shoulder, his hunting knife on his belt. Since then deadly weapons have been devised small enough to be carried effectively concealed in the ordinary pocket. The practice of carrying such weapons concealed is appreciated and indulged in mainly by the enemies of social order. Our State has been one of the slowest to act in meeting this comparatively new evil, but she has finally spoken in no uncertain language.[64]

The further removed legal commentators became from the Revolution, the less absolute their statements that the Second Amendment guaranteed an individual right to carry arms. By the turn of the century, the bearing of arms concealed was no longer recognized as a point worthy of serious debate, having been settled by most state supreme courts as an exercise of the police power. Open carry became the next controversial issue for the legal commentators.

Thomas Cooley, the noted nineteenth century law professor and Michigan Supreme Court Chief Justice, appears to have taken two contradictory positions on the meaning of the Second Amendment. In his third edition of Blackstone's *Commentaries*, published in 1884, Cooley's note on Blackstone's assertion of an individual right tells us:

> In the United States this right is preserved by express constitutional provisions. But it extends no further than to keep and bear those arms which are suited and proper for the general defense of the community against invasion and oppression, and it does not include the carrying of such weapons as are specially suited for deadly individual encounters, and therefore the carrying of these, concealed, may be prohibited.[65]

Yet Halbrook reports the third edition of Cooley's *General Principles of Constitutional Law*, published only seven years later, observed:

> The Right is General—It may be supposed from the phraseology of this provision that the right to keep and bear arms was only guaranteed to the militia; but this would be an interpretation not warranted by the intent... The meaning of the provision undoubtedly is that the people from whom the militia must be taken, shall have the right to keep and bear arms, and they need no permission or regulation for the purpose...[66]

Cooley's 1884 edition of Blackstone's *Commentaries* told us that only those weapons of general defense against "invasion and oppression" were protected, and the carriage of other weapons may be prohibited; Cooley's 1891 law text told us "no

64 *State v. Keet*, 269 Mo. 206, 213, 214, 190 S.W. 573 (1916).

65 William Blackstone, *Commentaries on the Laws of England*, 3d ed., edited by Thomas M. Cooley, (Chicago: Callaghan & Co., 1884), 1:93, note 24.

66 Thomas M. Cooley, *The General Principles of Constitutional Law*, 2nd ed., (1891), quoted in Halbrook, *That Every Man Be Armed*, 169.

permission or regulation" was required—a dramatic change. Unfortunately, attempts to locate Cooley's *General Principles of Constitutional Law* were unsuccessful; at a minimum, such a dramatic change in viewpoint by Cooley in only seven years would be worthy of serious examination.

William Draper Lewis' edition of Blackstone's *Commentaries*, published in 1897, in reference to the "right of subjects... having arms for their defence," repeats St. George Tucker's remarks, but then tells us,

A defense of the right to carry concealed deadly weapons—delivered, however, in a dissenting opinion in Andrews *v.* State, 3 Heisk. (Tenn.) 199 (1871). That the right of carrying arms as secured by the U.S. constitution, and generally by State constitutions, does not include the habitual carrying of concealed deadly weapons by private individuals.[67]

George Chase's *Commentaries on the Laws of England*, published in 1906, has yet another construction of the import of Blackstone's "right of subjects" to American law. After reciting the Second Amendment:

Similar provisions are contained in the constitutions of a number of the States. But it is generally held that statutes prohibiting the carrying of *concealed* weapons are not in conflict with these constitutional provisions, since they merely forbid the carrying of arms in a particular manner, which is likely to lead to breaches of the peace and provoke to the commission of crime, rather than contribute to public or personal defence. In some States, however, a contrary doctrine is maintained. (*State* v. *Shelby*, 90 Mo. 302; see 116 U.S. 252 [*Presser* v. *Illinois* (1886)]).[68]

William Carey Jones' *Commentaries on the Laws of England*, published in 1916, contains the single note:

The constitutional right to bear arms in this country does not mean the right to bear them for individual defense, but only for the defense of the community against invasion or oppression. The use of arms for the latter purpose may be restricted but not prohibited; of all other, arms may be prohibited. (Andrews v. State, 3 Heisk. 165.)[69]

The Missouri Supreme Court's decision in *State* v. *Keet* (1916) may be considered the final decision on the subject of the constitutionality of laissez-faire concealed carry, and a fitting ending it is, with a serious, and apparently honest attempt at locating all the decisions of the various state supreme courts. But while it ended serious dispute about the unregulated concealed carry of arms, it did not end disputes about the *regulated* concealed carry of arms, or open carry of arms—as the next three chapters will demonstrate.

The Missouri Supreme Court also claimed that the rise of concealed weapons laws was the result of technological advancement in the development of concealable deadly weapons.[70] As we saw in the conclusion to the previous chapter, this is simply not the case—technology alone was not a factor, and even the declining cost of handguns fails to explain the laws aimed at Bowie-knives.

Don Kates points to a number of statutes and illegal practices in the South from the close of Reconstruction up to World War I, designed to disarm blacks (and the

67 William Blackstone, *Commentaries on the Laws of England*, edited by William Draper Lewis, (Philadelphia: Rees Welsh & Co., 1897), 1:132, note 91.

68 William Blackstone, *Commentaries on the Laws of England*, 3d ed., edited by George Chase, (Albany, N.Y.: Banks & Co., 1906), note 11.

69 William Blackstone, Jones ed., 1:246, note 20.

70 *State* v. *Keet*, 269 Mo. 206, 213, 214, 190 S.W. 573 (1916).

occasional white union organizer). These included laws prohibiting sale of concealable handguns in Arkansas in 1881; handgun registration laws in Mississippi; heavy handgun sales taxes adopted in Alabama in 1893, and similarly in Texas in 1907, as an economic barrier to ownership; a complete ban on pistol sales "except to sheriffs and their special deputies" adopted in South Carolina in 1902. When all else failed, illegal confiscations were made by county sheriffs when the "wrong" people were found to own arms that might be used defensively.

But while the statutes aimed at open carry of firearms were rare before the 1890s (outside of the South), they appeared with increasing frequency in the North as labor unions increased, a substantial immigration of Eastern and Southern Europeans began to remake the image of America, and an increasingly vocal nativism reappeared nationally. Kates sees a combination of actual revolutionary violence (*i.e.*, armed robbery to fund radical groups) and xenophobia as an explanation for the rise of these laws in the North and West.[71] It is a tempting explanation; Ohio's "Tramp Law," in *State* v. *Hogan* (1900), which prohibited "tramps" from carrying guns, reflected a fear of hungry, jobless men, who might have taken what they wanted, if they had been armed. Similarly, the city ordinance in *City of Salina* v. *Blaksley* (1905) was principally a vagrancy law. Our first New York decision involves an Italian, who was of enough interest to the police to be followed until he could be arrested. The Florida decision *State ex rel. Russo* v. *Parker* (1909) has elements to it that suggest the ethnicity of the plaintiffs may have had some part in the refusal to issue a permit to carry a handgun. As we saw in the *Patsone* v. *Pennsylvania* (1914) decision, laws prohibiting resident aliens from owning arms appeared in a number of states shortly after the turn of the century.

Many clues suggest that the statutes passed during this period were for the purpose of dealing with problems of race and ethnicity. But before the question of motivations is stamped, "Case Closed," detailed histories of gun control in the various states must be done. As the evidence stands, we will have no problem getting a grand jury to indict gun control laws as an expression of racism; but until the evidence is brought forth for each of these states, there is insufficient evidence to convict.

---

71 Kates, "Toward a History of Handgun Prohibition...", 14-19.

VIII. "A PROPER REASON FOR CARRYING A PISTOL"

Several dramatic social and technological changes took place during the 1920s, and each of these changes had a significant impact on popular perceptions of the right to keep and bear arms, and the judicial interpretation of that right. The first was a increasing willingness to deny a right to bear arms at all, even openly. A second change was the nativism that had been triggered by the rising tide of Southern and Eastern European immigration. Third, Prohibition dramatically increased violent crime in America. Fourth, the introduction of the Thompson submachine gun, and its highly publicized criminal misuse, brought about the first significant federal gun control laws. Nor were these factors isolated from each other: for example, the gangsters were often immigrants, or children of immigrants, and their criminal activity reinforced the nativist claims.

One of the ironies of the period between the World Wars is that significant restrictions on the open carrying of handguns began to appear throughout the United States—and the National Rifle Association was one of the promoters. There is significant disagreement among different sources as to the origin of the Model Uniform Firearms Act, widely adopted by the different states in the period between World Wars I and II. One source asserts that in the first three decades of this century, the NRA and the United States Revolver Association (no longer in operation), developed a model statute called, "A Bill To Provide For Uniform Regulation of Revolver Sales," promoted by the National Conference of Commissioners on Uniform State Laws and adopted by most states.[1]

Another source indicates that it was called "A Uniform Act to Regulate the Sale and Possession of Firearms," and was a product of a committee appointed by the National Conference of Commissioners on Uniform State Laws in 1923, at the urging of the United States Revolver Association, with the final form adopted in 1930.[2] A third source, largely in agreement, tells us that California's concealed weapon permit system, adopted in 1923:

> was based on the Uniform Firearms Act (UFA) which purported to provide a uniform series of state laws on this subject... The UFA was a model act proposed by the United States Revolver Association in 1923. The Uniform Act was adopted by the National Commission on Uniform State Laws in the 1920s. Under the UFA and California law

---

1 Kates, "Handgun Prohibition and the Original Meaning of the Second Amendment", 82:209-10.
2 Gregory J. Petesch, ed., *Montana Code Annotated*, (Helena, Mont.: Montana Legislative Council, 1990), 371.

since 1923, one may possess a firearm in one's home or place of business. It may be loaded in one's home and in a place of business....

If not in an exempted category, one needs a license in order to carry the pistol or revolver concealed on one's person.[3]

This system of licensing provided some limitations, and much discretion, in the issuance of concealed weapons permits. It also contained many exemptions for peace officers, guards, and civilians transporting unloaded firearms to and from hunting and other recreational shooting activities. In many respects, the adoption of the Uniform Firearms Act represents the national expansion of the sort of gun control laws that we saw in the antebellum South. Significantly, California's version of the UFA did not prohibit *open* carry of a handgun;[4] in that respect, it was more liberal than the laws of Texas, Arkansas, and Tennessee. While perhaps a narrowing of the intent of the Second Amendment, it was not an abolition of the right to bear arms. But even this recognition of the right of open carry soon came under assault, with differing results in different state supreme courts.

In 1919, Forsyth County in North Carolina passed an ordinance that prohibited carrying of "Bowie knives, dirks, daggers, slung-shots, loaded canes, brass, iron, or metallic knucks, razors," and pistols outside of private property without a permit. In 1921, O.W. Kerner was attacked in Kernersville, Forsyth County. He went to his place of business, retrieved a pistol, and returned to where he had been attacked. At trial, "The court, being of the opinion that this statute was in conflict with the constitutional provision that 'the right to bear arms shall not be infringed,' directed a verdict of not guilty, and the state appealed."[5]

The North Carolina Supreme Court in *State* v. *Kerner* (1921) first denied the applicability of the Second Amendment to state laws, insisting that "indeed by all courts" it was agreed that the Bill of Rights only restricted the federal government. The Court then cited a number of cases, including *U.S.* v. *Cruikshank* (1876). By the absence of citations, it appears that the Court was unaware of the *Nunn* v. *State* (1846), *Cockrum* v. *State* (1859), *In Re Brickey* (1902), *State* v. *Chandler* (1850), or *State* v. *Jumel* (1858) decisions, which *had* held that the Second Amendment *was* a limitation on both the Federal and state governments.

The Court did, however, strike down the Forsyth County law based on the North Carolina Constitutional protections:

> The Constitution of this state, section 24, art. 1, which is entitled, "Declaration of Rights," provides, "The right of the people to keep and bear arms shall not be infringed," adding, "nothing herein contained shall justify the practice of carrying concealed weapons or prevent the Legislature from enacting penal statutes against said practice." This exception indicates the extent to which the right of the people to bear arms can be restricted; that is, the Legislature can prohibit the carrying of concealed weapons but no further. This constitutional guaranty was construed in State v. Speller, 86 N. C. 697, in which it was held that the distinction was between the "right to keep and bear arms" and the "practice of carrying concealed weapons." The former is a sacred right based upon the experience of the ages in order that the people may be accustomed

---

3 Assembly Office of Research, 6-8. A previous, very similar statute, prohibited unlicensed concealed carry in California cities as early as 1917; unlicensed concealed carry in unincorporated areas of the state was apparently not restricted. *Statutes of California Passed At The Extra Session of the Forty-First Legislature,* (San Francisco: Bancroft-Whitney Co., 1916), 221.

4 Assembly Office of Research, 6-8.

5 *State* v. *Kerner,* 181 N.C. 574, 107 S.E. 222, 223 (1921).

to bear arms and ready to use them for the protection of their liberties or their country when occasion serves. The provision against carrying them concealed was to prevent assassinations or advantages taken by the lawless; i.e., against the abuse of the privilege.[6]

The Court held that of all the weapons banned from carry by the Forsyth County ordinance, only the pistol was protected:

None of these except "pistol" can be construed as coming within the meaning of the word "arms" used in the constitutional guaranty of the right to bear arms. We are of the opinion, however, that "pistol" ex vi termini is properly included within the word "arms," and that the right to bear such arms cannot be infringed. The historical uses of pistols as "arms" of offense and defense is beyond controversy.

It is true that the invention of guns with a carrying range of probably 100 miles, submarines, deadly gases, and of airplanes carrying bombs and other modern devices, have much reduced the importance of the pistol in warfare except at close range. But the ordinary private citizen, whose right to carry arms cannot be infringed upon, is not likely to purchase these expensive and most modern devices just named. To him the rifle, the musket, the shotgun, and the pistol are about the only arms which he could be expected to "bear," and his right to do this is that which is guaranteed by the Constitution. To deprive him of bearing any of these arms is to infringe upon the right guaranteed to him by the Constitution.[7]

After asserting the absurdity of using the Second Amendment (the ancestor of the North Carolina Constitution's provision) to justify private citizens the right to practice "dropping bombs from a flying machine" or "to practice in the use of deadly gases," the North Carolina Supreme Court quoted from Thomas Cooley's *Constitutional Limitations* about the "history and intention of this provision":

Among the other safeguards to liberty should be mentioned the right of the people to keep and bear arms... The alternative to a standing army is 'a well-regulated militia'; but this cannot exist unless the people are trained to arms. The federal and state Constitutions therefore provide that the right of the people to bear arms shall not be infringed.[8]

The Court discussed the habituation of the people to bearing arms, and the use of privately owned arms in the American Revolution, the War of 1812, and:

In our own state, in 1870, when Kirk's militia was turned loose and the writ of *habeas corpus* was suspended, it would have been fatal if our people had been deprived of the right to bear arms and had been unable to oppose an effective front to the usurpation.... The maintenance of the right to bear arms is a most essential one to every free people and should not be whittled down by technical constructions. It should be construed to include all "arms" as were in common use, and borne by the people as such when this provision was adopted.[9]

The Court *did* make it clear that laws that prohibited "carrying of deadly weapons when under the influence of intoxicating drink, or to a church, polling place, or public assembly, or in a manner calculated to inspire terror..."[10] were not infringements on the right to bear arms. The Court also held that laws prohibiting "pistols

6 State v. Kerner, 181 N.C. 574, 107 S.E. 222 (1921).
7 State v. Kerner, 181 N.C. 574, 107 S.E. 222, 224 (1921).
8 State v. Kerner, 181 N.C. 574, 107 S.E. 222, 224 (1921).
9 State v. Kerner, 181 N.C. 574, 107 S.E. 222, 224 (1921). See Stephen E. Massengill, "The Detectives of William W. Holden, 1869-1870", North Carolina Historical Review, 63:4, [October 1985], 470, and Foner, 440-1, for details of this Reconstruction struggle.
10 State v. Kerner, 181 N.C. 574, 107 S.E. 222, 225 (1921).

of small size which are not borne as arms but which are easily and ordinarily carried concealed" would be Constitutional. But:

> To exclude all pistols, however, is not a regulation, but a prohibition, of arms which come under the designation of "arms" which the people are entitled to bear. This is not an idle or obsolete guaranty, for there are still localities, not necessary to mention, where great corporations, under the guise of detective agents or private police, terrorize their employees by armed force. If the people are forbidden to carry the only arms within their means, among them pistols, they will be completely at the mercy of these great plutocratic organizations. Should there be a mob, is it possible that law-abiding citizens could not assemble with their pistols carried openly and protect their persons and their property from unlawful violence without going before an official and obtaining license and giving bond?[11]

The Court expressed a republican view of the purpose of the right to bear arms:

> The usual method by which a country is overborne by force is to "disarm" the people. It is to prevent the above and similar exercises of arbitrary power that the people, in creating this government "of the people, by the people and for the people," reserved to themselves the right to "bear arms," that, accustomed to their use, they might be ready to meet illegal force with legal force by adequate and just defense of their persons, their property, and their liberties, whenever necessary. We should be slow indeed to construe such guaranty into a mere academic expression which has become obsolete.[12]

Which "great corporations" was the Court referring to? It is most likely that the Court was referring to the continuous labor violence in West Virginia, where deputy sheriffs, nominally public employees, were paid their salaries by coal companies, and were stationed on coal company property, while engaged in violence against strikers and union organizers. West Virginia was a site of continuing labor violence from 1890 into the early 1920s. Deputy sheriffs, paid by the coal companies to guard company facilities, appear to have thrown in extra-legal violence against union organizers, free of charge. Armed violence, on both sides, was not at all in short supply during this period, with coal companies using private detective agencies to intimidate, and on occasion, murder union organizers.[13]

It would be tempting to conclude that the threats of labor violence and actual clashes were a factor in the apparent change in judicial decisions concerning the right to keep and bear arms in the period after World War I. We have evidence that other countries adopted gun control laws for these very reasons. The New Zealand Police Department, in explaining the 1983 decision to replace long gun registration with firearms owner licensing, explained why the registration of all firearms was adopted in 1920: "Revolution had occurred in Russia and there was a fear that large scale industrial demonstrations or even riot could occur here."[14] It appears that similar concerns motivated the actions of the British Government in passing the Firearms Act of 1920.[15] Decisions such as *Presser* v. *Illinois* (1886) and

---

11 *State* v. *Kerner*, 181 N.C. 574, 107 S.E. 222, 225 (1921).

12 *State* v. *Kerner*, 181 N.C. 574, 107 S.E. 222, 225 (1921).

13 Winthrop D. Lane, *Civil War in West Virginia*, (New York: B. W. Huebsch, Inc., 1921; reprinted New York: Arno Press, 1969), 17-19, 48-9.

14 New Zealand Police Department, *Background To The Introduction of Firearms User Licensing Instead Of Rifle and Shotgun Registration Under The Arms Act of 1983*, (Wellington: n.p., 1983), 2-3.

15 Jan A. Stevenson, "Firearms Legislation in Great Britain", *The Handgunner*, [March/April 1988], 6. *The Handgunner* is a British private handgun owners publication, and as might be expected, they are hardly an unbiased source. However, the evidence cited includes British Cabinet minutes with

Commonwealth v. *Murphy* (1896) *do* suggest fear of radicalism; that such laws only restricted armed *groups*, not individuals, suggests that the principal concern was not individual criminals, but criminal organizations (as labor unions were perceived, in some circles).

State v. *Nieto* (1920) provides another example of the increasing reluctance to acknowledge a right to possess a handgun. A 1917 Ohio statute (107 O.L., 28) prohibited the carrying of "a pistol, bowie knife, dirk, or other dangerous weapon concealed on or about his person," with the usual exemptions for police officers.[16] Doubtless reflective of the labor strife then gripping the United States, "specially appointed police officers" were entitled to carry arms if they posted a $1000 bond, apparently to work as company police. General Code §13693 also provided an escape clause for private persons who carried concealed weapons:

> Upon the trial of an indictment for carrying a concealed weapon, the jury shall acquit the defendant if it appear that he was at the time engaged in a lawful business, calling or employment, and that the circumstances, in which he was placed, justified a prudent man in carrying such weapon for the defense of his person, property, or family.[17]

The defendant, Mike Nieto, "a Mexican in the employ of the United Alloy Steel Company," was asleep in a railroad car which was functioning as a company bunkhouse. Nieto was accused of threatening the camp cook's life while drunk on Christmas night, 1919. On the morning of December 26th, two company police officers searched the still intoxicated Nieto while he lay in his bed. A revolver was readily found concealed in his clothing.

The trial judge charged the jury to determine if the bunkhouse was Nieto's home or not, since "if that was his place of living, where he slept, then that was his home, and being his home he had a right, I say to you, as a matter of law, to have a pistol, either loaded or empty, with him and in his possession, or concealed on his person." Not surprisingly, the jury found Nieto innocent, and the prosecutor appealed. Unlike many of the other cases we have studied where the defendant was set free by a jury, Nieto was represented when this matter reached the Ohio Supreme Court, and the statute in question was challenged as a violation of the Ohio Constitution's Article I, §4: "The people have the right to bear arms for their defense and security; but standing armies, in the time of peace, are dangerous to liberty, and shall not be kept up; and the military shall be in strict subordination to the civil power."[18]

The majority opinion, written by Justice Avery, pointed to such decisions as *Dunstan* v. *State* (1900),[19] and *Carroll* v. *State* (1872) for support for the position that the state could even prohibit concealed carry in one's own home. With respect to the right to bear arms in general, the Court cited the Ohio Constitution and the Second Amendment, and asserted that the Second Amendment was only a

---

unambiguous statements that fear of "a revolutionary outbreak in Glasgow, Liverpool or London" caused the Minister of Transport to request a Firearms Act for the purpose of disarming the working classes.

16 *State* v. *Nieto*, 101 Ohio St. 409, 412, 130 N.E. 663 (1920).

17 General Code §13693, quoted at *State* v. *Nieto*, 101 Ohio St. 409, 416, 417, 130 N.E. 663 (1920).

18 *State* v. *Nieto*, 101 Ohio St. 409, 410, 411, 413, 130 N.E. 663 (1920).

19 Though they consistently misspelled it as *Dunston*.

restriction on the powers of the federal government, citing *Aymette* v. *State* (1840), *Fife* v. *State* (1876), *English* v. *State* (1872), and *City of Salina* v. *Blaksley* (1905).

But as we have previously seen, these decisions are mutually contradictory, and some contradict the position taken by the Ohio Supreme Court in this case. *Salina* denied any individual right existed under either state or federal constitutions; *English* accepted that both the Second Amendment and the Texas Constitution protected an individual right (at least for military arms) from state laws; *Fife* found the Arkansas Constitutional guarantee to be an individual right.

In addition to the question of whether this was an individual right, *English* and *Fife* both upheld what were effectively prohibitions on the carrying of handguns, either concealed or openly; yet the Ohio Supreme Court sought to use these as precedents for the position that some bearing of arms was Constitutionally protected:

> The statute does not operate as a prohibition against carrying weapons, but as a regulation of the manner of carrying them. The gist of the offense is concealment. The constitution contains no prohibition against the legislature making such police regulations as may be necessary for the welfare of the public at large as to the manner in which arms shall be borne.[20]

In spite of these dramatic contradictions, the Court declared, "We are thoroughly in accord with these decisions."

Next, the Court quoted from *State* v. *Hogan* (1900), in which a previous Ohio Supreme Court had recognized the constitutional right that: "A man may carry a gun for any lawful purpose, for business or amusement..." While no explicit statement was made that open carry was constitutionally protected, the majority opinion's careful distinction between concealed carry and other forms, clearly recognized that open carry was protected under the Ohio Constitution.

It would be tempting to leave this decision now—but the minority opinion of Justice Wanamaker brings up the issue that was alluded to in previous chapters— the issue of race. Justice Wanamaker's opinion is a *tour de force* of logical argument, starting with the basic premise of human rights:

> ORIGIN OF HUMAN RIGHTS. Human rights were born when humanity was born. Both were divine creations. They antedated states, kings, and parliaments. States, constitutions and statutes followed centuries after. The latter were human creations. Their primary and paramount purpose was to conserve those human rights, not to deny or destroy them.[21]

Justice Wanamaker then traced the significance of the preamble of the Declaration of Independence, the American peculiarity of written constitutions as limits to governmental power, and Cooley's writings on "State Constitutions Limitations On Power Rather Than Grants Of Power," finally arriving at the Ohio Constitutions of 1802 and 1851:

> "Section 4. The people have the right to *bear arms* for their defense and security;..."

> This is the language of the plain people of Ohio, put into their own constitution. The people's meaning is self-evident. It will not do to pervert the natural and ordinary meaning of the people's words by substituting therefor a judicial construction that negatives and nullifies these constitutional guarantees. The people clearly understood

---

20 *State* v. *Nieto*, 101 Ohio St. 409, 413, 130 N.E. 663 (1920).
21 *State* v. *Nieto*, 101 Ohio St. 409, 418, 130 N.E. 663 (1920).

these plain provisions. It is incredible that any court should be ignorant of them, or even doubtful concerning them.[22]

Wanamaker also argued that a crime, by the definitions of Ohio law, required an injury to others, and therefore the mere carrying of concealed weapons, without some other criminal purpose, was not properly within the police powers of the state.[23]

In conclusion, Justice Wanamaker pointed out the problems of the existing precedents on the subject:

I desire to give some special attention to some of the authorities cited, supreme court decisions from Alabama, Georgia, Arkansas, Kentucky, and one or two inferior court decisions from New York, which are given in support of the doctrines upheld by this court. The southern states have very largely furnished the precedents. *It is only necessary to observe that the race issue there has extremely intensified a decisive purpose to entirely disarm the negro, and this policy is evident upon reading the opinions.*[24] [emphasis added]

Justice Wanamaker observed that while many decisions were already present on which the majority could base its opinion, "Of course, opinions could be found in support of almost any doctrine if you will look long enough and far enough. Opinions never were wanting to support witchcraft and slavery."

His closing paragraphs sound profoundly current:

I hold that the laws of the state of Ohio should be so applied and so interpreted as to favor the law-abiding rather than the law-violating people. If this decision shall stand as the law of Ohio, a very large percentage of the good people of Ohio to-day are criminals, because they are daily committing criminal acts by having these weapons in their own homes for their own defense. The only safe course for them to pursue, instead of having the weapon concealed on or about their person, or under their pillow at night, is to hang the revolver on the wall and put below it a large placard with these words inscribed:

"The Ohio supreme court having decided that it is a crime to carry a concealed weapon on one's person in one's home, even in one's bed or bunk, this weapon is hung upon the wall that you may see it, and before you commit any burglary or assault, please, Mr. Burglar, hand me my gun."[25]

Less than ten years later, only one of those justices remained on the Ohio Supreme Court, and the opinion of the Court in *Porello* v. *State* (1929) took a much more accepting position with respect to concealed carry. A Rosario Porello had been arrested at 3:00 AM in Cleveland, and a revolver was found in the pocket of his car door. Porello was convicted in Cuyahoga County of carrying concealed weapons, in violation of the same General Code §12819. The Court of Appeals upheld that conviction, and so did the Ohio Supreme Court.

While Justice Allen's decision primarily focused on the technical definition of whether the weapon was in the possession of Porello, even though Porello was not actually seen driving the automobile, the issue of the Ohio Constitution's protections again was raised: "The first of these sections gives the people the right to bear arms for their defense and security. In view of §13693 which makes ample provision for the necessities of genuine self-defense, we see little soundness in this con-

22 *State* v. *Nieto*, 101 Ohio St. 409, 422, 130 N.E. 663 (1920).
23 *State* v. *Nieto*, 101 Ohio St. 409, 422, 423, 424, 426, 130 N.E. 663 (1920).
24 *State* v. *Nieto*, 101 Ohio St. 409, 430, 130 N.E. 663 (1920).
25 *State* v. *Nieto*, 101 Ohio St. 409, 435, 436, 130 N.E. 663 (1920).

tention."[26] Since Porello (who was apparently a bootlegger) had failed to prove that he was engaged in a lawful business at the time, he had been unable to take advantage of §13693. More importantly, the Ohio Supreme Court *appears* to have acknowledged that the right to bear arms might well include the *right* to carry them concealed—but the burden of proof was on the defendant to prove that he was engaged in a lawful action that a jury would consider "prudent."

The first New Jersey decision on the meaning of the right to keep and bear arms appears to have been *State* v. *Angelo* (1925). A Dominick Angelo pleaded guilty of carrying a concealed revolver, and upon sentencing, appealed on the grounds that his right to bear arms was infringed. Since New Jersey's Constitution had no such protection, it would appear that his argument was based on the Second Amendment. Starting what would become a tradition, the Supreme Court of New Jersey appears to have accepted the existence of such a right, denied that the right was absolute, but cited no precedents or authorities for its position:

> The right of a citizen to bear arms is not unrestricted. The state government, in the exercise of its police power, may provide such conditions precedent to the right to carry concealed weapons as the safety and welfare of the people of the state in its judgment require. The statute upon which the indictment was based is a valid exercise of the police power.[27]

There was a recognition that an individual right to bear arms existed, but that the state had the authority to regulate or prohibit the concealed carrying of arms.

In *Pierce* v. *State* (1929), The Oklahoma Court of Criminal Appeals continued down the path established in *Walburn* v. *Territory* (1899) and *Ex parte Thomas* (1908). Three police officers had gone to Fritz Pierce's property with a search warrant to search for a still. When they arrived, Pierce came to the door with a gun in his belt, "about half of the gun being visible." While the officers were searching for a still, Pierce went into his yard, still with the gun in his belt. At no point did Pierce attempt to use the gun, which he asserted he had purchased to protect himself from robbery. The police found no still or any other evidence of criminal behavior—except that Pierce had walked from his front door into the front yard, still on his property—so they arrested him, for carrying a "Colt's automatic revolver."

On appeal, Pierce pointed to article 2, §26 of the Oklahoma Constitution, arguing that there was a right to carry a gun openly in one's own house and yard. The Court of Criminal Appeals rejected this position, pointing to the *Ex parte Thomas* decision, and asserting that only "such arms as are recognized in civilized warfare" were protected by the Oklahoma Constitution—quite definitely a handgun was *not* protected.

But the Court didn't stop there; they went one step beyond, and asserted that under article 2, §26

> the Legislature has power to not only prohibit the carrying of concealed or unconcealed weapons [of the type specified in the deadly weapons statutes] but also has the power to even prohibit the ownership or possession of such arms. Some of the states under similar constitutional provisions have prohibited the ownership, but the Legislature of Oklahoma has not seen fit to go that far. As law now is in this state, a person may lawfully own and possess any of the weapons named... and may move such weapons from room to room in their place of residence, but may not wear them on their person

---

26 *Porello* v. *State*, 121 Ohio St. 280, 168 N.E. 135, 137, 138 (1929).
27 *State* v. *Angelo*, 3 N.J.Misc. 1014, 130 A. 458, 459 (1925).

and transport them about the yard as shown by the evidence to have been done by the defendant in this case.[28]

It's not clear to which state they were referring. New York State, it is true, had established a licensing procedure for purchase of handguns, and in that sense, ownership was regulated, but not prohibited.[29] South Carolina had prohibited the sale of pistols in 1902, but, apparently, not possession of those already owned.[30] Unlike the pretense made in Tennessee and Arkansas, not even military handguns were protected in public, and not even on one's own property. Only the weapons of "civilized warfare" were protected by the Oklahoma Constitution.

When last we visited Tennessee, the Legislature was seeking a way to ban the carrying of deadly weapons, and the Tennessee Supreme Court was attempting to draw a fine line between that which was constitutional, and that which was not. The results were a statute that required large military pistols to be carried in the most dangerous manner possible—openly, in the hand.

After fifty years of quiet from the Tennessee Supreme Court, the Court made two decisions that may be misleading, if not read carefully. In the first decision, *Glasscock* v. *City of Chattanooga* (1928), a Chattanooga city ordinance that banned the carrying of pistols was overturned. W.R. Glasscock, T.F. Brandon, and Dick Edwards, apparently independently of each other, were convicted of violating the ordinance in question. The decision tells us nothing about the manner in which the defendants were carrying pistols, whether openly, or concealed.

The Tennessee Supreme Court pointed to the 1870 Constitution, Article I, §26, recapitulated the *Andrews* v. *State* (1871) decision, and pointed out that the ordinance in question prohibited *all* carrying of pistols:

> There is no qualification of the prohibition against the carrying of a pistol in the city ordinance before us, but is made unlawful "to carry on or about the person any pistol"; that is, any sort of pistol in any sort of manner. Upon the authority of Andrews v. State..., we must accordingly hold the provision of this ordinance as to the carrying of a pistol invalid.[31]

While the Chattanooga ordinance was found unconstitutional, the Tennessee Court here did not expand the constitutional protections of the *Andrews* decision; only one mode of carrying a handgun was protected—openly, in the hand.

In *Burks* v. *State* (1931), the Tennessee Supreme Court made a ruling which has also been misunderstood. Halbrook asserts that a short-barreled shotgun "has been factually determined to fall within a state constitution protecting the right of citizens to 'keep and bear arms for their common defense.'"[32] This author's reading of the decision is considerably more narrow. Sheriff Norman of Fentress County served an arrest warrant on a Dewey Burks; when he took Burks into custody, he found that Burks was carrying a concealed short-barreled shotgun in a holster. While considerably larger than a pistol, it was still only 15 3/4 inches long, and so concealable, at least under overalls or an overcoat. (This is one of the classes of

---

28 *Pierce* v. *State*, 42 Okla. Crim. 272, 275 P. 393, 394, 395 (1929).

29 *People ex rel. Darling* v. *Warden of City Prison*, 139 N.Y.S. 277, 154 App. Div. 413, 422, 423, 29 N.Y.Cr. 74 (1913).

30 Kates, "Toward A History of Handgun Prohibition...", 15.

31 *Glasscock* v. *City of Chattanooga*, 157 Tenn. 518, 11 S.W.2d 678 (1928).

32 Stephen Halbrook, "What The Framers Intended: A Linguistic Analysis Of The Right To 'Bear Arms'", 158.

weapons brought under Federal regulation with the National Firearms Act of 1934). Tennessee law had specifically prohibited the carrying of "any kind of pistol," but failed to define what constituted a "pistol." After citing the decision in *Andrews* v. *State* (1871), the Court held that: "Penal statutes are to be construed strictly, and should be so definite as to give the citizen notice of the prohibited act. To say that one who carries a shotgun can be convicted under a statute prohibiting the carrying of a pistol violates this rule of construction."

The Court's decision in this case was a narrow statement of the deficiency of the statute that prohibited concealed carry—*not* a statement of a constitutional right to carry such weapons. The factual determination made by the Court in this decision was only that a shotgun is *not* a pistol based on a shotgun's lack of rifling, and that a shotgun fires shot, not a single bullet. No issue of constitutional rights appeared in the decision; what the Tennessee Supreme Court held, might explain the confusion: "Under this decision the citizen has a right to carry a shotgun, subject to regulation by the legislature. We are not aware of any such regulatory statute."[33]

In *People* v. *Woodward* (1937), the Idaho Supreme Court heard an appeal involving an insult that turned into a gunfight. George Woodward was convicted of assault with a deadly weapon. Most of this decision is not relevant to our subject; the portion that is of interest was the instructions to the jury:

> You are instructed that the defendant, under the Constitution of Idaho, was entitled to keep and bear firearms for his security and defense. The legislature, however, has the power to regulate the exercise of this right, and this you may consider in connection with the other instructions given you herewith.

The Idaho Supreme Court agreed that the defendant had reason to be concerned that the second sentence had biased the jury against him, and the Court recognized: "The jury might well have thought that this instruction signified that appellant had no right to have the gun in his possession at the time the trouble arose." The Court then pointed to *In Re Brickey* (1902) and held: "Under the Constitution, the right to bear arms may not be denied by the Legislature..." and reasserted the position taken in *Brickey*, that only the carrying of concealed weapons could be prohibited, other carrying of arms was protected and legal, and that the judge's instructions (of which this was simply one example), had prejudiced the jury. Woodward's conviction was reversed, and a new trial ordered.[34]

The next Idaho Supreme Court decision of relevance is *State* v. *Hart* (1945). There is just enough information presented in this case to make one suspect that the defendant, who appears to have been involved with shady elements in the slot machine business, was "set up." Indeed, two of the justices of the Idaho Supreme Court, Justices Ailshie and Holden, suspected as much, since many of the supposedly threatened parties, U.S. Army officers stationed at nearly Gowen Field, were not called as witnesses at trial.

The defendant Hart had apparently received a phone call threatening his life: he should "keep my nose out of the slot machine business or my body would be found out in the brush." Hart at that point made an effort to obtain a concealed weapon permit, first from the Boise police chief, then from the county sheriff; the police chief lacked the authority under Idaho law, and the sheriff was out of town.

---

33 *Burks* v. *State*, 162 Tenn. (9 Smith) 407, 408, 409, 410, 411 (1931).
34 *State* v. *Woodward*, 58 Ida. 385, 74 P.2d 92, 93, 94, 95, 97 (1937).

Later that evening, Boise police officers went to a reported disturbance at "the Gremlin's Roost, a so-called club in the Boise Hotel," and on arrival in the hotel lobby, they were informed by several people, including the previously mentioned U.S. Army officers, two uniformed policemen, and several civilians that Hart had threatened them with a blackjack or billy club. At this point, Hart walked out of the club, apparently unaware of his impending arrest. Hart was arrested without incident, and while being searched, a .25 Colt pistol was found in his vest pocket.

Hart argued that the ordinance prohibiting the carrying of concealed deadly weapons was unconstitutional, though it is unclear from the decision on what provision Hart based this argument. The majority opinion pointed to *In re Brickey* (1902), where the Court had insisted that either open carry or concealed carry had to be legal, to avoid running afoul of the Second Amendment and the Idaho Constitution, and *State* v. *Woodward* (1937), where the right to *open* carry had been acknowledged, but concealed carry had not, and upheld the conviction.

The dissenting opinion in this case, written by Justice Ailshie (who had also authored the *Woodward* decision), and concurred in by Justice Holden, was not even prepared to admit that *concealed* carry was not protected by the Idaho Constitution. To Justices Ailshie and Holden, the Boise ordinance against concealed carry of deadly weapons "is in excess of the authority of the city of Boise and violates the constitution, Art. I, sec. 11, and also run counter to the provisions of sec. 17-3102, I.C.A."

Justice Ailshie pointed out that Hart had attempted to obtain a permit, and his life had been threatened:

> It would be utter folly to talk about requiring a man to get a permit to carry a gun concealed to defend himself, when he is suddenly attacked by a ruffian with threats to take his life. What he needs is the right to act then and, unless he has a gun or other weapon with which to offer equal persuasive peril, his right of self-defense would vanish and so would he.[35]

The Court divided into two camps; one that argued that *open* carry was constitutionally protected, and another that argued that even *concealed* carry was constitutionally protected.

In *Watson* v. *Stone* (1941), as we have already discussed on page 155, the Florida Supreme Court found that a handgun carried in the glove compartment of an automobile was not carried upon the person, within the meaning of the Florida statute that prohibited carrying of a handgun without a permit. The defendant, Mose Watson, sought to overturn his conviction based on §20 of the Florida Constitution's Declaration of Rights. The Florida Supreme Court, using the *State ex rel. Russo* v. *Parker* (1909) and *Carlton* v. *State* (1912) precedents, found that the "Legislature has the constitutional power to enact laws regulating the carrying of weapons."

Yet, while acknowledging that the law was constitutional, the Florida Supreme Court held that the statute, by prohibiting the carrying of a weapon "on" or "about the person," did not prohibit the carrying of a weapon "under the seat, cushion, door, side floor, or pocket of the automobile." Justice Chapman, writing for the Court, also recognized that the practice was widespread and blameless:

---

35 *State* v. *Hart*, 66 Ida. 217, 157 P.2d 72, 73, 74, 75, 76 (1945).

The business men, tourists, commercial travelers, professional man on night calls, un-protected women and children in cars on the highways day and night, State and County officials, and all law-abiding citizens fully appreciate the sense of security afforded by the knowledge of the existence of a pistol in the pocket of an automobile in which they are traveling. It cannot be said that it is placed in the car or automobile for unlawful purposes, but on the other hand it was placed therein exclusively for defensive or protective purposes.[36]

Justices Terrell and Thomas came to a dissenting opinion, most of which is an at-tempt to justify that a pistol concealed in a glove compartment was a violation of the statute, and is uninteresting from the standpoint of constitutionality. However, Justice Terrell asserted that the majority opinion was "predicated on the interpreta-tion of [the statute] in the light of Section Twenty, Declaration of Rights, Consti-tution of Florida, and the Second Amendment to the Federal Constitution." Ter-rell then argued that the Second Amendment was only a restriction on Congress' authority, using the *U.S.* v. *Cruikshank* (1876), *Presser* v. *Illinois* (1886), and *Miller* v. *Texas* (1894) decisions of the U.S. Supreme Court.[37] But the majority opinion at no point mentioned the Second Amendment—only the Florida Constitution's provision. It appears that Terrell recognized the Second Amendment, while not applicable to a state law, was a protection of an individual right from laws passed by Congress.

In *Moore* v. *Gallup* (1943), a LeRoy Moore, Sr., appealed the decision of county judge Earl Gallup, who had turned Moore down for renewal of a pistol permit in Albany County, New York. It was agreed that Moore was "a person of good moral character" with no criminal history, previously licensed to possess pistols; "experienced and skillful in the use of pistols", and desired a permit for target shooting.

While Moore had earlier argued that the Second Amendment protected his right to keep and bear arms:

petitioner's brief on this appeal relies not upon those provisions but upon section 4 of the [New York] Civil Rights Law which, except for the substitution of "cannot" for "shall not", is *in ipisissimis verbis* as those of the Second Amendment. Accordingly, authoritative Federal decisions construing the Second Amendment may properly be applied to the State statute in the interest of homogeneity of interpretation.[38]

However, the appellate court pointed to the existing *U.S.* v. *Cruikshank* (1876) and *Presser* v. *Illinois* (1886) precedents to establish that the Second Amendment was a limitation on the national government only, not the state governments. The court then used the "collective militia" argument, with appropriate citations from Cooley's *Constitutional Law* and *State* v. *Workman* (1891) to bolster the argument that "swords, guns, rifles and muskets" were protected, "arms to be used in defend-ing the State and civil liberty—but not pistols and other such weapons as are ha-bitually carried by those who, in the vernacular of today, are termed gangsters." While citing and accepting the authority of *Nunn* v. *State* (1846), *Aymette* v. *State* (1840), *State* v. *Buzzard* (1842), *Andrews* v. *State* (1871), *State* v. *Shelby* (1886),

36 *Watson* v. *Stone*, 4 So.2d 700, 701, 702, 703 (Fla. 1941).
37 *Watson* v. *Stone*, 4 So.2d 700, 703 (Fla. 1941).
38 *Moore* v. *Gallup*, N.Y.S.2d 63, 267 App. Div. 64, 66, 67, 294 N.Y. 699 (1943). This is also the first case in which the court record shows the National Rifle Association playing a part; the NRA filed a *amicus curiae*, apparently on behalf of Mr. Moore.

and *State* v. *Keet* (1916) that concealed carry of arms was not constitutionally protected,[39] those same decisions that recognized the right to carry arms openly, and therefore to possess them, had no apparent influence on the court.

A minority opinion, written by Judge Hill, was much more in line with the historical development of the Second Amendment. While still seeing the issue in question as military defense, not individual protection, Judge Hill wrote:

> *The several statutes which are known as the Sullivan Law, were enacted in an effort to prevent, or make more difficult, the obtaining of weapons by the criminal classes or by those who might use them in connection with crime. If the statute is extended beyond that scope and field, it is unconstitutional and infringes the right of the people to keep and bear arms.* The need of the citizens to become proficient in the use of firearms is now brought strikingly to our attention. Six hundred thousand of our citizens in cities have sat in shelters at the top of tall buildings and in the country on lonely hillsides every hour, day and night, for more than eighteen months. Unless the home defense authorities were foolishly and unnecessarily panic-stricken there was some danger, no matter how slight, that a foreign foe would land or disloyal residents would take to the air in a hostile way. Under those circumstances, a man of the type of this petitioner who could shoot with accuracy, would be a more useful citizen than one who, if attacked, could only throw a bootjack at his assailant.[40] [emphasis added]

The next New York decision is one of those fascinating reminders of how far our society has come in tolerating, and even extending its full privileges to those who would advocate its overthrow. John F. Cassidy sought admission to the New York Bar, and was turned down, because of a history of fascist political agitation. In addition, Cassidy had been tried and found innocent of criminal charges of "conspiracy to overthrow the Government of the United States"; the evidence brought forth at his trial was used to prevent his admittance to the Bar.

In *Application of Cassidy* (1944), New York's appellate court ruled that his agitation and promotion of racist and fascist doctrines meant that he was unfit to be an attorney in New York State, and that there were limits to free speech; this right "is lost when it is abused by urging the use of illegal and unconstitutional methods." Cassidy's call for armed revolution was, in the opinion of the Court, such an abuse of free speech. It is within this context that the Court's opinion about the meaning of the Second Amendment must be evaluated. The Court held: "That amendment, however, does not grant a license to carry arms. "The right to keep and bear arms is not a right conferred upon the people by the federal constitution." The Court then cited *U.S.* v. *Cruikshank* (1876), and *People Ex Rel. Darling* v. *Warden of City Prison* (1913). In spite of the clear-cut language of the *Cruikshank* decision that this right was not "conferred" by the Constitution, because it pre-existed the Constitution, the Court, by quoting it out of context, gave the impression that the Second Amendment was not an individual right. This decision can hardly be seen as a carefully reasoned response to a law-abiding person, arguing for a right to bear arms in self-defense, but an attempt to dispose of a gadfly who narrowly escaped conviction on a charge of conspiracy to overthrow the government.[41]

---

39 *Moore* v. *Gallup*, N.Y.S.2d 63, 267 App. Div. 64, 68, 294 N.Y. 699 (1943).

40 *Moore* v. *Gallup*, N.Y.S.2d 63, 267 App. Div. 64, 71, 294 N.Y. 699 (1943).

41 *Application of Cassidy*, 51 N.Y.S.2d. 202, 268 App. Div. 282, 283, 284, 285, 286 (1944). Whether Cassidy was actually a fascist, or simply a hotheaded and ignorant anti-Communist, seems less than clear from the quotes in the majority and minority opinions.

In *State* v. *Plassard* (1946), the defendant Frank Plassard was convicted of "feloniously exhibiting a weapon" in Newton County, Missouri. Plassard was an occupant of a farm, over which some disputes within his family had clouded his legal possession of the property. In an ensuing argument about who was to plow part of the land, Plassard fired one shot from a .22 rifle, though in a direction clearly intended as a warning, not as an attempt at injury. A number of issues were decided by the Missouri Supreme Court; the one relevant to our interests is: "If he was defending his home and property he had a constitutional right to bear arms. Art. II, Sec. 17, Constitution 1875."[42] While the Missouri Court phrased this, "a constitutional right to bear arms," the arms were borne entirely on private property—but that right was clearly recognized by the Court.

In *People* v. *Liss* (1950), a Walter Liss had been convicted in Chicago of carrying a pistol "concealed on or about his person." The Illinois Supreme Court's decision, written, appropriately, by Justice Gunn, reversed the lower court judgments based on a variety of issues, including the location of the gun within the car, that the car Liss was driving was not his own, and that Liss' claim that he was unaware of the gun's presence had not been adequately regarded by the trial court. Of most interest to us, however, is the Illinois Supreme Court's assertion about the Second Amendment, and for what purpose the statute against concealed carry was intended:

> The second amendment to the constitution of the United States provides the right of the people to keep and bear arms shall not be infringed. This, of course, does not prevent the enactment of a law against carrying concealed weapons, but it does indicate it should be kept in mind, in the construction of a statute of such character, that it is aimed at persons of criminal instincts, and for the prevention of crime, and not against use in the protection of person or property. There is not an iota of evidence that the defendant was a criminal, or had associated with criminals, or that he came within any of the specific provisions against carrying a deadly weapon.[43]

Like the decision of the Pennsylvania Supreme Court in *Wright* v. *Commonwealth* (1875), this was a statement that, in some way not articulated by Justice Gunn, a concealed weapon statute that did not factor in the issue of criminal intent would be in some way violative of the Second Amendment—and that a state law should be considered subject to the limitations of the Second Amendment.

In *State* v. *Nickerson* (1952), a Clarence Nickerson was charged and convicted of assault after drawing a loaded revolver on one Fred Hochalter, who apparently had a law enforcement position with a nearby Indian reservation. The circumstances under which this took place—Hochalter knocked on the door, and Nickerson bade him enter, while training a handgun on the doorway—would certainly be considered assault under normal circumstances. In this particular case, the remote location, and Nickerson's reasonable concern that a criminal with whom he had experienced a number of confrontations was returning to do him injury, persuaded the Montana Supreme Court that Nickerson's actions were not criminal.[44] In justifying Nickerson's actions:

---

42 *State* v. *Plassard*, 355 Mo. 90, 195 S.W.2d 495, 496, 497 (1946).
43 *People* v. *Liss*, 406 Ill. 419, 94 N.E.2d 320, 322, 323 (1950).
44 *State* v. *Nickerson*, 126 Mont. 157, 158, 160, 168 (1952).

The law of this jurisdiction accords to the defendant the right to keep and bear arms and to use same in defense of his own home, his person and property.

The second amendment to the Constitution of the United States provides that "the right of the people to keep and bear arms, shall not be infringed."

The Constitution of Montana provides: "The right of every person to keep or bear arms in defense of his own home, person and property, ... shall not be called in question, but nothing herein contained shall be held to permit the carrying of concealed weapons." Art. II, sec. 13, Const. of Montana.[45]

In conjunction with their citation of the provisions of the Montana Constitution, including "but nothing herein contained shall be held to permit the carrying of concealed weapons," it is unambiguous that the Montana Supreme Court was recognizing the right to openly carry outside of private property, for self-defense— and also that the Court recognized this right was protected by both the state and federal constitutional guarantees.

The strong nativist movement that played a part in the KKK's resurgence in the 1920s appears to have also played a part in the passage of laws prohibiting resident aliens from possession of firearms. Our first such case during this period, *People* v. *Zerillo* (1922), considered this same issue as *Patsone* v. *Pennsylvania* (1914): was a "right of the people" limited to citizens or not? But where the *Patsone* decision had found that this right could be limited to citizens, *Zerillo* came to very different conclusions. A 1921 Michigan ordinance required a permit for non-citizens to possess a firearm—ostensibly to protect wildlife. That the law in question had another purpose—and that no halo was visible above the defendant's head—may be surmised from the description of the circumstances under which the defendant, "James Zerillo, alias Joseph Zerillo," was arrested:

It was made to appear in evidence that, about 5 o'clock in the morning of the 25th day of September, 1921, at the corner of Chase and Russell streets in the city of Detroit, defendant was seated at the wheel of a Marmon touring car, with four or five men in the car with shotguns. Defendant had no shotgun, but in the pocket of the door of the automobile was found a .38-caliber revolver, and this is the firearm the possession of which led to his conviction.

The complaint was laid under the game law, but did not charge the defendant with hunting for or capturing or killing any wild bird or animal, or intending to do so. Does the game law make it unlawful for an unnaturalized foreign-born resident of the state to possess a revolver? The act mentioned makes it a misdemeanor for an unnaturalized foreign-born resident to hunt for or capture or kill any wild bird or animals, either game or otherwise, of any description, excepting in defense of his person or property, "and to that end," such a person shall not own or be possessed of a shotgun or rifle of any make or a pistol or firearms of any kind. The act provides that, on the recommendation of two citizens, the sheriff of the county, upon a showing of necessity, may issue a permit to an unnaturalized, foreign-born resident to possess firearms.[46]

Zerillo claimed that his rights under the Michigan Constitution were violated: "Every person has a right to bear arms for the defense of himself and the state." In explicating the meaning of this provision, the Michigan Supreme Court cited the more detailed and expansive provision in the Colorado Constitution:

45 *State* v. *Nickerson*, 126 Mont. 157, 166 (1952).
46 *People* v. *Zerillo*, 219 Mich. 635, 189 N.W. 927, 928 (1922).

"That the right of no person to keep and bear arms in defense of his home, person, and property, or in aid of the civil power when there to lawfully summoned, shall be called in question; but nothing herein contained shall be construed to justify the practice of carrying concealed weapons." Article 2, §13.

There should be added to this, however, the right of the Legislature, under the police power, to regulate the carrying of firearms....

Firearms serve the people of this country a useful purpose wholly aside from hunting, and under a constitution like ours, granting to aliens who are bona fide residents of the state the same rights in respect to the possession, enjoyment, and inheritance of property as native-born citizens, and to *every person* the right to bear arms for the defense of himself and the state, while the Legislature has power in the most comprehensive manner to regulate the carrying and use of firearms, that body has no power to constitute it a crime for a person, alien or citizen, to possess a revolver for the legitimate defense of himself and his property. The provision in the Constitution granting the right to all persons to bear arms is a limitation upon the power of the Legislature to enact any law to the contrary.

The exercise of a right guaranteed by the Constitution cannot be made subject to the will of the sheriff. The part of the act under which the prosecution was planted is not one of regulation, but is one of prohibition and confiscation. It is not regulation to make it a crime for an unnaturalized foreign-born resident of the state to possess a revolver, unless permitted to have one by the sheriff of the county where he resides.[47]

In spite of the apparently shady nature of Zerillo, the conviction was set aside, and the defendant released.

The California Supreme Court came to a different conclusion in the case *In re Rameriz* (1924). A Gevino Rameriz was "charged, tried, and convicted in Kings County," California, and was sentenced to one to five years in prison for carrying "a certain automatic revolver some four inches in length of twenty-five caliber and loaded with powder and ball, the petitioner then and there being an unnaturalized foreign-born person."[48] On appeal, Rameriz's attorney argued that the statute that prohibited non-citizens from possessing concealable firearms was a violation of the Fourteenth and Second Amendments.[49] Most of the resulting decision centered on whether the state had the authority to discriminate against non-citizen residents of the state.

The part of interest to us is the Second Amendment, and citing *U.S.* v. *Cruikshank* (1876) and *Miller* v. *Texas* (1894), the California Supreme Court held: "It will suffice to state this point is without merit, since this amendment offers no protection against the exercise of power by the state governments but applies only to the exercise of power by the federal government," and then quoted from the *Cruikshank* decision. The Court also claimed that the "first ten articles of amendment were not intended to limit the powers of the state governments"—an assertion that could be made in 1924, but not today. The Court continued: "If there is an inhibition upon the legislature it must be found in the state constitution,

---

47 *People* v. *Zerillo*, 219 Mich. 635, 189 N.W. 927, 928 (1922).

48 *In re Rameriz*, 193 Cal. 633, 226 P. 914 (1924). There is not now, nor has there ever been, such a handgun. The Webley-Fosbery is the only known example of an "automatic revolver," a curious hybrid at the turn of the century, never produced in large numbers. See Blair, 375-7. The term "automatic revolver," however, was sometimes used at the turn of the century to refer to double-action revolvers. In this case, the weapon appears to be a Colt .25 ACP semiautomatic pistol, or one of the many very similar models produced by other manufacturers.

49 *In re Rameriz*, 193 Cal. 633, 636, 226 P. 914 (1924).

and not in the second amendment of the federal constitution. The constitution of this state contains no provision on the subject."

But even though there was no such provision in the California Constitution, the Court decided to pursue that line of reasoning:

> An examination of the numerous authorities in various states will show that the right to keep and bear arms as guaranteed by a state constitutional provision similar to the federal amendment refers only to the bearing of arms by the citizens in defense of a common cause, and not to their use in private broils and affrays.[50]

The Court then cited those cases which held to this limited view, and cited none of the cases which recognized this as an individual right of self-defense.

But curiously, after asserting that such a right was strictly for the purposes of common defense: "It may be remarked that an absolute prohibition of such right might be held to infringe a fundamental right." The Court then cited *Nunn* v. *State* (1846), and quoted the Georgia Supreme Court's remarks about self-defense.

The California Supreme Court's decision closed the subject of the nature of this right with the statement:

> It appears that although state constitutions declare that every citizen has the right to bear arms, in defense of himself and the state, and do not expressly or by implication deny to the legislature the right to enact laws in regard to the manner in which arms shall be borne, such regulation may be prescribed, and the absence of such a guarantee to the state constitution leaves the legislature entirely free to deal with the subject of bearing arms.[51]

While the Court did not deny that the Second Amendment protected an individual right, it was only protection from the Federal Government—not the actions of the state.

A 1919 Colorado statute prohibited resident aliens from hunting "any wild bird or animal, either game or otherwise," and for that purpose, prohibited resident aliens from owning any firearms. In *People* v. *Nakamura* (1936), Charles Nakamura, was charged with a violation of the statute. On the first count of "unlawful possession of three pheasants," he pleaded guilty; on the second count, unlawful possession of a firearm, he pointed to article 2, §13 and §27 of the Colorado Constitution. While §27, guaranteeing the right of aliens to property on equal terms with citizens, is not of interest to us, §13 is: "That the right of no person to keep and bear arms in defense of his home, person and property, or in aid of the civil power when thereto legally summoned, shall be called in question; but nothing herein contained shall be construed to justify the practice of carrying concealed weapons." The trial court quashed the second count of the indictment, based on §13 and §27; the prosecutor appealed.

The Colorado Supreme Court refused to accept the state's argument that the right in question was for common defense:

> The people contend that the "right" referred to in section 13 of the Constitution is not a personal right, but one of collective enjoyment for common defense, and that the act in question is a proper exercise of the police power.

50 *In re Rameriz*, 193 Cal. 633, 651, 652, 226 P. 914 (1924).
51 *In re Rameriz*, 193 Cal. 633, 652, 226 P. 914 (1924).

It is apparent that the statute above quoted was designed to prevent possession of fire-arms by aliens, as much, if not more, than the protection of wild game within the state.[52]

The Court did not cite Blackstone's remarks about the purpose of the English game laws, but the parallels to Blackstone's similar remarks are quite strong.

The Court now drew a line that recognized that "right of the people" included non-citizens:

> It is equally clear that the act wholly disarms aliens for all purposes. The state may pre-serve its wild game for its citizens, may prevent the hunting and killing of same by aliens, and for that purpose may enact appropriate laws, but in so doing, it cannot disarm any class of persons or deprive them of the right guaranteed under section 13, article 2 of the Constitution, to bear arms in defense of home, person, and property. The guaranty thus extended is meaningless if any person is denied the right to possess arms for such protection.   Under this constitutional guaranty, there is no distinction between unnaturalized foreign-born residents and citizens.[53]

One of the side effects of the rising crimes rates of the 1920s was an increasing willingness of the courts to split hairs concerning the arms that were *not* protected by the state constitutions. In *People* v. *Brown* (1931), a Bernard Brown was ar-rested and convicted of being in possession of a blackjack in an automobile; since this was his fourth felony conviction, Brown was given a life sentence. Not surpris-ingly, he appealed his conviction, arguing that possession of a blackjack was pro-tected under the Michigan Constitution's "right to bear arms for the defense of himself and the state" provision, so successfully used in *People* v. *Zerillo* (1922).

The Michigan Supreme Court, after acknowledging the historical setting of con-cerns about standing armies, also admitted, "Probably the necessity of self-protec-tion in a frontier society was also a factor." The *City of Salina* v. *Blaksley* (1905) decision was mentioned, and while acknowledging that significant differences ex-isted as to whether only members of state militias were protected by such a right, or all citizens, the Court held that, "the state, nevertheless, has the police power to rea-sonably regulate it."

The Court also described the militia of the state as "practically extinct," having

> been superseded by the National Guard and reserve organization. If called to service, the arms are furnished by the state... In times of peace, the militia, as such, is unarmed and the historical test would render the constitutional provision lifeless.[54]

While acknowledging the precedent set by the *Zerillo* case:

> Some arms, although they have a valid use for the protection of the state by organized and instructed soldiery in times of war or riot, are too dangerous to be kept in a settled community by individuals, and, in times of peace, find their use by bands of criminals and have legitimate employment only by guards and police. Some weapons are adapted and recognized by the common opinion of good citizens as proper for private defense of person and property. Others are the peculiar tools of the criminal. The police power of the state to preserve public safety and peace and to regulate the bearing of arms cannot fairly be restricted to the mere establishment of conditions under which all sorts of weapons may be privately possessed, but it may take account of the character and ordi-nary use of weapons and interdict those whose customary employment by individuals is to violate the law. The power is, of course, subject to the limitation that its exercise be reasonable, and it cannot constitutionally result in the prohibition of the possession of

---

52 *People* v. *Nakamura*, 99 Colo. 262, 62 P.2d 246, 247 (1936).
53 *People* v. *Nakamura*, 99 Colo. 262, 62 P.2d 246, 247 (1936).
54 *People* v. *Brown*, 253 Mich. 537, 235 N.W. 245, 246, 247 (1931).

those arms which, by the common opinion and usage of law-abiding people, are proper and legitimate to be kept upon private premises for the protection of person and property...

The list of weapons in section 16751, supra, is significant and demonstrates a definite intention of the Legislature to protect society from a recognized menace. *It does not include ordinary guns, swords, revolvers, or other weapons usually relied upon by good citizens for defense or pleasure.* It is a partial inventory of the arsenal of the "public enemy," the "gangster."[55] [emphasis added]

At first glance, this would seem a clear statement that possession of rifles, shotguns, handguns, and swords were protected by the Michigan Constitution—and it would a reasonable extrapolation to the Second Amendment as well. The danger lies in the phrase, "by the common opinion and usage of law-abiding people." No clear-cut rule is provided for determining what constitutes "common opinion and usage." Is an automatic weapon outside "common opinion and usage"? What happens as society becomes more urbanized, and handguns take precedence over long arms for defense? Might rifles and shotguns become outside "common opinion and usage"? If a particular class of weapon, which is admirably suited to the "military use" tests used in such late nineteenth century decisions as *Fife* v. *State* (1876) and *State* v. *Workman* (1891), is especially competent for criminal uses, and therefore becomes commonly used by criminals, are all non-criminal owners automatically outside "common opinion and usage"?

People v. *Brown* (1931) is one of those hard cases making bad case law. The defendant belonged behind bars—but within the law the Legislature had written, the only choices were to overturn the law, and release a "habitual offender,"[56] or uphold a law that was a general prohibition (applying to everyone, not just criminals) on possession of a particular type of weapon.

Similarly, the California Court of Appeals, in *People* v. *Ferguson* (1932), upheld a prohibition on possession of metal knuckles:

Firearms have their legitimate uses; hence the law regulates their use and prescribes who shall be prohibited their possession. But there is impressed upon slung-shots, sandbags, blackjacks and metal knuckles the indubitable *indicia* of criminal purpose. To every person of ordinary intelligence these instruments are known to be the tools of the brawl fighter and cowardly assassin and of no beneficial use whatever to a good citizen or to society. The legislature may take note of and act upon such common facts... It can regulate and proscribe the use of a thing so that its beneficial use may be enjoyed and its detrimental use prohibited. It follows that if the beneficial use of a thing is entirely lacking or grossly proportionate to its harmful use the police power may absolutely prohibit its possession.[57]

At first glance, this "social utility" test would seem perfectly reasonable—but the measure of "legitimate" and "illegitimate" is necessarily a value judgment by the court, and one that is fraught with potential for being swayed by the emotions of the moment. It is significant that the same argument, "of no beneficial use whatever," is today argued for prohibition of handguns, a position that the California Court of Appeals appears to have rejected with its acknowledgement that, "Firearms have their legitimate uses..."

55 *People* v. *Brown*, 253 Mich. 537, 235 N.W. 245, 246, 247 (1931).
56 *People* v. *Brown*, 253 Mich. 537, 235 N.W. 245 (1931).
57 *People* v. *Ferguson*, 129 Cal.App. 300, 304 (1933).

At the beginning of the 1920s, a technological change burst on the scene, destined to change public perceptions of the right to keep and bear long guns: the submachine gun. Unlike the nineteenth century arguments about whether handguns qualified as "arms of the soldier," there could be no serious question about the submachine gun's military function. The Thompson submachine gun had been developed by Brig. Gen. John T. Thompson, principally with World War I in mind, but the war was over before the Thompson was ready. In spite of its military intent, most of the militaries of the world were unable to see a hand-carried, nine pound automatic weapon with a range of several hundred yards as a useful combat weapon:

> To peddle the new gun in peacetime, it was necessary to think up something else it might be good for. With more enthusiasm than perspective, Auto-Ordnance decided that the submachine gun was, in fact, good for anything. Especially anything hard to hit, or that needed to be killed in quantity, or thoroughly intimidated. At practically any range, Auto-Ordnance claims could have been boiled down to a single slogan: Anything a gun can do, the Thompson can do better.[58]

Auto-Ordnance aggressively marketed the "Tommy Gun" to police departments throughout the world, but in the U.S. in particular, for the dramatic expansion of the road system in the U.S. meant that armed robbers could knock over a bank, and be "quickly out of town, or even out of state." Before the development of two-way radios, it was effectively impossible for a local police department to catch such criminals. Perhaps reflective of the lessened concern in those days for civil liberties and lawsuits from innocent bystanders, police officers would attempt to end such chases by firing from moving police cars with handguns—an exercise nearly as futile as it was dangerous.

Auto-Ordnance decided that a submachine gun was the perfect solution to armed robbers on the run, and in a spectacular 1922 demonstration conducted in Tenafly, New Jersey, used a motorcycle sidecar mounted submachine gun to riddle, incapacitate, and explode a "getaway" car. Reporters invited were "enormously impressed that the antibandit gun would now permit police not only to shoot fleeing criminals but also burn them to a crisp." Similarly, concerns about riot control, labor strife, and the example of the Russian Revolution made police and private security organizations likely prospects for sales of the Thompson. The intimidating capabilities of the weapon were felt by many reviewers to be sufficient to deter all but the most foolish of criminals.

Auto-Ordnance also advertised the virtues of the Thompson for home defense— one especially memorable ad which appeared in 1920-21, titled, "The Thompson Submachine Gun, The Most Effective Portable Fire Arm In Existence," showed a cowboy standing on a ranch house porch, blasting away at what are presumed to be bandits.[59] Since handgun purchase required a license in New York City, but submachine guns did not, a civilian market rapidly developed by default.

---

58 William J. Helmer, *The Gun That Made The Twenties Roar,* (Toronto: The Macmillan Co., 1969), 75.

59 Helmer, 72-76, plate after 86. There is a widely held belief in some circles that the Thompson full auto was sold through the Sears, Roebuck & Co. catalog at one time. In light of the sales restrictions in effect from the very beginning, it seems more likely that this infamous ad, done in a style that might fit into a 1920s Sears catalog, is the source of this recurring rumor.

While no government regulation was then in effect, Auto-Ordnance did make some attempts at restricting the ownership of these weapons. The early catalogs contained the statement: "Thompson Guns are for use by those on the side of law and order and the Auto-Ordnance Corporation agents and dealers are authorized to make sales to responsible parties only." Not surprisingly, submachine guns soon began to appear in criminal hands. Rumrunners were using Thompsons for self-defense by 1924, and starting in 1925, they became a glamorous weapon for gang warfare in Chicago, New York, and a few other metropolitan centers. While some Thompsons were clearly and unquestionably purchased through legal channels, there is evidence that Auto-Ordnance's efforts at restricting the weapons to "responsible parties" may have been somewhat effective: retail prices ranged from $175 to $227 in 1928, while alarmist articles about the Thompson indicated that gangsters paid from $1000 to $2000 each. Many gangsters simply stole Thompsons and Browning Automatic Rifles from National Guard armories and police stations. The widespread corruption of police departments and individual police officers also meant that Thompsons sold through official channels were rapidly diverted to gangsters.[60]

Prohibition also led to a dramatic increase in violent crime as gangsters fought over sales territories; murder rates had risen from 6 per 100,000 people to 10 per 100,000 people in the period 1919 to 1933,[61] declining rapidly with the end of Prohibition. Attitudes towards the turf wars changed dramatically near the end of the Roaring Twenties, largely because of the St. Valentine's Day Massacre, committed with this awesome new weapon, the submachine gun: "But the St. Valentine's Day Massacre—seven men lined up and shot in the back—violated all the rules of fair play and sportsmanship, and civic reformers at last found more than token support." Not surprisingly, many spectacular gangland shootings reported in the press became a "Tommy gun," regardless of the weapon actually used, fueling popular support for restrictions on the Thompson.[62]

Movies made between 1927 and 1935 often glorified gangster violence, with the Thompson an essential prop for such films; John Ellis, social historian of the machine gun tells us: "The excessively cinematic exploits of the mid-West bandits forced certain public figures and Hollywood moguls to ponder on the social effects of their films."[63] In response to criticisms that Hollywood glamorized gangsters, the film industry adopted the Breen Code, which sought to demonstrate, "that crime does not pay."[64]

---

60 Helmer, 78-91, 95-98, 123-4, 270. One of the early, well-publicized drive-by shootings with the Thompson killed a bootlegger, a minor politician, and William McSwiggin, Assistant State's Attorney for Illinois. What the three men were doing together—fascinating speculations are possible—has never been explained. Presumably, today's politicians have learned the importance of not meeting with drug dealers in free fire zones.

61 Bureau of Justice Statistics, 15.

62 Helmer, 91-92, 100-1. A similar phenomenon was noticed by the author after Patrick Purdy's 1989 Stockton schoolyard murders; many shootings were initially reported as committed with "assault weapons," then corrected later.

63 John Ellis, *The Social History of the Machine Gun*, (New York: Pantheon Books, 1975), 160-2. Ellis' work explores the social and political consequences of the development of the machine gun, with an emphasis on how it made both the European colonization of Africa possible, and the dramatic impact it had on the collapse of the old order during World War I.

64 Walker, 182-3.

State and local authorities had utterly failed in controlling the now highly mobile armed robbers, and "states rights" attitudes against federal involvement in local law enforcement had made it politically impossible to pass national anti-crime legislation until Franklin Roosevelt was elected in 1932. Roosevelt's Attorney General, Homer S. Cummings, took advantage of two widely publicized kidnappings and the Kansas City Massacre (the killing of three policemen and a federal agent by Pretty Boy Floyd) to declare a "war on crime."

How much more armed robbery was there? Helmer argues that "if any tidal wave occurred, it was probably in crime statistics, which the Justice Department began compiling on a national basis for the first time in 1930." Helmer also argues that many of the desperadoes of this time were neither as successful or bloodthirsty as they were portrayed, but instead were part of FBI Director J. Edgar Hoover and Attorney General Cummings' campaign for the creation of a truly effective national police force. Since the legal channels for Thompsons had by now significantly tightened up, such famous "Tommy Gun" criminals as John Dillingers obtained their weapons by raiding police stations.[65]

While support for restrictions on automatic weapons seems to have been largely motivated by concerns about public safety (perhaps artificially heightened by sensationalistic, inaccurate news reports and movie portrayals of the criminal use of automatic weapons), there is reason to wonder if other, baser motives may have been involved. The Auto-Ordnance Co. opposed a New York State bill banning machine guns in 1928 claiming that the proposed law was, "motivated by commercial favoritism for the manufacturers of such arms as sawed-off shotguns."[66] Sawed-off shotguns, of course, would have been the logical alternative weapon for bank guards and other legitimate users of submachine guns. When the second generation of submachine guns, largely manufactured in Europe, begin to appear in the summer of 1933, the president of Federal Laboratories (by then Auto-Ordnance's exclusive sales agent), suggested to the Attorney General "that an embargo be placed by the President on the importation of all submachine guns in the U.S., pointing out that this action would be necessary if they hoped to make any progress in their drive against crime."[67] Since Auto-Ordnance's sales had been voluntarily restricted to police agencies and industrial security firms by this point,[68] restrictions on private sales of submachine guns would have been entirely an advantage for Auto-Ordnance.

In response to a murder problem that had already peaked, although they didn't know it, Congress passed the National Firearms Act of 1934, requiring a license to transfer or transport interstate short-barreled rifles & shotguns, machine guns, or silencers. The license procedure involved a $200 transfer tax, and appropriate tax stamp.[69] The original request of Attorney General Cummings was for this procedure to apply to all concealable firearms, including handguns, silencers, and "any weapon designed to shoot automatically, or semiautomatically, 12 or more shots

---

65 Helmer, 103, 107-110, 114. Walker, 183-4, comes to much the same conclusion about the supposed increase in crime rates.

66 *New York Times*, January 26, 1928, quoted in Helmer, 144.

67 U.S. Senate, Special Committee to Investigate the Munitions Industry, *Hearings*, Pursuant to S.R. 206 (73-74th Cong., 1934-43), Pt. 7, 1903-1904, quoted in Helmer, 156.

68 Helmer, 152.

69 *U.S. v. Miller*, 307 U.S. 174, 175 (1939).

without reloading." The concerns expressed during Congressional hearings show that it was *concealable* automatic weapons, such as the Auto-Ordnance, at which the law was primarily aimed. Because of concerns expressed by some Congressmen that including handguns under this regulatory scheme would become burdensome to law-abiding people, and "cause an awful revolt all over the United States amongst private citizens," handguns were removed from the law.[70]

Why such a complicated procedure, instead of a direct ban on private ownership of machine guns? In hearings before the House Ways & Means Committee in 1934, Representative Harold Knutson inquired why the government should "permit the sale of the machine guns to any one outside of the several branches of the Government..." Representative Sumners suggested that the authority of the Federal Government only extended to collecting of revenue, and therefore it must be "possible at least in theory for these things to move in order to get internal revenue?" and Attorney General Cummings confirmed the reasoning.[71]

Cummings and Assistant Attorney General Joseph B. Keenan, both agreed that there were legitimate concerns about the Constitutionality of a law that directly prohibited private ownership of machine guns. An exchange between Rep. Treadway and Keenan reveals how limiting even proponents of the National Firearms Act found the Constitution to be:

Mr. TREADWAY.... Why not exclude them from manufacture?

Mr. KEENAN. We have not the power to do that under the Constitution of the United States. Can the Congressman suggest under what theory we could prohibit the manufacture of machine guns?

Mr. TREADWAY. You could prohibit anybody from owning them.

Mr. KEENAN. I do not think we can prohibit anybody from owning them. I do not think that power resides in Congress.[72]

Earlier, Cummings explained why the National Firearms Act was constructed in a form similar to the Harrison Anti-Narcotic Act, and how this form evaded what Rep. Lewis called, "a provision in the Constitution... about the right to carry firearms":

Attorney General CUMMINGS... If we made a statute absolutely forbidding any human being to have a machine gun, you might say there is some constitutional question involved. But when you say, "we will tax the machine gun" and when you say that "'the absence of a license showing payment of the tax has been made indicates that a crime has been perpetrated'", you are easily within the law.

Mr. LEWIS. In other words, it does not amount to prohibition, but allows of regulation.

---

70 *National Firearms Act*, "Hearings Before The House Committee on Ways and Means", 73rd Cong. 2d Sess., (1934), 6, 15-16, 22, 100-1.

71 *National Firearms Act*, 13-14. This exchange was used in *U.S.* v. *Rock Island Armory, Inc.*, 773 F.Supp. 117, 120 (C.D. Ill. 1991) to limit the Federal Government's regulatory authority over machine gun manufacture. *Rock Island Armory, Inc.* is not strictly a right to keep and bear arms case, but rather an attempt to determine the limits of the Federal Government's regulatory authority. In a criminal prosecution of Rock Island Armory, Inc., for a violation of the 1986 ban on new machine gun manufacturing, Judge Mihm found that: because the National Firearms Act of 1934 had been adopted under the theory that *only* taxation of gun ownership was within the Federal Government's authority; the Federal Government had stopped accepting new registrations and associated taxes for new machine guns; the 1986 ban was therefore unconstitutional.

72 *National Firearms Act*, 100.

Attorney General CUMMINGS. That is the idea. We have studied that very carefully.[73]

Significantly for later discussions of registration proposals, Attorney General Cummings agreed that with respect to mandatory registration, "I am afraid it would be unconstitutional."[74]

The first case to come before the Supreme Court concerning the National Firearms Act of 1934 was *U.S.* v. *Miller* (1939). Jack Miller and Frank Layton were charged with violation of this law for "unlawfully transporting a firearm in interstate commerce without having registered the firearm," the firearm in question being a short-barreled shotgun. The District Court of the Western District of Arkansas accepted the defendants' argument that the National Firearms Act of 1934 was "an attempt to usurp police power reserved to the States," contrary to the Second Amendment, and quashed the indictment. The trial judge had taken it under judicial notice (the legal equivalent of "everyone knows this, I don't need expert testimony about it") that a short-barreled shotgun was a militia weapon. The prosecution appealed this decision; Miller and Layton were off the hook, and no appearance was made on their behalf before the Supreme Court.[75]

This lack of appearance, and therefore a lack of brief on behalf of the defendants, appears to have been a fatal injury to the Second Amendment; the citations given by the Court concerning the Second Amendment is a list that only the U.S. Attorney could have provided, for only the decisions that took the most hostile view towards the right to keep and bear arms were included: *Aymette* v. *State* (1840), *Presser* v. *Illinois* (1886), *Fife* v. *State* (1876), *City of Salina* v. *Blaksley* (1905), *People* v. *Brown* (1931), *State* v. *Duke* (1875), and *State* v. *Workman* (1891). *Robertson* v. *Baldwin* (1897) was also cited, with no apparent awareness that, contrary to the note in which it appears, it has nothing to do with the militia. The Georgia case *Jeffers* v. *Fair* (1862), a Confederate draft case with no applicability to gun restrictions, was also cited. *None* of the many decisions that recognized an individual right to keep arms, or to bear arms, was cited in the *Miller* decision.

Up until 1937, the Supreme Court had struck down a number of components of President Roosevelt's New Deal as unconstitutional extensions of federal authority. In response to Roosevelt's criticism, and after Roosevelt's unsuccessful attempt at "packing" the Court, the Court appears to have decided that it was better to stop swimming against the current of the New Deal, and began to find New Deal laws constitutional, resuming "its former, very limited role in passing on acts of social and economic legislation." In the period 1937-1939, the retirement and death of a number of Supreme Court justices enabled Roosevelt to appoint a Court more in line with activist governmental policies.[76]

From reading the decision in *U.S.* v. *Miller* (1939), it appears that the Court was anxious to uphold the National Firearms Act of 1934, while recognizing that the Second Amendment protected an individual right. As a consequence, this decision was made on the narrowest of grounds. Four essential issues were decided by the Court: the constitutionality of the registration requirement & tax; that regulating transfers of short-barreled shotguns & rifles did not violate the Second Amendment

---

73 *National Firearms Act*, 18-19.
74 *National Firearms Act*, 13.
75 *U.S.* v. *Miller*, 307 U.S. 174, 175, 176, 177 (1939).
76 Edmond Cahn, ed., *The Great Rights*, (New York: MacMillan Co., 1963), 9. Viault, 269-270.

"in absence of any reasonable relationship between such weapons and a well-regulated militia"; that it was not "within judicial notice that a shotgun having a barrel less than eighteen inches in length is any part of ordinary military equipment"; and that the purpose of the Second Amendment was "to assure continuation and render possible the effectiveness of the militia."

The Court upheld the constitutionality of the Federal Government regulating taxation and regulation of firearms transfers, using the Harrison Narcotic Act as precedent.[77] This is not surprising, since both acts used the mechanism of tax stamps to avoid a direct Federal prohibition on possession—a mechanism that allowed the government to indirectly prohibit possession by refusing to issue tax stamps, then prosecuting for failure to have the tax stamp. *Nigro* v. *U.S.* (1928), in upholding the Harrison Narcotic Act, had recognized that the federal law regulating "opiate and other drugs" was only valid as a tax measure, "for otherwise it would be no law at all."[78]

In some of the more convoluted language the Court has used to justify a position, the majority decided:

> In the absence of any evidence tending to show that possession or use of a "shotgun having a barrel of less than eighteen inches in length" at this time has some reasonable relationship to the preservation or efficiency of a well regulated militia, we cannot say that the Second Amendment guarantees the right to keep and bear such an instrument. Certainly it is not within judicial notice that this weapon is any part of the ordinary military equipment or that its use could contribute to the common defense.[79]

The Court did *not* say that a short-barreled shotgun was unprotected—just that no evidence had been presented to demonstrate such a weapon was "any part of the ordinary military equipment" or that it could "contribute to the common defense." What argument would they have used if Miller and Layton had been charged with possession of a Thompson submachine gun, or if the original trial court had heard expert testimony about the use of short-barreled shotguns in trench warfare?

More interesting is the Court's historical summary of the concerns that led to the Second Amendment. While taking the republican position—that the Second Amendment was principally concerned with maintaining a militia that would render a dangerous standing army unnecessary—the Court recognized:

> The signification attributed to the term Militia appears from the debates in the Convention, the history and legislation of Colonies and States, and the writings of approved commentators. These show plainly enough that the Militia comprised all males physically capable of acting in concert for the common defense. "A body of citizens enrolled for military discipline." And further, that ordinarily when called for service these men were expected to appear bearing arms supplied by themselves and of the kind in common use at the time.[80]

But what does the *Miller* decision mean? The republican school asserts, after quoting the "In the absence of any evidence..." paragraph from *Miller*:

> What we have then is a two tiered test: first for the weapon and second for the weapon holder. Even assuming that clear convincing proof had shown that sawed-off shotguns were not merely part of the military arsenal but in fact were standard issue as common as

---

77 *U.S.* v. *Miller*, 307 U.S. 174, 179 (1939).
78 *Nigro* v. *U.S.*, 276 U.S. 332, 341, 48 S.Ct. 388, 390 (1928).
79 *U.S.* v. *Miller*, 307 U.S. 174, 179 (1939).
80 *U.S.* v. *Miller*, 307 U.S. 174, 180 (1939).

K-rations and helmets and furthermore it was a court martial offense to be found
without it, it still would not have done Mr. Miller a whit of good. Mr. Miller fails mis-
erably in the weapon holder test. He was not acting in the role of the member of the
"militia," much less a regulated militia," and least of all the "well regulated militia," described by the Court and the Second Amendment.

The most that can be said for whose right emerged in *Miller* is that of the state militia's
and their own arsenal.[81]

But at no point was Miller's membership in any state militia ever raised as an issue. If the Court had considered membership in a state-recognized military force a
necessity for protection under the Second Amendment, it could have disposed of
the *Miller* case with a simple statement: Mr. Miller is not part of such a militia, and
is therefore not protected by the Second Amendment. *Even accepting the republican
view*, "the right of the people to keep and bear arms" was intended, as the Court
acknowledges in its decision, to have arms widely distributed among the
population.

Another member of the republican school argues, with reference to the same
paragraph: "The difficulty with such an interpretation is that were a weapon to have
such a 'reasonable relationship' it would be a protected weapon under the second
amendment."[82] But that is exactly what the Court had ruled in *Miller*—that such
weapons are protected. If not, the Court could have disposed of the case quickly by
simply asserting that the Second Amendment did not protect the right of
individuals to keep and bear arms.

The obtuse decision in *Miller* led to two conflicting decisions by the federal appellate courts, and because they were not overturned by the Supreme Court, it is
important to examine them carefully. Levin argues with respect to the decision
Cases v. *U.S.* (1st Cir. 1942):

> The court also recognized that such an interpretation would prohibit the federal gov-
> ernment from prohibiting private ownership of heavy weapons "even though under the
> circumstances of such possession or use it would be inconceivable that a private person
> could have any legitimate reason for having such a weapon." The court then decided it
> would be impossible to formulate any general test to determine the limits of the second
> amendment and each case would have to be determined on its individual merits.[83]

The *Cases* decision is often cited by proponents of restrictive federal gun control
laws, and because the conclusions it reached are significantly at variance with the
decision in *U.S.* v. *Miller* (1939), it is worthy of analysis. The defendant, one Jose
Cases Velazquez, had shot another person at a beach club in Carolina, Puerto Rico,
and was prosecuted for violation of the Federal Firearms Act of 1938, which prohibited convicted felons from possession of firearms. What could have been a
straightforward statement that convicted felons lost their right to keep and bear
arms, instead turned into a repudiation of the Second Amendment as protecting an
individual right:

> The Federal Firearms Act undoubtedly curtails to some extent the right of individuals to
> keep and bear arms but it does not follow from this that it is bad under the Second
> Amendment which reads "A well regulated Militia, being necessary to the security of a
> free State, the right of the people to keep and bear Arms, shall not be infringed."

---

81 Beard & Fields, 34.
82 Levin, 126-7.

The right to keep and bear arms is not a right conferred upon by the people by the federal constitution. Whatever rights in this respect the people may have depend upon local
legislation; the only function of the Second Amendment being to prevent the federal
government and the federal government only from infringing that right.[84]

And then to back up this assertion, the Circuit Court cited *U.S.* v. *Cruikshank*
(1876), and *Presser* v. *Illinois* (1886). But there is a subtle difference between the
assertion made in *Cruikshank*, that, "The right of bearing arms for a lawful purpose
is not a right granted by the Constitution; neither is it any manner dependent upon
that instrument for its existence,"[85] and the assertion made by the Circuit Court in
Cases. In *Cruikshank*, the Supreme Court argued that the Second Amendment only
protected individuals from actions by the Federal Government. In *Cases*, the Circuit Court denied that any such right was "conferred" by the Second Amendment,
and held that only "local legislation" might *grant* such a right.

Next, the *Cases* Circuit Court asserted that, "in a dictum in *Robertson* v. *Baldwin*,
165 U.S. 275, 282,... indicated that the limitation imposed upon the federal government was not absolute and this dictum received the sanction of the court in the
recent case of *United States* v. *Miller*..."[86] But as we have seen, in *Robertson* v.
Baldwin (1897), the Supreme Court had listed the right to keep and bear arms in
the midst of a series of other individual rights, with a list of "well-recognized exceptions" to each of these rights. Where the Court in *Robertson* v. *Baldwin* emphasized
that "right of the people to keep and bear arms" did not include "carrying of concealed weapons,"[87] the *Cases* Circuit Court inverted the intent, and argued that this
meant that the right was subject to such regulation and restriction as seemed
appropriate.

The *Cases* Circuit Court next acknowledged that the decision in *U.S.* v. *Miller*
(1939) meant that the Federal Government

> cannot prohibit the possession or use of any weapon which has reasonable relationship to
> the preservation or efficiency of a well regulated militia. However, we do not feel that
> the Supreme Court in this case was attempting to formulate a general rule applicable to
> all cases. The rule which it laid down was adequate to dispose of the case before it and
> that we think was as far as the Supreme Court intended to go. At any rate the rule of the
> Miller case, if intended to be comprehensive and complete would seem to be already
> outdated, in spite of the fact that it was formulated only three and a half years ago,
> because of the well known fact that in the so called "Commando Units" some sort of
> military use seems to have been found for almost any modern lethal weapon.[88]

Here we find the Circuit Court's first major error in reasoning. The *Miller* decision
made a very narrow ruling—not that a sawed-off shotgun was outside the protections of the Second Amendment, but that it was not within judicial notice that such
a weapon was a militia weapon. Expert testimony at trial would have established
that such a weapon was a militia weapon.[89] The Circuit Court then continued and

---

83 Levin, 127.
84 *Cases* v. *U.S.*, 131 F.2d 916, 921, 922 (1st Cir. 1942).
85 *U.S.* v. *Cruikshank*, 92 U.S. 542 (1876).
86 *Cases* v. *U.S.*, 131 F.2d 916, 922 (1st Cir. 1942).
87 *Robertson* v. *Baldwin*, 165 U.S. 275, 281, 282 (1897).
88 *Cases* v. *U.S.*, 131 F.2d 916, 922 (1st Cir. 1942).
89 At least 40,000 shotguns were purchased by the U.S. Government for service in World War I,
many being used as "trench brooms." Newton, 44-45.

unwittingly provided a clear statement of the meaning of the *Miller* decision that *should* clearly invalidate contemporary bans on so-called "assault rifles," semiautomatic versions of the battle rifles used by many of the world's armies:

> In view of this, if the rule of the Miller case is general and complete, the result would follow that under present day conditions, the federal government would be empowered only to regulate the possession or use of weapons such as a flintlock musket or a matchlock harquebus. But to hold that the Second Amendment limits the federal government to regulations concerning only weapons which can be classed as antiques or curiosities,—almost any other might bear some reasonable relationship to the preservation or efficiency of a well regulated militia unit of the present day,—is in effect to hold that the limitation of the Second Amendment is absolute.[90]

But even this statement contains a critical flaw. Throughout the history of the right to bear arms, state supreme courts both recognized that such a right existed, and that it was within the authority of the state to regulate the manner in which that right could be exercised, as long as such regulation was either "reasonable,"[91] or did "not... nullify the right, nor materially embarrass its exercise."[92]

Finally, the Circuit Court made a statement about the nature of the arms protected:

> Another objection to the rule of the Miller case as a full and general statement is that according to it Congress would be prevented by the Second Amendment from regulating the possession or use by private persons not present or prospective members of any military unit, of distinctly military arms, such as machine guns, trench mortars, anti-tank or anti-aircraft guns, even though under the circumstances surrounding such possession or use it would be inconceivable that a private person could have any legitimate reason for having such a weapon. It seems to us unlikely that the framers of the Amendment intended any such result. Considering the many variable factors bearing upon the question it seems to us impossible to formulate any general test by which to determine the limits imposed by the Second Amendment but that each case under it, like cases under the due process clause, must be decided on its own facts and the line between what is and what is not a valid federal restriction pricked out by decided cases falling on one side or the other of the line.[93]

It would appear that the circuit court in *Cases* was unaware of the definition of "arms" in Webster's 1828 dictionary, or the reasoning of the North Carolina Supreme Court in *State* v. *Kerner* (1921). The problem of regulating "heavy weapons" without doing damage to the Second Amendment could then have been resolved. The *Cases* decision had clearly taken great liberties with the *Miller* decision. Why then, did the Supreme Court decline to hear it? Unfortunately, the Court provided no answer to that question. But since Cases was a felon in possession of a firearm, the Court may have felt no need to bother considering such a trivial issue—much as the various "felon in possession of a gun" cases have been largely decided at the appellate level in the various states.

The same year, the Fourth Circuit Court of Appeals decided *U.S.* v. *Tot* (4th Cir. 1942). Where *Cases* had refused to recognize the Second Amendment as absolute, but still admitted it had some applicability to individuals, the *Tot* decision was unprepared to admit even that. Frank Tot was a convicted felon found in possession

---

90 *Cases* v. *U.S.*, 131 F.2d 916, 922 (1st Cir. 1942).
91 *Carroll* v. *State*, 28 Ark. 99, 101 (1872).
92 *Haile* v. *State*, 38 Ark. 564, 565, 566 (1882).
93 *Cases* v. *U.S.*, 131 F.2d 916, 922 (1st Cir. 1942).

of a handgun, and was convicted of violating the Federal Firearms Act of 1938. While the Second Amendment was only one of the issues raised, the decision is an astonishing one:

> It is abundantly clear both from the discussions of this amendment contemporaneous with its proposal and adoption and those of learned writers since that this amendment, unlike those providing for protection of free speech and freedom of religion, was not adopted with individual rights in mind, but as a protection for the States in the maintenance of their militia organizations against possible encroachments by the federal power. The experiences in England under James II of an armed royal force quartered upon a defenseless citizenry was fresh in the minds of the Colonists. They wanted no repetition of that experience in their newly formed government.[94]

The sources given for these assertions are a series of law review articles and three citations from Elliot's *Debates on the Federal Constitution*. As we saw in the beginning chapters, such a position is supported by the debates, but includes the assumption that the general populace would have arms under their individual control for the purpose specified, *and* the assumption of the common law right to bear arms for self-defense. But the next two sentences demonstrate an internal inconsistency, as well as an ignorance of the history of right to keep and bear arms decisions:

> The almost uniform course of decisions in this country, where provisions similar in language are found in many of the State Constitutions, bears out this concept of the constitutional guarantee. A notable instance is the refusal to extend its application to weapons thought incapable of military use.[95]

As we have seen, there was an "almost uniform course of decisions," but it was in the direction of recognizing an individual right to bear, and therefore, to possess arms for defensive purposes. The exceptional decisions have been the ones that limited the arms to those appropriate to "military use." *Even accepting this incorrect statement*, the decisions that recognized a right to possess military weapons, such as the Arkansas and Oklahoma decisions, demonstrate by analogy that the Second Amendment was intended to protect individual possession of arms for the purpose of restraining tyranny. Indeed, while the Circuit Court cited *Aymette* v. *State* (1840) as evidence to support their view that only state militias were protected, the Tennessee Supreme Court in that decision held that the purpose of individuals "being armed, they may as a body rise up to defend their just rights, and compel their rulers to respect the laws."[96]

This period, from the end of World War I to the beginning of the civil rights movement in the late 1950s defies easy characterization. Rural states, like North Carolina, Idaho, and Montana, were prepared to recognize that the right to bear arms, at least openly, was in every sense, a right—even when the characters involved were less than shining examples of law-abiding citizens (*e.g.*, the defendants in the two Idaho decisions). More urban states, on the other hand, took a more restrictive approach, where the discretion of the police in issuing permits was more and more trusted by the courts. Why the relative lack of state supreme court decisions during this period? One possibility was the dramatic decline in murder rates in the U.S.

---

94 *U.S.* v. *Tot*, 131 F.2d 261, 266 (4th Cir. 1942).
95 *U.S.* v. *Tot*, 131 F.2d 261, 266 (4th Cir. 1942).
96 *Aymette* v. *State*, 2 Hump. (21 Tenn.) 154, 156, 158 (1840).

from the end of Prohibition until the 1960s.[97] Law-abiding people who are not afraid of criminal attack do not generally insist on a right to carry a gun, either openly or concealed.

Don Kates sees the migration northward of Southern gun control laws as a symptom of a society which was becoming increasing hostile to "foreigners," labor organizers, and revolutionaries. In Kates' view, the significant cultural and religious differences between the immigrants that came in large numbers from the 1880s until 1924 (when immigration restrictions took effect), generated tremendous discomfort among the Brahmins of American society, who were overwhelmingly Protestant, and of Northwestern European origin.[98] If we accept Kates' theory, the cutoff of immigration might well have eased the perceived need for more gun control laws, as American society became more homogenous.

Corroborating evidence is available to substantiate Kates' "immigration discomfort" theory; Wade Ellis' introduction to Judge Marcus Kavanagh's 1928 book, *The Criminal and His Allies*, included the assertion:

While European writers and thinkers have adopted the fashion lately of deprecating with polite condescension the reign of lawlessness in the United States, it is pertinent and timely to observe that, aside from offenses committed by negroes, two-thirds of the crimes in the United States are committed by persons born in Europe, or by their immediate descendants.[99]

The appendices of the book included a table showing country of origin of various categories of criminals, with Italy, Poland, Russia, Mexico, and Sweden, disproportionately involved. Judge Kavanagh supported a prohibition on manufacturing concealable firearms for ten years, with a relaxation of the requirements for search warrants, apparently with the goal of allowing something like a general warrant, so that the particular details of the place to be searched, and the items to be seized, would not be needed. Anyone found in possession of a concealable firearm, anywhere, would be sentenced to one to five years in prison.[100]

Something of Kavanagh's view of civil liberties may be deduced from the introduction's enthusiastic digest of Kavanagh's proposals, including "substitution of a five-sixth for a unanimous verdict in all [non-capital] felony cases," elimination of jury trials for some criminal cases, enhanced power to the judge in selecting the jury, discouraging "trivial appeals" by expanding the power of the appellate courts "to consider only the ends of justice to be served without regard to form or precedent, and even to reduce or enlarge the penalty imposed," and finally, "a modification of the old rule about self-incrimination as an inviolable protection of the accused...."[101]

How serious was the crime problem? There was, indeed, a dramatic increase in murder rates from 1900 to 1933. From 1900 to 1905, murder rates remained flat, between 1.1 and 2 per 100,000 population, and then rose to 5 per 100,000 population in only two years. While the murder rate rose and fell throughout the next 25 years, the general trend was upward, reaching a peak of 9.7 per 100,000 people

97 Bureau of Justice Statistics, 15.
98 Kates, "Toward a History of Handgun Prohibition...", 15-19.
99 Marcus Kavanagh, *The Criminal and His Allies*, (Indianapolis: Bobbs-Merrill Co., 1928), ix.
100 Kavanagh, 356-8, 403-4.
101 Kavanagh, xiii-xiv.

in 1933.[102] If the adoption of the Uniform Firearms Act in the 1920s by most states had any effect on murder rates, it would appear to have been overwhelmed by other factors.

Compared to the relative peace of the first few years of the twentieth century, it must have seemed as though something had gone very wrong. For the generation that were young adults in 1900, the dramatic increase in murder rates from 1905-1920 must have seemed incomprehensible—and that the murder rates continued to rise, must have seemed to justify almost any action. Having established that, indeed, *something* had to be done, what was the proper course of action? Why did the regulation of handgun carrying seem an appropriate response?

Based on his proposals for judicial reform, it is unlikely that Kavanagh was a member of the American Civil Liberties Union—and here is one of the most interesting changes between 1928 and 1988. Where handgun control and even prohibition seems to have been largely supported by conservatives in the early part of this century, it has become popularly perceived as a litmus-test of liberalism today.

Kates argues that a combination of KKK nativism, and businessmen concerned about armed robbery and union struggle, were major forces in pushing this expansion of gun control laws, and none of these were of a liberal persuasion.[103] But Kates also points to the internal struggle within the Democratic Party over Prohibition as a factor in the development of modern liberalism's interest in gun control measures:

> Loath as we modern liberals are to admit it, Prohibition was the *cause celebre* of four generations of American liberals, the brightest and the best, the most progressive and humane, political figures of their times... Others who saw in Demon Rum the cause of domestic and acquaintance homicide... included William Lloyd Garrison, Henry Ward Beecher, Theodore Parker, Frederick Douglass, Jane Addams, William Jennings Bryan, and at least in their youth, Eleanor Roosevelt and Hugo Black...
>
> It was only after the failure of Prohibition became manifest that many of the people who had supported it found in handgun prohibition a similar promise of cutting through the complex social, cultural, and institutional factors that produce violent crime. The addition of this veteran core of social reformers to the already very influential forces calling for handgun prohibition seemed to make a national Sullivan Law a real possibility in the heady early New Deal days of expanding federal power.... The likelihood that handgun prohibition might divert attention from Prohibition was to F.D.R. not a disadvantage, but an attraction.[104]

This may also explain the near collapse of awareness of the Second Amendment as a protection of individual liberties during this period, since both major political factions in American politics had embraced gun control, if not gun prohibition, though for different reasons.

George Seldes' *You Can't Do That!*, published in 1938, was intended as an warning of the collapse of American civil liberties, caused by the forces of "reaction." In the appendix, Seldes tells us, "These are the sections of the Bill of Rights of the Federal Constitution which constitute the basis of civil liberty," and

---

102 Bureau of Justice Statistics, 15.
103 Kates, "Toward a History of Handgun Prohibition...", 17-22.
104 Kates, "Toward a History of Handgun Prohibition...", 22-23. The Sullivan Law, discussed on page 158, restricted handgun ownership in New York.

then lists the First, Fourth, Fifth, Sixth, Eighth, and Fourteenth Amendments. Next, Seldes lists in a more simplified form, "I. The Rights—Personal Liberty," and includes, "5. The Right to Bear Arms and to Organize the Militia."[105] Leaving out the Second Amendment might have been more understandable, if not for this curiously reworded condensation of it—as if Seldes considered the right guaranteed by the Second Amendment to be collective in nature only. When we consider the close relationship between the right to bear arms and labor organizing activity that existed into the 1930s, Seldes' apparent reluctance to recognize the Second Amendment as an individual right is all the more curious.

A revival of interest in the Bill of Rights as history started in the 1950s; first, Robert Rutland's *The Birth of the Bill of Rights* appeared in 1955, then Edward Dumbauld's *The Bill of Rights And What It Means Today* was published in 1957. Yet Rutland's first edition called the Second and Third Amendments, "obsolete."[106] Dumbauld also listed the Second and Third Amendments under the heading "Unused Provisions." Yet an indication that the Second Amendment was not yet entirely dead may be found in the same work. Dumbauld acknowledged that the Court had taken two contradictory positions: that the Second Amendment was a limitation on federal power in *U.S.* v. *Cruikshank* (1876), as opposed to the narrower decision in *U.S.* v. *Miller* (1939), and he suggested that there was opportunity for further development of this right.[107]

The period between World War I and the Civil Rights Movement might be best characterized as the Second Amendment's coma. The 1960s could be seen then, as the time that the Second Amendment came very close to dying, without regaining consciousness.

---

105 George Seldes, *You Can't Do That!*, (New York: Modern Age Books, 1938), 245-6.
106 Robert Allen Rutland, *The Birth of the Bill of Rights 1776-1791*, (Chapel Hill, N.C.: University of North Carolina Press, 1955), 229.
107 Edward Dumbauld, *The Bill of Rights And What It Means Today*, (Norman, Okla.: University of Oklahoma Press, 1957), 60-61.

IX. Civil Rights, Civil Disturbances

In spite of the comatose condition of the right to keep and bear arms, there were voices, some in positions of authority, expressing the opinion that the Second Amendment protected an individual right. An example was Justice Hugo Black's entry in the James Madison Lectures at New York University in 1960. Justice Black, explained his opposition to a "balancing of interests" approach to the Constitutional protections:

> Some people regard the prohibitions of the Constitution, even its most unequivocal commands, as mere admonitions which Congress need not always observe.... For example, it is sometimes said that Congress may abridge a constitutional right if there is a clear and present danger that the free exercise of the right will bring about a substantive evil that Congress has authority to prevent. Or it is said that a right may be abridged where its exercise would cause so much injury to the public that this injury would outweigh its injury to the individual who is deprived of the right....
>
> I cannot accept this approach to the Bill of Rights. It is my belief that there are "absolutes" in our Bill of Rights, and that they were put there on purpose by men who knew what words meant, and meant their prohibitions to be "absolutes."[1]

Black then articulated the meaning of the various amendments of the Bill of Rights as they restrict the federal government: "The use of the words, 'the people,' in both these Amendments strongly emphasizes the desire of the Framers to protect individual liberty." After repeating the Second Amendment, Black contended: "Although the Supreme Court has held this Amendment to include only arms necessary to a well-regulated militia, as so construed, its prohibition is absolute." While Justice Black did not explicitly call this "absolute" protection an individual right, the entire rest of the lecture repeatedly emphasized that the Bill of Rights protects *individual* rights.

To those who see the Second Amendment as "increasingly irrelevant":

> I cannot agree with those who think of the Bill of Rights as an 18th century straitjacket, unsuited for this age.... The evils it guards against are not only old, they are with us now, they exist today....
>
> Experience all over the world has demonstrated, I fear, that the distance between stable, orderly government and one that has been taken over by force is not so great as we have assumed.[2]

---

1 Hugo L. Black, "The Bill of Rights and the Federal Government", in Cahn, 44-45.
2 Black, 50-51, 54-55, 61-62.

Earl Warren's James Madison Lecture, delivered in 1961, took a more ambiguous position. After discussing concerns about standing armies, fears of a "military independent and superior to the civil power," and concerns of the population about the new government:

> They were reluctant to ratify the Constitution without further assurances, and thus we find in the Bill of Rights Amendments II and III, specifically authorizing a decentralized militia, *guaranteeing the right of the people to keep and bear arms*, and prohibiting the quartering of troops in any house in time of peace without the consent of the owner.[3] [emphasis added]

In 1962, Justice William O. Douglas gave another installment in the James Madison Lecture series, discussed his view of the deficiencies of a Bill of Rights:

> So far as the Bill of Rights is concerned, the individual is on his own when it comes to the pursuit of happiness.... The closest the Framers came to the *affirmative* side of liberty was in "the right of the people to bear arms." Yet this too has been greatly modified by judicial construction.[4]

Nor were these views strictly judicial and academic in nature. Washington State, which had adopted a fairly typical version of the Uniform Firearms Act in 1935, revised the concealed weapon permit statute in 1961 so that it was no longer within the discretion of the police or courts to refuse a concealed weapon permit; as long as the applicant was legally qualified to own a handgun, a permit *had* to be issued.[5]

Three great disruptions startled American society between 1954 and 1975. The first great shock was the Civil Rights Movement, as the status quo of customary and legally enforced racial segregation came under attack through civil disobedience, judicial action, and legislation. The changes brought about were profoundly disturbing to the status quo, and not surprisingly, violence and intimidation, some of it at the point of a gun, were major components of this shock.

A second great shock, though one for which the effects are still being debated, was the dramatic expansion of civil liberties through the decisions of the Warren Court. To liberals, these decisions represented a redemption of the promise of the Bill of Rights, as each decision extended its protections to include not only actions by the federal government, but also actions by the state and local governments. To conservatives, these decisions represented not only the destruction of traditional values with respect to family, sexual morality, and the proper limits on expression, but also a threat to the efficient removal of violent criminals from society.

But as the Civil Rights Movement began to subside, and the Supreme Court's dramatic expansions of civil liberties begin to hit their peak, yet another dramatic challenge to the status quo appeared: the anti-war/countercultural movement. The anti-war movement merged with parts of the Civil Rights Movement. A rising countercultural movement turned into a sexual revolution, provoked by the development of the birth control pill and widespread middle-class illegal drug use. A strident New Left movement developed.[6] Simultaneously, there was a decline in the 1950s moral and religious consensus, and a dramatic expansion of demands for

---

3 Earl Warren, "The Bill of Rights and the Military", in Cahn, 94.
4 William O. Douglas, "The Bill of Rights Is Not Enough", in Cahn, 146-7.
5 Wash. RCW Ann. 9.41.070 (1991).
6 Walker, 229-32, 236.

tolerance and social acceptance from groups heretofore ignored or actively suppressed.

The anti-war movement's failure to stop the war bred cynicism and bitterness, and by the late 1960s, violent factions of the Left began to use bombs to express their disapproval of "the System," and employed armed robbery as a method of raising funds. The Civil Rights Movement failed to immediately alleviate the second-class status of blacks, and the non-violent leadership of Martin Luther King, Jr., was increasing supplanted by black leaders with a considerably more menacing style.

One especially powerful example of this can be found in the speeches of Malcolm X and the writings of Stokley Carmichael. Malcolm X spoke April 3, 1964, at the Cory Methodist Church in Cleveland, Ohio:

> [W]here the government has proven itself unwilling or unable to defend the lives and the property of Negroes, it's time for Negroes to defend themselves. Article number two of the constitutional amendments provides you and me the right to own a rifle or a shotgun. This doesn't mean you're going to get a rifle and form battalions and go out looking for white folks, although you'd be within your rights—I mean, you'd be justified; but that would be illegal and we don't do anything illegal.[7]

An interview Malcolm X gave on March 19, 1964, and published in May of that year, addressed much the same issue:

> Article 2 of the Constitution—it says concerning the right to bear arms in the Bill of Rights: "A well-regulated militia being necessary to the security of a free state, the right of the people to keep and bear arms shall not be infringed." Negroes don't realize this, that they are within their constitutional rights to own a rifle, to own a shotgun. When the bigoted white supremists [sic] realize that they are dealing with Negroes who are ready to give their lives in defense of life and property, then these bigoted whites will change their whole strategy and their whole attitude.[8]

The second rally of the Organization of Afro-American Unity, held on July 5, 1964, includes a telling comment about why Malcolm X felt that New York City was considering restrictive licensing of rifles:

> The City Council right now is considering a law that's designed to make it illegal for you to walk with a rifle or have a rifle. Why just now? As long as it's been legal to own a rifle, why all of a sudden does the great white father want to pass a law making rifle-carrying illegal? Because of you; he's afraid of you getting rifles. Every law that they pass is aimed at you.[9]

Two years later, Stokley Carmichael articulated a new ideology called "Black Power" in the *New York Review of Books*. He explained the reason for the adoption of the black panther as a political party name in Alabama:

> A man needs a black panther on his side when he and his family must endure—as hundreds of Alabamians have endured—loss of job, eviction, starvation, and sometimes death, for political activity. He may also need a gun and SNCC reaffirms the right of black men everywhere to defend themselves when threatened or attacked.
>
> As for initiating the use of violence, we hope that such programs as ours will make that unnecessary; but it is not for us to tell black communities whether they can or cannot use any particular form of action to resolve their problems. Responsibility for the use of

---

7 Malcolm X, *Malcolm X Speaks*, (New York: Grove Press, Inc., 1965), 43.
8 Malcolm X, *By Any Means Necessary*, (New York: Pathfinder Press, Inc., 1970), 11.
9 Malcom X, *By Any Means Necessary*, 91.

violence by black men, whether in self-defense or initiated by them, lies with the white community.[10]

Self-defense should not have been a controversial position to take, nor the right to defend oneself with a gun; such actions would have given the KKK good reason to consider less hazardous activities than cross-burnings and murder of civil rights activists. Refusing to exclude *initiation* of violence, especially in such close proximity to an assertion of a right to a gun, seemed to many Americans at the time to be a veiled threat of race war.

During this period, race riots broke out in many American cities. Their visceral impact cannot be underestimated. This author remembers clearly the pillar of smoke rising from the Watts riots, and his parents discussing where in the house he should hide if the riots spread to Santa Monica.[11] Review of the news magazines and newspapers of the time show that these were not isolated incidents; the 1967 race riots occupied the cover of *Newsweek*, week after week.

By the mid-1960s, murder rates had begun a dramatic rise—one that continued until 1980. Murder rates had declined from 9.7 per 100,000 in 1933, to 4.5 in 1958, then began constantly increasing, reaching 10 per 100,000 by the mid-1970s, and eventually peaking at 10.2 per 100,000 in 1980.[12] Whether this was the result of the expansion of civil liberties, the collapse of 1950s moral standards, or simply an artifact of the post-war Baby Boomers reaching their peak crime years[13] is a highly debatable point. But considering the rapidity with which fundamental aspects of American society changed, and the prospect that the rate of change might continue unabated, it would have been very surprising if the Second Amendment protections did not experience substantial injury during this period.

How afraid was the status quo? The Gun Control Act of 1968 came hard on the heels of the assassination of Robert F. Kennedy, Martin Luther King, Jr., and a wave of race riots in the aftermath of King's death. The Supreme Court tells us, in *Lewis* v. *U.S.* (1980), that Congress "was concerned that the receipt and possession of a firearm by a felon constitutes a threat... to the continued and effective operation of the Government of the United States."[14] Most disturbing of all, there is evidence that Sen. Thomas J. Dodd, a Nuremberg trials prosecutor, had the Library of Congress translate the 1938 Nazi weapons laws shortly before the very similar Gun Control Act of 1968 was written by Dodd's committee.[15]

In 1967, race riots in American cities dotted maps in *Newsweek*, and the greatest imaginable fear hit the California Legislature: "Two dozen armed Negroes entered the State Capitol at noon today and 10 made their way to the back of the Assembly Chamber before they were disarmed and marched away by the state police." The demonstration was in protest of a bill to be considered that day by the Assembly that would have prohibited the open carry of loaded firearms in cities. Bobby Seale,

10 Stokley Carmichael, "What We Want", *New York Review of Books*, September 22, 1966, in *Annals of America*, 18:375.

11 Unlike a number of other people of the time who purchased firearms because of the Watts riots, this author's parents never even considered it.

12 Bureau of Justice Statistics, 15.

13 Walker, 228.

14 *Lewis* v. *U.S.*, 445 U.S. 55, 67, 100 S.Ct. 915, 921 (1980).

15 Jews for the Preservation of Firearms Ownership, "The War on Gun Ownership Still Goes On!", *Guns and Ammo*, [May 1993], 30-31.

a heretofore unknown black militant, leading the Black Panthers (almost as unknown as Seale) read a statement at a hastily arranged press conference. The demonstration was intended as a protest against "police brutality." Seale and his compatriots insisted that they had a right to defend themselves. Their weapons (including "pistols, rifles, at least one sawed-off shotgun") were returned to them, after they were escorted from the building.[16]

The bill, which became California Penal Code §12031, almost certainly benefitted from the Panthers' actions; political astuteness was never one of their strong points. Governor Ronald Reagan was on the steps of the statehouse at the time the Panthers' were escorted from the building: "Reagan also said it was a 'ridiculous way to solve problems that have to be solved among people of good will.' He added he was against 'even the implied threat weapons might be directed again fellow Americans.'"[17] (As we saw at the beginning of this work, the "implied threat" that the population might rise up against a tyrannical government composed of "fellow Americans" was the principal reason for the Second Amendment.)

By the time the bill reached the State Senate, on July 27, 1967, the U.S. Army had been sent into Detroit to restore order, rioting had broken out in dozens of American cities, and bombings and random gunfire from disaffected blacks had even reached California's sleepy little capital of Sacramento. In the context of these threats to public safety, the surprise is not that the law in question was passed, but that there were legislators prepared to argue against it; the final vote in the state senate was 29-7. While some proponents of the bill argued that it would have no effect on anyone with a gun for a "lawful reason," such as hunting or target shooting, several conservative Republicans (unlike Governor Reagan) argued otherwise. State Senator John G. Schmitz argued, predictably enough, "It would destroy the Second Amendment to the Constitution—the right to bear arms," and "The right of self-defense is not an unlawful reason." But surprisingly enough, Schmitz also referred to what was going on in Detroit as, "A revolution, not a riot."[18]

It is in the context of these dramatic cultural shocks that the following decisions appeared; it should therefore be no surprise to find that legislatures and courts became increasingly skeptical of the right to bear arms. In *Matthews* v. *State* (1958), the defendant was charged and convicted of "assault and battery with intent to commit murder and carrying pistol without license" in Vanderburgh County, Indiana. It appears that Jasper Leroy Matthews, the defendant, intended to kill one person, but shot another. While the "intent to commit murder" charge would certainly seem the most serious charge, most of the majority decision of the Indiana Supreme Court, and nearly all of the minority opinion, involve the relatively minor charge of carrying a pistol without a license.

The majority opinion was concerned with four questions, of which the second two were squarely involved with the Indiana Constitution's right to keep and bear arms clause:

> Appellant further asserts that the Legislature has attempted to delegate discretionary duties to the Superintendent of State Police without providing sufficient standards under

---

16 "Capitol Is Invaded", *Sacramento Bee*, May 2, 1967, A1.
17 "Capitol Is Invaded", *Sacramento Bee*, May 2, 1967, A10.
18 "Bill Barring Loaded Weapons In Public Clears Senate 29-7", *Sacramento Bee*, July 27, 1967, A6.

which such discretion is to be exercised and, therefore, the Uniform Firearms Act violates §1, Art. 4 of the Constitution of Indiana, and the Due Process Clause of the 14th Amendment of the United States Constitution.[19]

The Model Uniform Firearms Act had been adopted by Indiana in 1935, and specified that no person was to carry a pistol outside of his "place of abode or fixed place of business" without a license. Application for the license to carry was to be made to the chief of police or sheriff, with the final decision made by the superintendent of the state police, "if it appears that the applicant has a proper reason for carrying a pistol and is of good character and reputation and a suitable person to be so licensed."

The majority decided that question of whether an applicant had a "proper reason" and was of "good character and reputation" were matters of fact, for which "the Superintendent of State Police, with his special training and experience, and with the facilities which he has at his command for securing information, is capable and qualified to determine..."

On the fourth question to be decided by the Court:

> Appellant further asserts that the Firearms Act violates Art. I, §32 of the Indiana Constitution which provides that "The people shall have a right to bear arms, for the defense of themselves and the State," because it restricts the right of the people to bear arms for their own defense....

> The purpose of the Firearms Act is to achieve a maximum degree of control over criminal and careless uses of certain types of firearms, while at the same time making them available to persons where needed for protection....

> The Legislature has the power, in the interest of public safety and welfare, to provide reasonable regulations for the use of firearms which may be readily concealed, such as pistols.[20]

The Court then provided a substantial list of decisions to buttress their position— but not all the decisions cited actually fit. *McIntyre* v. *State* (1908), *State* v. *Tully* (1939), and *State* v. *Buzzard* (1842) were cited, and to varying degrees, support the Court's opinion.

State v. *Hart* (1945) was cited, but the Idaho Supreme Court had ruled that while regulation of the *mode* of carrying arms was constitutional, the precedent of *In Re Brickey* (1902) was still in effect, and such regulation could not preclude *some* mode of bearing arms. *Hill* v. *State* (1874) was cited; even though the *Hill* decision had accepted that there were places where open carry could be prohibited, it had also recognized that the right to carry arms openly "in the fields, and in the woods, on the highways and byeways [*sic*], at home and abroad" was Constitutionally protected, under both Federal and Georgia Constitutions. Similarly, the Georgia Supreme Court had admitted that a regulation so incompatible with the use of arms as to preclude their defensive use would be "a denial of the right to bear arms altogether."[21] *City of Salina* v. *Blaksley* (1905) was cited, but the *Salina* decision had denied that any individual right was protected by the Kansas constitutional guarantee, and the Indiana Supreme Court's majority opinion at no point denied that an individual right was protected.

---

19 *Matthews* v. *State*, 237 Ind. 677, 148 N.E.2d 334, 335 (1958).

20 *Matthews* v. *State*, 237 Ind. 677, 148 N.E.2d 334, 336, 337, 338 (1958).

21 *State* v. *Hill*, 53 Ga. 472, 475, 476, 480, 481 (1874).

Finally, *U.S.* v. *Miller* (1939), which upheld the licensing of machine guns and short-barreled rifles & shotguns was cited. But *Miller* had upheld a Federal law on the narrowest of grounds—that short-barreled shotguns were not "militia" weapons. The serious question of how far such regulation of militia weapons could be carried was not addressed in *Miller.*

The majority appears to have ignored the guarantee of a right "to bear arms," as distinguished from the right to "keep" arms:

> The provisions of §10-4736, supra, do not restrict nor prohibit appellant or any other person from having a pistol in his home or "fixed place of business" for the defense of himself and the State. Neither does such Act attempt to restrict or prohibit the use of firearms other than pistols, as they are defined in §1 of the Act.[22]

The Court implied that *possession* of a pistol at home or one's own business was protected by the Indiana Constitution, but not necessarily the *carrying* of a pistol: "Article I, §32... does not say that the people shall have a right to bear pistols, or any other specific kind or type of arms." The Court refused to abide by the reasoning of the *State* v. *Hart* (1945) and *State* v. *Hill* (1874) decisions, which had recognized that *some* bearing of pistols was protected. The Indiana Supreme Court implied that bearing of *some* type of arms was protected, though exactly what kind, was left unclear.[23]

The minority opinion, written by Chief Justice Emmert, is considerably more protective of the right to keep and bear arms. It is also much longer, with more historical detail in defense of its opinion. While in agreement with the majority opinion about the first two questions (with respect to the indictment and sentencing for assault and battery), Chief Justice Emmert vigorously disagreed on the issue of whether the Uniform Firearms Act was Constitutional.

Chief Justice Emmert first pointed out, concerning Art. I, §32:

> It is to be noted that this constitutional protection is in the identical language of §20 of Article 1 of the 1816 Constitution of Indiana. The Indiana constitutional right to bear arms is not based only in aid of the militia as is the Second Amendment to the Federal Constitution.... Nor does the Indiana Constitution guaranteeing the inalienable right of self-defense, specifically grant the General Assembly the right to regulate the carrying of weapons.[24]

In a footnote, the Chief Justice contrasted Indiana's provision with the Oklahoma and Texas Constitutions, which specifically gave their legislatures authority to regulate the carrying of arms:

> The constitutional right to bear arms in Indiana is stated in clear and simple language, and neither this court nor the Legislature, even if it enacts a Uniform Firearms Act, has any right to disregard a single well-chosen word, nor deprive an accused of a right granted by the Constitution. We should "not bend the constitution to suit the law of the hour...". If constitutional rights are to mean anything, they must protect the guilty as well as the innocent.[25]

Indeed, as we seen throughout the period after the Civil War, words like "reasonable" were used by state supreme courts to avoid admitting that the clear-cut

---

22 *Matthews* v. *State*, 237 Ind. 677, 148 N.E.2d 334, 338 (1958).
23 *Matthews* v. *State*, 237 Ind. 677, 148 N.E.2d 334, 338 (1958).
24 *Matthews* v. *State*, 237 Ind. 677, 148 N.E.2d 334, 338, 339 (1958).
25 *Matthews* v. *State*, 237 Ind. 677, 148 N.E.2d 334, 339 (1958).

language of the various state constitutions meant what it said, or that the character of the population had changed so that the people could no longer be trusted to carry arms:

> The decisions from other jurisdictions are not uniform on the right to keep and bear arms any more than the constitutional provisions are stated in the same language. Few of the decisions make any historical analysis of the cause for constitutional guarantees of the right to bear arms being considered so important by the Forefathers, nor do they consider the future effect of the precedent being made as to the right of the Legislature to make more drastic regulations and prohibitions. But the Supreme Court of Michigan has well noted the constitutional right to bear arms in America had its origin in the fear of a standing army as well as a necessity of self-protection in a frontier society. See People v. Brown, 131...[26]

Chief Justice Emmert then covered the historical origins of the Second Amendment, starting with the English Bill of Rights (1689). Next, the Chief Justice cited the Pennsylvania Constitutions of 1776 and 1790, and the problem of an insufficiency of arms for defense against Indians, and against the British. Emmert also pointed to evidence that pistols were in common use by members of the Continental Army, and therefore:

> the right to bear arms as first recognized by the Forefathers not only included cutting swords, muskets, rifles and shotguns, but also pistols. Arms were not necessary for the equipment of the militia... but the necessities of each man being in a position to protect himself and his property were so obvious that the Forefathers chose not to rely upon mere legislation to guarantee the right....

> It was early held that the 1831 statute prohibiting anyone except travelers from wearing or carrying concealed weapons was constitutional. State v. Mitchell, 1833, 3 Blackf. 229. The militia was never on duty armed with concealed weapons. The bearing of arms was unconcealed. This in no way limited the right to bear arms unconcealed, and not until the present Uniform Firearms Act has any statute attempted to abolish what the Constitution protects.

> Since 1816 this State has gotten along very well maintaining law and order under the various statutes prohibiting the carrying of concealed weapons, while at the same the owners of pistols had the right to carry them hunting or target shooting unconcealed without a permit and without being branded a criminal. The 1925 Firearms Act (Ch. 207, Acts 1925), did not prevent carrying unconcealed pistols, and under it the crime rate for crimes of violence was less than it had been under the 1935 Uniform Act. The effect of such unconstitutional regulation as prescribed by the latter Act has always been to disarm the law-abiding citizen, while the criminal pays no attention to the law. Such legislation really provides greater security for the outlaw.[27]

The Chief Justice then addressed and refuted the pragmatic argument, which we have seen throughout this work, and which can be found espoused by nearly all political persuasions in modern America when a Constitutional right becomes inconvenient:

> It is often assumed in some of the cases that a change in the constitutional right to bear arms must be made in the exercise of the police power of the State for the protection of the health, safety and general welfare of the people. The same argument could be presented for the impairment of the constitutional right to be free from unreasonable searches and seizures, which has roots in the pre-Revolutionary Writs of Assistance used to oppress the people of Massachusetts. What is overlooked is the obvious fact that the

---

26 *Matthews v. State*, 237 Ind. 677, 148 N.E.2d 334, 339 (1958).
27 *Matthews v. State*, 237 Ind. 677, 148 N.E.2d 334, 340, 341 (1958).

constitutional right to bear arms is in itself an exercise of the sovereign police power, and being a part of the Constitution, the Legislature has been prohibited from legislating any part of it out of existence.

Next, the Chief Justice demolished the "only arms of that time are protected" school of thought:

> Nor can it be maintained that the right to bear arms only protects the use of muskets, muzzle-loading rifles, shotguns and pistols, because they were the only ones used by the Colonists at the time. It might as well be argued that only a house of the architectural vintage of the Revolution would be protected against a present unreasonable search and seizure. Modern guns suitable for hunting and defense are within the protection of the Bill of Rights just the same as the owner of a modern ranch house type home is protected against unlawful searches.

Chief Justice Emmert pointed out the fallacy of the majority opinion, that the constitutional protection does not specifically include pistols:

> If the Legislature can prohibit the carrying of an unconcealed pistol without a permit, with equal logic it can prohibit the carrying of an unconcealed rifle or shotgun without a permit. The advocates of a Police State by restrictive legislation or administrative rules always seem around and busy trying to restrict freedom and constitutional rights. Their plan is always cleverly designed to take a small ship at a time, for "many strokes overthrow the tallest oaks."

> If we are to heed the lessons of modern history, it is self-evident our Bill of Rights should be construed liberally in favor of the individual and against restrictive legislation. When the Boston Police Strike resulted in areas of local anarchy within the city, the only protection for private property was the owner's armed guard. We have often been cited to the example of England and her restrictive firearms legislation as the cause for reducing crimes. But it is within the memory of most of us that after Dunkirk, Americans with hunting arms were urged to give them to England to rearm a disarmed population in order to repel Hitler's planned invasion. Had Hitler succeeded, the population would have been disarmed again for Dictators can tolerate no arms among the subject people. Modern History clearly discloses a prime modus operandi of the Communist State is the disarming of its civilian population.[28]

The Chief Justice completed his stinging criticism of "the advocate of the Police State, whether he be a misguided reformer or a ruthless dictator" with the observation that:

> The philosophy that the ends justifies the means can only result in the progressive destruction of constitutional liberties. Many more convictions could be obtained if courts would construe away the protection against self-incrimination and unreasonable searches, but Bills of Rights were adopted to protect the individual against oppression by his Government, whether he be guilty or innocent. If the courts ignore well settled precedents for the construction of constitutional rights, they become government by judges, and not by law. If the constitutional safeguards are to be diminished, it should be done by constitutional amendment, and not by validating legislation that contravenes what the Forefathers and the people made the supreme law of this State.[29]

Unfortunately, the Chief Justice was alone on the Indiana Supreme Court, and the right to keep and bear arms went into a coma—to be restored to consciousness in *Schubert* v. *DeBard* (1980).

---

28 *Matthews* v. *State*, 237 Ind. 677, 148 N.E.2d 334, 341, 342 (1958).
29 *Matthews* v. *State*, 237 Ind. 677, 148 N.E.2d 334, 342, 343 (1958).

The following two New York decisions are remarkable in a number of ways. Both were decided very, very low in the hierarchy of the courts, and both are splendid examples of legal writing as literature. In *Application of Grauling* (1959), the New York City police commissioner had denied renewal of a pistol license to one Walter Grauling because his 16-year-old son had been twice charged with unnamed "violations of law," but apparently not convicted. Grauling had also been a victim of a burglary in which two pistols had been stolen, but subsequently recovered. Much of the decision by Samuel Hofstadter can only be characterized as a sermon on the moral collapse of American society. After four pages of musing about the moral failures of 1959 America, free of legal argument, precedent, or authority, the guts of the decision finally appear:

> The right to bear arms is a precious one, guaranteed by the United States Constitution. But while we are a society still pioneering in the realm of space and spirit, we are no longer a frontier community. The great master of the law correctly observed that "Most rights are qualified" (American Bank & Trust Co. v. Federal Bank, 256 U.S. 350, 358, 41 S.Ct. 499, 500, 65 L.Ed. 983), and this right, too, is subject to regulation.[30]

But how severe can such regulation be, and yet not conflict with this right "guaranteed by the United States Constitution"? No answer is given, but one of Hofstadter's footnotes argued for extending the handgun licensing law to include rifles and shotguns, which was done in the 1967 New York City Gun Control Law.

Other than the assertion that "Most rights are qualified," there are no precedents cited anywhere in this decision. How then was this decision developed? Perhaps the heart of the matter comes from the third paragraph from the end, where Judge Hofstadter expresses a view of the nature of violence and guns that tells us more about Hofstadter than anything else:

> One of the obvious methods of combatting violence is to remove the weapons of violence. In the struggle against evil we need help—not to be tempted as we are prone to be in our daily lives. The means of avoidance of temptation is itself a weapon against evil. That is the prayer for grace uttered by many every day—the inward meaning, perhaps, of "Lead us not into temptation."[31]

Judge Hofstadter apparently saw firearms as the serpent in the New York City Garden of Eden, tempting and luring the owner into criminality—the handgun straining at the confines of a drawer, begging its owner to take it out and murder someone. It would be tempting to cite *Application of Grauling* (1959) as a decision that recognized the Second Amendment as protecting an individual right against state law, subject to "reasonable" regulation. But there is nothing "reasonable" about the decision made in this case, and it is hard to take seriously a decision so deficient in legal reasoning.

Compared to the decisions of the New York courts in *Moore* v. *Gallup* (1943) and *Application of Cassidy* (1944), our next New York decision at first *appears* to be a radical departure. This case started out in small claims court, and was appealed to the Queens Municipal Court. As Ferdinand Hutchinson described the sequence of events:

> outside his home he saw some men dumping the rubbish and garbage from the cans he had put out a short time before; that he remonstrated with them and asked them to stop

---

30 *Application of Grauling*, 17 Misc.2d 215, 183 N.Y.S.2d 654, 658 (1959).
31 *Application of Grauling*, 17 Misc.2d 215, 183 N.Y.S.2d 654, 658 (1959).

what they were doing and replace the debris; that they threatened him and called him a name that reflected upon his race and ancestry; that as they advanced he retreated into the hallway, that they came in after him, still menacing him, that he retreated further into his apartment and locked the door, that they broke in the door and entered his apartment. He withdrew further into another room and there, getting possession of a hunting rifle which he owned, he ordered them out. They left his apartment still threatening him, and took up a position in the common hall. That he opened the door leading to the hall from the rear room where he had sought shelter, and leveling the gun ordered them to leave. They refused and he fired the gun into the ceiling.

The police subsequently decided that Hutchinson had been refused entry to a party, and therefore decided to threaten a large crowd of people attempting to go to the party—even though the investigating officer admitted that he had no direct evidence of this, and "his investigation showed that plaintiff's apartment door had been forced and broken open."

That something was fishy about the criminal case filed by the police may be inferred from the judge's comment:

> It is significant that no evidence was given by the people allegedly driven out by the plaintiff or by those claiming to have been injured, or who were allegedly giving the party upstairs. They were not produced upon the trial. They hover vaguely in the background of the testimony, muttering direful threats and charges, like an ancient Greek chorus. There is no intimation of their race, creed, color or anything else by which they might be identified.[32]

Hutchinson was charged with felonious assault and "discharging a gun within the city limits," and his hunting rifle turned over to the Property Clerk. When the case came to trial, "no one appeared against the defendant." The charges were dropped, but the Property Clerk, Thomas Rosetti, refused to turn over Hutchinson's rifle, on the grounds that the rifle was forfeited for being used in the commission of a crime—a crime for which the defendant faced no accusers, and in which the police department apparently didn't have enough confidence to actually pursue a trial.

The decision is a marvelously droll piece of writing—which, alas, limitations of space preclude reproducing here. The decision compared forfeiture of Hutchinson's rifle, even though no crime was proved, and no serious attempt was made to prove a crime, "to the Queen of Hearts in Alice in Wonderland, who, at the trial before the King insisted, 'Sentence first, verdict afterward.'" After articulating the reasons why Judge Fitzpatrick found Hutchinson's testimony "credible," and the absurdity of forfeiting the rifle when found innocent:

> In the face of the Corporation Counsel's insistence upon the provisions of the Administrative Code forbidding the discharge of firearms within the city limits, the court suggests that anyone in a situation of immediate peril is not going to stop to look up the Administrative Code to ascertain whether or not he may fire a rifle within the city limits. To so hold would be to give lip service only to the constitutional guarantees.

> The Constitution permits citizens the right to bear arms. It is well known that next to his horse, the possession most valued by the pioneer was his gun. It was often his only guarantee against premature baldness at the hands of whooping Indians bent upon avenging wrongs, real or imagined, their courage heightened by liberal doses of "fire water."... The founding fathers therefore wisely risked no major crises within the new nation by rashly depriving the pioneer or patriot of his right to retain his rifle, thereby

---

32 *Hutchinson v. Rosetti*, 205 N.Y.S.2d 526, 24 Misc. 949, 950, 951 (1960).

preserving domestic tranquility and the infant population from the depredations of out-
raged natives....

The Corporation Counsel insists that the Administrative Code is entitled to great
weight. It undoubtedly is, but in this court's humble opinion it is in this instance
fighting out of its division, and is hopelessly outclassed by the Constitution and the Bill
of Rights.[33]

It would be tempting, at first glance, to see this opinion as a humorous, not entirely
serious method of disposing of an absurd abuse of governmental power—but note
that the opinion did not go against the existing precedents that recognized the
authority of the Sullivan Law to "regulate" *handgun* ownership, as found in *People
Ex Rel. Darling* v. *Warden of City Prison* (1913), perhaps even to an abusive level, as
found in *Moore* v. *Gallup* (1943).

As we saw in *Wright* v. *Commonwealth* (1875), concealed carry of firearms,
without a criminal intent, was recognized as protected by the Pennsylvania
Constitution's right to keep and bear arms provision. Yet the Pennsylvania decisions that appeared during the turbulent 1960s and 1970s seemed unaware of the
Wright decision, and the spirited discussions at the 1873 constitutional convention.
As the 1960s wore on, concerns about crime and civil unrest bore fruit in restrictive
gun ordinances. In 1965, Philadelphia passed an ordinance that licensed transfer of
all firearms within and into the city. In 1967, Philadelphia prohibited the carrying
of firearms on public streets, with exceptions for those with state permits to carry
firearms, licensed hunters, those "actively engaged in a defense of his life or
property from imminent peril or threat," police officers, and the military.

In 1968, the state added to the Uniform Firearms Act of 1939 provisions that
prohibited carrying of firearms "during an emergency proclaimed by a municipal or
state governmental executive," with exceptions for those "actively engaged" in self-
defense, and those licensed to carry; and that prohibited carrying under all conditions "in a city of the first class" (Philadelphia), except for those licensed by the
state.[34]

The next decision attempting to use the Pennsylvania Constitution's arms provision was at the heights of the social chaos that characterized this period. The decision *Commonwealth* v. *Ray* (1970) disposed of two similar but unrelated cases. Frederick Ray was charged and convicted of carrying a concealed deadly weapon, unlawfully carrying a firearm without a license, and transferring a firearm without a license from the city. Hosie Jeffcoat was charged with the same offenses, as well as
"carry of firearms in public in Philadelphia County." At trial, the Court of Common Pleas dismissed the carrying weapons charges of the Uniform Firearms Act,
held that the Philadelphia ordinance requiring a license to transfer firearms was unconstitutional, and directed a not guilty verdict for carrying concealed weapons.
Not surprisingly, the Commonwealth appealed.

On appeal, the Superior Court[35] refused to allow an appeal of a directed verdict;
more relevant to our interests is how the Superior Court dealt with the various fire-

33 *Hutchinson v. Rosetti*, 205 N.Y.S.2d 526, 24 Misc. 949, 952, 953, 954 (1960).

34 *Commonwealth* v. *Ray*, 218 Pa.Super. 72, 272 A.2d 275, 277, 278 (1970). See Penn. Statutes
Annotated 53§101 (1974) for the classification of Pennsylvania cities.

35 The term "Superior Court," as used in Pennsylvania, may be confusing to non-Pennsylvanians.
This is an appellate court with jurisdiction over most criminal case, but not all. Attempts to tease out
the exact structure of the Pennsylvania appeals process have left this author quite confused. Those who

arms charges. The Philadelphia licensing procedure for firearms transfers was overturned—but not based on the Pennsylvania's constitutional protection of the right
to keep and bear arms, but because the city ordinance attempted "to extend its
authority beyond the city limits and enlarges the powers granted by acts of the
General Assembly..."[36] The Superior Court acknowledged:

> The right of citizens of Pennsylvania to bear arms in defense of themselves, their prop-
> erty and the State predates any Constitution of the Commonwealth, and has been em-
> bodied in every Constitution we have had and is in Article I, §1, and Article I, §21 of
> the present Constitution of Pennsylvania....

> That the right to bear arms guaranteed by the Constitution is not an unlimited right is
> almost universally accepted. That a reasonable regulation in a gun control law is a valid
> exercise of the police power of the Commonwealth prescribing for the good order and
> protection of its citizens. Commonwealth v. Butler, 189 Pa.Super. 399, 150 A.2d 172
> (1959); Wright v. Commonwealth, 77 Pa. 470 (1875).[37]

But in *Butler*, the constitutionality of the concealed weapons statute was not
raised, or decided;[38] in *Wright* v. *Commonwealth* (1875), the Pennsylvania Supreme
Court appears to have held that criminal intent *and* concealed carry of a firearm
were required to form a crime; and the intent of the 1873 Pennsylvania
Constitutional Convention was that concealed carry would remain constitutionally
protected. Yet the Superior Court here implied that the Uniform Firearms Act was
constitutional.

The next paragraphs discussed the constitutionality of the provisions of the
Uniform Firearms Act with respect to prohibiting the carrying of arms during a
state of emergency:

> The lower court based its conclusion that the 1968 Amendments... were unconsti-
> tutional because the second portion thereof did not contain as an exception to the right
> of a citizen to bear arms in defense of himself or his property.

> This right is a constitutional one and cannot be diminished by any act of the Legislature.
> If it was included it would be mere surplusage, for it is presumed that all acts of the
> Legislature are subject to the clear mandate of the Constitution and included by
> reference thereto.

> We are bound to afford this legislation the presumption of constitutionality.[39]

So what does this mean? The Court here uphold the provisions with respect to a
state of emergency, but is silent about the provisions that prohibit a person from
carrying firearms in public in a "city of the first class" at all times, and which, without question, restricted the right of a citizen to defend himself.

In *Morrison* v. *State* (1960) the Texas Court of Criminal Appeals drew upon the
Michigan Supreme Court's *People* v. *Brown* (1931) decision to hold that a
submachine gun was one of the weapons of the "gangster," not protected by the
Texas Constitution's guarantee of a right to arms. Charles Walter Morrison had

---

desire to share in the confusion are referred to *The Pennsylvania Manual: 1970-71*, (Pennsylvania Dept.
of Property and Supplies, 1971), 473-4.
    36 *Commonwealth* v. *Ray*, 218 Pa.Super. 72, 272 A.2d 275, 276, 277, 278 (1970).
    37 *Commonwealth* v. *Ray*, 218 Pa.Super. 72, 272 A.2d 275, 278, 279 (1970).
    38 *Commonwealth* v. *Butler*, 189 Pa.Super. 399, 150 A.2d 172 (1959).
    39 *Commonwealth* v. *Ray*, 218 Pa.Super. 72, 272 A.2d 275, 276, 279 (1970).

used the submachine gun to render his wife's car inoperable, so as to discourage her from leaving him. The Texas Court of Criminal Appeals decision recognized and reiterated the language from *Brown* that protected weapons were, "those arms which by the common opinion and usage of law-abiding people, are proper and legitimate to be kept upon private premises for the protection of persons and property."[40]

When George B. Davis, III and John Allen Johnson were "apprehended in a remote part of Dade County, Florida, each had a pistol in his hand and each carried a pistol in an unconcealed holder." Unfortunately, no other information is provided as to how they came to the attention of the police. Both were charged under a Florida statute, §790.05, which prohibited the carrying of pistols without a permit from the county commissioners. Davis and Johnson argued that the statute was a violation of §20 of the Declaration of Rights of the Florida Constitution, which provides:

> The right of the people to bear arms in defence of themselves, and the lawful authority of the State, shall not be infringed, but the Legislature may prescribe the manner in which they may be borne.

The Florida Supreme Court held:

> Doubtless the guarantee was intended to secure to the people the right to carry weapons for their protection while the proviso was designed to protect the people also—from the bearing of weapons by the unskilled, the irresponsible, and the lawless. It seems sensible that to secure the protection intended in the contrasting final statement of the section the regulatory procedure should be placed under the control of the county commissioners as was done in Sec. 790.06, supra.

> We think this controversy may be epitomized by the statement that the appellants planted their thrust upon the first statement of Sec. 20 of the Declaration of Rights while the State in its parry stood firmly on the second.

> We are referred to no decision of this court passing directly on the validity of the Act although it seems to have first appeared in Chapter 4147, Acts of 1893.

The Court decided that "the public safety and general welfare are appropriately guarded by the control imposed by the statute" and refused to overturn the ordinance. The Court expressed a complete lack of interest in why the original statute applied only to "pistols and repeating rifles": "We are concerned with whether or not the legislature went too far, not with whether or not that body did not go far enough. The wisdom of the law is a matter of legislative not judicial concern."[41] The Court failed to recognize (or admit) that the first part of the guarantee was meaningless, if there was no legal manner remaining to bear arms.

In *State* v. *Cole* (1959), the North Carolina Supreme Court heard an appeal from, "James Cole, James Garland Martin, and others to the State unknown," who had been convicted of inciting a riot in Robeson County, North Carolina. James Cole and other Klansmen had engaged in, "inflammatory speeches and cross-burnings," with the apparent purpose of provoking the Indians of Robeson County into a confrontation. The decision is lengthy, with most of it not relevant to our concerns. To the extent that Cole, Martin, and the other defendants were engaged in inciting a riot, they were violating the law by carrying arms "in a county where

---

40 *Morrison* v. *State*, 170 Tex.Cr.R. 218, 339 S.W.2d 529, 530, 531, 532 (1960).
41 *Davis* v. *State*, 146 So.2d 892, 893, 894 (Fla. 1962).

the defendant Cole had been preaching racial dissension and hatred and conducting cross-burnings for the purpose of frightening certain Indian families in the community."

Cole's appeal argued that his conviction had denied his right to keep and bear arms:

> The defendant Cole's exception... is to the instruction given by the court with respect to the right to bear arms. The pertinent part of the instruction was as follows: "...the Constitution and laws of this State guarantee to a person the right to bear arms and right to assemble peaceably for the purpose of registering their grievances. I instruct you that does not give any individual, or any body of individuals, the right to bear arms for unlawful purposes in any respect anywhere."[42]

The North Carolina Supreme Court cited *State* v. *Huntly* (1843) with respect to the carrying of arms "to the annoyance and terror and danger of its citizens," and concluded that Cole's exception concerning the charge to the jury was without merit.[43]

What is additionally interesting about the riot that led to Cole's arrest, is the reaction of the Indian community to Cole's efforts. Robeson County Sheriff Malcolm G. McLeod had approached Cole before the riot, and asked him to call off the rally; Cole had insisted, "I am due some protection for a lawful assembly." McLeod had argued that it was hardly a lawful assembly, and warned Cole, "I believe if I had one hundred and fifty men, I couldn't keep the Indians of Robeson County from coming in on that field."

According to McLeod, there were approximately 200 people at the rally; they were outnumbered by armed Indians who had gathered across the road. In the ensuing riot, hundreds of shots were fired, and two people, one a reporter, the other a bystander, were slightly injured by gunfire.[44] It would appear that not just the KKK believed in the right to keep and bear arms, and further, that the Klan had more to gain from restrictive gun control than their intended victims.

The next North Carolina decision, *State* v. *Dawson* (1967), also involved the KKK, but unlike Cole, Dawson and his associates don't seem to have been suicidally inclined. Edward W. Dawson and a number of his friends were engaged in some late night vandalism and terrorism. After spray painting the letters "KKK" on the inside of a padlocked door, Dawson and his friends opened fire into an occupied dwelling, narrowly missing some of the residents. Dawson and his friends were convicted, and on appeal, sought to overturn the convictions on the grounds that one of the crimes charged was not a crime. The crime charged was that Dawson

> on 24 November 1966, "did unlawfully & willfully arm themselves with unusual and dangerous weapons, to wit: Pistols and Rifles and, for the wicked and mischievous purpose of terrifying and alarming the citizens of Alamance County, did ride or go about the public highways of Alamance County without lawful excuse armed with said weapons in a manner as would cause a terror and annoyance and danger to the citizens of said County..."[45]

While Dawson and his associates were convicted of other crimes, and appealed their convictions for those other crimes, only this crime is relevant to the "right to keep

42 *State* v. *Cole*, 249 N.C. 733, 107 S.E.2d 732, 740, 741 (1959).
43 *State* v. *Cole*, 249 N.C. 733, 107 S.E.2d 732, 741 (1959).
44 *State* v. *Cole*, 249 N.C. 733, 107 S.E.2d 732, 737 (1959).
45 *State* v. *Dawson*, 272 N.C. 535, 537, 538 (1967).

and bear arms." The North Carolina Supreme Court held that the crime in question was a violation of the "common-law misdemeanor"—Edward III's Statute of Northampton (1328). Considering the circumstances under which Dawson and associates were carrying these weapons—breaking and entering, vandalizing, and firing into occupied dwellings—it would seem a clear-cut case, hardly in need of much elucidation. But the Court provided a very detailed explanation of their reasoning.

The Court discussed Hawkins summary of *Sir John Knight's case*, and its application in *State* v. *Huntly* (1843). The Court also acknowledged that *Simpson* v. *State* (1833), came to a similar conclusion: "that it was no offense at all at common law for a man to go armed in public places with dangerous and unusual weapons when there was no attempt to use them, even though it was alleged to have been done to the terror of the people."[46] The Court agreed with the assertion of Dawson's attorney that since the North Carolina Constitutional provision protecting the right to keep and bear arms had changed since *Huntly*, that this might impact the meaning of the right. The 1776 North Carolina Constitution protected the "right to bear arms for the defense of the state":

> In 1868, the above provision was replaced by the first sentence of Art. I §24 of the present Constitution: "A well regulated militia being necessary to the security of a free state, the right of the people to keep and bear arms shall not be infringed; and, as standing armies in time of peace are dangerous to liberty, they ought not to be kept up, and the military shall be kept under strict subordination to, and governed by, the civil power." To the foregoing, the Constitutional Convention of 1875 added a second sentence: "Nothing herein contained shall justify the practice of carrying concealed weapons, or prevent the Legislature from enacting penal statutes against said practice."

> Defendant in this cases makes no contention that Art. I §24 of our present Constitution abolished the common-law crime of carrying weapons to the terror of the people or that it protects him from Indictment No. 50 [carrying of arms "to the terror of the people"]. Notwithstanding, we now consider whether this revision in the Constitution changed the common law as it existed in this State in 1843.

As Rawle's commentaries showed, even the early commentators who found that the Second Amendment protected an individual right to carry weapons, recognized that it had not repealed the common law prohibition on carrying arms "to the terror of the people":

> It is obvious that the second amendment to the Federal Constitution... furnished the wording for the first part of the N.C. Constitution, Art. I §24. Historical data and the reports of the deliberations and discussions which resulted in the wording of the second amendment and similar provisions in the constitutions of the original states lead to the conclusion that the purpose of these deliberations... was to insure the existence of a state militia as an alternative to a standing army.

The Court articulated the civic republicanism theory of the Second Amendment—but only with respect to avoiding the evil of a standing army, and with no apparent acknowledgment of the importance of keeping the government restrained:

> Today, of course, the State militia (of which the National Guard is the backbone) is armed by the State government and privately owned weapons do not contribute to its effectiveness. While the purpose of the constitutional guarantee of the right to bear arms

---

46 *State* v. *Dawson*, 272 N.C. 535, 537, 541, 542, 543, 544 (1967).

was to secure a well regulated militia and not an individual's right to have a weapon in order to exercise his common-law right of self-defense, this latter right was assumed.[47]

After citing a number of precedents with respect to the right of the state to regulate the manner of carrying arms, and arguing that "a citizen's right to carry arms is subject to reasonable regulation," the Court came to the point of the decision of interest to us:

> The right of a citizen to keep and bear arms is not at issue in this case. The question is whether he has a right to bear arms to the terror of the people. Our decisions make it quite clear that any statute, or construction of a common-law rule, which would amount to a destruction of the right to bear arms would be unconstitutional...[48]

If concealed carry could be regulated or forbidden by the North Carolina Legislature, and weapons "unconcealed... would endanger the whole community," what right to bear arms remains? It would seem a legitimate argument that open carry could be considered "to the terror of the people," but in that case, all that remains is concealed carry.

The minority opinion, by Justices Lake and Higgins, while agreeing that Dawson and friends were certainly guilty on the other counts, argued that unlike *State* v. *Huntly* (1843), Dawson and friends were not exhibiting their weapons for the purposes of terrorizing anyone, even though their *discharge* of those weapons achieved that effect. Further, Lake and Higgins asserted that the 1868 Constitution's revision, with the Second Amendment's language replacing the old "right to bear arms" clause, was even more liberal than the old provision:

> Seven years later, in the Convention of 1875, this sentence was added: "Nothing herein contained shall justify the practice of carrying concealed weapons, or prevent the Legislature from enacting penal statutes against said practice." It appears indisputable that the Convention of 1875 regarded the then established right of the people to keep and bear arms as absolute, so much so that the Legislature could not even forbid the carrying of a concealed weapon without the express authority being granted to it in the Constitution by amendment.[49]

After acknowledging that *State* v. *Speller* (1882) and *State* v. *Kerner* (1921) had recognized that the state might "regulate this right to bear arms," Justice Lake & Higgins tell us:

> I am unable to understand how a right can be regulated without being infringed. The language of the present Constitution appears to be plain and unequivocal. It does not say that the right to bear arms cannot be infringed except for the promotion of peace and good order in the community. It says the right shall not be infringed. It is immaterial whether that is wise or unwise. That is what the Constitution says.[50]

In *Harris* v. *State* (1967), the Nevada Supreme Court upheld a statute licensing the possession of tear gas. In that decision, they asserted that the Second Amendment applied only to the Federal Government, "and does not restrict state action." Further: "The right to bear arms does not apply to private citizens as an individual right." For that opinion, they cited *U.S.* v. *Miller* (1939), with no particular page

---

47 *State* v. *Dawson*, 272 N.C. 535, 545, 546 (1967).
48 *State* v. *Dawson*, 272 N.C. 535, 546, 548, 549 (1967).
49 *State* v. *Dawson*, 272 N.C. 535, 551, 552 (1967).
50 *State* v. *Dawson*, 272 N.C. 535, 552, 553 (1967).

cited for that position—and a position that is unsupported by reading the *Miller* decision.[51]

The year 1968 was a busy one for state courts about the meaning of the right to keep and bear arms; that it was also a year of race riots, antiwar riots, assassinations, and campus violence, did not bode well for the original intent of the Second Amendment. In 1966, New Jersey had adopted a gun control law that required purchasers of firearms to obtain

> firearms purchaser identification cards, which required the applicant to state... whether he had ever been a member of any organization advocating or approving the commission of acts of force and violence either to overthrow the government of the United States or of the State, or which sought to deny others their rights under the Constitutions of either the United States or of the State.[52]

The language alone showed the concern—America had entered the turbulent and divisive 1960s, and a great many Americans weren't too sure how far they trusted other Americans. Those of us who grew up in that confused time are not surprised; a younger generation may find it hard to imagine that anyone seriously worried about armed revolution.

In *Burton* v. *Sills* (1968), Arthur Burton and a number of associates, as the Citizens Committee for Firearms Legislation, filed suit against the requirements of the new law. While the decision went no higher than Superior Court, it showed the unwillingness of the New Jersey courts to make a serious attempt at refuting the constitutional arguments. Burton argued that the new New Jersey law violated:

> the Second Amendment to the United State Constitution and the rights of citizens of New Jersey provided for in Amendments I, IV, V, IX and XIV and Article I, Secs. 8 and 10 of the United States Constitution. They claim that the law's restraints and restrictions exceed the State's regulatory powers and constitute "a partial abolition of a basic right."...

> We find no substantial merit in the claim that this law wrongfully infringes upon the individual's constitutional rights under any of the provisions specified. Under the State's police powers, the common good takes precedence over private rights. One's home may be destroyed to prevent a conflagration. One's freedom of locomotion may be impeded to prevent the spread of a contagious disease. Our basic freedoms may be curtailed if sufficient reasons exists therefor. Only in a very limited sense is a person free to do as he pleases in our modern American society. Regulation by the government is price we pay for living in an organized community.[53]

Incredibly, the court cited *not a single precedent* for its decision—not even the existing U.S. Supreme Court precedents to hold that the Second Amendment applied only to the Federal Government.

In 1968, the U.S. Supreme Court made a decision that is *not* a Second Amendment decision—but is of great importance to the history of gun control, and to our next decision, *Grimm* v. *City of New York* (1968). In *Haynes* v. *U.S.* (1968) a Miles Edward Haynes had been convicted of unlawful possession of a sawed-off shotgun, in violation of the National Firearms Act of 1934, 26 U.S.C. §5851, which made it illegal to possess any firearm not registered under 26 U.S.C. §5841.[54] Haynes had

---

51 *Harris* v. *State*, 432 P.2d 929, 930 (Nev. 1967).
52 *Burton* v. *Sills*, 99 N.J.Super. 459, 460 (1968).
53 *Burton* v. *Sills*, 99 N.J.Super. 459, 461, 462 (1968).
54 *Haynes* v. *U.S.*, 390 U.S. 85, 88, 88 S.Ct. 722, 725 (1968).

argued at trial that his Fifth Amendment protection against self-incrimination had been violated by the requirement that he register a weapon he could not legally possess. When his motion to dismiss the charge was denied, Haynes pleaded guilty. The Fifth Circuit Court of Appeals upheld the conviction, and the Supreme Court agreed to hear the case.

Haynes argued, and the Supreme Court agreed, that registration of a sawed-off shotgun, as required by 26 U.S.C. §5841,[55] would provide information to the Federal Government that would incriminate him under 26 U.S.C. §5851, the unlawful possession section. Consequently, punishing Haynes for unregistered possession, when registering the gun would doubtless lead to criminal prosecution, violated Haynes' Fifth Amendment protection against self-incrimination. While the Court acknowledged that there were circumstances where a person might register such a weapon without having violated the prohibition on illegal possession or transfer, both the prosecution and the Court acknowledged such circumstances were "uncommon." The Court concluded: "We hold that a proper claim of the constitutional privilege against self-incrimination provides a full defense to prosecutions either for failure to register a firearm under §5841 or for possession of an unregistered firearm under §5851."[56]

This 8-1 decision (with only Chief Justice Earl Warren dissenting) is, depending on your view of Fifth Amendment, either a courageous application of the intent of the self-incrimination clause, or evidence that the Supreme Court had engaged in *reductio ad absurdum* of the Fifth Amendment. Under this ruling, a person who could not legally possess a firearm, under either federal or state law,[57] could not be punished for failing to register it. As the Court explained, *if* a registration requirement existed, a person who was violating the law by possession of such a weapon could not be punished for it, nor for failure to register.

While the Court does not directly address the issue, it appears that the same defense would apply to a criminal in unlawful possession of a gun in a jurisdiction that required registration. Consider a state that required registration of firearms, and made it illegal for a felon to be in possession of a firearm. The convicted felon could not be convicted for failure to register; but a law-abiding person who was in lawful possession on the date of registration and failed to register *could* be punished. In short, the person at whom, one presumes, such a registration law is aimed, is the one who *cannot* be punished; the person at whom such a registration law is not principally aimed, *can* be punished.

Also in 1968, the 1967 New York City Gun Control Law was challenged. This statute sought to bring shotguns and rifles under the same sort of licensing restrictions as the Sullivan Act had done to handguns. Edward Grimm and a number of others filed suit against the City of New York, asking the courts to overturn the city ordinance. Grimm, *et. al.*, raised a number of objections to the law, including that it was contrary to the Second Amendment.

The trial court asserted that the Second Amendment was not a restriction on state action. The court also cited *People Ex Rel. Darling* v. *Warden of City Prison* (1913), with respect to the authority to regulate handgun ownership, but neglected

---

55 *Haynes* v. *U.S.*, 390 U.S. 85, 96, 88 S.Ct. 722, 724, 725, 726 (1968).
56 *Haynes* v. *U.S.*, 390 U.S. 85, 100, 88 S.Ct. 722, 730, 732 (1968).
57 *Haynes* v. *U.S.*, 390 U.S. 85, 98, 88 S.Ct. 722, 730 (1968).

to mention that the same decision had recognized that "the arms of a militiaman or soldier" were constitutionally protected.

The court held that the legislative intent of the law was "that there existed an evil in the misuse of rifles and shotguns by criminals and persons not qualified to use these weapons and that the ease with which the weapons could be obtained was of concern..."[58] This would ordinarily not be a particularly interesting case; it did not reach very high in the New York court system; but at the end of the decision is a remarkable statement:

> Finally, in a post-argument letter, plaintiffs' attorney called this court's attention to the decision in Haynes v. United States.... In this court's reading of the *Haynes* decision, it is inapposite to the statute under consideration here. The registration requirement in *Haynes* was "...directed principally at those persons who have obtained possession of a firearm without complying with the Act's other requirements, and who therefore are immediately threatened by criminal prosecutions... They are unmistakably persons 'inherently suspect of criminal activities.'" (p. 96) (390 U.S. 85, 88 S.Ct. 722, 730, 19 L.Ed.2d 923.) The City of New York's Gun Control Law is not aimed at persons inherently suspect of criminal activities. It is regulatory in nature. Accordingly, *Haynes* does not stand as authority for plaintiffs' position.[59]

In three pages, the court went from "an evil in the misuse of rifles and shotguns by criminals" to "not aimed at persons inherently suspect of criminal activities."

A later New York decision, *Guida* v. *Dier* (1975), in Saratoga County, came to a different understanding of the Second Amendment and the New York Civil Rights Law. Salvatore Guida, an antique dealer in Warren County, had applied for a permit to carry a pistol. He asserted he had been robbed twice, once at gunpoint. Warren County Judge John Dier had denied Guida a permit, first based on an investigation by the Warren County Sheriff's Dept., and the second time based on the recommendation of the New York State Police.

Guida appealed, arguing that his rights under the Second Amendment, and article 2, §4 of the New York Civil Rights Law had been violated. On appeal to the court of a neighboring county:

> That contention is without merit. The right guaranteed by the Second Amendment to the United States Constitution and further defined in Section 4 of Article 2 of the Civil Rights Law does not extend to pistols or other readily concealable hand weapons. Rather, those guarantees protect only the right to be armed with weaponry suitable for use by the militia in warfare and for the general defense of the community. (*Moore* v. *Gallup*, 267 App. Div. 64, 45 N.Y.S.2d 63, affd. 293 N.Y.S. 846, 59 N.E.2d 439.)[60]

As we have previously seen, in *Moore v. Gallup* (1943), the New York courts *had* recognized that a right to possess long guns was constitutionally protected. However, neither *Guida* v. *Dier* (1975) nor *Grimm* v. *City of New York* (1968) went to New York's highest court, and so the apparent conflict between them has yet to be resolved.

In *State* v. *Bolin* (1968), the Kansas Supreme Court again heard a decision in which the Kansas Bill of Rights guarantee was argued. While the case has been discussed in a previous chapter—the statute in question made it illegal for convicted felons to possess firearms—the Kansas Supreme Court pointed to the *City of Salina*

---

58 *Grimm* v. *City of New York*, 56 Misc.2d 525, 289 N.Y.S.2d 358, 361 (1968).
59 *Grimm* v. *City of New York*, 56 Misc.2d 525, 289 N.Y.S.2d 358, 364 (1968).
60 *Guida* v. *Dier*, 84 Misc.2d 110, 375 N.Y.S.2d 826, 827, 828 (1975).

v. *Blaksley* (1905) precedent, and again held that no individual right was protected.[61]

In *Photos* v. *City of Toledo* (1969), a Toledo, Ohio, city ordinance required handgun owners to obtain an identification card. It also prohibited violent ex-felons, minors, and those convicted of more than one violent misdemeanor or "drunk and disorderly" within the previous year, from possessing a handgun. Unlike New York's Sullivan Law, the Toledo ordinance gave no discretionary authority to the police department; if a person was not in one of the prohibited categories, issuance of the identification card was required. Exceptions were made for travellers passing through Toledo, new residents, and gun dealers.[62]

The plaintiffs, George T. Photos and Bennie J. Martin, attacked the law on a number of points, of which the ones of interest to us are: "The plaintiffs allege the ordinance violates the plaintiffs' right to bear arms as provided by the Ohio Constitution; that the plaintiffs' constitutional right not to be compelled to testify against themselves is violated by this ordinance;..."[63]

The Lucas County Court of Common Pleas generally upheld the ordinance:

> With reference to issue two, the law is well settled that the state's power to prohibit carrying of concealed weapons does not violate the constitutional provisions of Ohio regarding the right to bear arms... Further, the ordinance in question does not go as far as the state statute and is less restrictive than the state prohibition. Almost all state constitutions, with variations in phraseology, contain a guaranty similar in substance and effect to that found in the Ohio Constitution. Whatever may be the source or nature of the right to bear arms, or the precise character of those arms in connection with which the right is to be exercised, the manner of bearing arms is subject to regulation by the states or their political subdivisions, under their police power, provided the regulation is reasonable.[64]

The Court had cleverly taken "the right to bear arms" from the plaintiffs' argument, and concluded that there was authority to regulate *possession* on private property because the authority to regulate concealed carry was within the state's authority. While the plaintiffs had not raised the issue of the Second Amendment, the Court pointed to *U.S.* v. *Miller* (1939), *U.S.* v. *Cruikshank* (1876), and *Presser* v. *Illinois* (1886) as precedents for the position that the Second Amendment did not restrict state law.

On the Fifth Amendment issue, the Court asserted that application for a handgun owner's identification card did not make a person "inherently suspect of criminal activities." The use of this quotation suggests that the Court was aware of the decision *U.S.* v. *Haynes* (1968), but they did not cite it. In any case, unless the plaintiffs had been prohibited persons within the Toledo ordinance, the Fifth Amendment would have provided them no protection. The decision closed with remarks that asserted that the ownership of a handgun was a "privilege," and a long quotation from *Burton* v. *Sills* (1968), including the infamous: "Only in a very limited sense is a person free to do as he pleases in our modern society."[65]

---

61 *State* v. *Bolin*, 200 Kan. 369, 436 P.2d 978, 979 (1968).
62 *Photos* v. *City of Toledo*, 19 Ohio Misc. 147, 250 N.E.2d 916, 918, 919, 920, 921 (Ct.Comm. Pleas 1969).
63 *Photos* v. *City of Toledo*, 19 Ohio Misc. 147, 250 N.E.2d 916, 923, 924 (Ct.Comm.Pleas 1969).
64 *Photos* v. *City of Toledo*, 19 Ohio Misc. 147, 250 N.E.2d 916, 925, 926 (Ct.Comm.Pleas 1969).
65 *Photos* v. *City of Toledo*, 19 Ohio Misc. 147, 250 N.E.2d 916, 927 (Ct.Comm.Pleas 1969).

Later that same year in the Ohio case *State* v. *Schutzler* (1969), Gale Leroy Schutzler attempted to quash an indictment for failure to register a submachine gun in accordance with O.R.C. 2923.04, which required registration of automatic weapons and a $5000 bond, "conditioned to save the public harmless by reason of any unlawful use of such weapon..."

Before the Montgomery County Court of Common Pleas, Schutzler argued that the registration requirement violated his Fifth Amendment rights, based on *Haynes* v. *U.S.* (1968); that the $5000 bond discriminated against the poor, and was therefore a denial of the equal protection of the laws; and that the law was contrary to Article 1, §4 of the Ohio Constitution guaranteeing the right to bear arms. The Court of Common Pleas did not agree with any of Schutzler's arguments. Where the *Haynes* decision was based on the fact that Haynes was an ex-felon, and therefore his possession of a sawed-off shotgun was illegal, Schutzler's only violation of the law was his failure to register the submachine gun and post bond. Had he been an ex-felon, the *Haynes* decision would have protected him.

The Court also disagreed about the bond:

> Schutzler, upon his own evidence, cannot be classified as poor. Furthermore the bond requirement of the statute is not directed against any one classification of persons, business, professions or hobbies. The unlawful or negligent use of machine guns can be injurious to persons. Thus the bond for the permit is in effect compulsory insurance for the exercise of the right to use such gun.[66]

It is frightening to consider what would happen to freedom of press if this reasoning were applied to newspapers and pamphleteers, and a bond to cover the costs of libel judgements were required as a condition of owning a printing press. The argument that such a law does not discriminate against the poor because it is not directed at them is this century's version of, "The majestic egalitarianism of the law, which forbids rich and poor alike to sleep under bridges, to beg in the streets, and to steal bread."[67]

On the subject of the Ohio Constitution's protection of the right to bear arms:

> But this right does not prevent the legislature from making such police regulations as may be necessary for the welfare of the public at large concerning the manner in which arms shall be borne and the use thereof. State v. Nieto, 101 Ohio St. 409, 130 N.E. 663; Porello v. State, 121 Ohio St. 280, 168 N.E. 135. The right cannot be deprived but it enjoins a duty in execution of which that right is to be exercised.[68]

It is wise that the Court did not provide any particular citation within *State* v. *Nieto* (1920), because the Ohio Supreme Court in *Nieto* had only recognized the constitution as allowing "police regulations as may be necessary for the welfare of the public at large as to the manner in which arms shall be borne."[69] Throughout *Nieto*, only the issue of *bearing* arms was found to be within the authority of "police regulations."

In *Porello* v. *State* (1929), the issue was again only whether concealed carry of arms was constitutionally protected—there was nothing in this decision that recognized or accepted that the police powers of the state went as far as regulation of the

---

66 *State* v. *Schutzler*, 249 N.E.2d 549, 552, 553 (Ohio Ct.Comm.Pleas 1969).
67 Anatole France, *Le Lys Rouge* (1894), ch .7.
68 *State* v. *Schutzler*, 249 N.E.2d 549, 552 (Ohio Ct.Comm.Pleas 1969).
69 *State* v. *Nieto*, 101 Ohio St. 409, 413, 130 N.E. 663 (1920).

possession of arms. Indeed, *Porello* quoted *State* v. *Hogan* (1900) that, "A man may carry a gun for any lawful purpose, for business or amusement, but he cannot go about with that or any other dangerous weapon to terrify and alarm a peaceful people."[70] Unless Schutzler was carrying his submachine gun (an action that would certainly "terrify and alarm"), it is hard to see what relevance *Porello* has to Schutzler's violation of the registration law.

The first Michigan decision of interest to us after *People* v. *Brown* (1931) was *People* v. *McFadden* (1971). The defendant, Roscoe McFadden, was pulled over for driving without headlights. When he was unable to produce a driver's license, he was arrested, and searched. The search found a revolver; as he was taken to the police car, he attempted to drop a packet of cocaine and amphetamines.

Not surprisingly, McFadden was convicted of carrying a concealed weapon, and drug possession. McFadden's appeal was largely based on his claim that the search was illegal. But McFadden also argued that "the statute governing the licensing of concealed weapons is void for vagueness," and was therefore unconstitutional. It does not appear that McFadden argued that there was a constitutional right to bear arms, nor is there any evidence in the decision by the Michigan Court of Appeals that McFadden had actually been denied a concealed weapons permit.

The statute in question, M.C.L.A. §28.-426, established several minimum criteria for a concealed weapons permit, including citizenship, over 21 years old, a resident of Michigan at least six months, approval of the local law enforcement agency head, and that "it appears that the applicant has good reason to fear injury to his person or property, or has other proper reasons, and that he is a suitable person to be so licensed..." This phrase apparently provided the basis for the argument that the statute was "vague," because "good reason" is not defined, and "suitable person to be so licensed" created no standards for making such a decision.

The Appeals Court was not sympathetic to McFadden's argument, arguing that, "Because of the state's legitimate interest in limiting access to weapons peculiarly suited for criminal purposes, the right to bear arms, like all other rights, is subject to the reasonable exercise of the police power." The Court cited *People* v. *Brown* (1931) as the precedent for this position.[71] Yet the *Brown* decision had turned on what weapons could be prohibited, and had explicitly placed revolvers outside the list of items of which the state could prohibit.[72] *Brown* also acknowledged the right to bear arms for self-defense, but that the right was "subject, however, to the valid exercise of the police power of the state to regulate the carrying of firearms." But it did not identify at what point the "police power" to regulate carrying conflicted with the right to bear arms in self-defense. The Michigan Court of Appeals also pointed to the *U.S.* v. *Miller* (1939) decision as supporting their position concerning police power to regulate the carrying of arms, but the *Miller* decision involved the power to license or prohibit the possession (not *bearing*) of a short-barreled shotgun—and the *Brown* decision had explicitly denied that the state had a right to prohibit *possession* of revolvers.

A series of federal appellate court decisions during the early 1970s and into 1980 affirmed that the Second Amendment did not guarantee the right of convicted fel-

---

70 *Porello* v. *State*, 121 Ohio St. 280, 168 N.E. 135, 138 (1929).
71 *People* v. *McFadden*, 31 Mich. App. 512, 188 N.W.2d 141, 142, 143, 144 (1971).
72 *People* v. *Brown*, 253 Mich. 537, 235 N.W. 245, 247 (1931).

ons to possess firearms. While continuing the use of the language from *U.S. v. Miller* (1939), that weapon ownership must have some "reasonable relationship to the preservation or efficiency of a well regulated militia,"[73] these decisions emphasize that the various federal laws were intended "to eliminate firearms from the hands of criminals, while interfering as little as possible with the law abiding citizen."[74]

U.S. v. Lewis (1980), made it to the Supreme Court, and again, the Court used the language from *Miller* to reject a Second Amendment appeal from a felon in possession of a firearm. However, in *U.S. v. Johnson* (4th Cir. 1974), and apparently only in this decision, the assertion is made that, "The Second Amendment only confers a collective right of keeping and bearing arms,"[75] and erroneously cited *U.S. v. Miller* (1939) as the source of this reasoning. While these decisions have frequently been cited as evidence that the Second Amendment guarantees no individual right to possess arms, and a federal law prohibiting handguns is therefore constitutional,[76] the most that can be accurately determined from these decisions is that the courts have upheld the authority of the Federal Government to prohibit convicted felons from possessing firearms.

In the period after the Civil War, and during the great wave of immigration at the turn of the century, we saw evidence that social dislocation caused the right to keep and bear arms to be interpreted more and more narrowly. It is therefore no great surprise to find that one of the most dramatic social changes our society has ever experienced, along with the steepest continuous rise in murder rates of this century, would have resulted in a drastic response—but what response? It could have been argued that a dramatic increase in violent crime rates justified a dramatic increase of the right of law-abiding citizens to carry arms. This was definitely *not* the society's response; in fact, it was quite the opposite.

If we understand restrictions on the bearing of arms, and a narrowing or denial of the underlying right as an expression of one group's desire to stifle dramatic cultural changes coming from other groups, the results are much more comprehensible. If the right to bear arms is reduced to a mere privilege, then a black man, or a long-haired hippie has no strong claim to a permit to carry a gun for self-defense. But because such a permit is merely a privilege, not a right, a "respectable" white businessman would still be able to obtain a permit, without the courts worrying too much about equal protection of the laws.

---

73 *Cody* v. *U.S.*, 460 F.2d 34, 37 (8th Cir. 1972); *U.S.* v. *Johnson*, 497 F.2d 548, 550 (4th Cir. 1974).

74 *U.S.* v. *Weatherford*, 471 F.2d 47, 51 (7th Cir. 1972).

75 *U.S.* v. *Johnson*, 497 F.2d 548, 550 (4th Cir. 1974).

76 Beard and Fields, 31.

X. THE RIGHT COMES OUT OF ITS COMA?

By the early 1970s, the Civil Rights Movement had largely eliminated the legally imposed forms of racial discrimination, though socially customary racism and the effects of decades of legally imposed racism remained. Reduced U.S. participation in the Vietnam War caused a dramatic subsidence in the antiwar movement. The counterculture was largely absorbed or co-opted by the mainstream culture. The sexual and pornographic revolutions no longer shocked most Americans, and increasingly, a generation that had abhorred the sexual promiscuity of their children got divorced and hit the discos.

One cultural change had not fizzled out: the dramatic increase of crime rates. Murder rates continued to rise dramatically in the mid-1970s. After a small reduction in the late 1970s, murder rates again rose to a heretofore unknown level, exceeding 10 murders per 100,000 population. Then, as the economy entered the severe recession of the early 1980s, murder rates began to decline, dropping below 8 per 100,000 for the first time since the 1960s.[1] The trend was short-lived, and murder rates began to rise, slowly and tentatively, in 1987.[2]

Yet during this period the right to keep and bear arms was coming out of its coma. It didn't happen in every state, but in enough that those state courts that recognized or reaffirmed the right cannot be called idiosyncratic. The first decision representing this new trend, *City of Las Vegas* v. *Moberg* (1971), took place in New Mexico. Leland James Moberg had entered a police station in Las Vegas, New Mexico, wearing a holstered pistol, to report a theft from his automobile. A Las Vegas ordinance prohibited the carrying of any deadly weapon, openly or concealed, including, "guns, pistols, knives with blades longer than two and half inches, slingshots, sandbags, metallic metal knuckles, concealed rocks, and all other weapons, by whatever name known, with which dangerous wounds can be inflicted."

Moberg appealed his conviction based on article II, §6 of the New Mexico Constitution: "The people have the right to bear arms for their security and defense, but nothing herein shall be held to permit the carrying of concealed weapons." The New Mexico Court of Appeals agreed that: "Ordinances prohibiting the carrying of concealed weapons have generally been held to be a proper exercise of police power..." and cited *State* v. *Hart* (1945) and *Davis* v. *State* (1962) as precedents, but agreed that:

---

1 Bureau of Justice Statistics, 15.
2 *Crime in the United States 1988*, (Washington: Government Printing Office, 1989), 8.

As applied to arms, other than those concealed, the ordinance under consideration purports to completely prohibit the "right to bear arms."

It is our opinion that an ordinance may not deny the people the constitutionally guaranteed right to bear arms, and to that extent the ordinance under consideration is void...[3]

The Court of Appeals cited *State* v. *Rosenthal* (1903), *In Re Brickey* (1902), *State*
v. *Woodward* (1937), and *State* v. *Kerner* (1921) as precedents for its position.
Much like the *Brickey* case, this decision was short, and contained little in the way
of analysis and explanation.

That same year, New Mexico's Constitution was amended to strengthen what
was already a very strong arms provision. The state legislature proposed and the
people approved revision of Art. I, §6 to: "No law shall abridge the right of the citizen to keep and bear arms for security and defense, for lawful hunting and recreational use and for other lawful purposes, but nothing herein shall be held to permit
the carrying of concealed weapons."[4] Not only were the valid reasons to bear arms
extended to include hunting, recreation, and "other lawful purposes," but the word
"their" just before "security and defense" was taken out, making it even more clear
that this was not a collective right, but an individual right.

The decision *Rinzler* v. *Carson* (1972) by the Florida Supreme Court can be
quoted out of context as implying an absolute right to possess semiautomatic weapons. But a more careful analysis of the decision shows a considerably more
equivocal result.

A Leonard Rinzler of Jacksonville, Florida, owned a submachine gun, registered
with the Federal Government in accordance with the National Firearms Act of
1968. He kept it at his business, and used it in self-defense in 1969. To Rinzler's
credit, he fired at his attacker's feet, apparently without injuring his attacker. Rinzler was arrested, and the gun was seized by Sheriff Dale Carson. The criminal
charges against Rinzler were eventually dismissed, but in the meantime the Florida
Legislature enacted Florida Statute §790.221, which prohibited possession of "any
short-barreled rifle, short-barreled shotgun, or machine gun which is, or may
readily be made, operable." Sheriff Carson also asserted that a Jacksonville
ordinance prohibiting possession of a submachine gun prevented return of the gun.

Rinzler sued for return of his submachine gun, and on appeal, argued that the
right to keep and bear arms provision of the 1968 Florida Constitution (Art. I, §8)
made the statute in question unconstitutional. The Florida Supreme Court held
that the statute in question was "a valid exercise of the police power of the state."
In particular:

Although the Legislature may not entirely prohibit the right of the people to keep and
bear arms, it can determine that certain arms or weapons may not be kept or borne by
the citizen. We have specifically held that the Legislature can regulate the use and the
manner of bearing certain specific weapons.[5]

The Court then cited the *Nelson* v. *State* (1967) precedent, which banned convicted
felons from possessing concealable firearms; *Davis* v. *State* (1962), which required a
license to carry pistols and repeating rifles; and *Carlton* v. *State* (1912), which pro-

---

3 *City of Las Vegas* v. *Moberg*, 82 N.M. 626, 627, 628, 485 P.2d 737 (App. 1971).
4 New Mexico Const., Art. I, §6 (1992).
5 *Rinzler* v. *Carson*, 262 So.2d 661, 663, 664, 665 (Fla. 1972).

hibited concealed carry of weapons. That the Florida Supreme Court had crossed a very dramatic line—the one that separated convicted felons from law-abiding citizens, and carrying in public from possession at home—appears to have been recognized by the justices:

> In each of the four cited cases there is inherent in the holding of this Court the proposition that the right to keep and bear arms is not an absolute right, but is one which is subject to the right of the people through their legislature to enact valid police regulations to promote the health, morals, safety and general welfare of the people. It seems to us to be significant that the type of firearms, the possession of which is outlawed by Section 790.221, Florida Statutes, F.S.A., is that weapon which is too dangerous to be kept in a settled community by individuals, and one which, in times of peace, finds its use by a criminal.[6]

In defense of this position, the Court cited *People* v. *Brown* (1931) and *Morrison* v. *State* (1960). *People* v. *Brown* (1931) raised questions about which weapons, "by common opinion and usage by law-abiding people are proper and legitimate to be kept upon private premises for the protection of persons and property," and gave a partial list. *Morrison* v. *State* (1960) echoed *Brown*, specifically excluding a submachine gun from the "proper and legitimate" arms constitutionally protected. Similarly, the Florida Supreme Court also provided evidence of what it considered to be "proper and legitimate," and what was not:

> We hold that the Legislature may prohibit the possession of weapons which are ordinarily used for criminal and improper purposes and which are not among those which are legitimate weapons of defense and protection and protected by Section 8 of the Florida Declaration of Rights. A machine gun, particularly a hand-barreled one [*sic*], which is, or which may readily be made, operable, is peculiarly adaptable to use by criminals in the pursuit of their criminal activities. The Legislature may in the exercise of the police power of the State make its possession or ownership unlawful.

Having given a single example of a weapon which was clearly *not* protected, the Court proceeded to define weapons which *might* be protected:

> The definition of the term "machine gun" used in the statute as being "any firearm, as defined herein, which shoots or is designed to shoot, automatically or semi-automatically, more than one shot, without manually reloading, by a single function of the trigger," could be construed to prohibit any person owning or possessing any semi-automatic hand gun. *But such a construction might run counter to the historic constitutional right of the people to keep and bear arms.* We cannot believe that it was the intention of the Legislature in enacting this statute to deny such right, and it is our duty in construing the statute to preserve its constitutionality, if reasonably possible. *We, therefore, hold that the statute does not prohibit the ownership, custody and possession of weapons not concealed upon the person, which, although designed to shoot more than one shot semi-automatically, are commonly kept and used by law-abiding people for hunting purposes or for the protection of their persons and property, such as semi-automatic shotguns, semi-automatic pistols and rifles.*[7] [emphasis added]

The Court had upheld the status quo, recognized a right to the ordinary weapons of hunting and self-defense, but denied a right to possess a category of weapon nearly ideally suited to the Framers' intent for private ownership of arms, which was overthrowing the government.

---

6 *Rinzler* v. *Carson*, 262 So.2d 661, 665, 666 (Fla. 1972).
7 *Rinzler* v. *Carson*, 262 So.2d 661, 666 (Fla. 1972).

Rinzler had argued that the use of the word "keep" in the "right of the people to keep and bear arms" had implied some right to possess arms at home, and that state regulation of the bearing of arms implied that the keeping of arms at home was beyond the state's power. The Court rejected this position:

> It is evident that the purpose of adding this word to the phrase is to bring the protection in line with the phraseology used in the Second Amendment to the Constitution of the United States. The Supreme Court of the United States has held, in construing that amendment, that the right of the people to keep and bear arms is not infringed by the prohibition of statute which make it unlawful to possess certain kinds of firearms. Presser v. Illinois, 116 U.S. 252, 6 S.Ct. 580, 29 L.Ed. 615. The statute is not per se unconstitutional.[8]

Presser v. *Illinois* (1886) makes no such statement. The Illinois law which the U.S. Supreme Court upheld in *Presser* prohibited bodies of men marching with arms. Indeed, the *Presser* Court had specifically recognized that, "A state cannot prohibit the people therein from keeping and bearing arms to an extent that would deprive the United States of the protection afforded by them as a reserve military force."[9] The Florida Supreme Court was grasping at straws; to assert that a person's private possession of a submachine gun would not have been protected by the *Presser* decision, requires a most peculiar notion of what arms would be appropriate to "a reserve military force." After this detailed discussion of what the right to keep and bear arms protected, the Florida Supreme Court then held that registration of the submachine gun under the National Firearms Act of 1968 meant that the state law was not violated by Rinzler's ownership of it, and ordered new hearings, apparently to see that the weapon was returned to Rinzler.[10]

Earlier the same year, the Florida District Court of Appeals gave an opinion concerning the constitutionality of the statute, but in reference to a short-barreled rifle, in *State* v. *Astore* (1972). The defendant, Ronald Astore, had argued that the ordinance violated the Florida right to bear arms provision. The decision admitted that

> there are no controlling Florida cases "on all fours" with the question as posed. We nonetheless think that there are sufficient judicial guidelines concerning the first two aspects therefore, in somewhat similar and analogous cases, so that our opinion is, at this stage, unnecessary. As to the contention that that law violates the constitutional right to bear arms, see United States v. Miller... See also, Davis v. State...[11]

The *U.S.* v. *Miller* (1939) decision is reasonably close; both involved possession of short-barreled shoulder weapons. But where the *Miller* decision involved a registration law which still provided a method for lawful ownership, the Florida statute was a complete prohibition, with exceptions for those with federal permits. The *Davis* v. *State* (1962) is even less appropriate of a case, since the ordinance upheld by the Florida Supreme Court in that case regulated the *carrying* of arms, not their private possession.

The *Astore* decision never directly addressed the issue of the limits of regulation allowed under the Florida Constitution, but the statement that the "statute is not unreasonable on theory that it prohibits handguns of all sorts made from any rifle

---

8 *Rinzler* v. *Carson*, 262 So.2d 661, 666, 667 (Fla. 1972).
9 *Presser* v. *Illinois*, 116 U.S. 252 (1886).
10 *Rinzler* v. *Carson*, 262 So.2d 661, 667, 668 (Fla. 1972).
11 *State* v. *Astore*, 258 So.2d 33, 34 (Fla.App. 1972).

parts,"[12] suggests that a statute that prohibited handguns, at least as an accidental consequence of the statute, would be "unreasonable."

In *City of Lakewood* v. *Pillow* (1972), the Colorado Supreme Court overturned a city ordinance that prohibited carrying or possession of any handgun, "except within his own domicile," with the usual exemptions for travel to and from "any range, gallery, or hunting areas." Also exempted were people licensed by the city, and of course, the police.

The Colorado Supreme Court overturned this ordinance by holding

> that it is so general in its scope that it includes within its prohibitions the right to carry on certain businesses and to engage in certain activities which cannot under the police powers be reasonably classified as unlawful... Furthermore, it makes it unlawful for a person to possess a firearm in a vehicle or in a place of business for the purpose of self-defense. Several of these activities are constitutionally protected. Colo. Const. art. II, §13.[13]

Perhaps an indication of the Colorado Supreme Court's view of the proper limits of "police power"—that superelastic basis for many of the laws limiting the right to bear arms—can be found in the following paragraph:

> A governmental purpose to control or prevent certain activities, which may be constitutionally subject to state or municipal regulation under the police power, may not be achieved by means which sweep unnecessarily broadly and thereby invade the area of protected freedoms... *Even though the governmental purpose may be legitimate and substantial, that purpose cannot be pursued by means that broadly stifle fundamental personal liberties when the end can be more narrowly achieved.*[14] [emphasis added]

While not one of the stronger defenses of the right to bear arms in this period, and doubtless small comfort to the defendants in the case, *City of Akron* v. *Dixon* (1972) narrowly reaffirmed the "right to bear arms" under Ohio Constitution, Article I, §4. The ordinance in dispute was Akron City Code 1185.04:

> No person shall carry on or about his person a pistol, knife having a blade two and one-half inches in length or longer, knuckles, or a billy or other dangerous weapon; provided however, that upon the trial of this charge, the defendant shall be acquitted if it appears that he was at the time engaged in a lawful business, calling, employment, or occupation, and that the circumstances in which he was placed justified a prudent man in possessing such a weapon for the defense of his person or family.[15]

Clearly, such an ordinance provided substantial leeway for a jury to free the "right" sort of person, while convicting others, whose actions failed to conform to the jury's notion of prudence. The defendants in four separate cases had argued that the statute was in violation of the Ohio Constitution. Judge McFadden ruled otherwise:

> The ordinance is much more prolix than the succinct and lucid language of the Constitution. Types of weapons are listed, mention is made of the possible existence of lawful business, circumstances justifying a prudent man acting to defend himself or family and much more, but it could all be summarized to prohibiting the bearing of arms except to

---

12 *State* v. *Astore*, 258 So.2d 33 (Fla.App. 1972).
13 *City of Lakewood* v. *Pillow*, 180 Colo. 20, 501 P.2d 744, 745 (1972).
14 *City of Lakewood* v. *Pillow*, 180 Colo. 20, 501 P.2d 744, 745 (1972).
15 Akron City Code 1185.04, quoted in *City of Akron* v. *Dixon*, 36 Ohio Misc. 133, 303 N.E.2d 923, 924 (1972).

defend one's self or one's family. How is this different from the Constitution? I see no essential distinction.[16]

There is, of course, one subtle difference—the Akron ordinance puts the burden on the defendant to prove that he was within the protection of the Constitution— in essence, to prove his innocence. Nonetheless, Judge McFadden left the door open for an employed person to prove his innocence, and thus, the right to bear arms was maintained, in a limited sort of way.

In *Mosher* v. *City of Dayton* (1976), the Ohio Supreme Court upheld a Dayton ordinance that required handgun purchasers to obtain an identification card. This would seem to be a repeat of *Photos* v. *City of Toledo* (1969), which had advanced no further than the Court of Common Pleas, but in fact the Toledo ordinance had required all existing handgun owners to register themselves; the Dayton ordinance did not include present handgun owners. This dramatically weaker ordinance thus provided an opportunity for the Ohio Supreme Court to uphold a gun control law, and still avoid a direct confrontation with the Ohio Constitution. The Court observed: "The ordinance does not deprive any individual of the protection of Section 4, Article I of the Ohio Constitution. All that the ordinance requires is that the person seeking to possess a handgun be identified under the provisions of the ordinance."[17]

After citing *State* v. *Nieto* (1920), and using it to show that the state had the authority to regulate the carrying of arms:

> The Dayton ordinance in the present case is still less restrictive, for it does not limit the bearing of arms, but only requires that anyone who wishes to acquire a weapon first obtain an identification card in order to demonstrate that he is entitled to possess such a weapon. This is a reasonable police regulation which finds ample justification in the public interest of keeping dangerous weapons out of the hands of convicted felons and others forbidden to own and carry them…. Reasonable gun control legislation is within the police power of a legislative body to enact….[18]

To this point, the decision would seem a reasonable response to a genuine public safety issue—preventing, or at least discouraging those who were prohibited from handgun ownership, from purchasing a handgun. But the decision continues, in a more ominous vein: "[A]ny such restriction imposes a restraint or burden upon the individual, but the interest of the governmental unit is, on balance, manifestly paramount. See *Burton* v. *Sills* (1968)…" The assertion that the interest of the government is "paramount" over the individual is a doctrine completely contrary to the notion of a Bill of Rights. What purpose does a Bill of Rights serve if an individual's "restraint or burden" is always to be considered of less importance than the interests of the government?

The Ohio Supreme Court reiterated the *U.S.* v. *Miller* (1939) and *Presser* v. *Illinois* (1886) decisions of the U.S. Supreme Court—but with a slight twist. Where *Presser* had claimed that the Second Amendment was not a limitation on state laws, the Ohio Supreme Court seems to have recognized that *Miller* and *Presser* created limits to which state laws were subject:

---

16 *City of Akron* v. *Dixon*, 36 Ohio Misc. 133, 303 N.E.2d 923, 924 (1972).
17 *Mosher* v. *City of Dayton*, 48 Ohio St.2d 243, 358 N.E.2d 540, 542, 543 (1976).
18 *Mosher* v. *City of Dayton*, 48 Ohio St.2d 243, 358 N.E.2d 540, 543 (1976).

We also find no merit in the appellants' claim that the ordinance violates the federal Constitution (Second Amendment to the United States Constitution...). A state regulation of the ownership and use of firearms does not violate the Second Amendment unless it infringes upon the maintenance of a well-regulated militia, the right which the Second Amendment seeks to protect.... No provision of the Dayton ordinance conceivably interferes with that right.[19]

It appears that the Ohio Supreme Court recognized that "militia" weapons in private hands would be protected from overbroad state regulation under the Second Amendment—a position that was clearly taken in *Presser*. So why was the Dayton ordinance acceptable? Perhaps because the Court did not consider handguns to be militia weapons, but more likely because, "Appellants have failed to show that their right to acquire and possess handguns is violated by the provisions of the Dayton ordinance." The Dayton ordinance was not an actual obstacle to purchasing such weapons.

Justice Celebrezze wrote a dissenting opinion, but while he referred to the right to bear arms as "one of the fundamental civil rights," his argument against the ordinance was primarily that it was superfluous, in some areas in conflict with state law, and his belief that, "all limitations placed upon that right be not only reasonable, but also necessary."[20]

The first decision of the courts with respect to the Rhode Island Constitution's right to keep and bear arms is surprisingly recent: *State* v. *Storms* (1973). A Lesley E. Storms "was convicted in the Superior Court, Providence and Bristol Counties,... of unlawfully, and without a license, carrying a pistol...." Storms appealed his conviction, arguing that the statute which required a license to carry a handgun was unconstitutional—but he failed to specify whether he appealed to the Federal Constitution, or the Rhode Island Constitution, and under which provision he sought protection.

Justice Joslin wrote the Rhode Island Supreme Court's decision:

The defendant's initial challenge is that the legislation which makes it unlawful for him to carry a pistol or revolver on his person, unless licensed to do so, infringes upon the right of self defense guaranteed to all person by art. I, sec. 23 of the state constitution. That challenge may be summarily rejected since the constitutional provision relied upon declares only that the enumeration of rights in the Declaration of Rights "shall not be construed to impair or deny others retained by the people," and manifestly this guarantee in no sense assures a right of self defense.[21]

That Article I, §23 of the Rhode Island Constitution was clearly intended as a parallel to the Ninth Amendment to the Federal Constitution, would seem beyond question. Some Federalist arguments against a Bill of Rights ridiculed the notion that a written list was required in the Constitution: "Freedom of the press was not mentioned, 'Nor is liberty of conscience, or of matrimony, or of burial of the dead,' Ellsworth declared, but 'it is enough that congress have no power to prohibit either, and can have no temptation.'"[22]

The Court disposed of the right to keep and bear arms provision:

---

19 *Mosher* v. *City of Dayton*, 48 Ohio St.2d 243, 358 N.E.2d 540, 543 (1976).
20 *Mosher* v. *City of Dayton*, 48 Ohio St.2d 243, 358 N.E.2d 540, 543, 544 (1976).
21 *State* v. *Storms*, 308 A.2d 463, 464 (R.I. 1973).
22 Rutland, rev. ed., 142.

Moreover, defendant, even had he relied upon art. I, sec. 22 of the state constitution, which safeguards the right of the people to keep and bear arms, might not be on sound ground. Then he would have been burdened with persuading us of the weakness of what is apparently the prevailing view, viz., that a constitutional guarantee to keep and bear arms is not infringed upon by legislation which, in broad terms, forbids the unlicensed carrying of a pistol or revolver upon one's person excepting only in his home and place of business or upon his land.[23]

In support of this position, the Court cited *Burton* v. *Sills* (1968) (in which no precedents were cited, and for which no state constitutional provision was available), and *Matthews* v. *State* (1958), but the Court also acknowledged the presence of the decision *State* v. *Kerner* (1921).

Storms' last grasped straw was to argue that the Legislature had given too much authority to local licensing authorities to decide who had "proper reason for carrying a pistol." The Court rejected this argument, primarily based on *Matthews* v. *State* (1958).[24] The poor preparation of the defendant to argue the right to bear arms would appear to have fatally damaged his case; there was certainly no shortage of decisions that could have been cited along with *Kerner*.

The decision *State* v. *Beorchia* (Utah 1974) was the only decision of this period to examine the issue of possession by resident aliens. Romeo Beorchia was convicted of being an alien in possession of dangerous weapons—in this case, a handgun and a shotgun. Beorchia's brother was arrested for deserting military service. While serving the warrant, it was noticed that there were firearms present in the residence of the Beorchias. A warrant was obtained, and a few days later, Romeo Beorchia was arrested.

On appeal, Beorchia attempted to overturn Utah Code 76-10-503, which prohibited aliens from possessing firearms, by arguing that it violated both the Fourteenth Amendment and Art. I, §6 of the Utah Constitution: "The people have the right to bear arms for their security and defense, but the Legislature may regulate the exercise of this right by law."

The Utah Supreme Court unanimously refused to overturn the statute, asserting, "It is quite evident from the language above set forth that the Legislature had sufficient power to enact the statute in question." There was no attempt to justify this position by reference to precedents involving similar constitutional provisions, and no awareness of the previous decisions involving aliens and state arms provisions in other courts.

Beorchia also claimed that his rights had been violated under the Fourteenth Amendment, guaranteeing equal protection of state laws. The Utah Supreme Court cited *Patsone* v. *Pennsylvania* (1914) and *In Re Rameriz* (1924), a California Supreme Court decision, both of which had upheld statutes prohibiting aliens from owning guns.[25] One of the serious errors, however, was their citation of *Rameriz*. Not only was the case miscited as *Ex Parte Rameriz*, but *Rameriz* had been overturned two years before *Beorchia* in *People* v. *Rappard*, (Cal. App. 1972), based on the Fourteenth Amendment, and a provision of the California Constitution.[26]

---

23 *State* v. *Storms*, 308 A.2d 463, 464 (R.I. 1973).

24 *State* v. *Storms*, 308 A.2d 463, 466, 467 (R.I. 1973).

25 *State* v. *Beorchia*, 530 P.2d 813, 814, 815 (Utah 1974).

26 *People* v. *Rappard*, 28 Cal.App.3d 302 (1972), summarized in Cal. Penal Code Ann. §12021, note 4.

Eight years later, the Utah Supreme Court returned to the subject of aliens in possession of a firearm in *State* v. *Vlacil* (Utah 1982). With the exception of retired Justice J. Allan Crockett, apparently filling in a vacancy on the bench, every Utah Supreme Court Justice had changed. The defendant, Frank Vlacil, a citizen of Czechoslovakia, was apparently involved in an altercation at a bar in Price, Utah. As a result, Vlacil was "forcibly ejected from the club." Shortly thereafter, a bullet was fired through a window, and according to the people inside, Vlacil was seen outside with what was described as a "burp gun," or automatic weapon. In the resulting confrontation, Vlacil apparently shot a James Cruz in the shoulder. Later that night, Vlacil was arrested and charged with possession of a dangerous weapon under the same statute that was used in *State* v. *Beorchia* (1974). He was convicted of this violation, but apparently, no other crime.[27]

Vlacil's argument against the statute's constitutionality was that his right to self-defense under Art. I, §6 was denied by such a statute, and that the Federal Government alone had authority to regulate aliens, an issue not of interest to us.[28] The decision of the Court was heavily fractured, with Chief Justice Hall filing one opinion, Justice Oaks filing a concurring opinion, retired Justice Crockett concurring in the decisions of Hall and Oaks, and Justices Stewart and Howe filing an opinion concurring only in the result—upholding Vlacil's conviction.

Hall's decision was a curious mixture of judicial activism and judicial restraint. Because Vlacil had argued that his right to self-defense was denied by the statute, and the alleged actions of Vlacil were not even close to self-defense, Hall insisted: "[T]he element of self-defense is not present in the instant case, we do not address that narrow issue, focusing instead on the *facial* constitutionality of the statute."[29] [emphasis in the original]

Hall refused to explore an issue not specific to Vlacil's case—admirable judicial restraint. But then, even though Vlacil's argument made reference *only* to the Utah Constitution, Hall engaged in a lengthy discussion of why the Second Amendment was not an individual right, but only a right of the states to maintain a militia. On the subject of the Utah Constitution, Hall used the *State* v. *Beorchia* (Utah 1974) precedent, with no apparent awareness that the *Rameriz* precedent on which it was based, had been overturned.[30]

Justice Oaks' concurring opinion was considerably more careful with respect to the significance of the Second Amendment: "Defendant has not relied on the Second Amendment. It is therefore inadvisable to discuss that amendment in this case, especially when its applicability to state regulation is doubtful at best."[31] But unlike Hall, who argued that the Second Amendment was not an individual right:

> The weight of authority holds that an *individual's Second Amendment right to bear arms is guaranteed only against federal, not state*, encroachment.... In view of those authorities,

---

27 *State* v. *Vlacil*, 645 P.2d 677, 678, 679, 683 (Utah 1982). Justice Stewart, concurring in the result only, asked the question: "No jury and no judge has ever determined that the facts recited [related to the shooting] are true. If, indeed, they are true, it is incomprehensible why the prosecution did not charge the defendant with a far more serious crime."

28 *State* v. *Vlacil*, 645 P.2d 677, 679, 680 (Utah 1982).

29 *State* v. *Vlacil*, 645 P.2d 677, 679 note 2 (Utah 1982).

30 *State* v. *Vlacil*, 645 P.2d 677, 679, 680 (Utah 1982).

31 *State* v. *Vlacil*, 645 P.2d 677, 681 (Utah 1982).

any comments about the meaning of the Second Amendment in this case are *obiter dictum....* [emphasis added]

Although it is possible that the Second Amendment may yet be held to apply to state regulation in some manner,... it is unwise to address that complicated issue in a case where it has not been fully briefed.[32]

While agreeing with Hall that Vlacil's offensive actions prevented him from using the Utah Constitution's arms provision, Oaks acknowledged that a case similar to *People* v. *Zerillo* (1922), with a peaceful alien prosecuted for possession of a firearm, might result in a different ruling.

Justice Stewart's opinion (concurred in by Justice Howe), agreed in the result—upholding Vlacil's conviction—but Stewart wished for a more clear-cut case on which to decide the Utah Constitutional provision's meaning, in particular because, "[T]he Court declines to reassess *State* v. *Beorchia...* (1974), a case which should be reassessed because of the absence of any analysis in support of the conclusion there reached."[33]

The Utah Constitution's right to keep and bear arms provision was amended in 1984. The old right to keep and bear arms provision had been: "The people have the right to bear arms for their security and defense, but the Legislature may regulate the exercise of this right by law."[34] The new wording was individual, and covered a broader range of legitimate uses: "The individual right of the people to keep and bear arms for security and defense of self, family, others, property, or the state, as well as for other lawful purposes shall not be infringed; but nothing herein shall prevent the legislature from defining the lawful use of arms."[35]

The only case law involving this new provision is *State* v. *Wacek* (Utah 1985), in which the Utah Supreme Court avoided directly discussing the effects of this new language, by observing that the defendant, James Christopher Wacek, had been convicted under a statute prohibiting convicted felons from possessing a firearm before the new constitutional provision had taken effect.[36] Other than affirming that the old constitutional provision had clearly allowed convicted felons to be prohibited from possession of arms, the Utah Supreme Court has not taken a position on the general applicability of this clause.

In *Carson* v. *State* (1978), the Georgia Supreme Court gave a decision that continued down the path taken in *Strickland* v. *State* (1911), towards a relativist, narrow understanding of the right to bear arms—but still maintained that the possession and carrying of at least *some* class of arms was constitutionally protected.

The defendant Carson was arrested as a result of alcohol on his breath; a search of his trunk found stolen license plates. A subsequent search of the car found a short-barreled shotgun. Carson was convicted of possession of the shotgun, a violation of the Georgia Firearms and Weapons Act, apparently passed in 1968.[37]

Carson's appeal argued a number of points, of which the constitutionality of the prohibition on short-barreled shotguns appears to have been a minor part. Carson argued that the Act violated Art. I, §I, paragraph V of the 1976 Georgia

---

32 *State* v. *Vlacil*, 645 P.2d 677, 681 note 1 (Utah 1982).
33 *State* v. *Vlacil*, 645 P.2d 677, 682, 684 (Utah 1982).
34 Utah Constituion, Art. I, §6, quoted in *State* v. *Beorchia*, 530 P.2d 813, 814 (Utah 1974).
35 Utah Constitution, Art. I, §6 (1991).
36 *State* v. *Wacek*, 703 Pac.2d 296, 297, 298 (Utah 1985).
37 *Carson* v. *State*, 241 Ga. 622, 247 S.E.2d 68, 70, 72 (1978).

Constitution: "The right of the people to keep and bear arms, shall not be infringed, but the General Assembly shall have power to prescribe the manner in which arms may be borne."

This clause will be recognized as significantly different from the provisions of the 1868 and 1877 Constitutions in that there was no longer any language concerning the militia; the right is unmistakably individual in nature. The Court pointed to their *Strickland* v. *State* (1911) and *Hill* v. *State* (1874) decisions, and quoted from the Strickland decision to hold that "under the general police power of regulation of the state, the question in each case being 'whether the particular regulation involved is legitimate and reasonably within the police power, or whether it is arbitrary, and, under the name of regulation, amounts to a deprivation of the constitutional right.'"

Where *Nunn* v. *State* (1846) had taken the largest possible understanding of the right to keep and bear arms, and neither *Hill* nor *Strickland* had directly addressed the issue of limits on arms in one's own home, the Court in this case decided:

> It was not arbitrary or unreasonable to prohibit the keeping and carrying of sawed-off shotguns, which are of a size such as can easily be concealed and which are adapted to and commonly used for criminal purposes. The Act does not prohibit the bearing of *all* arms. Even the *Nunn* case, 1 Ga. 243, supra, held that a law is unconstitutional "so far as it cuts off the exercise of the right of the *altogether* to bear arms..." (Emphasis supplied.)[in *Carson*][38]

A similar view of the limits of the "police power" with respect to gun prohibition was presented in *Quilici* v. *Village of Morton Grove* (7th Cir. 1982). In 1981, the village of Morton Grove, Illinois, prohibited the private ownership of handguns, with exceptions for gun stores, gunsmiths, licensed firearms collectors, and licensed gun clubs. Handgun owners resident in Morton Grove and nearby communities immediately filed suit to block enforcement of the law. While they sought to fight this matter in the Illinois state courts, Morton Grove arranged to have a total of three suits consolidated before a Federal judge, who granted summary judgement for Morton Grove.

On appeal to the Seventh Circuit Court of Appeals, Quilici argued that the Morton Grove ordinance was a violation of the Second Amendment, and the 1970 Illinois Constitution, art. I, §22: "Subject only to the police power, the right of the individual citizen to keep and bear arms shall not be infringed."[39]

Of some interest is the *amicus curiae* briefs. The Illinois State Rifle Association (the NRA state affiliate) and Handgun Control, Inc., filed *amici* briefs. Of more interest is a brief filed by "the States of Arizona, Connecticut, Hawaii, Idaho, Louisiana, Missouri, Montana, Nevada, North Carolina, Oregon and Wyoming collectively." Their objection appears to have been that the federal courts were deciding the meaning of the Illinois Constitution, instead of letting the Illinois courts interpret the Illinois Constitution.[40]

Unlike some of the earlier disputes as to whether a handgun was a constitutionally protected type of arm, Judge Bauer quickly resolved this question by examination of the debates from the 1970 Illinois Constitutional Convention: "Our con-

---

38 *Carson* v. *State*, 241 Ga. 622, 247 S.E.2d 68, 72, 73 (1978).
39 *Quilici* v. *Village of Morton Grove*, 695 F.2d 261, 263, 264, 265 (7th Cir. 1982).
40 *Quilici* v. *Village of Morton Grove*, 695 F.2d 261, 265 note 2 (7th Cir. 1982).

clusion that the framers intended to include handguns in the class of protected arms is supported by the fact that in discussing the term the Proceedings refer to *People* v. *Brown*...(1931) and *State* v. *Duke*...(1875)."[41] The sections of *Brown* and *Duke*, recognizing that handguns were commonly kept for self-defense, discussed in previous chapters, were then quoted. So how did the Court of Appeals find that the Morton Grove ordinance was constitutional, when handguns were clearly intended to be a protected class of arms?

> Having determined that section 22 includes handguns within the class of arms protected, we must now determine the extent to which a municipality may exercise its police power to restrict, or even prohibit, the right to keep and bear these arms. The district court concluded that section 22 recognizes only a narrow individual right which is subject to substantial legislative control. It noted that "[t]o the extent that one looks to the convention debate for assistance in reconciling the conflict between the right to arms and the exercise of the police power, the debate clearly supports a narrow construction of the individual right...". It further noted that while the Proceedings cite some cases holding that the state's police power should be read restrictively, those cases were decided under "distinctly different constitutional provisions" and, thus, have little application to the case...

> We agree with the district court that the right to keep and bear arms in Illinois is so limited by the police power that a ban on handguns does not violate that right. In reaching this conclusion we find two factors significant. First, section 22's plain language grants only the right to keep and bear arms, not handguns. Second, although the framers intended handguns to be one of the arms conditionally protected under section 22, they also envisioned that local governments might exercise their police power to restrict, or prohibit, the right to keep and bear handguns.[42]

The Court quoted from the Illinois Constitutional Convention debates, wherein a delegate named Foster, speaking for the majority, stated that before the 1970 Constitution's adoption, there was nothing that prohibited the state from banning all arms; that §22 would allow a ban on a particular class of arms, including handguns; but that "an absolute and complete ban on the possession of all firearms" alone would be prohibited. Any other regulation would be legal.[43]

This is strikingly reminiscent of the position taken in the decision *Matthews* v. *State* (1958), where the Indiana Supreme Court held that the right to bear arms did not include the right to bear a pistol, "or any other specific kind or type of arms."[44] But as long as *some* class of arms remained legal, Morton Grove was free to do as they wished. Could they prohibit all handguns, rifles, and shotguns, except for single shot black powder shotguns with barrels exceeding 40" in length, without violating the constitutional provision? Apparently so. If freedom of the press were similarly "protected," there would be nothing to prevent a city from banning all publications except those drawn by hand, or printed on color offset presses—and no one would consider those to be reasonable restrictions.

On the subject of the Second Amendment's applicability, the Court pointed to *Presser* v. *Illinois* (1886), and held, as dozens of courts before it had done, that the Second Amendment was not a restriction on state laws. However, the various parties who were seeking the overturn of the Morton Grove ordinance pointed to the

---

41 *Quilici* v. *Village of Morton Grove*, 695 F.2d 261, 266, 267 (7th Cir. 1982).
42 *Quilici* v. *Village of Morton Grove*, 695 F.2d 261, 267 (7th Cir. 1982).
43 *Quilici* v. *Village of Morton Grove*, 695 F.2d 261, 267 (7th Cir. 1982).
44 *Matthews* v. *State*, 237 Ind. 677, 148 N.E.2d 334, 338 (1958).

other parts of the *Presser* decision. One of the appellants pointed out that, "*Presser* also held that the right to keep and bear arms is an attribute of national citizenship which is not subject to state restriction," and also argued that the handgun ban interfered "with the ability of the United States to maintain public security..." by preventing individuals from defending themselves and the community. This was a stretch of the position taken in *Presser*, which had clearly meant that the limitations in question were with reference to the duty of every member of the militia to form "a reserve military force." Yet the Supreme Court in *Presser* recognized that a state could not "prohibit the people therein from keeping and bearing arms..."[45] Both the district court and the Court of Appeals in *Quilici* asserted that this claim was, "based on dicta quoted out of context."

Quilici, *et. al.*, also argued that:

> *Presser* is no longer good law because later Supreme Court cases incorporating other amendments into the fourteenth amendment have effectively overruled *Presser*.... *Presser* is illogical... the entire Bill of Rights has been implicitly incorporated into the fourteenth amendment to apply to the states...[46]

The Court of Appeals quickly disposed of each claim. To the assertion that *Presser* is no longer good law, because of subsequent selective incorporation, the Court of Appeals pointed to several decisions where the Supreme Court had rejected the idea of complete incorporation—though only one decision, *Malloy* v. *Hogan* (1964), took place after the start of the Warren Court's dramatic expansion of the Bill of Rights. (But in *Malloy*, the Court cited *Presser*—indicating that it remained a valid precedent.)

The Court then asserted:

> Since we hold that the second amendment does not apply to the states, we need not consider the scope of its guarantee of the right to bear arms. For the sake of completeness, however, and because appellants devote a large portion of their briefs to this issue, we briefly comment on what we believe to be the scope of the second amendment.[47]

The Court of Appeals then used a textual analysis of the Second Amendment to hold that, "the right to bear arms is inextricably connected to the preservation of a militia." They also pointed to *U.S.* v. *Miller* (1939), and pointed to the "ordinary military equipment" statement as evidence that the Second Amendment was for militia purposes only.

To demonstrate that the Second Amendment was built on the assumption of an individual right, the appellants had included in their briefs a discussion of English common law, and the debates surrounding adoption of the Second and Fourteenth Amendment. The Court of Appeals concluded: "This analysis has no relevance on the resolution of the controversy before us. Accordingly, we decline to comment on it, other than to note that we do not consider individually owned handguns to be military weapons."[48]

And there the Court of Appeals completed its discussion of the Second Amendment—with a refusal to examine the historical evidence that the Second Amendment was understood to include an individual right to arms, as well as a republican

---

45 *Presser* v. *Illinois*, 116 U.S. 252 (1886).
46 *Quilici* v. *Village of Morton Grove*, 695 F.2d 261, 269, 270 (7th Cir. 1982).
47 *Quilici* v. *Village of Morton Grove*, 695 F.2d 261, 270 (7th Cir. 1982).
48 *Quilici* v. *Village of Morton Grove*, 695 F.2d 261, 270 note 8 (7th Cir. 1982).

right to arms for the purpose of restraining tyranny—and a refusal to admit that handguns were military weapons, in spite of more than 200 years of continuous use of handguns by the United States armed forces, military use of handguns in the English military from at least 1584 forward,[49] and dozens of decisions in state courts recognizing that at least *some* handguns were constitutionally protected as military arms.

Judge Coffey wrote a dissenting opinion. While his opinion pointed to the problems of privacy produced by such a ban, and evidence that the intent of the "police power" clause was not to allow municipalities to impose restrictions on guns more severe than those adopted by the state,[50] at no point did Judge Coffey present any argument based on the Second Amendment, or based on the inconsistencies that result from acknowledging that "police power" to regulate, could extend so far as to prohibit a particular class of arms. The Supreme Court refused to hear an appeal.

The next case, *Schubert* v. *DeBard* (1980), is all the more surprising when we consider the facts which appear in the decision. A Joseph L. Schubert, Jr., had applied for a concealed weapons permit in Indiana. He was denied a permit by the superintendent of the Indiana State Police, and he appealed this decision first to Superior Court, where he lost, then to the Indiana Court of Appeals, where Presiding Judge Garrard wrote the majority opinion, which recognized that "applicant for license to carry a handgun for self-protection could not be denied such a license on ground that he did not have a proper reason to be licensed; self-protection was constitutionally a 'proper reason' within meaning of licensing statute."

Before examining the constitutional basis on which the Court of Appeals made its decision in this case, it is interesting to examine Schubert's character, as described by the decision. After detailing evidence that Schubert had previously possessed a concealed weapons permit, and apparently had been a police officer with two different police agencies:

> A report summarizing a background investigation made of appellant when he applied for a private detective's license in 1971... concluded that appellant was a "chronic liar" suffering from a "gigantic police complex." The report, as well as testimony of a police officer at the hearing, indicated that on occasion, when he had been licensed to carry a gun, appellant had carried and displayed his pistol at inappropriate times which did not require the use of a gun for personal safety or to expedite the duties of his employment.... Several of those interviewed during the course of the investigation, including former employers and the sheriff who both created and revoked his deputy sheriff's commission, felt appellant had "mental problems."

First, the Indiana Court of Appeals held that a licensing procedure for carrying handguns: "is not violative of the right to bear arms as guaranteed by the Second Amendment or Art. I, Sec. 32 of the Indiana Constitution,"[51] and cited *Matthews* v. *State* (1958). But instead of simply resting their decision on this point on the existing precedent, the Court of Appeals chose to engage in a more detailed analysis of this provision of the Indiana Constitution.

---

49 Russell, 198-218, describes the various models of pistols adopted by the U. S. Army during the period 1799-1847. Norman and Pottinger, 182, 190, 206.

50 *Quilici* v. *Village of Morton Grove*, 695 F.2d 261, 271, 272, 277 (7th Cir. 1982).

51 *Schubert* v. *DeBard*, 398 N.E.2d 1339, 1340 (Ind.App. 1980).

Schubert argued that the Indiana Constitution protected his right to bear arms for self-defense, and this was been the reason he gave when applying for a concealed handgun permit. The Court of Appeals thus addressed the issue of whether Superintendent DeBard could refuse to issue a permit, because Schubert did not have a proper reason for desiring such a permit. To that purpose, they pointed to the journal of the 1850 Indiana Constitutional Convention, which explained the purpose of the arms provision in question (originally §12):

"The twelfth section, providing that no law should restrict the right of the people to bear arms, *whether in defense of themselves or the state*, next came up in order." (emphasis added)[in the Court's decision]

and concluded:

We think it clear that our constitution provides our citizenry the right to bear arms in their self-defense. Furthermore, in *Matthews* v. *State, supra*, our Supreme Court held that if it is determined under I[ndiana] C[ode] 35-23-4.1-5 that the applicant has met the conditions of the statute, the superintendent has no discretion to withhold the license...

In Schubert's case it is clear from the record that the superintendent decided the application on the basis that the statutory reference to "a proper reason" vested in him the power and duty to subjectively evaluate an assignment of "self-defense" as a reason for desiring a license and the ability to grant or deny the license upon the basis of whether the applicant "needed" to defend himself.

Such an approach... would supplant a right with a mere administrative privilege which might be withheld simply on the basis that such matters as the use of firearms are better left to the organized military and police forces even where defense of the individual citizen is involved.

While the Court of Appeals held that Schubert had provided a proper reason for being licensed, they noted: "We recognize, however, that there was conflicting evidence on Schubert's suitability to be licensed and that those issues were not attempted to be resolved in the original determination."

While Judge Hoffman concurred in Judge Garrard's decision, his opinion was even more radical: "I agree that *Matthews* v. *State* (1958)... stands for the proposition set out in the majority opinion, however, I would join in Judge Emmert's dissent in that opinion." As we saw in a previous chapter, Chief Justice Emmert took the position that even a license for *open* carry of a handgun, was contrary to the Indiana Constitution.

Judge Staton dissented. It is possible to quote Judge Staton's opinion out of context as recognizing a right to bear arms:

Without question, Article 1, Section 32 of the Indiana Constitution gives our citizens "a right to bear arms, for the defense of themselves." I reiterate that Superintendent DeBard did not find otherwise.[52]

Judge Staton, however, argued that DeBard's decision to not grant a license was based on the evidence that Schubert lacked a *need* for self-defense, not that self-defense was an insufficient reason. Instead, Judge Staton argued that where the majority opinion in *Matthews* v. *State* (1958) had recognized that the Superintendent of State Police was especially qualified to determine whether an applicant had

52 *Schubert* v. *DeBard*, 398 N.E.2d 1339, 1342 (Ind.App. 1980).

"proper reason" for a permit, they had meant, whether "good cause" existed. Judge Staton correctly read the intention of the majority in *Matthews*. The Indiana Court of Appeals simply chose to put the intent of the Indiana Constitution above the *Matthews* precedent.[53]

Judge Staton correctly identified the result of this Court of Appeals decision:

[T]he State Police Superintendent would be compelled to grant licenses to carry handguns to any "proper" person who simply alleged a need for self-defense. I suggest that "proper" persons are many; on the other hand, those with a genuine need to carry a handgun on their persons outside their home or business may be very few. If an *alleged* need for self-defense was all that was necessary, most of our citizens would qualify for the license; the Superintendent could not—except upon proof of mental incompetency or previous criminal acts—deny an application. For all practical purposes, the upshot of the Majority's approach, were it given effect, would be the de-regulation of handguns.[54] [emphasis in original]

Exactly. As we will see, later in the 1980s, several states have adopted regulations of carrying arms that are *exactly* such—limitations only upon those who have demonstrated, by their individual actions, that they could not be trusted with arms.

That Judge Staton's concern was not, primarily, protection of the *Matthews* precedent, may be deduced from his remarks in support of limited issuance of licenses to carry handguns, including the assertion, "that numerous studies have confirmed that handgun restrictions promote the public safety and welfare," and from his use of the *National Commission on the Causes and Prevention of Violence* final report, which argued for a very limited right to even *possess* handguns on private property. Perhaps a final comment on Judge Staton's perception of those people who are neither mentally incompetent, nor convicted criminals, is his assertion that: "If, as the Majority has suggested, any suitable person could obtain a license to carry a handgun in public merely be alleging a need for self-defense, the purposes of the statute would not be served; rather, concealed handgun crimes would run rampant."[55]

Judge Staton's concern was *not* that criminals or the mentally incompetent would engage in "concealed handgun crimes," but that those adults who were not in either category, would do so—and herein lies the heart of the differing attitudes about the carrying of arms today. One side argues that those who have demonstrated, by their individual actions, an inability to be trusted with weapons, should be prohibited from possessing a permit to carry a handgun; the other side argues that not just criminals and mental incompetents, but *all* people, are assumed to be untrustworthy to carry a handgun. The former side trusts most people to carry a gun; the latter side believes that permits to carry a gun should be issued only under extremely limited circumstances.

The second Indiana decision during this period shows the dramatic recovery of the right to bear arms: *Kellogg* v. *City of Gary* (1990). This was a civil action for damages, and included a great many issues not relevant to our concerns, but at its heart is the fundamental issue of whether bearing arms is a right, or a privilege. The mayor of Gary, Indiana, Richard G. Hatcher, and the acting police chief, Virgil L. Motley, decided that concealed handgun license application forms would

53 *Schubert* v. *DeBard*, 398 N.E.2d 1339, 1343 (Ind.App. 1980).
54 *Schubert* v. *DeBard*, 398 N.E.2d 1339, 1344 (Ind.App. 1980).
55 *Schubert* v. *DeBard*, 398 N.E.2d 1339, 1344, 1345 (Ind.App. 1980).

no longer be available after January 1, 1980. The apparent reason was "to control the number of handguns on the streets in Gary." Since, one presumes, criminals could not obtain such licenses, it is unclear how such an action would reduce the number of guns in the hands of criminals on the streets. The only practical effect would be to reduce the number of law-abiding people carrying guns on the streets of Gary.

The Gary Police Department continued to process forms; they simply no longer made blank forms available, and by so doing, made it impossible for citizens of Gary to obtain the application form. An injunction by Gary gun owners was obtained requiring the Superintendent of State Police to provide forms to the police chief, and similarly requiring the police chief to make these forms available to those who sought them. Even after the injunction, however, "the city and its official improperly recommended certain applications for denial and in some instances completely failed to forward the applications to the superintendent of state police."[56] But, the improper negative recommendations were ignored by the Superintendent, and licenses were then issued.

The plaintiffs in this civil action, residents of Gary who had been denied application forms and proper processing of those applications, argued that their rights to equal protection of the law had been denied in violation of the Fourteenth Amendment, since they were denied access to the same licensing available to other Indiana residents.[57] The plaintiffs also argued that their rights under the Second Amendment, and the Indiana Constitution's arms provision had been violated. They contended that they had a property interest in a concealed handgun license, and that the denial of the right to bear arms was a deprivation of a liberty and property interest, for which monetary compensation should be awarded.

The Indiana Supreme Court held that the Second Amendment was not applicable to state action, but only to federal action. Unlike some of the other state supreme courts, the Indiana Supreme Court recognized that the Second Amendment, while not a limitation on state laws, was a protection of an individual right against the Federal Government, and subscribed to the understanding that the arms protected must have "some reasonable relationship" to the preservation of the militia—the military weapons test that we saw so frequently in some of the nineteenth century decisions.

The Indiana Constitution was another matter: "We agree with the Court of Appeals' analysis in *Schubert*, and now find that this right of Indiana citizens to bear arms for their own self-defense and for the defense of the state is an interest in both liberty and property which is protected by the Fourteenth Amendment to the Federal Constitution."[58] After mentioning the *Quilici* v. *Village of Morton Grove* (7th Cir. 1982) decision, the Court recognized:

> This interest is one of liberty to the extent that it enables law-abiding citizens to be free from the threat and danger of violent crime. There is also a property interest at stake, for example, in protecting one's valuables when transporting them, as in the case of a businessman who brings a sum of cash to deposit in his bank across town.

---

56 *Kellogg* v. *City of Gary*, 462 N.E.2d 685, 688, 689, 690 (Ind. 1990).
57 *Kellogg* v. *City of Gary*, 462 N.E.2d 685, 691 (Ind. 1990).
58 *Kellogg* v. *City of Gary*, 462 N.E.2d 685, 692, 694 (Ind. 1990).

The right to bear arms for the defense of one's self and his property, however, is not absolute. The state may regulate the exercise of this right. It has done so by statute.[59]

In the cradle of the American revolution, where the personally owned arms of the Minutemen "fired the shot heard 'round the world," during the Bicentennial year of 1976, the Massachusetts Supreme Judicial Court denied that an individual right to keep and bear arms was protected by either the Second Amendment, or the state constitution.   In *Commonwealth* v. *Davis* (Mass. 1976), Hubert Davis was convicted of illegal possession of a short-barreled shotgun. After appeal to the Appeals Court, arguing that the law was a violation of the right to keep and bear arms, the Supreme Judicial Court took it up for direct review. As is usually the circumstance in illegal weapons possession cases, the discovery of the short-barreled shotgun was as a result of enforcement of an unrelated law. In this case, Davis' apartment was searched for illegal drugs, and during the search, the illegal shotgun was found.

The diligent reader will recall that the Massachusetts Constitution's provision includes the phrase, "for the common defence." Even though we have seen much evidence that indicates this phrase had a meaning that included an individual right, the Massachusetts Supreme Judicial Court, based partly on Levin's *Chicago-Kent Law Review* article, came to a conclusion which is neither liberal, nor republican in interpretation:

> Article 17 expresses the distrust in its second sentence. It refers to the preference in the first: the declared right to keep and bear arms is that of the people, the aggregate of citizens; the right is related to the common defense; and that in turn points to service in a broadly based, organized militia. Provisions like art. 17 were not directed to guaranteeing individual ownership or possession of weapons.[60]

It is frightening to imagine how this Court would interpret the equivalent "right of the people" in the U.S. Bill of Rights; perhaps only large corporations or government-owned newspapers would be protected by the First Amendment. *City of Salina* v. *Blaksley* (1905) was cited as justification for this collective interpretation; it would appear that the minority opinion in that decision, asking why the state needed to protect its right to organize a militia from itself, made no impression on Justice Kaplan. *Burton* v. *Sills* (1968) was also cited, even though that decision did not address the meaning of "right of the people" at all.

The Massachusetts Supreme Judicial Court did, however, acknowledge that the militia furnished their own weapons in Revolutionary times, citing *U.S.* v. *Miller* (1939) and *State* v. *Dawson* (1967). But while the *Miller* decision is on point, *Dawson* contains a damaging assertion of a common-law right to arms.[61]

In much the same way that the Kansas Supreme Court insisted that the National Guard now took the place of the militia, the Massachusetts Court held:

> A law forbidding the keeping by individuals of arms that were used in the militia service might then have interfered with the effectiveness of the militia and thus offended the art. 17 right. But that situation no longer exists; our militia, of which the backbone is the National Guard, is now equipped and supported by public funds.[62]

---

59 *Kellogg* v. *City of Gary*, 462 N.E.2d 685, 694 (Ind. 1990).
60 *Commonwealth* v. *Davis*, 343 N.E.2d 847, 848, 849 (Mass. 1976).
61 *State* v. *Dawson*, 272 N.C. 535, 546 (1967).
62 *Commonwealth* v. *Davis*, 343 N.E.2d 847, 849 (Mass. 1976).

Perhaps reflecting Levin's confidence in a democratic society, the Court showed no recognition of the Framers' concerns about the need to keep the government checked and balanced by a widespread distribution of arms in the hands of the people. With respect to the Second Amendment, the Court asserted:

> This was adopted to quiet the fears of those who thought that the Congressional powers under article I, §8, clauses 15 and 16, with regard to the State militias, might have the effect of enervating or destroying those forces. The amendment is to be read as an assurance that the national government shall not so reduce the militias.

The Court miscited *U.S.* v. *Cruikshank* (1876) and the various U.S. Supreme Court decisions that held the Second Amendment was a restriction only on the Federal Government, and the Court appears to have been unaware of the many state supreme court decisions that recognized the Second Amendment as a limitation on state gun control laws. The Court held:

> The chances appear remote that this amendment will ultimately be read to control the States, for unlike some other provisions of the bill of rights, this is not directed to guaranteeing the rights of individuals, but rather, as we have said, to assuring some freedom of State forces from national interference. Apart from such interference, Congress is not inhibited by the amendment from regulating firearms by exercise of its interstate commerce or other powers, and it has done so a considerable scale, with judicial approval.[63]

How did they go so far afield? Much of the reasoning clearly came from Levin's law review article.

In 1975, the New Hampshire Legislature proposed an amendment to the state constitution: "All persons have the right to keep and bear arms in defense of themselves, their families, their property and the state, but the legislature may prescribe the manner in which they may be borne and may prohibit convicted felons from carrying or possessing them." It appears that opposition to the language allowing the legislature "to prescribe the manner in which they may be borne" prevented this amendment from going to a vote of the people until revisions were made in 1978. At least one proponent argued that without "the explicit legislative authority to regulate," all the existing statutes regulating carrying of arms would be repealed by the proposed amendment.[64]

In *State* v. *Sanne* (1976), the New Hampshire Supreme Court heard an appeal from a Stephen G. Sanne, a non-resident of the state who had been arrested "for carrying two loaded pistols without a license to do so." Sanne, who represented himself, argued that the Second Amendment protected his right to carry without a license.[65] While there is no indication in the decision whether Sanne was carrying concealed or openly, it appears that New Hampshire did not at that time, and does not now, prohibit open carry of a pistol. Further, the annotation on the statute prohibiting concealed carry upon the person cites *Sanne* as to its constitutionality.[66]

Of some historical interest, David Souter, then Attorney General, now a U.S. Supreme Court Justice, presented the state's argument that: "It is too well established to require elaboration that a state statute reasonably regulating the right to

---

63 *Commonwealth* v. *Davis*, 343 N.E.2d 847, 850 (Mass. 1976).
64 Halbrook, *A Right To Bear Arms*, 119-20.
65 *State* v. *Sanne*, 116 N.H. 583, 364 A.2d 630 (1976).
66 New Hampshire Revised Statutes Ann. (1988), 159:4.

bear arms does not violate the Second Amendment to the United States Constitution which is not a grant of a right, but 'a limitation only upon the power of Congress and the National Government...'"[67] Souter presented the usual citations of *U.S.* v. *Miller* (1939), *Presser* v. *Illinois* (1886), and two new citations, *U.S.* v. *Johnson* (4th Cir. 1974), and *Commonwealth* v. *Davis* (Mass. 1976). The New Hampshire Supreme Court upheld Sanne's conviction.

In 1978, the proposed constitutional amendment was put to a vote of the people of New Hampshire; while the vote was 160,628 in favor and 87,807 against it, it failed to win the two-thirds majority required. In 1981, the amendment was reintroduced, but without the two clauses permitting the state to regulate the manner of carrying, and excluding felons. The following year, the voters ratified the text, "All persons have the right to keep and bear arms in defense of themselves, their families, their property and the state," as Part I, article 2a of the New Hampshire Constitution. While Halbrook argues that the history of the excised controversial clauses with respect to felons and regulation suggests that "some forms of legislative regulation of the right may be constitutionally suspect,"[68] the New Hampshire Supreme Court appears not to have shared in that understanding.

In *State* v. *Smith* (1990), the New Hampshire Supreme Court upheld the conviction of a felon in possession of a firearm. In particular, the Court held that:

> The available legislative history of Part I, article 2-a, proposed by the legislature in 1981 and approved by the voters in 1982, is not particularly helpful. However the history of RSA 159:3 (Supp.1988) persuades us that the legislature did not intend the constitutional amendment to invalidate the statute.

The Court presented as evidence that the same session of the legislature that approved the amendment, also deleted a provision of RSA 159:3 that had allowed felons to purchase a firearm with written permission from a city official.[69] Legislative intent was clearly important.

The more interesting question is whether, as some legislators had suggested in the 1970s debates, the amendment "overrides all of those statutes. The Constitution prevails. Those statutes go out."[70] On this issue, the Court did an about face regarding the importance of legislative history:

> We note that New Hampshire voters, and not their legislature, made part I, article 2-a an amendment to the state constitution. Therefore, since our inquiry in this case cannot end with a determination of legislative intent, we turn to standard constitutional analysis. As the defendant concedes, the State constitutional right to bear arms is not absolute and may be subject to restriction and regulation. Assuming that the right to bear arms is no more absolute than the right of free speech, N.H. CONST. pt. I, arts. 22 & 23, a restriction such as that provided by RSA 159:3 (Supp.1988) may be sustained if it "narrowly serve[s] a significant governmental interest..." *State* v. *Comley*, 130 N.H. 688, 691, 546 A.2d 1066, 1069 (1988). The governmental interest served by the statute, protection of human life and property, is patently significant.[71]

What, realistically, had this amendment done? Perhaps nothing, because the definition of "governmental interest"—protection of human life and property—al-

---

67 *State* v. *Sanne*, 116 N.H. 583, 364 A.2d 630 (1976).
68 Halbrook, *A Right To Bear Arms*, 120-1.
69 *State* v. *Smith*, 571 A.2d 279, 280 (N.H. 1990).
70 Halbrook, *A Right To Bear Arms*, 120.
71 *State* v. *Smith*, 571 A.2d 279, 281 (N.H. 1990).

lows the legislature to pass a wide variety of restrictions and regulations on arms bearing, with no apparent limits. Especially disturbing is that the legislative intent was considered worthy of consideration with respect to a felon in possession of a firearm, but not with respect to the boundaries of state regulation on law-abiding citizens.

The Connecticut Constitution of 1818 included a guarantee of the right of every citizen "to bear arms in defense of himself and the State." This provision was retained in the 1955 and 1965 Constitutions. But until *Rabbitt* v. *Leonard* (1979), there were no cases dependent on that clause. In this case, the decision advanced only to Superior Court—and still remains the highest decision of the Connecticut courts on the subject.[72]

A Joseph M. Rabbitt's permit to carry a handgun was revoked, without notice. In response, Rabbitt sought a writ of mandamus[73] to force the reinstatement of his permit, and argued that his "fundamental right to bear arms and to defend himself" under the Connecticut Constitution had been denied. The Court pointed to a number of decisions by the U.S. Supreme Court and the Appeals Courts to demonstrate that the Second Amendment was not a restriction on state laws, including *U.S.* v. *Cruikshank* (1876), and *U.S.* v. *Miller* (1939). The Court also pointed to a number of other state constitutions and decisions to show the variety of such provisions, and to argue that these decisions did not "imply the absolute right of an individual to carry a gun."

But the Court then discussed the Connecticut Constitution's provision:

> The language of article first, §15, of the Connecticut constitution, which states that "[e]very citizen has a right to bear arms in defense of himself and the state," is different from that of the second amendment and the other state constitutional provisions discussed above. The use of the conjunction "and" gives every citizen a dual right; he has the right to bear arms to defend the state, a clear reference to the militia; and he may also bear arms to defend himself. It appears that a Connecticut citizen, under the language of the Connecticut constitution, has a fundamental right to bear arms in self-defense, a liberty interest which must be protected by procedural due process.[74]

While the revocation without notice was upheld, the Superior Court had recognized that due process was a requirement before a person's right to carry a pistol could be denied.[75]

In *Application of Atkinson*, 291 N.W.2d 396 (Minn. 1980), the Minnesota Supreme Court heard an appeal concerning Berton M. Atkinson application for a concealed weapons permit. The case is interesting because Minnesota did not find it necessary to restrict the carry of arms until 1975. Apparently, until this late date, no permit was required to "carry or possess a pistol in a public place..."

Atkinson had applied for a concealed weapons permit "to continue his pre-1975 practice of carrying a loaded pistol in the glove compartment of his automobile 'while traveling appreciable distances away from [his] home on public roads and highways.'" In 1978, Atkinson applied to the Bloomington Police Chief for a permit; he was turned down, on the grounds that he had failed to demonstrate a "personal safety hazard," and therefore lacked a good reason. Atkinson appealed to

---

72 *Rabbitt* v. *Leonard*, 36 Conn. Sup. 108, 110 (1979). Conn. Const. Ann., Art. I, §15.
73 A writ compelling performance of some action.
74 *Rabbitt* v. *Leonard*, 36 Conn. Sup. 108, 110, 111, 112 (1979).
75 *Rabbitt* v. *Leonard*, 36 Conn. Sup. 108, 116 (1979).

the Hennepin Municipal Court, then the district court, and finally to the Minnesota Supreme Court.

The Minnesota Supreme Court decided that the constitutional issue was: "Is there an absolute constitutional or common-law right to carry a loaded gun on public highways?"[76] While Atkinson's appeal had *not* been based on the Second Amendment, but apparently on the common-law right, the Minnesota Court pointedly argued that the Second Amendment had no application to this case. The Court held that the Second Amendment was not a restriction on the States, and cited *Miller* v. *Texas* (1894) and *Burton* v. *Sills* (1968).

As we have seen in a previous chapter, in *Miller* v. *Texas* (1894), the U.S. Supreme Court had held that not only was the Second Amendment not a restriction on the states, but neither were the First, Fourth, or Fifth Amendments. The Minnesota Court appears to have been unaware of the extent to which the *Miller* v. *Texas* (1894) decision reflects the pre-incorporation understanding of the Bill of Rights. Using *Burton* v. *Sills* (1968) as evidence that the Second Amendment was not a restriction on state laws was not one of the more careful citations. While Burton had argued the Second Amendment as an individual protection, the New Jersey appellate court decision neither affirmed nor denied that the Second Amendment was a restriction on the states.

The Minnesota Supreme Court also denied that the Second Amendment was in any sense a protection of individual rights: "Even as against the United States, furthermore, the Second Amendment protects not an individual right but a collective right, in the people as the group, to serve as militia." As evidence for this, they cited *U.S.* v. *Miller* (1939), but gave no particular location within this case for their position—and as we saw when we studied *U.S.* v. *Miller* in a previous chapter, the Supreme Court studiously avoided answering the question of whether an individual right was protected or not by the Second Amendment, though the implication was strong that it does.

On the question of whether there was a common-law right to bear arms, the Court cited a number of law review articles on the subject.[77] Blackstone's *Commentaries* appears not to have come to the Court's attention, nor Hawkins' *Treatises of the Pleas of the Crown*, or any of the other pieces of evidence that show a common-law right was recognized at the time of the American Revolution.

In *Morris* v. *State* (1977), the Alabama Court of Criminal Appeals overturned a conviction for resisting arrest. The defendant, James Harrell Morris, argued that the arrest he was resisting by a Baldwin County deputy sheriff was illegal, because he was carrying a pistol openly, and was therefore within the law. The Court of Criminal Appeals asserted: "He had a right to carry the pistol unconcealed at the time and place of arrest. Defendant was under no duty to submit to any other than a lawful arrest."[78] But while the Court clearly identified where the right to resist an unlawful arrest came from, it did not explain the origin of the right to carry a pistol openly; it is entirely possible that the Court merely meant that open carry of a pistol was not illegal.

---

76 *Application of Atkinson*, 291 N.W.2d 396, 397, 398 (Minn. 1980).
77 *Application of Atkinson*, 291 N.W.2d 396, 398, 399 (Minn. 1980).
78 *Morris* v. *State*, 342 So.2d 417, 418 (Ala. Cr. App. 1977).

Next, the Alabama Court of Criminal Appeals heard *Hyde* v. *City of Birmingham*, 392 So.2d 1226 (Ala. Crim. App. 1980). At first glance, the law in question appears to be a modern version of the common law prohibition on carrying arms "to the terror of the people." The ordinance prohibited the possession of a firearm "in a public place or within public view under circumstances tending to provoke breach of the peace." But the more we look into the circumstances of the case, and the reasoning by which the Appeals Court upheld the ordinance, the more interesting it becomes:

> In the summer of 1979, a young black woman, Bonita Carter, was shot and killed by a white police officer outside one of two Jerry's convenience stores located in the Kingston area of Birmingham, Alabama. Following that incident, racial tension was acute in the city and open acts of violence and racial conflict occurred in the area near the two Jerry's convenience stores. The two stores were located within five blocks of each other. The Bonita Carter shooting incident and the racial disturbances that followed were widely reported by various news media.[79]

William Wayne Hyde was arrested on July 6, 1979, in a pickup truck near one of the stores where disturbances had occurred, because there was a shotgun visible within the truck. Upon search, three pistols were also found. Hyde possessed a valid permit for the pistols, but was charged with possessing the shotgun in an area where the sight of it might cause violence.

Hyde testified that he was on his way to target practice, and was in the area to pick up a friend. He had stopped at the store to get "ice, grapefruit juice and cigarettes." He was convicted by the Birmingham Municipal Court of disturbing the peace, by having firearms "where the natural tendency of such possession would be to provoke a breach of the peace."

On appeal, Hyde argued that the ordinance in question was unconstitutional, and pointed to Article I, §26 of the Alabama Constitution of 1901: "That every citizen has a right to bear arms in defense of himself and the state." The Criminal Appeals Court did not agree: "It is well-settled and 'universally recognized,' however, that this right of a citizen to bear arms in defense of himself and the state is subject to reasonable regulation under the police powers of the state." The Court then pointed to the decision in *State* v. *Reid* (1840), where the right to concealed carry had been denied; the Court also quoted the *Reid* decision to the effect that: "A statute which, under the pretence of regulating, amounts to a destruction of the right, or which requires arms to be borne so as to render them wholly useless for the purpose of defence, would be clearly unconstitutional."[80]

Yet, in spite of the contradiction between the *Reid* protection of open carry, and the ordinance in question, the Criminal Appeals Court upheld the ordinance as a valid exercise of the police power. The Court cited *Abernathy* v. *State* (1962) as evidence that circumstances can make a legal act into an illegal act, and asserted:

> The "natural tendency" of the appellant's open display of the shotgun in question would be to not only provoke, but to invite a breach of the peace. We are of the opinion that

---

79 *Hyde* v. *City of Birmingham*, 392 So.2d 1226, 1227, 1228 (Ala. Cr. App. 1980).

80 *State* v. *Reid*, 1 Ala. 612 (1840), quoted in *Hyde* v. *City of Birmingham*, 392 So.2d 1226, 1227, 1228 (Ala. Cr. App. 1980).

the City of Birmingham does not run afoul of this state's constitution by its adoption of this ordinance which seeks to prevent lawless armed confrontation.[81]

But *Abernathy* v. *State* (1962) is perhaps the most embarrassing possible case to use as an example of a lawful action inciting a breach of the peace. The Abernathy was Ralph Abernathy, and the action was a peaceful civil rights demonstration—the Freedom Riders, attempting to exercise their rights in interstate travel.[82] The analogy is strong. The cause of the riots was not Abernathy's actions, but that of the rioters who refused to allow Abernathy and the Freedom Riders to exercise their rights. Similarly, the Birmingham ordinance sought to deny the right to bear arms not because the bearing of arms was necessarily the problem, but out of fear that others would respond to a lawful action with violence.

Is this a natural tendency? The minority opinion, written by Judge DeCarlo and concurred in by Judge Bookout, was that, "This argument, I suggest, has no more merit than the argument that short skirts on women incite would-be attackers to rape." Certainly, one would have to wonder about the rationality of anyone whose response to seeing Hyde's shotgun was a criminal attack on Hyde; rational people maintain a wary distance or a pleasant demeanor towards anyone armed with a shotgun. Judge DeCarlo also pointed to the decision of the Alabama Criminal Appeals Court in *Morris* v. *State* (1977), and asserted that it recognized a right to carry pistols openly (though it is unclear whether *Morris* meant a constitutionally protected right, or merely that Morris' actions were not prohibited).[83]

Examination of the legislative history of Maryland's weapons control laws suggests that the first statute prohibiting concealed carry was not passed until 1886, late for a former slave state, but early for a free state. Similarly, it does not appear that open carry of a handgun was prohibited until 1972.[84] It is therefore not at all surprising that until 1979, there were no constitutional challenges of the statutes regulating the carrying of arms.

In *Onderdonk* v. *Handgun Permit Review Board* (1979), we learn the importance of hiring an attorney, instead of representing yourself. William H. Onderdonk appealed a concealed weapon permit denial from the Superintendent of the Maryland State Police to the Handgun Permit Review Board, then to the Baltimore City Court, and having been denied in each place, he appealed to the Maryland Court of Special Appeals.

Mr. Onderdonk's argument showed no understanding of the basis on which a court would reverse such a denial. He presented a total of ten arguments, only one of which was a legal argument (and even that poorly presented). The rest of his arguments were assertions of the absurdity of gun control laws, with no basis on which such assertions could be used to overturn a law.

Onderdonk sought a permit to carry a handgun for self-defense; the Maryland State Police decided that Onderdonk did not have a "good and sufficient reason." In Baltimore City Court, Judge Greenfeld determined that he "was not at liberty to substitute his judgment on the facts for that of the Board so long as the Board's decision 'is not arbitrary.'" Judge Greenfeld also asserted that Onderdonk's "reading

---

81 *Hyde* v. *City of Birmingham*, 392 So.2d 1226, 1228, 1229 (Ala. Cr. App. 1980).
82 *Abernathy* v. *State*, 42 Ala. App. 149, 155 So.2d 586, 587 (1962).
83 *Hyde* v. *City of Birmingham*, 392 So.2d 1226, 1229 (Ala. Cr. App. 1980).
84 Md. Ann. Code art. 27, §36, §36B.

of the Second Amendment is 'much too broad and [it] does not extend to the absolute right of private citizens to carry guns.'"

The Appeals Court described Onderdonk as "indignant," and his presentation as,
"He uses, if not abuses, the Court as a sounding board for his thoughts...."
Perhaps some of the irritation the Court felt can be found in their description of the
one argument Onderdonk advanced that was related to the Second Amendment:

> Onderdonk posits to us that Md.Ann.Code art. 27, §§36B-F are unconstitutional be-
> cause they conflict with the Second Amendment. Onderdonk advances only his argu-
> mentative personal view of the constitutionality... of the Maryland Handgun Law. We
> are not furnished a reference to any authority that supports his position, nor has he cited
> us any appellate decision in Maryland or elsewhere that has considered the issue pro or
> con.[85]

While agreeing that Onderdonk did not require a license to own a handgun in
his home, or to transport a gun unloaded, the Appeals Court did not recognize that
he had any Constitutional right to do either of these acts. On the issue of whether
the Second Amendment was applicable or not, the Appeals Court was in the
mainstream: "A plethora of cases hold that a statute, such as Maryland's, which
reasonably regulates the 'right to bear arms' does not violate the Second
Amendment's limitation on the federal government."[86]

In light of Onderdonk's lack of precedents the list of decisions cited are all
against Onderdonk: *Miller* v. *Texas* (1894), *Presser* v. *Illinois* (1886), *U.S.* v.
Cruikshank (1876), *U.S.* v. *Johnson* (4th Cir. 1974), *City of Salina* v. *Blaksley*
(1905), *Commonwealth* v. *Davis* (Mass. 1976), and *Burton* v. *Sills* (1968).

In July of 1980, the Oregon Supreme Court heard the case *State* v. *Kessler*
(1980). This decision is one of the most historically thorough Second Amendment
decisions in the entire twentieth century. Instead of relying simply on precedent
from other courts, the Oregon Supreme Court's decision made extensive use of the
historical record, and traced the origins of the Oregon Constitutional provision,
Article I, §27, "The people shall have the right to bear arms for the defence of
themselves, and the State,"[87] back to the Second Amendment.

The facts of the case are relatively simple:

> The defendant was involved in an off and on verbal argument with his apartment man-
> ager in the course of the day on November 13, 1978. The dispute escalated into name
> calling, colorful words, and object throwing. At one point the defendant kicked the
> elevator door in the apartment building. The police were called and arrested the de-
> fendant. The defendant asked the police to get his coat from his apartment. The offi-
> cers found two "billy clubs" in the defendant's apartment.[88]

Randy Kessler was convicted in a non-jury trial on a disorderly conduct charge, and
"possession of a slugging weapon" (Oregon Revised Statutes 166.510). On appeal,
Kessler sought to overturn both convictions; only the second charge, "possession of
a slugging weapon" is of interest to us here. The Oregon Court of Appeals found
ORS 166.510 a reasonable exercise of the police power of the state. Kessler
appealed to the Oregon Supreme Court, arguing that the statute violated his right

---

85 *Onderdonk* v. *Handgun Permit Review Board*, 44 Md. App. 132, 407 A.2d 763, 764 (1979).
86 *Onderdonk* v. *Handgun Permit Review Board*, 44 Md. App. 132, 407 A.2d 763, 764 (1979).
87 *State* v. *Blocker*, 291 Or. 255, 258 (1981).
88 *State* v. *Kessler*, 289 Or. 359, 370 (1980).

to possess arms in his home for personal defense,[89] contrary to the Oregon Constitution.

The Oregon Supreme Court acknowledged that the meaning of the Oregon Constitutional provision in question had never been explored by the Oregon courts. For this reason, the Court decided it was time to ask and answer three questions:

(a) To whom does the right belong?

(b) What is the meaning of "defense of themselves"?

(c) What is the meaning of "arms," and what, if any, weapons of current usage are included in this term?[90]

The Court recognized that the Second Amendment "has not yet been held to apply to state limitations on the bearing of arms," and that the Oregon Constitutional provision differed substantially in wording from both the Second Amendment, and many other state constitutional "right to keep and bear arms" provisions. The Court recognized:

> We are not unmindful that there is current controversy over the wisdom of a right to bear arms, and that the original motivations for such a provision might not seem compelling if debated as a new issue. Our task, however, in construing a constitutional provision is to respect the principles given the status of constitutional guarantees and limitations by the drafters; it is not to abandon these principles when this fits the needs of the moment.[91]

The Court traced Oregon's provision back to the Indiana state constitution of 1816, and from there to the state constitutions of Kentucky (1799) or Ohio (1802), backward through the Second Amendment to the English Bill of Rights.[92] The Court then cited *People* v. *Brown* (1931) to justify the position that concern about standing armies represented a major part of the motivation behind the Second Amendment, but also reflected a personal self-defense requirement.[93]

The Court then took up the question of what constitutes "arms," and concluded:

> Therefore, the term "arms" as used by the drafters of the constitutions probably was intended to include those weapons used by settlers for both personal and military defense. The term "arms" was not limited to firearms, but included several handcarried weapons commonly used for defense. The term "arms" would not have included cannon or other heavy ordnance not kept by militiamen or private citizens.[94]

The Court went on to argue that since the "revolutionary war era ended at a time when the rapid social and economic changes of the so-called Industrial Revolution began," that "advanced weapons of modern warfare have never been intended for personal possession and protection." The Court described how:

> The development of powerful explosives in the mid-nineteenth century, combined with the development of mass-produced metal parts, made possible the automatic weapons, explosives, and chemicals of modern warfare...

---

89 *State* v. *Kessler*, 289 Or. 359, 361, 370, 371 (1980).

90 *State* v. *Kessler*, 289 Or. 359 (1980).

91 *State* v. *Kessler*, 289 Or. 359, 361, 362 (1980).

92 *State* v. *Kessler*, 289 Or. 359, 365, 367 (1980).

93 *State* v. *Kessler*, 289 Or. 359, 366, 368 (1980).

94 *State* v. *Kessler*, 289 Or. 359, 368 (1980).

These advanced weapons of modern warfare have never been intended for personal possession and protection. When the constitutional drafters referred to an individual's
"right to bear arms," the arms used by the militia and for personal protection were basi-
cally the same weapons. Modern weapons used exclusively by the military are not
"arms" which are commonly possessed by individuals for defense, therefore, the term
"arms" in the constitution does not include such weapons.[95]

What the Court overlooked is that while military needs drove the development of
modern automatic weapons, they were not exclusively governmental in ownership,
nor is it clear that the Industrial Revolution led to unanticipated new weapons. As
early as 1663, "a man named Palmer presented a paper to the Royal Society"
describing what is recognizably the operating principle of the modern gas-operated
semiautomatic firearm. Similarly, James Puckle's "A Portable Gun or Machine
called a Defence," patented in May 1718, bears many similarities to the Gatling
gun, the first of the practical machine guns. While ridiculed at the time as an
impractical design, a scheme for separating investors from their money, it certainly
demonstrates that the *concept* of repeating firearms was in existence, even if the
mechanical details remained to be worked out.

While it is certainly true that machine guns were originally designed with military
purposes in mind, there is substantial evidence that machine guns, from the
beginning had a civilian market: "As early as 1863 H.J. Raymond, the owner of the
New York Times, had bought three Gatling guns to protect his offices against feared
attacks by mobs of people protesting against the Conscription Act of March of that
year, of which the *Times* had come out in support." Machine guns played a role in
suppressing strikes throughout the period between the Civil War and the 1930s,
not only in the hands of National Guard units, as we have previously seen, but also
in the hands of company goon squads—a clearly civilian use.[96]

The Thompson submachine gun is the best example of this more complex
relationship between private and public ownership; since the hoped for government
contracts did not materialize, attempts were made to market them to private owners
for self-defense, as we have previously seen.[97]   Private ownership of automatic
weapons in the United States, while somewhat unusual, and heavily regulated, is
legal—this author personally knows several such legal owners. In Switzerland, of
course, automatic weapons in private hands (though governmentally owned) are
not only common, but required by law.[98] While privately owned machine guns
require a permit for Swiss citizens, such permits are not particularly difficult to
obtain.[99]

Because the Oregon Constitution's provision included "defense of themselves,"
the Court concluded that defensive arms, even though "unlikely to be used as a militia weapon," would include any weapon commonly used for defense. The Court

---

95 *State* v. *Kessler*, 289 Or. 359, 369 (1980).

96 Ellis, 13-15, 42-44.

97 Helmer, 75-76, plate after 86.

98 John McPhee, *La Place de la Concorde Suisse*, (New York: Farrar, Straus, Giroux, 1984), 40-41.
The Swiss militia system is widely believed to have been a source for the ideas contained in the stillborn
Militia Act of 1792. In reading McPhee's description, it would appear that not only does militia service play a role in developing individual self-reliance, but the very limited standing army has made it
impractical for the Swiss to engage in an adventurist foreign policy.

99 David B. Kopel and Stephen D'Andrilli, "The Swiss And Their Guns", *American Rifleman*,
[February 1990], 38-39.

also held that the right to keep arms was not unrestricted or unregulated, and cited *State* v. *Cartwright* (1966), as precedent for laws prohibiting firearms possession by felons.

In the particular case before them, the Court affirmed Kessler's conviction for disorderly conduct, but held that because a billy club was within the definition of "arms," and the clubs in question were in his home, that, "the defendant's possession of a billy club in his home is protected by Article I, section 27, of the Oregon Constitution," and reversed his conviction on the possession charge.[100]

However, possession of a weapon in one's home is not the same as the unrestricted right to carry it outside one's home, and the Court cited Edward III's Statute of Northampton (1328), forbidding carrying of firearms "for the purpose of terrifying the people," and a 1678 Massachusetts law that prohibited shooting "near any house, barn, garden, or highway in any town" where a person might be accidentally hit. But more to the point of our interest:

> The courts of many states have upheld statutes which restrict the possession or manner of carrying personal weapons. The reasoning of the courts is generally that a regulation is valid if the aim of public safety does not frustrate the guarantees of the state constitution. For example, many courts have upheld statutes prohibiting the carrying of concealed weapons, *see, e.g., State v. Hart*, 66 Idaho 217, 157 P2d 72 (1945); and statutes prohibiting possession of firearms by felons, *see, e.g., State v. Cartwright*, 246 Or 120, 418 P2d 822 (1966).[101]

The Court suggested that there are statutes regulating the carrying of arms which *would* be unconstitutional—but the Court didn't describe those statutes.

While *State* v. *Kessler* (1980) was being appealed to the Oregon Supreme Court, a similar case was working its way up through the courts. In *State* v. *Blocker* (1981), Michael Blocker had been convicted of possession of a billy club in his car, in violation of the same statute that had snared Kessler. The Court of Appeals waited for *Kessler* to be decided, and when it was, the Court of Appeals overturned Blocker's conviction, citing *Kessler* as precedent. The State appealed the decision.

Much of the *State* v. *Blocker* (1981) decision involved defining what constitutes "vague" and "overbroad" laws, but the opinion of the Oregon Supreme Court remained that while the Legislature could prohibit the carrying of a concealed weapon, they had not done so in this case—the statute in question had banned possession of a billy club anywhere—and had apparently neglected to ban concealed carry of such a weapon. The Court did acknowledge that some types of regulation of the bearing of arms was legal, and gave some examples of then current Oregon statutes that were constitutional:

> This state has several such regulatory statutes, with which we are not concerned in this case: ORS 166.220(1) prohibiting possession of a dangerous weapon with intent to use such weapon unlawfully against another; ORS 166.240, prohibiting carrying certain weapons concealed about one's person; ORS 166.250, prohibiting carrying any firearm concealed upon the person or within any vehicle without a license to do so.

> On the other hand, ORS 166.510, with which we are here concerned, is not, nor is it apparently intended to be, a restriction on the manner of possession or use of certain weapons. The statute is written as a total proscription of the mere possession of certain

---

100 *State* v. *Kessler*, 289 Or. 359, 369, 370, 372 (1980).
101 *State* v. *Kessler*, 289 Or. 359, 369, 370 (1980).

weapons, and that mere possession, insofar as a billy is concerned, is constitutionally protected.[102]

Carrying arms with some criminal intent could be prohibited; carrying concealed could be prohibited; but some form of carry was protected, or the statute would be contrary to the constitutional protection to bear arms for self-defense.

Three years later, in *State v. Delgado* (1984), the Oregon Supreme Court used very similar reasoning in a switchblade case. Joseph Luna Delgado was stopped on October 3, 1983 by police, since he "appeared disorderly." During a patdown search, the officer found a switch-blade knife in the defendant's back pocket, and Delgado was convicted of possessing a switch-blade knife, a prohibited weapon.

On appeal, the conviction was reversed, based on the *Blocker* and *Kessler* decisions; the prosecution asked the Oregon Supreme Court to review the question of whether switch-blades were constitutionally protected arms. Since the *Kessler* decision had recognized that "hand-carried weapons commonly used by individuals for personal defense" were constitutionally protected, the state argued that switch-blades were not commonly used for defense, and were therefore outside the protection of the Oregon Constitution.

The Oregon Supreme Court rejected the prosecution's evidence that switch-blade knives are "almost exclusively the weapon of the thug and delinquent," calling the material "no more than impressionistic observations on the criminal use of switch-blades." But next the Court took up the distinction between "offensive" and "defensive" arms:

> More importantly, however, we are unpersuaded by the distinction which the state urges of "offensive" and "defensive" weapons. All hand-held weapons necessarily share both characteristics. A kitchen knife can as easily be raised in attack as in defense. The spring mechanism does not, instantly and irrevocably, convert the jackknife into an "offensive" weapon. Similarly, the clasp feature of the common jackknife does not mean that it is incapable of aggressive and violent purposes. It is not the design of the knife but the use to which it is put that determines its "offensive" or "defensive" character.[103]

The Court brought up the fundamental issue that determined whether a class of weapon was constitutionally protected or not:

> The appropriate inquiry in this case at bar is whether a kind of weapon, as modified by its modern design and function, is of the sort commonly used by individuals for personal defense during either the revolutionary and post-revolutionary era, or in 1859 when Oregon's constitution was adopted. In particular, it must be determined whether the drafters would have intended the word "arms" to include the switch-blade knife as a weapon commonly used by individuals for self defense.[104]

After a history of pocket knives, fighting knives, sword-canes, and Bowie knives, the Court concluded:

> It is clear, then, that knives have played an important role in American life, both as tools and as weapons. The folding pocket-knife, in particular, since the early 18th century has been commonly carried by men in America and used primarily for work, but also for fighting.

---

102 *State v. Blocker*, 291 Or. 255, 257, 258, 259, 260 (1981).
103 *State v. Delgado*, 298 Or. 395, 692 P.2d 610, 611, 612 (1984).
104 *State v. Delgado*, 298 Or. 395, 692 P.2d 610, 612 (1984).

The brings us to the switch-blade knife... If ORS 166.510(1) proscribed the possession of mere pocket-knives, there can be no question but that the statute would be held to conflict directly with Article I, section 27. The only difference is the presence of the spring-operated mechanism that opens the knife. We are unconvinced by the state's argument that the switch-blade is so "substantially different from its historical antecedent" (the jackknife) that it could not have been within the contemplation of the constitutional drafters. They must have been aware that technological changes were occurring in weaponry and in tools generally. The format and efficiency of weaponry was proceeding apace. This was the period of development of the Gatling gun, breech loading rifles, metallic cartridges and repeating rifles. The addition of a spring to open the blade of a jackknife is hardly a more astonishing innovation than those just mentioned....

This court recognizes the seriousness with which the legislature views the possession of certain weapons, especially switch-blades. The problem here is that ORS 166.510(1) absolutely proscribes the mere possession or carrying of such arms. This the constitution does not permit.[105]

The next Oregon decision, *Barnett* v. *State* (1985), was a bit different, and went no higher than the Oregon Court of Appeals. The plaintiff, Harry E. Barnett, was suing for relief from a conviction for carrying a blackjack; apparently he had been convicted before the Oregon Supreme Court had recognized the invalidity of the laws proscribing various weapons, and now sought relief from the disabilities of that prior conviction, which the Court of Appeals granted.[106]

The last of the Oregon decisions is *State* v. *Smoot* (1989), which answered the questions raised by *State* v. *Delgado* (1984), concerning the limits of the right to bear switch-blade knives. Dayne Arthur Smoot was convicted in Lane County, Oregon, of carrying a switch-blade knife concealed in a trouser pocket. The Oregon Court of Appeals upheld the conviction, since only the manner of carrying this constitutionally protected arm was regulated: "A person may possess and carry a switchblade as long as it is not concealed."[107]

The Arizona Court of Appeals concluded that a nunchaku[108] was not a constitutionally protected arm in *State* v. *Swanton* (1981). A Gary Dwayne Swanton had been convicted in Pima County Superior Court of unlawful possession of a nunchaku, in violation of Arizona Revised Statute 13-3102, which declared the nunchaku to be a "prohibited weapon." On appeal, Swanton argued that not only was the statute's exception for "lawful exhibitions, demonstrations, contests or athletic events" vague, but that his constitutional right to keep and bear arms was violated, and pointed to the Second Amendment and "Art. 2, Sec. 26 of the Arizona Constitution."

The Appeals Court rejected all of Swanton's arguments, and in a unanimous decision, cited *Harris* v. *State* (1967) as evidence that the Second Amendment did not protect individuals from state law. As for the Arizona Constitution: "With respect to our state constitution, the term 'arms' as used means such arms as are recognized in civilized warfare and not those used by a ruffian, brawler or assassin." The Appeals Court then cited *Ex parte Thomas* (1908), *Strickland* v. *State* (1911), *Fife* v.

---

105 *State* v. *Delgado*, 298 Or. 395, 692 P.2d 610, 613, 614 (1984).

106 *Barnett* v. *State*, 72 Or. App. 585, 695 P.2d 991 (Or.App. 1985).

107 *State* v. *Smoot*, 97 Or. App. 255, 258, 775 P.2d 344, 345 (1989).

108 This is an Oriental weapon, consisting of two sticks attached by a chain or cord. Laws similar to Arizona's prohibiting possession of a nunchaku are easy to find.

State (1876), and *State* v. *Kerner* (1921) to buttress this limited understanding of "arms." As perhaps a reminder of how the obligation of a state Attorney General to defend the state's laws sometimes conflicts with his own beliefs, the Arizona Attorney General whose staff persuaded the Court of Appeals that the Second Amendment did not extend to the states, and that the nunchaku was not a protected arm, was Robert K. Corbin—as of 1992, NRA First Vice President.[109]

In *Dano* v. *Collins* (Ariz. App. 1990), Franklin Dano and Paul Huebl brought suit against Tom Collins, the Maricopa County District Attorney, and Richard G. Godbehere, the Maricopa County Sheriff, requesting that the "state statute which prohibits the carrying of concealed weapons be declared in violation of the State Constitution." The Maricopa Superior Court dismissed the complaint. It was appealed to the Arizona Court of Appeals, where the "police power" was again cited as the basis for regulating, though not prohibiting, the carrying of arms:

> Arizona's prohibition on the carrying of concealed weapons does not frustrate the purpose of the constitutional provision. We do not read the Arizona constitutional guarantee as granting an absolute right to bear arms under all situations. The right to bear arms in self-defense is not impaired by requiring individuals to carry weapons openly. Appellants are free to bear exposed weapons for their defense.

The Arizona Court of Appeals went on to assert that the right to bear arms was not absolute, and cited the *State* v. *McAdams* (1986), *State* v. *Reid* (1840), *Matthews* v. *State* (1958), and *State* v. *Gohl* (1907) decisions as precedents.[110] The first two decisions were in complete harmony; both had recognized a right to open carry. *Gohl* had avoided a direct statement, but implied that open carry was protected. However, the *Matthews* decision had denied a right to open carry without a permit.

The Louisiana Supreme Court decision *State* v. *Hamlin* (1986) involved an indictment of Carolyn Hamlin and Anthony Reddix for the "possession of unregistered shotgun having a barrel of less than 18 inches in length..." The trial judge accepted their argument that the statute was "overbroad," violated their right to not self-incriminate, and quashed the indictment. On appeal to the Louisiana Supreme Court, Justice Marcus, writing for the majority, pointed to the *State* v. *Amos* (1977) decision to dispose of the Second Amendment. The Louisiana Constitution of 1974, article I, §11 was then quoted: "The right of each citizen to keep and bear arms shall not be abridged, but this provision shall not prevent the passage of laws to prohibit the carrying of weapons concealed on the person."

People v. *Brown* (1931) was again cited to justify regulation of weapons considered especially prone to criminal abuse, and the debates of the 1973 Louisiana Constitutional Convention were consulted to find that after debating the subject, a proposal to prohibit "licensing or registration or impose special taxes" of firearms had been voted down. Hamlin's effort to use the *Haynes* v. *U.S.* (1968) precedent was similarly unsuccessful, because the Louisiana statute in question specifically prohibited the use of registration information for any sort of criminal prosecution for failure to register.[111]

---

109 *State* v. *Swanton*, 129 Ariz. 131, 629 P.2d 98, 99 (App. 1981). Robert K. Corbin, "Firearms Civil Rights Legal Defense Fund", *American Rifleman*, [January 1992], 40.
110 *Dano* v. *Collins*, 166 Ariz. 322, 820 P.2d 1021, 1023, 1024 (App. 1990).
111 *State* v. *Hamlin*, 497 So.2d 1369, 1371, 1371, 1372 (La. 1986).

Maine's constitutional provision guaranteeing the right to bear arms "for the common defense" was raised in *State* v. *Friel* (1986). At first glance, this decision by Justice Glassman that upheld the conviction of an ex-felon for being in possession of a firearm, would appear to fit well into the other decisions covered in the chapter, "Problems of Judicial Interpretation." But the Maine Supreme Judicial Court pointed to the declaration that "the right to keep and bear arms" was "for the common defense," and cited the Massachusetts Supreme Judicial Court's decision in *Commonwealth* v. *Davis* (Mass. 1976) and the existing Maine precedent in *State* v. *McKinnon* (1957), to hold that the right so protected was limited to "service in a broadly based, organized militia."[112] As we have seen in a previous chapter, there is considerable reason to wonder if this understanding of the phrase accurately reflects the intent of the framers of the Massachusetts Constitution. Another problem is that the Maine Supreme Court in *McKinnon* had utterly refused to make any ruling of the meaning of this clause, since the facts in the case were insufficient to determine if the Maine Constitution's provision was applicable.[113] Later the same year, in *State* v. *Goodno* (1986), a conviction for carrying a concealed handgun was upheld, based again on the *Presser* and *Friel* precedents. A Michael Goodno had been arrested for failure to appear on a traffic warrant, and a concealed handgun discovered at that time.[114]

The Maine Supreme Judicial Court's position in these cases appears not to have sat well with the people of Maine:

> In 1987 the people of this state voted to amend article I, section 16, of the Maine Constitution to provide that "[e]very citizen has a right to keep and bear arms; and this right shall never be questioned." *By their vote the people struck four words, "for the common defense," from the original provision, with the apparent intent of establishing for every citizen the individual right to bear arms, as opposed to the collective right to bear arms for the common defense.*[115] [emphasis added]

While the decision in *State* v. *Brown* (1990) was again primarily whether the Maine Constitution protected the right of ex-felons to possess firearms, the decision by Chief Justice McKusick pointed to the ballot arguments used in the 1987 election to demonstrate that the change meant that an individual right was now protected, but that the change in question did not bar "reasonable regulation." What constituted "reasonable regulation" was not answered by the Court, other than to observe: "Plainly, the people of Maine who voted for the amendment never intended that an inmate at Maine State Prison or a patient at a mental hospital would have an absolute right to possess a firearm."[116] A subsequent decision by the Maine Supreme Judicial Court, *Hilly* v. *City of Portland* (1990), provides no more insight into the limits of that right, except to the extent that a concealed weapon permit could be required to carry concealed, and an applicant could be required to be photographed as a condition of getting a permit.[117]

State v. *McAdams* (1986) is the rarest of cases we have studied—one of only two criminal matters in which a female was the defendant:

---

112 *State* v. *Friel*, 508 A.2d 123, 125, 126 (Me. 1986).
113 *State* v. *McKinnon*, 153 Me. 15, 123 A.2d 885 (1957).
114 *State* v. *Goodno*, 511 A.2d 457, 458 (Me. 1986).
115 *State* v. *Brown*, 571 A.2d 816 (Me. 1990).
116 *State* v. *Brown*, 571 A.2d 816, 817, 818 (Me. 1990).
117 *Hilly* v. *City of Portland*, 582 A.2d 1213, 1215, 1216 (Me. 1990).

On June 11, 1985, defendant was stopped by two deputies of the Campbell County [Wyoming] sheriff's office for driving a vehicle without license plates. During the course of their inquiry, one of the deputies noticed that defendant had a knife in a sheath inside the right breast pocket of her jacket. Defendant advised the deputies that she was a cocktail waitress and that she carried the knife for her protection.

Lisa McAdams was charged with carrying a concealed deadly weapon. At trial, she sought dismissal of the charge on the grounds that the statute was a violation of Art. 1, §24 of the Wyoming Constitution: "The right of citizens to bear arms in defense of themselves and of the state shall not be denied." The trial court granted the motion. The State appealed to the Wyoming Supreme Court, arguing that:

> [T]he constitutional right to bear arms is subject to the legitimate exercise of the State's police power. The State argues that, pursuant to its police power, it can restrict the time and manner in which weapons are possessed without infringing upon any constitutional guarantee.[118]

McAdams' argument was that the language of the Wyoming Constitution leaves

> no room for restricting the bearing of arms. It is her contention that, so long as the weapon is possessed for defensive purposes, the constitutional right to such possession cannot be restricted in any respect. In support of her contention, she points to the history of territorial legislation regulating the possession of firearms. Apparently, defendant's claim is that because the possession of a concealed deadly weapon for defensive purposes was not prohibited in 1890, it cannot be prohibited in 1986. More succinctly, defendant seems to be saying that because the right to carry concealed weapons for defensive purposes existed when the constitution was adopted, that right cannot now be infringed upon under the guise of regulation.

This would seem an iron-clad argument. As we have previously seen, concealed weapons statutes appear to be a twentieth century phenomenon in most of the North and West. But the Wyoming Supreme Court did not accept this argument:

> In the first place, a constitution is not a lifeless or static instrument, the interpretation of which is confined to the conditions and outlook prevailing at the time of its adoption; rather, a constitution is a flexible, vital, living document, which must be interpreted in light of changing conditions of society. 16 Am.Jur.2d, Constitutional Law §96 (1979).

Here we have one of the fundamental disagreements, which reappears on issue after issue of constitutional law in American history: should the Bill of Rights be interpreted based on original intent, or "changing conditions"? The "changing conditions" theory provides an open door for an activist judiciary, by allowing the "rewriting" of the constitution through judicial interpretation. The "original intent" theory, while still subject to abuse, instead emphasizes the historical evidence for what was intended, and therefore how the Bill of Rights should be interpreted.

The Wyoming Supreme Court explicated its theory that the right to bear arms was not absolute:

> In the second place, defendant's argument incorrectly presumes that the right to carry concealed arms for defensive purposes did exist when the constitution was adopted. An absolute right to bear arms, concealed or otherwise, has never been recognized, even at common law. State v. Rupp, Iowa, 282 N.W.2d 125 (1979). In the case of Carfield v. State, Wyo., 649 P.2d 865 (1982), dealing with the constitutionality of a statute prohibiting a felon from carrying a weapon, this Court held that, by its very terms, Art. 1,

---

118 State v. McAdams, 714 P.2d 1236, 1237 (Wyo. 1986).

§24 of the Wyoming Constitution grants to citizens only a limited right to bear arms in defense of themselves and of the state. Because there was no claim by the appellant that he possessed the weapon for the purpose of defending the state or himself, the Court found it unnecessary to address the question we are presented with in the present case.[119]

In *State* v. *Rupp* (1979) and *Carfield* v. *State* (1982), the question was not whether the right to bear arms was absolute, but whether convicted felons could be prohibited from bearing arms as a loss of civil rights for past criminal behavior. Even the assertion that the Wyoming Constitution "grants only a limited right to bear arms in defense of themselves," based on *Carfield* is highly questionable. In the *Carfield* decision, the Wyoming Supreme Court had cited *Hyde* v. *City of Birmingham* (1980), but the rest of the decisions cited related to ex-felons in possession of arms.[120]

The Wyoming Supreme Court then went on to argue that constitutional rights were always subject to the police power, and quoted *State* v. *Langley*, 53 Wyo. 332, 84 P.2d 767 (1938), an alcohol regulation case: "That power, giving the legislature the right to enact laws for the health, safety, comfort, moral and general welfare of the people, is an attribute of sovereignty, is essential for every civilized government, is inherent in the legislature except as expressly limited, and no express grant thereof is necessary."[121]

But, having used the argument that appears repeatedly throughout American history—that rights are not absolute, but relative, and therefore subject to majority abridgement if the magic expression "health, safety, comfort, moral and general welfare" is properly invoked—the Court acknowledged: "The police power cannot, however, be invoked in such a manner that it amounts to the destruction of the right to bear arms. *People v. Brown...* (1931); *State v. Dawson...* (1968)." The Court also quoted *State* v. *Wilforth* (1881): "A statute which, under the pretense of regulating, amounts to a destruction of the right, or which requires arms to be so borne as to render them wholly useless for purposes of defense, would be clearly unconstitutional."

The remainder of the *McAdams* decision argued that there is a balancing act between the rights of the individual, and the rights of the society, in the interest of order. In the opinion of the Wyoming Supreme Court, the responsibility for determining where this balance of majority will and individual rights was to be struck, was with the judiciary. Finally, the Court asserted that the prohibition on concealed carry was "not... unreasonable."[122] Without directly saying so, the Court had recognized a right to bear arms for defensive purposes; but explicitly recognized that regulation must be "reasonable," and that such regulation must not require "arms to be so borne as to render them wholly useless for purposes of defense..."

A radically different example of how the "police power" of the state and a constitutional protection of a right to bear arms were dealt with can be found in the West Virginia decision, *City of Princeton* v. *Buckner* (W.Va. 1988). Article III, §22 of the West Virginia Constitution, approved by the voters on November 4, 1986, reads: "A person has the right to keep and bear arms for the defense of self, family, home and state, and for lawful hunting and recreational use."

---

119 *State* v. *McAdams*, 714 P.2d 1236, 1237 (Wyo. 1986).
120 *Carfield* v. *State*, 649 P.2d 865, 871, 872 (Wyo. 1982).
121 *State* v. *McAdams*, 714 P.2d 1236, 1237 (Wyo. 1986).
122 *State* v. *McAdams*, 714 P.2d 1236, 1237, 1238 (Wyo. 1986).

A Harold L. Buckner was pulled over and arrested for drunk driving in Princeton, Mercer County, West Virginia. During a search, a .22 caliber pistol was found in the driver's jacket pocket, which he did not have a license to carry. A judge refused to allow a charge of "carrying a dangerous and deadly weapon," under West Virginia Code 61-7-1, on the grounds that the statute in question violated the recently enacted constitutional provision. The prosecutor filed a writ of mandamus with the Circuit Court of Mercer County, to compel the judge to pursue the criminal charge. The Circuit Court agreed that the statute in question was in conflict with the constitutional provision, and sought an opinion from the West Virginia Supreme Court of Appeals.

Where the Oregon Supreme Court's decision in *State* v. *Kessler* (1980) provides one of the first detailed historical analyses of the right to keep and bear arms in many decades, the West Virginia Court wrote, in a sense, a companion opinion, emphasizing the judicial precedents associated with the various state constitutional provisions. The Court acknowledged that concealed weapons statutes in West Virginia went back to 1882, and detailed the history of those West Virginia decisions related to bearing arms.[123] In discussing the *State* v. *Workman* (1891) decision, the Court pointed out that the *Workman* decision defined "arms" in relation to the "well-regulated militia" clause of the Second Amendment, and thus excluded a number of weapons ("pistols, Bowie-knives, brass knuckles, billies") which the West Virginia Supreme Court of 1891 did not believe were "militia weapons." But the West Virginia Supreme Court of 1988 pointed to a significant difference in the definition of "arms" in this case:

> [I]t is important to note that the definition of "arms" presented in *Workman* focuses on the "well regulated militia" language of the second amendment. No parallel language appears in our state constitutional amendment. Because the second amendment does not operate as a restraint upon the power of states to regulate firearms,... the definition of "arms" set forth in *Workman* is not particularly helpful in the case now before us. Moreover, the broad language embodied in our current Right to Keep and Bear Arms Amendment makes any further reexamination of the *Workman* decision unnecessary.[124]

The Court cited the Colorado decision, *City of Lakewood* v. *Pillow* (1972); the Idaho decision, *In Re Brickey* (1902); the Michigan decision, *People* v. *Zerillo* (1922); the Vermont decision, *State* v. *Rosenthal* (1903); and the series of Oregon decisions of the 1980s. The Court concluded that the statute prohibiting the carrying of dangerous or deadly weapons without a license was so broad as to be in conflict with the constitutional provision:

> Based upon the foregoing, we conclude that the language embodied in *W. Va. Code*, 61-7-1 [1975] sweeps so broadly as to infringe a right that it cannot permissibly reach, in this case, the constitutional right of a person to keep and bear arms in defense of self, family, home and state, guaranteed by art. III, §22.[125]

The Court did not deny that the state had the authority to regulate, in some manner, the bearing of arms:

> We stress that our holding above in no way means that the right of a person to bear arms is absolute... Other jurisdictions concluding that state statutes or municipal ordinances

---

123 *City Of Princeton* v. *Buckner*, 377 S.E.2d 139, 140, 141, 142 (W.Va. 1988).
124 *City Of Princeton* v. *Buckner*, 377 S.E.2d 139, 142, 143 (W.Va. 1988).
125 *City Of Princeton* v. *Buckner*, 377 S.E.2d 139, 143, 144 (W.Va. 1988).

have violated constitutional provisions guaranteeing a right to bear arms for defensive purposes, though not specific in what way this is to be done, have recognized that a government may regulate the exercise of the right, provided the regulations or restrictions do not frustrate the guarantees of the constitution provision.[126]

After asserting that "the constitutional right to keep and bear arms is not absolute," the Court cited a number of decisions upholding such regulations, though the range of regulations in those cases range from *Carfield* v. *State* (1982), which prohibited concealed carry, to *Commonwealth* v. *Ray* (1970), which did not recognize a right to carry arms at all:

> We stress, however, that the legitimate governmental purpose in regulating the right to bear arms cannot be pursued by means that broadly stifle the exercise of this right where the governmental purpose can be more narrowly achieved....
>
> [A] governmental purpose to control or prohibit certain activities, which may be constitutionally subject to state regulation under the police power, may not be achieved by means which sweep unnecessarily broadly and thereby invade the realm of protected freedoms, such as the right to keep and bear arms guaranteed in our State *Constitution.*[127]

The Court declared that a complete prohibition on carry of a pistol without a permit was unconstitutional; but it appears that the Court believed that those laws that regulated carrying, including licensing of concealed carry, might be constitutional, as long as they were not "overbroad."

Clarification of the intent of the West Virginia Supreme Court came two years later, in *Application of Metheney* (1990). West Virginia's 1989 statute established a concealed weapon permit process intended to conform with the *Buckner* decision. The new law required the applicant to be a U.S. citizen, a resident of West Virginia, and of the county where the application was made, over 18, "not addicted to alcohol, a controlled substance or a drug," no prior felony convictions, or other violent offenses involving deadly weapons, "[t]hat the applicant desires to carry such deadly weapon for the defense of self, family, home or state, or other lawful purpose," "physically and mentally competent",[128] and demonstrate competence in "handling and firing such firearms."[129]

Several applicants for concealed weapons permits had appealed rejections by circuit court judges, arguing that the statute: "W.Va.Code §61-7-4 does not permit the circuit court any discretion in the granting of the licenses outside the specific provisions of the statute. They further claim a constitutional right to carry a concealed deadly weapon." The Court denied that there was a constitutional right to carry a *concealed* deadly weapon, even though the *Buckner* decision had dealt with such a circumstance. The Court held that the state could "reasonably regulate" carry of a deadly weapon, including the licensing of concealed carry.

On the issue of discretionary authority, the Court found that the statute was somewhat ambiguous. The circuit court had the authority to hear evidence as to whether an applicant's purpose was "defense of self, family, home or state, or other lawful purpose," and thus, the circuit court could deny an application if the evi-

---

126 *City Of Princeton* v. *Buckner*, 377 S.E.2d 139, 145 (W.Va. 1988).
127 *City Of Princeton* v. *Buckner*, 377 S.E.2d 139, 146. 149 (W.Va. 1988).
128 West Virginia Code Ann. §61-7-4 (1992).
129 *Application of Metheney*, 391 S.E.2d 635, 636, 637 (W.Va. 1990).

dence demonstrated that the purpose was not satisfied. The West Virginia Supreme Court then ordered the circuit courts to consider again these applications, "consistent with this opinion."[130] However, "if the judge determines that the eight specific requirements found [in the statute] have been satisfied, then the circuit court must issue the license."[131]

The issue of which arms were protected was again taken up in *People* v. *Smelter* (1989), a Michigan Court of Appeals decision which held that stun guns were not constitutionally protected. Timothy Smelter argued that his possession of a stun gun was protected by article 1, §6 of the Michigan Constitution of 1963: "Every person has a right to keep and bear arms for the defense of himself and the state." The Court of Appeals pointed to *People* v. *Brown* (1931), and unanimously held that: "The right to regulate weapons extends not only to the establishment of conditions under which weapons may be possessed, but allows the state to prohibit weapons whose customary employment by individuals is to violate the law."[132] How the Michigan Court of Appeals found that a "stun gun" constituted a weapon customarily used "to violate the law" was not explained. Since a stun gun requires physical contact to be effective, and is nominally a non-lethal weapon, this seems like a somewhat questionable decision of fact.

Our long history of North Carolina decisions ends with *State* v. *Fennell* (1989), a decision of the North Carolina Court of Appeals. Jeffrey Fennell was convicted "of possession of a weapon of mass death and destruction..." In this case, the weapon was a short-barreled shotgun. Fennell had been spotted carrying a "sawed-off shotgun" at a Goldsboro community recreation center, and the police were called. After a brief chase, Fennell was apprehended, and the disassembled sawed-off shotgun was located. Fennell was convicted. Fennell's appeal argued a variety of points, of which the principal interest to us is the constitutionality of the statute under which he was charged:

> Fennell contends that the statute is an overly-broad restriction of his constitutional right to bear arms under both the Second Amendment to the Constitution of the United States and Article I, Section 30 of the North Carolina Constitution....

> Fennell concedes that the Second Amendment does not protect his right to carry a sawed-off shotgun. Indeed, it is generally understood that the Second Amendment guarantees the right to bear arms only in connection with a "well regulated militia."[133]

The Court then cited *U.S.* v. *Miller* (1939)—though with no apparent recognition that *Miller* had ruled primarily on the issue of whether expert testimony was required to make the decision that a sawed-off shotgun was a militia weapon.

> It is true, however, that the North Carolina Constitution has been interpreted to guarantee a broader right to individuals to keep and bear arms. "North Carolina decisions have interpreted the right to bear arms to the people in a collective sense—similar to the concept of a militia—and also to individuals." *State* v. *Dawson*,... (1968). Yet, as the Supreme Court of this state also noted, "These decisions have... consistently pointed out that the right of individuals to bear arms is not absolute, but is subject to regulation."...

---

130 *Application of Metheney*, 391 S.E.2d 635, 637, 638 (W.Va. 1990).
131 West Virginia Code Annotated, §61-7-4 (1992).
132 *People* v. *Smelter*, 175 Mich.App. 153, 437 N.W.2d 341, 342 (1989).
133 *State* v. *Fennell*, 95 N.C.App. 140, 382 S.E.2d 231, 232 (1989). Other than minor differences in punctuation and capitalization, the two provisions are identical.

The regulation must be "'reasonable and not prohibitive, and must bear a fair relation to the preservation of the public peace and safety.'"....

But, as Fennell pointed out, the statute in question was "an absolute prohibition on short-barreled shotguns..." Fennell argued "that the State may regulate firearms only as to time, place or manner." There was a fundamental problem here: how could an absolute prohibition be found constitutional in light of the *Dawson* decision?

> First, the statute does not completely ban a class of weapons protected by the Constitution. Rather, it permits possession of shotguns, with the exception of those which have been tampered with so as to shorten the barrel. "[A] sawed-off shotgun seems a most plausible subject of regulation as it may be readily concealed and is especially dangerous because of the wide and nearly indiscriminate scattering of its shot." *Commonwealth* v. *Davis*...(1976)... Accordingly, we hold that this regulation is reasonable and bears a fair relation to the preservation of the public peace and safety.

The Court also cited *State* v. *Astore* (1972) and *State* v. *Hamlin* (1986) in support of this position. But while *Hamlin* and *Astore* had accepted the existence of an individual right to keep arms, which was merely regulated by the statutes concerning short-barreled shotguns, the *Davis* decision had denied such a right existed.

The Court pointed to *State* v. *Kerner* (1921) as evidence that the size of a firearm could be regulated, and therefore held:

> Thus, the State can regulate the length of a particular firearm as long as there is a reasonable purpose for doing so. We are not convinced by Fennell's argument that such a restriction leads us down the "slippery slope" and gives the legislature full license to restrict any and all firearms possessed by individuals.[134]

There were limits to the restrictions which the legislature could enact, as long as *some* members of a class of arms were still legal.

The West Virginia Supreme Court in the *Buckner* decision had observed:

> It is important to note that the state of Delaware recently adopted a constitutional amendment strikingly similar to our West Virginia provision, *see Del. Const.* art. I, §20.... The Delaware weapons statute, *Del.Code Ann.* tit. 11, §1441 (1987) is analogous to our weapons regulations in that it requires an applicant to obtain a license in order to carry a concealed weapon.[135]

Indeed, three months later, a case based on that constitutional amendment was before the New Castle County Superior Court. A Joan McIntyre, initially licensed to carry a concealed handgun in 1975 after being attacked and harassed, was denied renewal of her license by the Delaware Dept. of Justice.[136] The argument was presented that good cause no longer existed, since the attack had been so many years before. Of most interest to us, McIntyre pointed to the clause added to the Delaware Constitution by a two-thirds vote of both houses of the legislature in 1986 and 1987: "A person has the right to keep and bear arms for the defense of self, family, home and state, and for hunting and recreational use."[137]

The response of the New Castle Superior Court judge was: "The Court notes that 'the right to keep and bear arms' does not of necessity require that such arms

---

134 *State* v. *Fennell*, 95 N.C.App. 140, 382 S.E.2d 231, 233 (1989).
135 *City Of Princeton* v. *Buckner*, 377 S.E.2d 139, 148 (W.Va. 1988).
136 *Application of McIntyre*, 552 A.2d 500, 501 (Del. Super. 1988).
137 Halbrook, *A Right To Bear Arms*, 121.

may be kept concealed. 11 *Del.C.* §1441 relates only to the carrying of concealed deadly weapons; and as such is supported by a legitimate State interest."[138] While this case went no higher, the Delaware courts here recognized that the state constitutional amendment did protect a right to carry openly.

The Nebraska Supreme Court decision *State* v. *LaChapelle* (1990), like several others during this period, was the result of an amendment to the state constitution, adopted at the November 1988 general election:

> All persons are by nature free and independent, and have certain inherent and inalienable rights; among these are life, liberty, the pursuit of happiness, and the right to keep and bear arms for security or defense of self, family, home, and others, and for lawful common defense, hunting, recreational use, and all other lawful purposes, and such rights shall not be denied or infringed by the state or any subdivision thereof. To secure these rights, and the protection of property, governments are instituted among people, deriving their just powers from the consent of the governed.[139]

It certainly lacks the conciseness of the Second Amendment, but would seem to make up for it in clarity! The defendant, Roger C. LaChapelle, was convicted of possession of a short-barreled shotgun, which he was using at the time to threaten a woman.

On appeal to the Nebraska Supreme Court, LaChapelle attempted to use the aforementioned amendment to the Nebraska Constitution as a defense. The Court pointed to their decision *State* v. *Comeau* (1989) as evidence that statutes regulating possession of firearms were constitutional. But where *Comeau* had found that felons in possession of a firearm were not protected by the Nebraska Constitution, this case was different: LaChapelle was not a felon or ex-felon in possession of a firearm.

The Nebraska Supreme Court also cited the language in West Virginia's *City of Princeton* v. *Buckner* (W.Va. 1988) to the effect that "reasonable regulatory control" was constitutional—even though the issue there was the carrying of weapons, which had been found to be constitutionally protected. The Massachusetts decision *Commonwealth* v. *Davis* (Mass. 1976) was cited, even though the Massachusetts Constitution was held to *not* protect an individual right, unlike the Nebraska Constitutional provision.

The decisions *State* v. *Fennell* (1989), *Carson* v. *State* (1978), *State* v. *Astore* (1972), *Morrison* v. *State* (1960), and their intellectual ancestor, *People* v. *Brown* (1931), were also cited to defend the position that some weapons were "commonly used for criminal purposes."[140] These decisions, at least, were not in obvious contradiction to the Nebraska Constitution—but the Nebraska Supreme Court made its decision based entirely on these precedents, that a short-barreled shotgun was not included among the protected firearms. Unlike other state supreme court decisions during this period which were provoked by amendments made through the initiative process, no attempt was made to justify this position based on election materials or statements.

In *State* v. *Rupe* (1984), the Washington Supreme Court heard an appeal from a Mitchell Edward Rupe, convicted "of two counts of aggravated first-degree murder and two counts of first-degree robbery..." in Thurston County. Because Rupe was

---

138 *Application of McIntyre*, 552 A.2d 500, 501 (Del. Super. 1988).
139 *State* v. *LaChapelle*, 234 Neb. 458, 451 N.W.2d 689 (1990).
140 *State* v. *LaChapelle*, 234 Neb. 458, 462, 451 N.W.2d 689, 690, 691 (1990).

sentenced to death, the resulting decision is complex and sought to cover a tremendous range of constitutional and procedural issues—as well such a decision should—execution is forever.

The crime itself was heinous, and assuming that the courts reached the correct decision about Rupe's guilt in this matter, it was an amateurish and clumsy bank robbery, intended to resolve his overdrawn checking account with the bank—his blood-stained checkbook was "lying open on the customer's side of the counter." Rupe confessed to the robbery-murder, then recanted his confession in court. To add to the horror of this crime, the first person to happen on the crime scene was the husband of one of the murder victims.

A total of 15 issues were raised by the defendant on appeal, most of which are irrelevant to our interests. The Washington Supreme Court found in Rupe's favor on only one of the issues raised—and that was the issue that is of interest to us. During the sentencing phase, the content of the defendant's gun collection was admitted as evidence,[141] for the purpose of giving the jury "an insight into defendant's personality..." (Significantly, none of the guns in the collection was used in the murder, and none of them were even similar to the gun used in the murder).

The Court's opinion, written by Justice Rosellini agreed that:

> this evidence was irrelevant, prejudicial, and violative of his due process rights...

> The challenged evidence included the admission of several weapons: (1) a CAR 15 semiautomatic rifle (civilian version of the military's M-16), (2) a 12-gauge shotgun with one shortened barrel, (3) a .22 caliber rifle, and (4) a pistol with interchangeable barrels. The last item belonged to defendant's landlord. In addition to the weapons themselves, the prosecution presented the testimony of several experts on firearms who alleged that, though the weapons were legal, they were not suitable for hunting or sport.

> Michael J. Peck of the Department of Game observed that the CAR 15 was a legal varmint gun but not commonly used. He stated that the CAR 15 was "designed as an antipersonnel rifle."

The defense responded "that he used the CAR 15 for hunting varmints. He explained that he purchased the gun because it was very similar to the M-16 he carried during his 8 1/2 years in the military."[142]

The prosecution expert witness Peck claimed that the shotgun "with the shortened barrel...was not legal for hunting birds in the state because it was not 'plugged.'" Another prosecution witness, however, agreed that it would have been legal for deer hunting. The defense, however, established that the shotgun "was in fact plugged..."[143] Unfortunately, the decision does not tell us whether the "shortened barrel" was shorter than the 18" minimum required by federal law, or was simply shorter than was commonly used for bird hunting. Since no weapons violation appears to have been charged because of the shotgun, and because one of the prosecution expert witnesses acknowledged it was "a type which would be used

---

141 *State* v. *Rupe*, 101 Wash.2d 664, 683 P.2d 571, 576, 577, 578 (1984).

142 *State* v. *Rupe*, 101 Wash.2d 664, 683 P.2d 571, 594, 595 (1984).

143 *State* v. *Rupe*, 101 Wash.2d 664, 683 P.2d 571, 594 (1984). A "plug" in a pump or semiautomatic shotgun reduces its capacity to three rounds. This is a requirement for bird hunting in many states; it is not a requirement for a self-defense shotgun, since self-defense is not considered a "sport." It is also not a requirement for hunting deer.

to hunt deer," it is likely that the shotgun barrel was of a legal length, such as are commonly sold for home defense.

The prosecution's essential purpose in presenting these intimidating weapons in the penalty phase was that Rupe was "a dangerous man because the CAR 15 was 'an assault weapon to gun groups of people down in combat situations.'" The Washington Supreme Court rejected this admission of the gun collection:

> Our analysis starts with the well-established rule that constitutionally protected behavior cannot be the basis of criminal punishment. See *Hess v. Indiana*...(1973) (constitutional guaranties of freedom of speech forbid states to punish use of words or language not within narrowly limited classes of speech); *Stanley v. Georgia*...(1969) (State may not punish mere possession of obscene material in privacy of home).[144]

After explaining how evidence introduced in a trial may not "'chill' or penalize the assertion of a constitutional right," the Court applied this principle to the case at hand:

> Here the challenged evidence directly implicates defendant's right to bear arms. Const. art. 1, §24 provides:
>
>> The right of the individual citizen to bear arms in defense of himself, or the state, shall not be impaired, but nothing in this section shall be construed as authorizing individuals or corporations to organize, maintain or employ an armed body of men.
>
> This constitutional provision is facially broader than the Second Amendment, which restricts its reference to "a well regulated militia."[145]
>
> Although we do not decide the parameters of this right, here, defendant's behavior—possession of legal weapons—falls squarely within the confines of the right guaranteed by Const. art. 1, §24....
>
> Defendant was thus entitled under our constitution to possess weapons, without incurring the risk that the State would subsequently use the mere fact of possession against him in a criminal trial unrelated to their use. Our conclusion follows from the clear language of Washington's constitution. In addition, it coincides with the interpretation placed on a similar provision contained in the Oregon constitution.[146]

The Washington Supreme Court then cited the *State* v. *Kessler* (1980) decision of the Oregon Supreme Court, and agreed that:

> [T]his evidence is both irrelevant and highly prejudicial... The guns in question had no connection with the crime and were all, admittedly, legally owned. We see no relation between the fact that someone collects guns and the issue of whether they deserve the death sentence. Furthermore, we take judicial notice of the overwhelming evidence that many nonviolent individuals own and enjoy using a wide variety of guns. This fact has no bearing on the issue of whether any of them deserve to live or die.
>
> While the State urges that if this evidence was irrelevant, it was nonetheless nonprejudicial, we cannot agree with this proposition. Personal reactions to the ownership of guns vary greatly. Many individuals view guns with great abhorrence and fear. Still others may consider certain weapons as acceptable but others as "dangerous." A third type may react solely to the fact that someone who has committed a crime has such

---

144 *State* v. *Rupe*, 101 Wash.2d 664, 683 P.2d 571, 595 (1984).

145 In note 8, the Court also acknowledged that the *Quilici* v. *Village of Morton Grove* (7th Cir. 1982) decision suggested "that the federal right to bear arms may be more limited than our own provisions."

146 *State* v. *Rupe*, 101 Wash.2d 664, 683 P.2d 571, 596 (1984).

weapons. Any or all of these individuals might believe that defendant was a dangerous individual and therefore deserved to die, just because he owned the guns. This was, in fact, the crux of the prosecutor's argument to the jury for defendant's death. Consequently, we reject the State's argument that no prejudice resulted from admission of these weapons.[147]

With such a complex case, it would be expecting too much for the Court to come to complete agreement. While Justices Dore, Dimmick, and Cunningham concurred with Justice Rosellini's decision, Chief Justice Williams and Justice Brachtenbach concurred in result only, and Justice Dolliver wrote a separate opinion, concurring in the result only. Dolliver's disagreements with the majority opinion were primarily that he felt the death penalty was unconstitutional, and whether to admit a polygraph test involving a witness. Of relevance to our interests: "I agree the evidence of defendant's gun collection should not have been admissible... at the sentencing stage. I do not agree that Const. art. 1, §24 is the appropriate vehicle by which to reach this conclusion." While asserting, "I do not necessarily disagree with the construction placed by the majority on this constitutional provision," Justice Dolliver argued that it was unnecessary to go to the Constitution, when existing criminal procedure provided an adequate reason to strike down the admission of the gun collection. Justices Stafford and Pearson concurred in Dolliver's opinion that there was no need to bring in the Washington Constitution's protections of the right to arms.[148]

This was a clear-cut decision that the Washington Constitution protected the right to possess what is commonly known as an "assault weapon." But in the next Washington decision, it was badly misused. A Leslie Riggins ran afoul of a Seattle ordinance in *City of Seattle* v. *Riggins* (Wash.App. 1991). Seattle Municipal Code 12A.14.080(B) made it unlawful to carry "concealed or unconcealed on his/her person any dangerous knife, or carry concealed on his/her person any deadly weapon other than a pistol;..." A "dangerous knife" was further defined as "any fixed-blade knife and any other knife having a blade more than three and one-half inches (3 1/2") in length." There were exemptions for "licensed hunters and fishermen actively engaged in such pursuits, persons carrying knives unconcealed pursuant to a lawful occupation, and those carrying knives in a secure wrapper or toolbox."[149]

Riggins was carrying a knife in a belt sheath, "partially concealed on his belt." Riggins was approached by three police officers, and informed that he was in violation of the law. Riggins was then arrested, and issued a citation at the police station. At a non-jury trial in Seattle Municipal Court, Riggins testified that "he had been at his brother's house earlier that day, and that he had intended to go fishing with his brother in the Puyallup area; however, they did not go fishing, but ended up using the knife to assist in roofing his brother's house."[150] Either of these activities would seem to have been covered by the exemptions. Riggins also argued that the ordinance in question violated the right to bear arms provision of the Washington Constitution.

Riggins was convicted. On appeal to King County Superior Court, he again raised these issues. The Superior Court concluded that the ordinance was a

---

147 *State* v. *Rupe*, 101 Wash.2d 664, 683 P.2d 571, 597 (1984).
148 *State* v. *Rupe*, 101 Wash.2d 664, 683 P.2d 571, 598, 599 (1984).
149 *City of Seattle* v. *Riggins*, 818 P.2d 1100, 1101 note 1 (Wash.App. 1991).
150 *City of Seattle* v. *Riggins*, 818 P.2d 1100, 1101 (Wash.App. 1991).

"reasonable restriction on the right of Defendant to bear arms," and that the safety of the citizens of Seattle outweighed his right to bear arms. The Washington Court of Appeals refused to find the ordinance in conflict with the Washington Constitution, but the manner in which they phrased that refusal makes clear that there was some limits to the authority of city ordinances: "Notwithstanding the seemingly absolute language of this constitutional provision, the right to bear arms is subject to reasonable regulation by the state under its police power."[151]

The Appeals Court then cited *State* v. *Rupe* (1984), and *State* v. *Krantz* (1945) for why this "seemingly absolute language" didn't mean what it said. But *Krantz* had only addressed the issue of whether an ex-felon could be prohibited from the possession of arms—a considerably different case than the one before us, and *Rupe*, as we saw, only cited the *Krantz* decision, and a few other decisions from other states, in defense of this position. No new position was taken by *Rupe*; the Appeals Court would have been far better off to cite *Krantz* and the decisions from the other states directly.

Riggins also objected to the ordinance "because it is an absolute prohibition against the mere possession or carrying of fixed-blade knives." Riggins pointed to the *State* v. *Delgado* (1984) decision by the Oregon Supreme Court, where a statute prohibiting possession of a switchblade was overturned as unconstitutional, and argued that the Seattle ordinance violated "his right to bear arms because it is an absolute prohibition against the mere possession or carrying of fixed-blade knives." Where the Oregon Supreme Court had held that regulation of the mode of carrying was constitutional, a complete ban on possession or carrying was not.

The Washington Court of Appeals refused to overturn the Seattle ordinance, and would not admit that the *Delgado* decision would have overturned such an ordinance in Oregon, insisting that the ordinance "does not amount to a total ban on the possession of knives" but "merely seeks to regulate the carrying of fixed-blade knives."[152] Where *Delgado* had recognized that at least some *method* of carry had to be legal, the Washington Court of Appeals regarded the small number of exemptions available for some categories of people as sufficient for the ordinance to remain constitutional.

This is the last case we will directly consider, and it may be regarded as something of a symbol of what has happened to the integrity of the courts. While recognizing that some limited individual right to bear arms existed, only by the most bizarre reasoning could the Court of Appeals find that the right to bear arms had not been "impaired" by such an ordinance.

During this period, from 1971 to 1991, the Second Amendment was no longer in a coma; increasingly, state courts recognized that the power of legislatures and local government to regulate the carrying of arms was subject to the limitations of their state constitutions. Of more interest from the standpoint of the Second Amendment was that some of these decisions recognized that these clauses were derived from, and analogous to, the Second Amendment. Also of interest is that many of these decisions were not appealed beyond the appellate level. For the first time, a large number of appellate court decisions were either insufficiently interest-

---

151 *City of Seattle* v. *Riggins*, 818 P.2d 1100, 1101 (Wash.App. 1991).
152 *City of Seattle* v. *Riggins*, 818 P.2d 1100, 1102 (Wash.App. 1991).

ing for the state supreme courts to hear an appeal, or sufficiently frightening in their
implications that prosecutors were reluctant to take a chance on appeal.

What brought the right to keep and bear arms out of its coma? During the
1970s, there was a dramatic expansion of efforts to take away handguns not just
from criminals, racial minorities, and radicals, but from the general population.
This effort brought about a revival of interest in the federal and state guarantees.
Nelson T. "Pete" Shields, director of Handgun Control, Inc. for many years, explained the techniques to be used and his eventual goal in an interview with the
New Yorker:

> Our ultimate goal—total control of handguns in the United States—is going to take
> time. My estimate is from seven to ten years. The first problem is to slow down the
> increasing number of handguns being produced and sold in this country. The second
> problem is to get handguns registered. And the final problem is to make the possession
> of *all* handguns and *all* handgun ammunition—except for the military, policemen, li-
> censed security guards, licensed sporting clubs, and licensed gun collectors—totally ille-
> gal.[153]

The passage of the Morton Grove, Illinois, ordinance banning private handgun
ownership, and the unwillingness of the Federal courts to overturn this ordinance,
appears to have motivated an increased interest in supporting the right to keep and
bear arms in those areas where gun control was never popular. One extreme
reaction was Kennesaw, Georgia, where, in response to the Morton Grove handgun
ban, the city council passed an ordinance requiring every household to have a
gun.[154] As we have seen, several states adopted constitutional amendments recognizing a right to keep and bear arms during this period that led to decisions affirming, to a greater or lesser degree, the right to bear arms.

Another factor affecting this period was that the National Rifle Association, after
a long period of inactivity on the issue, began to aggressively pursue the addition of
"right to keep and bear arms" provisions to those state constitutions that lacked
them. In addition to those constitutional amendments that led to previously discussed court decisions, Idaho and New Mexico amended their right to arms provisions during this period. Art. I, §11 of the Idaho Constitution was amended in
1978 to:

> The people have the right to keep and bear arms, which right shall not be abridged; but
> this provision shall not prevent the passage of laws to govern the carrying of weapons
> concealed on the person nor prevent passage of legislation providing minimum sentences
> for crimes committed while in possession of a firearm, nor prevent the passage of
> legislation providing penalties for the possession of firearms by a convicted felon, nor
> prevent the passage of any legislation punishing the use of a firearm. No law shall im-

---

153 Richard Harris, "A Reporter At Large: Handguns", *The New Yorker*, July 26, 1976, 57-58. A
fascinating interview, Shields also describes the founder of Handgun Control, Inc., as a "retired CIA
official" who was its first director without pay. For those people who regard the CIA as a secret
government with nefarious motives, this will doubtless make them wonder about the origins of
Handgun Control's current policies in support of prohibition of those rifles which are most necessary
to restrain tyranny. Hard as it may be to believe today, when much of Handgun Control's energy is
devoted to prohibiting rifles and shotguns, Handgun Control was completely uninterested in any other
category of weapon in the early days.

154 "Second thoughts in Gunsville", *The Economist*, March 29, 1989, 28. In spite of the title, no
one interviewed in Kennesaw expressed any doubts about the efficacy or wisdom of the city ordinance
requiring gun ownership.

pose licensure, registration or special taxation on the ownership or possession of firearms or ammunition. Nor shall any law permit the confiscation of firearms, except those actually used in the commission of a felony.[155]

It appears that the Idaho Supreme Court decisions recognizing that concealed carry was not constitutionally protected were simply written explicitly into the Idaho Constitution. No case law exists to explain why it was felt necessary to make the prohibition on concealed carry or felons possessing firearms explicit. At the same time, the language was strengthened to leave no room for future prohibitions or discriminatory taxes on gun ownership.

New Mexico's constitutional provision, already held by the New Mexico Court of Appeals to be a protection of open carry against local ordinances, was amended in 1986 to make even more explicit that state law pre-empted all other local regulation of the right to keep and bear arms. A single sentence was added to Art. I, §6: "No municipality or county shall regulate, in any way, an incident of the right to keep and bear arms."[156]

Hawaii, North Dakota, and Nevada added right to keep and bear arms provisions to their state constitutions during this period. Hawaii adopted the text of the Second Amendment as Art. I, §17 in 1978. In spite of Hawaii's very restrictive handgun laws, there was *no* case law as late as 1991 in which the courts ruled on the meaning of this provision.[157]

Nevada adopted Article I, §11, clause 1, at the 1982 general election: "1. Every citizen has the right to keep and bear arms for security and defense, for lawful hunting and recreational use and for other lawful purposes."[158] No case law has yet attached itself to this provision of the Nevada Constitution.

The North Dakota Constitution was amended by initiative at the November 1984 elections:

All individuals are by nature equally free and independent and have certain inalienable rights, among which are those of enjoying and defending life and liberty; acquiring, possessing and protecting property and reputation; pursuing and obtaining safety and happiness; *and to keep and bear arms for the defense of their person, family, property, and the state, and for lawful hunting, recreational, and other lawful purposes, which shall not be infringed.*[159] [italics indicate amendment]

As was previously discussed, the *State* v. *Ricehill* (N.D. 1987) decision of the North Dakota Supreme Court held that laws prohibiting convicted felons from possessing firearms were constitutional—and was careful to limit its discussion to the issue of whether convicted felons could be prohibited from arms possession.

There was also an increased recognition by some state governments that a concealed weapon permit was not simply a privilege, but a right. The Washington Legislature had already led the way with a change to a non-discretionary concealed weapon permit issuance policy in 1961.[160] In 1983, Washington Attorney General Ken Eikenberry issued an opinion that asserted applicants for a concealed weapon

---

155 Idaho Const. Art. I, §11 (1979).
156 New Mexico Const., Art. I, §6 (1992).
157 Hawaii Const., Art. I, §17 (1991).
158 Nevada Const., Art. I, §11 (1986).
159 North Dakota Const., Art. I, §1 (1984), quoted in *State* v. *Ricehill*, 415 N.W.2d 481, 482 (N.D. 1987).
160 Wash. RCW 9.41.070 (1991).

permit were not required to have a photograph taken; not required to be a resident of the county where they applied for a permit; not required to produce a driver's license; and not required to supply their social security number.[161] While providing this information would speed up the process of doing a background check, it was not mandatory. On the contrary, throughout the Attorney General's opinion, the word "mandatory" was used to describe the obligation of the state to issue permits.

Other evidence of how the constitutional provisions were recognized as guaranteeing such a right is found in the pamphlet given out to applicants for a concealed weapon permit in Washington State: the first two paragraphs consist of the Second Amendment, and the Washington Constitution's right to bear arms provision.[162] The right to bear firearms, subject to a very minimal regulation, had been fully redeemed in Washington State.

The academic community has also played a part in the Second Amendment's revival, with increasingly careful attention paid towards the original intent of the Second Amendment. Where Rutland's first edition of *The Birth of the Bill of Rights*, in 1955, had called the Second and Third Amendments "obsolete,"[163] the second edition, published in 1983, took a more cautious approach to the Second Amendment:

> Ambivalent feelings toward the right to bear arms (Second Amendment) reveal a gap in the citizens' view of what is right and wrong. Stalked by the ghosts of two Kennedys and Martin Luther King, Americans wonder where a prohibition on handguns should come from—the Congress or the courts? And if such a prohibition were passed by Congress, would the law be as full of loopholes as the Eighteenth Amendment?[164]

The Winter 1986 edition of *Law and Contemporary Problems* was devoted to the question of gun control. While most of the issue was related to issues of modern law and criminology, some of the papers studied the history of the Second Amendment. Of more interest from the standpoint of scholarly study, is the Foreword by John Kaplan, a Stanford law professor:

> Ten years ago it might have been said with some accuracy that there was virtually no informed scholarly debate about gun control. Although most observers recognized that there were political obstacles to the enactment of laws designed to restrict civilian ownership of firearms, the overwhelming weight of scholarly opinion was that gun control measures, if enacted, would be beneficial. Indeed, among academics and journalists writing on the issue, it was frequently said that the more drastic the gun control measure the better, thus aiming toward a society in which to the greatest extent possible guns were removed from civilian hands. This issue of *Law and Contemporary Problems* shows how far the debate has come in only a decade.

> The underpinnings of the arguments for major restrictions on civilian firearms ownership are now under attack at almost every point that previously had been taken for granted. It is no longer so obvious that most gun control measures are free from constitutional doubt. Although there are no hints in the case law that the judiciary shares this perception, recent scholarship on the original meaning of the second amendment

---

161 Wash. AGO 1983 No. 21, 1.

162 Washington Dept. of Wildlife, *Firearms Safety, The Law and You*, (n.p.: n.d.), 2. The author obtained this pamphlet when applying for a non-resident concealed weapon permit in 1992. In compliance with the law, the permit was issued less than 60 days later.

163 Rutland, 229.

164 Rutland, rev. ed., 236-7. Of the three public figures mentioned by Rutland in connection to a ban on handguns, two were murdered with rifles, not handguns.

indicates that many of the framers contemplated the granting of an individual as well as a state right.[165]

Sanford Levinson's "The Embarrassing Second Amendment," in the December 1989 issue of *Yale Law Journal*, also showed the increased willingness of the academic community, even liberal academics, to take seriously the claim that the Second Amendment protected an individual right. Similarly, Robert Cottrol and Raymond Diamond's "The Second Amendment: Toward An Afro-Americanist Reconsideration" in the December 1991 *Georgetown Law Journal*, demonstrated that Levinson's article was not just a flash in the pan, but part of a growing body of academic research that recognized the right to bear arms as a fundamental individual right.

Nor was this recognition limited to the academic community, or a few political activists. In 1985, the National Rifle Association declared as one of its goals a dramatic change of concealed weapon permit issuance laws, on a state by state basis. Where the NRA-backed Model Uniform Firearms Acts of the 1920s had allowed great discretion to the issuing agencies to decide whether an applicant was "of good moral character and good cause" existed for the issuance of a permit,[166] the goal now was elimination of discretionary abuse, by establishing a more consistent, uniform set of standards for issuance of permits.[167] Even the California Legislature's research service (hardly in the hip-pocket of the NRA), agreed that the old system of nearly unlimited discretion in issuance of permits was in need of reform.[168]

During this period, a shift to the political arena to protect the right to keep and bear arms—perhaps assisted by the increasing recognition of these rights by various state courts—led to significant liberalization of the concealed weapons permit statutes in Florida, Virginia, Pennsylvania, Oregon, Idaho, and Montana. It is indisputable that West Virginia's new concealed weapons permit law was a result of the *City of Princeton* v. *Buckner* (W.Va. 1988) decision.

While there are minor differences from state to state, each of these states has effectively redeemed the right to bear arms, by making it possible for law-abiding citizens, often with a simple training requirement, to obtain a concealed handgun permit. Yet murder rates did not rise significantly in any of these states after liberalization of their laws; in several of the states (Florida being among the dramatic), murder rates fell starting with the first year of the new law.[169]

---

165 John Kaplan, "Foreword", *Law and Contemporary Problems*, 49:1 [Winter 1986], 1.
166 Assembly Office of Research, 6.
167 David Conover, "To Keep And Bear Arms", *American Rifleman*, [September 1985], 40.
168 Assembly Office of Research, 4.
169 Clayton E. Cramer and David B. Kopel, *Concealed Handgun Permits for Licensed, Trained Citizens: A Policy that is Saving Lives*, Independence Issue Paper 14-93, (Golden, Colo.: Independence Institute, 1993).

XI. AT THE CROSSROADS

The history of the right to keep and bear arms is disappointing. In spite of overwhelming evidence concerning original intent, much of the judicial interpretation of the Second Amendment and the state analogs has been repeated efforts to avoid the original intent and explicit language of these protections. In this century especially, original intent has increasingly been formally abandoned by the courts as a basis for constitutional interpretation.

While the right to bear arms has been primarily an issue of handguns, the right of private possession is a considerably more complicated matter. In general, the legislatures and courts have distinguished weapons into the following classes, for purposes of regulating private possession: long guns, handguns, machine guns, and other arms. The nineteenth century decisions were seldom concerned with long guns and never with machine guns; handguns, Bowie knives, daggers, sword-canes, billy clubs, blackjacks, slungshots, and a bewildering array of other non-firearms were the principal concerns. The twentieth century decisions have seldom involved long gun possession, with the exception of automatic weapons.

A recurring distinction has been made between the right to "military pistols"—large handguns appropriate to warfare—and small, sometimes cheap pistols of the sort best suited to concealed carry. Attempting to draw a distinction between these two types of handguns is a nearly impossible task, since at one time or another, nearly every sort of handgun has been pressed into military service.

Before the Civil War, a consensus had developed, almost entirely in the slave states, that *concealed* carry of arms was not constitutionally protected, but that open carry of arms was protected (though this guarantee did not include blacks, either slave or free). In this period, only two decisions refused to recognize a right to open carry;[1] only one of those suggested that there was no right to possess arms, and that was the *State* v. *Buzzard* (1842) decision. Three decisions narrowed the right of open carry to "citizens" (whites),[2] and similarly narrowed the right to private possession of arms. All other decisions recognized that at a minimum, a right to private possession of rifles, shotguns, and large military pistols existed. Significant to today's debate about whether "assault weapons" may be constitutionally banned,

---

1 *Aymette* v. *State*, 2 Hump. (21 Tenn.) 154 (1840); *State* v. *Buzzard*, 4 Ark. 18 (1842).

2 *State* v. *Newsom*, 27 N.C. 250, 5 Iredell 181 (1844); *Cooper and Worsham* v. *Mayor of Savannah*, 4 Ga. 68 (1848); *Dred Scott* v. *Sandford*, 60 U.S. (19 How) 393 (1857).

military firearms were the one type of arm that *all* courts (except for *Buzzard*) agreed were constitutionally protected.

In the *State* v. *Smith* (1856) decision, a distinction between military pistols and more concealable pistols was made, with only military pistols constitutionally protected; arms other than firearms were also found to be unprotected. Eight of the decisions gave no indication if other arms were protected; *Bliss* v. *Commonwealth* (1822) and *Simpson* v. *State* (1833) recognized that a number of other arms were protected. *Aymette* v. *State* (1840) recognized that other arms commonly used in military service were protected, and *Cockrum* v. *State* (1859) recognized that even the dreaded Bowie knife was a constitutionally protected arm.

After the Civil War, again, almost entirely in the slave states, the state courts developed a more mixed set of precedents, some of which recognized a right to open carry, and some of which upheld laws banning open carry. The strong similarity of these laws to the pre-war "free black" laws, and the immediate post-war Black Codes, is striking. It appears that the motivation for such laws was to disarm blacks, even at the expense of nominally disarming whites, but this is not irrefutably proven.

The first three decades of the twentieth century saw the general acceptance of laws licensing concealed carry of arms throughout the West and North and, in a considerably less uniform manner, the licensing of open carry of arms in many states. The turbulent period from 1958-1975 saw state after state abolish the one remaining component of the right to bear arms: open carry. Finally, the 1970s through 1991 saw a resurgence of awareness of the right to bear arms, and an increasing willingness of some legislatures to make issuance of concealed weapons permits non-discretionary.

While few states made attempts to restrict ownership of firearms (other than machine guns) in the twentieth century, those that have done so (*i.e.*, New York), have provided disturbing evidence of a desire to "regulate" the right to the point where no right remains.

Until very recently, there has been no serious dispute about the right of citizens to own rifles and shotguns. Free blacks before the Civil War were another matter; and even after the Civil War, by extralegal procedures, free blacks were frequently disarmed. In the period from 1900-1934, there was a burst of nativist sentiment against "foreigners," and this was expressed in laws that sometimes prohibited non-citizens from owning guns. But with a very few exceptions, the right of citizens to possess rifles and shotguns, especially weapons of a military nature, appropriate to "civilized warfare," had been recognized. Even those state courts that held that handguns were not protected, have nearly always recognized that privately possessed military long guns were protected under either the Second Amendment or state constitution's provision, or both.

In our entire study of judicial interpretation of the right to keep and bear arms, only six final decisions have denied the right of law-abiding citizens to possess non-concealable rifles and shotguns in their homes.[3] Seventy-one decisions have either

---

3 *State* v. *Buzzard*, 4 Ark. 18 (1842);, *Carroll* v. *State*, 28 Ark. 99 (1872);, *Pierce* v. *State*, 42 Okla. Crim. 272, 275 P. 393 (1929);, *Application of Grauling*, 17 Misc.2d 215, 183 N.Y.S.2d 654 (1959);, *Burton* v. *Sills*, 99 N.J.Super. 459, 240 A.2d 432 (1968), and *Commonwealth* v. *Davis*, 343 N.E.2d 847 (Mass. 1976);.

recognized such a right, or upheld an existing precedent in that state's courts that had recognized such a right—and in two of those cases, this right explicitly protected *only* weapons useful to a militia.[4] The remaining decisions have not addressed the issue at all, for throughout most of the history of this country, no one was foolish enough to attempt to take away the rifles and shotguns of the people—until the current hysteria about "assault weapons," most of which are rifles or shotguns admirably suited to militia use in overthrowing the government.

Handguns have a somewhat more checkered history. Seventy-one decisions have recognized a right to possess military handguns in the home; ten decisions have either explicitly or implicitly refused to recognize such a constitutional right.[5] In the category of "other pistols"—those that because of concealability or non-military application, cannot be considered military service pistols, the results are even more split. In addition to the ten decisions which have refused to recognize a right to possess military pistols, thirteen other decisions recognized military pistols as constitutionally protected, but not those pistols unsuited to military use.[6] In opposition stand 53 decisions that recognized pistols of all sorts as constitutionally protected for private ownership.

In some states, the right of private possession *seems* secure, but the decisions that have recognized that right have been so equivocal and limited that the "police power" might in time of crisis, magically expand to deny that right. In other states, the right of private possession of firearms is in grave danger. The danger comes not from a lack of precedents recognizing the existence of such a right; the danger comes from a generation that has been told, repeatedly, that no such right exists, or has ever existed.

Issues of race, ethnicity, union organizing, nativism, and sometimes even commercial advantage for manufacturers of American firearms[7] appear as factors in the passage of laws restricting the possession and carrying of arms. It is significant that the most severe restrictions in the United States on firearms today are in those urban areas where racial tensions are strongest: Boston, New York City, and

---

4 *U.S.* v. *Miller*, 307 U.S. 174 (1939); *Moore* v. *Gallup*, N.Y.S.2d 63, 267 App. Div. 64, 294 N.Y. 699, 60 N.E.2d 847 (1943).

5 Decisions refusing to recognize such a right: *State* v. *Buzzard*, 4 Ark. 18 (1842); *Carroll* v. *State*, 28 Ark. 99 (1872); *State* v. *Workman*, 35 W.Va. 367, 14 S.E. 9 (1891); *Pierce* v. *State*, 42 Okla. Crim. 272, 275 P. 393 (1929); *Moore* v. *Gallup*, N.Y.S.2d 63, 267 App. Div. 64, 294 N.Y. 699, 60 N.E.2d 847 (1943); *Hutchinson* v. *Rosetti*, 205 N.Y.S.2d 526, 24 Misc. 949 (1960); *Grimm* v. *City of New York*, 56 Misc.2d 525, 289 N.Y.S.2d 358 (1968); *Burton* v. *Sills*, 99 N.J.Super. 459, 240 A.2d 432 (1968); *Commonwealth* v. *Davis*, 343 N.E.2d 847 (Mass. 1976); *Quilici* v. *Village of Morton Grove*, 695 F.2d 261 (7th Cir. 1982).

6 Military pistols protected, but other pistols were not: *State* v. *Smith*, 11 La. An. 688 (1856); *Andrews* v. *State*, 3 Heisk. (50 Tenn.) 165, 8 Am. Rep. 8 (1871); *Page* v. *State*, 3 Heisk. (50 Tenn.) 198 (1871); *English* v. *State*, 35 Texas 472, 14 Am. Rep. 370 (1872); *State* v. *Wilburn*, 7 Bax. 57, 32 Am. Rep. 551 (Tenn. 1872); *State* v. *Duke*, 42 Tex. 455 (1875); *Fife* v. *State*, 31 Ark. 455, 25 Am. Rep. 556 (1876); *Wilson* v. *State of Arkansas*, 33 Ark. 557, 34 Am. Rep. 52 (1878); *Holland* v. *State*, 33 Ark. 560 (1878); *Haile* v. *State*, 38 Ark. 564, 42 Am. Rep. 3 (1882); *Dabbs* v. *State*, 39 Ark. 353, 43 Am. Rep. 275 (1882); *Ex Parte Thomas*, 21 Okl. 770, 97 P. 260 (1908); *Glasscock* v. *City of Chattanooga*, 157 Tenn. 518, 11 S.W.2d 678 (1928).

7 While not addressed in this work, there is reason to believe that many of the restrictions on the importation of surplus military firearms and small handguns adopted as part of the Gun Control Act of 1968 were motivated as much by a desire to protect American manufacturers as to disarm poor Americans.

Washington, DC. While recent laws aimed at long guns has been pushed "over the top" by incidents of mass murder, usually committed by whites, these laws have been intended primarily to disarm criminal gangs that are almost always black.

Why is the right to keep and bear arms an issue where democracy and minority rights conflict? At first glance, it would seem unlikely that they would conflict. A survey taken in 1988 asked Americans if they supported a ban on handguns; 59% were opposed, and 37% in support. Yet a 1989 survey asked if, "Cheap handguns known as Saturday Night Specials" should be banned: 71% supported such a ban, 25% opposed it. In the same survey, 75% supported a ban on plastic handguns (which do not exist, except in the fevered imagination of Handgun Control, Inc.); and 72% supported a ban on "Semi-automatic assault guns, such as the AK-47."[8] The disparity reflects the ease with which emotion-laden labels (e.g. "AK-47") and media-manufactured distinctions can sway people into supporting policies and goals which, in a less emotion-laden context, would be opposed.[9]

As we stand at the crossroads, it is important to remember that the Supreme Court has a long history of wriggling out of unpleasant decisions; U.S. v. Miller (1939) is just one example. The Court has made other decisions that have provoked political change to counteract those decisions; the Warren Court's recognition of the rights of criminal suspects and the Roe v. Wade (1973) decision played a role in the conservative political shift of American national politics, that culminated in the election of President Reagan in 1980. Most dramatically, the Court in Dred Scott v. Sandford (1857) made a decision so diametrically opposed to the sentiments of abolitionists, that the only resolution possible was the Civil War.[10]

Some rights are so essential that when they are denied or revoked, there may well be no possible alternative but armed revolution; the tools of self-defense and revolution are in that category of "fundamental rights." The American Revolution was sparked by the attempt of the British Army to confiscate militia weapons and supplies at Lexington and Concord; more recently, the Barcelona uprising during the Spanish Civil War was provoked by the government's attempt to confiscate private arms.[11] This is not surprising; the scenario becomes, "Use it or lose it."

The history of the twentieth century is rife with totalitarian governments, torture, and extermination camps. To many Americans, government confiscation of arms conjures up images of the Soviet Union and Nazi Germany. The claim that, "It can't happen here," is not persuasive to those who see striking similarities between the Weimar Republic and modern America. Attempts at disarming the population, *especially* of those weapons that are best suited to the task of revolution, creates an intransigence concerning *any* restrictions on arms, even those restrictions which are

---

8 Timothy J. Flanagan and Kathleen Maguire, eds., *Sourcebook of Criminal Justice Statistics 1989*, (Washington: Government Printing Office, 1990), 174.

9 See my forthcoming "Ethical Problems of Mass Murder Coverage In The Mass Media", in *Journal of Mass Media Ethics*, 9:1 [Winter 1993-94], for an examination of how disproportionate coverage of firearms mass muders in *Time* and *Newsweek* in the period 1984-91 caused at least one copycat mass murder—and may have caused others.

10 Smith, 431-2. The *Dred Scott* decision also produced considerable anger among Northern racists as well, because slavery could now migrate north, bringing blacks with it; Justice Taney made no one happy with his decision.

11 George Orwell, *Homage To Catalonia*, (San Diego, Cal.: Harcourt Brace Jovanovich, 1980), 150.

unquestionably constitutional, and perhaps even of some slight value in reducing criminal use of firearms.

Similarly, the openly stated goal of Handgun Control's Nelson Shields to prohibit private ownership of handguns,[12] creates powerful opposition to *any* sort of mandatory registration law—especially in light of the *Haynes* v. *U.S.* (1968) decision, which appears to exempt *only* the criminal from punishment for not registering a gun. What purpose is served by a law that punishes only the law-abiding, and fails to punish the criminal?

In the years since *U.S.* v. *Miller* (1939) the U.S. Supreme Court has refused to hear any case challenging a law that prohibited law-abiding citizens from possessing or carrying guns. As we have seen, the Federal Courts of Appeals have upheld a number of restrictions on firearms possession by felons, with varying theories as to why they are constitutional. After the dramatic expansion of the right to keep and bear arms by a number of state supreme courts, a series of mass murders committed with so-called "assault rifles," again raised the question of what constitutes "the right to keep and bear arms."

Many of the weapons banned by such laws as California's Roberti-Roos Assault Weapons Control Act, Connecticut's very similar 1993 law, and New Jersey's even more comprehensive assault weapon ban, are semiautomatic versions of battle rifles in current or recent military use in a number of the world's armies, including our own. That such weapons have "some reasonable relationship to the preservation or efficiency of a well regulated militia"—the test endorsed by *U.S.* v. *Miller* (1939) for whether private ownership of a weapon was protected by the Second Amendment—would seem undisputable. However, the federal district and appellate courts that heard the lawsuit challenging California's law held that the Second Amendment was a restriction only on the Federal Government, not on the states, and was therefore not incorporated by the Fourteenth Amendment, but acknowledged that, based on the ruling in *U.S.* v. *Verdugo-Urquidez* (1990), "The Court accepts that definition of those who are protected from Congress or other parts of the National Government from infringing on their rights to bear arms."[13]

The Supreme Court has a number of choices, if various assault weapon ban cases reach it. The Court can recognize the Second Amendment as a limitation on the powers of the Federal Government *only*, precluding any federal ban. Having done so, it can either use the republican theory, recognize that the Framers intended for the tools of revolution to be widely distributed, and use the *U.S.* v. *Miller* (1939) precedent to hold that "militia weapons" are protected; or it can use the liberal theory, and recognize that nearly any hand-carried weapon qualifies as constitutionally protected. This would leave a number of state laws, such as California's, intact—

---

12 Harris, 57-58. Also see NBC News President Michael Gartner, "Glut of guns: What can we do about them?", *USA Today*, January 16, 1992, 9A, and George F. Will, "How to control guns", Santa Rosa (Cal.) *Press-Democrat*, March 21, 1991, B5, for recent examples of influential and prominent Americans calling for repeal of the Second Amendment in order to, respectively, ban handguns, or to implement "strict gun control..." At least there was a recognition that the Second Amendment was an obstacle to both schemes. Rep. Major Owens (D-NY) introduced House Joint Resolution 438 (102d Cong., 2d sess.) to repeal the Second Amendment, but it received little support. Its introduction was an admission that the Second Amendment was either an obstacle to restrictive federal gun control measures, or was perceived by some Americans as such.

13 *Fresno Rifle and Pistol Club, Inc.* v. *Van de Kamp*, 746 F.Supp. 1415, 1419 (E.D.Cal. 1990).

but raise serious questions of the constitutionality of statutes in Massachusetts and New York, where the state analogs to the Second Amendment would clearly need to be interpreted in an equivalent manner.

The Court can recognize the Second Amendment as incorporated under the Fourteenth Amendment. If it does so, it can either use the republican theory, and therefore strike down the state laws that prohibit or restrictively license rifles, shotguns, and large military pistols; or the liberal theory, and strike down a great many laws on a wide variety of weapons, much as the Oregon Supreme Court did in the 1980s. This would also lead to serious questions about the constitutionality of statutes that provided discretion to the authorities in the issuance of permits to carry or purchase firearms.

The Supreme Court has the option to continue ducking decisions about the Second Amendment—and allow circuit courts to make decisions that would have seemed incomprehensible to the Framers—as they did when they denied the appeal of *Quilici* v. *Village of Morton Grove* (7th Cir. 1982) and upheld the Appeals Court's decision that handguns are not military weapons. Without direction from the Supreme Court, the decisions may eventually diverge sufficiently that, for practical purposes, the constitutionality of gun control laws will differ depending on the circuit.

Finally, the Supreme Court has a fourth option—to hear a case, overturn the existing precedents of *U.S.* v. *Cruikshank* (1876) and *Presser* v. *Illinois* (1886), and ignore the overwhelming number of state supreme court decisions that have recognized "the right to keep and bear arms" as an *individual* right. But this last option has risks. Many millions of Americans will become angry, afraid, and will lose confidence in the integrity of their government—and those millions will be forced to look to the arms they possess on that day and make the choice: "Use it, or lose it." Unlike other factions whose rights have been stepped on throughout American history, owners of "assault weapons" are in a position to experimentally determine if firearms can be used to overturn a modern government. Win or lose, the results will be unpleasant.

The American Revolution was started by the British Government forcing the colonists to make such a choice. Will we see history repeat itself?

SELECTED BIBLIOGRAPHY

Abbott, Richard H., *The Republican Party and the South, 1855-1877*, (Chapel Hill, N.C.: University of North Carolina Press, 1986).

Adams, Graham, *Age of Industrial Violence 1910-15*, (New York: Columbia University Press, 1966).

Annals of America, (Chicago: Encyclopedia Britannica, Inc., 1976).

Assembly Office of Research, *Smoking Gun: The Case For Concealed Weapon Permit Reform*, (Sacramento: State of California, 1986).

Allen, William B., ed., *Works of Fisher Ames*, (Indianapolis: Liberty Classics, 1983).

Avary, Myrta Lockett, *Dixie After The War*, (New York: Doubleday, Page & Co., 1906; reprinted New York: Da Capo Press, 1970).

Beccaria, Cesare, trans. by Henry Palolucci, *On Crimes And Punishments*, (New York: Bobbs-Merrill Co., 1963).

Bendix, Reinhard, *Kings or People: Power and the Mandate to Rule*, (Berkeley, Cal.: University of California Press, 1978).

Benedict, Michael Les, *The Fruits of Victory: Alternatives in Restoring the Union, 1865-1877*, (New York: J.B. Lippincott Co., 1975).

Bickford, Charlene Bangs, & Veit, Helen E., ed., *Documentary History of the First Federal Congress 1789-91*, (Baltimore: Johns Hopkins University Press, 1986).

"Bill Barring Loaded Weapons In Public Clears Senate 29-7", *Sacramento Bee*, July 27, 1967, A6.

Blackstone, William, *Commentaries on the Laws of England*, edited by St. George Tucker, (Philadelphia: William Young Birch & Abraham Small, 1803; reprinted Buffalo, N.Y.: Dennis & Co., 1965).

_____, *Commentaries on the Laws of England*, edited by Herbert Broom and Edward A. Hadley, (Albany, N.Y.: John D. Parsons, 1875).

_____, *Commentaries on the Laws of England*, 3d ed., edited by George Chase, (Albany, N.Y.: Banks & Co., 1906).

_____, *Commentaries on the Laws of England*, 3d ed., edited by Thomas M. Cooley, (Chicago: Callaghan & Co., 1884).

_____, *Commentaries on the Laws of England*, edited by William Carey Jones, (San Francisco: Bancroft-Whitney Co., 1916).

_____, *Commentaries on the Laws of England*, edited by William Draper Lewis, (Philadelphia: Rees Welsh & Co., 1897).

Blair, Claude, ed., *Pollard's History of Firearms*, (New York: Macmillan Co., 1983).

Brandt, Nat, *The Town That Started The Civil War*, (Syracuse, N.Y.: Syracuse University Press, 1990).

Brecher, Jeremy, *Strike!*, (San Francisco: Straight Arrow Books, 1972).

Brewer, J. Mason, *Negro Legislators of Texas*, (Dallas, Texas: Mathis Publishing Co., 1935; reprinted San Francisco: R&E Research Associates, n.d.)

Broderick, Francis L., *Reconstruction and the American Negro, 1865-1900*, (London: Macmillan Co., 1969).

Brooke, Christopher, *Europe in the Central Middle Ages: 962-1154*, 2nd ed., (New York: Longman Group, 1987).

Bruce, Robert V., *1877: Year of Violence*, (Indianapolis: Bobbs-Merrill Co., 1959; reprinted Chicago: Quadrangle Books, Inc., 1970).

Bureau of the Census, *Negro Population in the United States 1790-1915*, (Washington: Government Printing Office, 1918; reprinted New York: Arno Press, 1968).

Bureau of Justice Statistics, *Report to the Nation on Crime and Justice*, 2nd ed., (Washington: Government Printing Office, 1988).

Burger, Warren E., "The Right To Bear Arms", in *Parade*, January 14, 1990, 4-6.

Cahn, Edmond, *The Great Rights*, (New York: MacMillan Co., 1963).

Callcott, Wilfrid Hardy, *Church and State in Mexico: 1822-1857*, (Duke University Press: 1926; reprinted New York: Octagon Books, 1971).

"Capitol Is Invaded", *Sacramento Bee*, May 2, 1967, A1, A10.

Carey, John, ed., *Eyewitness to History*, (Cambridge, Mass.: Harvard University Press, 1988).

Carter, Dan T., *When The War Was Over: The Failure of Self-Reconstruction in the South, 1865-1867*, (Baton Rouge: Louisiana State University Press, 1985).

Cartwright, Joseph H., *The Triumph of Jim Crow*, (Knoxville, Tenn.: University of Tennessee Press, 1976).

Catton, Bruce, *Glory Road*, (Garden City, N.J.: Doubleday & Co., 1952),

Cheng, Nien, *Life and Death In Shanghai*, (New York: Grove Press, 1986).

Conover, David, "To Keep And Bear Arms", *American Rifleman*, [September, 1985], 40.

Cooke, Jacob E., ed., *The Federalist*, (Middletown, Conn.: Wesleyan University Press, 1961).

Corbin, Robert K., "Firearms Civil Rights Legal Defense Fund", *American Rifleman*, [January, 1992], 40.

Cottrol, Robert J., and Raymond T. Diamond, "The Second Amendment: Toward An Afro-Americanist Reconsideration", in *Georgetown Law Journal*, 80:2 [December, 1991], 309-61.

Cramer, Clayton E., ed., *By The Dim And Flaring Lamps: The Civil War Diary of Samuel McIlvaine*, (Monroe, N.Y.: Library Research Associates, 1990).

_____, "Ethical Problems of Mass Murder Coverage In The Mass Media" in *Journal of Mass Media Ethics*, 9:1 [Winter 1993-94].

Cramer, Clayton E., and David B. Kopel, *Concealed Handgun Permits for Licensed, Trained Citizens: A Policy that is Saving Lives*, Independence Issue Paper 14-93, (Golden, Colo.: Independence Institute, 1993).

Craven, Avery, *Reconstruction: The Ending of the Civil War*, (New York: Holt, Rinehart, and Winston, 1969).

Cress, Lawrence Delbert, "An Armed Community: The Origins and Meaning of the Right to Bear Arms", *Journal of American History*, 71:1 [June 1984], 22-42.

Cress, Lawrence Delbert, and Shalhope, Robert E., "The Second Amendment and the Right to Bear Arms: An Exchange", *Journal of American History*, 71:3 [December, 1984], 587-93.

Dacus, Joseph A., *Annals of the Great Strikes*, (Chicago: L.T. Palmer & Co., 1877; reprinted New York: Arno Press, 1969).

Dumbauld, Edward, *The Bill of Rights And What It Means Today*, (Norman, Okla.: University of Oklahoma Press, 1957).

Elkins, Stanley M., *Slavery*, (Chicago: University of Chicago Press, 1968),

Elliot, Jonathan, *The Debates of the Several State Conventions on the Adoption of the Federal Constitution*, (New York: Burt Franklin, 1888).

Ellis, John, *The Social History of the Machine Gun*, (New York: Pantheon Books, 1975).

Flanagan, Timothy J., and Maguire, Kathleen, eds., *Sourcebook of Criminal Justice Statistics 1989*, (Washington: Government Printing Office, 1990).

Fletcher, Andrew, *Selected Political Writings and Speeches*, edited by David Daiches, (Edinburgh: Scottish Academic Press, 1979).

Foner, Eric, *Reconstruction*, (New York: Harper & Row, 1988).

Ford, Paul, ed., *Pamphlets On The Constitution of the United States*, (Brooklyn, N.Y.: 1888; reprinted New York: Da Capo Press, 1968).

_____, *Essays on the Constitution of the United States*, (New York: Burt Franklin, 1892).

Foster, Carol D., Siegel, Mark A., Plesser, Donna R., & Jacobs, Nancy R., *Gun Control: Restricting Rights or Protecting People*, (Plano, Texas: Information Aids, Inc., 1987).

Freeman, A. C., ed., *American Decisions*, (San Francisco: A.L. Bancroft & Co., 1879).

Gales, Joseph, ed., *Debates and Proceedings in the Congress of United States*, (Washington: Gales & Seaton, 1834).

Gartner, Michael, "Glut of guns: What can we do about them?", *USA Today*, January 16, 1992, 9A.

Gates, Jr., Henry Louis, ed., *The Classic Slave Narratives*, (New York: Penguin Books, 1987).

Green, Jonathan, *The Dictionary of Contemporary Slang*, (New York: Stein & Day, 1984).

Halbrook, Stephen P. "The Fourteenth Amendment and the Right to Keep and Bear Arms: The Intent of the Founders", in *The Right To Keep And Bear Arms*, 68-82.

_____, *That Every Man Be Armed*, (University of New Mexico Press, 1984; reprinted Oakland, Cal.: The Independent Institute, 1984).

_____, "What The Framers Intended: A Linguistic Analysis Of The Right To 'Bear Arms'", *Law And Contemporary Problems*, 49:1 [Winter 1986], 151-162.

_____, *A Right To Bear Arms*, (Westport, Conn.: Greenwood Press, 1989).

Hall, Kermit L., ed., *The Oxford Companion to the Supreme Court of the United States*, (New York: Oxford University Press, 1992).

Harris, Richard, "A Reporter At Large: Handguns", *The New Yorker*, July 26, 1976, 53-58.

Helmer, William J., *The Gun That Made The Twenties Roar*, (Toronto: The Macmillan Co., 1969).

Historical Statistics of the United States, Colonial Times to 1970, (Washington: Government Printing Office, 1975).

Hobson, Charles F., & Rutland, Robert A., ed., *The Papers of James Madison*, (Charlottesville, Va.: University Press of Virginia, 1977).

Ingersoll, Thomas N., "Free Blacks in a Slave Society: New Orleans, 1718-1812", *William and Mary Quarterly*, 48:2 [April, 1991], 173-201.

Jews for the Preservation of Firearms Ownership, "The War on Gun Ownership Still Goes On!", *Guns and Ammo*, [May, 1993].

Kaeuper, Richard W., *War, Justice, and Public Order: England and France in the Later Middle Ages*, (Oxford: Clarendon Press, 1988).

Kaminski, John P., and Saladino, Gaspare J., ed., *The Documentary History of the Ratification of the Constitution: Commentaries on the Constitution*, (Madison, Wisc.: State Historical Society of Wisconsin, 1984).

Kaplan, John, "Foreword", *Law and Contemporary Problems*, 49:1 [Winter 1986], 1-3.

Kates, Don B., Jr., "Toward a History of Handgun Prohibition", in Kates, Don B., Jr., ed., *Restricting Handguns: The Liberal Skeptics Speak Out*, (North River Press, 1979).

_____, "Handgun Prohibition and the Original Meaning of the Second Amendment", in *Michigan Law Review*, 82 [November 1983].

_____, "The Second Amendment: A Dialogue", in *Law and Contemporary Problems*, 49:1 [Winter 1986], 143-50.

Kavanagh, Marcus, *The Criminal and His Allies*, (Indianapolis: Bobbs-Merrill Co., 1928).

Kettner, James H., *The Development of American Citizenship, 1608-1870*, (Chapel Hill, N.C.: University of North Carolina Press, 1978).

Kopel, David B., and Stephen D'Andrilli, "The Swiss And Their Guns", *American Rifleman*, [February, 1990].

"Kuwait begins search for illegal weapons", *USA Today*, July 2, 1991, 4A.

Lane, Winthrop D., *Civil War in West Virginia*, (New York: B. W. Huebsch, Inc., 1921; reprinted New York: Arno Press, 1969).

Laquer, Walter, and Rubin, Barry, ed., *The Human Rights Reader*, (New York: New American Library, 1979).

Levin, John, "The Right To Bear Arms: The Development Of The American Experience", *Chicago-Kent Law Review*, [Fall-Winter 1971], reprinted in *The Right To Keep And Bear Arms*, 110-29.

Levinson, Sanford, "The Embarrassing Second Amendment", in *Yale Law Journal*, [December 1989], 99:637-659.

"The Liberation of the Emir", *Newsweek*, March 18, 1991, 26.

Lomenzo, John P., *Manual for the Use of the Legislature of the State of New York: 1969*, (Albany, NY: n.p., 1969).

Lott, Davis Newton, *The Presidents Speak: The Inaugural Address of the American Presidents from Washington to Kennedy*, (New York: Holt, Rinehart & Winston, 1961).

Machiavelli, Niccolo, *Machiavelli: The Chief Works And Others*, transl. Allan Gilbert, (Durham, N.C.: Duke University Press, 1965).

Maclay, William, *Journal of William Maclay*, (New York: Frederick Ungar Publishing Co., 1965).

Maestro, Marcello, *Cesare Beccaria and the Origins of Penal Reform*, (Philadelphia: Temple University Press, 1973).

Malcolm X, *Malcolm X Speaks*, (New York: Grove Press, Inc., 1965).

_____, *By Any Means Necessary*, (New York: Pathfinder Press, Inc., 1970).

Massengill, Stephen E., "The Detectives of William W. Holden, 1869-1870", *North Carolina Historical Review*, 63:4, [October 1985].

McAdam, E. L., Jr., and Milne, George, ed., *Johnson's Dictionary*, (New York: Pantheon Books, 1963).

McDonald, Forrest, *A Constitutional History of the United States*, (New York: F. Watts, 1982; reprinted Malabar, Fla.: Robert E. Krieger Publishing Co., 1986).

McFeely, William S., *Frederick Douglass*, (New York: W.W. Norton & Co., 1991).

McPhee, John, *La Place de la Concorde Suisse*, (New York: Farrar, Straus, Giroux, 1984).

Meyer, Michael C., and Sherman, William L., *The Course of Mexican History*, 4th ed., (New York: Oxford University Press, 1991).

Morgan, Edmund S., "Slavery and Freedom: The American Paradox", *Journal of American History*, 59 [June, 1972], 5-29, reprinted in Stanley N. Katz, John M. Murrin, and Douglas Greenberg, ed., *Colonial America: Essays in Politics and Social Development*, 4th ed., (New York: McGraw-Hill, Inc., 1993).

Mundy, John H., *Europe in the High Middle Ages: 1150-1309*, 2nd ed., (New York: Longman Group, 1991).

Nalty, Bernard C., *Strength For The Fight: A History of Black Americans in the Military*, (New York: Macmillan, 1989).

National Firearms Act, "Hearings Before The House Committee on Ways and Means", 73rd Cong. 2d Sess., (1934).

Newton, Michael, *Armed and Dangerous: A Writer's Guide to Weapons*, (Cincinnati: Writer's Digest Books, 1990).

New Zealand Police Department, *Background To The Introduction of Firearms User Licensing Instead Of Rifle and Shotgun Registration Under The Arms Act of 1983*, (Wellington: n.p., 1983).

Norman, A. V. B., and Don Pottinger, *English Weapons & Warfare: 449-1660*, (New York: Dorset Press, 1979).

Orwell, George, *Homage To Catalonia*, (San Diego: Harcourt Brace Jovanovich, 1980).

The Pennsylvania Manual: 1970-1971, (Pennsylvania Dept. of Property and Supplies, 1971).

Petesch, Gregory J., ed., *Montana Code Annotated*, (Helena, Mt.: Montana Legislative Council, 1990).

Pocock, J. G. A., *The Machiavellian Moment: Florentine Political Thought and the Atlantic Republican Tradition*, (Princeton, N.J.: Princeton University Press, 1975).

Quarles, Benjamin, *The Negro in the Making of America*, 3rd ed., (New York: Macmillan Publishing, 1987).

Ramsdell, Charles William, *Reconstruction in Texas*, (New York: Columbia University Press, 1910; reprinted Gloucester, Mass.: Peter Smith, 1964).

Rawle, William, *A View of the Constitution*, 2nd ed., (Philadelphia: n.p., 1829).

The Right To Keep And Bear Arms, 97th Congress, 2d Sess. (1982), (Washington: Government Printing Office, 1982).

Russell, Carl P., *Guns On The Early Frontier*, (Berkeley, Cal.: University of California Press, 1957; reprinted Lincoln, Nebr.: University of Nebraska Press, 1980).

Rutland, Robert Allen, *The Birth of the Bill of Rights 1776-1791*, (Chapel Hill, N.C.: University of North Carolina Press, 1955).

_____, *The Birth of the Bill of Rights 1776-1791*, rev. ed., (Boston: Northeastern University Press, 1983).

Seldes, George, *You Can't Do That!*, (New York: Modern Age Books, 1938).

Shalhope, Robert E., "The Ideological Origins of the Second Amendment", *Journal of American History*, 69:3 [December 1982], 599-614.

_____, "The Armed Citizen in the Early Republic", in *Law and Contemporary Problems*, 49:1 [Winter 1986], 126-141.

Shapiro, Herbert, *White Violence and Black Response*, (Amherst, Mass.: University of Massachusetts Press, 1988).

Simkin, Jay, and Zelman, Aaron, *"Gun Control": Gateway to Tyranny*, (Milwaukee, Wisc.: Jews for the Preservation of Firearms Ownership, 1992).

Simpson, J. A., & Weiner, E. S. C., ed., *Oxford English Dictionary*, 2nd ed., (Oxford: Clarendon Press, 1989).

Smith, Page, *The Constitution: A Documentary and Narrative History*, (New York: William Morrow & Co., 1978).

Speer, Albert, transl. Richard & Clara Winston, *Inside The Third Reich*, (New York: Macmillan Co., 1970),

Stampp, Kenneth M., *The Era of Reconstruction, 1865-1877*, (New York: Vintage Books, 1965).

Statutes of California Passed At The Extra Session of the Forty-First Legislature, (San Francisco: Bancroft-Whitney Co., 1916).

Stevenson, Jan A., "Firearms Legislation in Great Britain", *The Handgunner*, [March/April 1988].

Story, Joseph, *Commentaries on the Constitution of the United States*, (Boston: n.p., 1833).

Thorpe, Francis Newton, ed., *The Federal and State Constitutions, Colonial Charters, and Other Organic Laws of the States, Territories, and Colonies*, (Washington: Government Printing Office, 1909).

"Underground in Kuwait", *Newsweek*, December 31, 1990, 43.

Usner, Jr., Daniel H., *Indians, Settlers, & Slaves in a Frontier Exchange Economy: The Lower Mississippi Valley Before 1783*, (Chapel Hill, N.C.: University of North Carolina Press, 1992).

Veit, Helen, Bowling, Kenneth R., & Bickford, Charlene Bangs, ed., *Creating The Bill of Rights: The Documentary Record from the First Federal Congress*, (Baltimore: Johns Hopkins University Press, 1991).

Viault, Birdsall S., *American History Since 1865*, (New York: McGraw-Hill, 1989).

Walker, Samuel, *Popular Justice: A History of American Criminal Justice*, (New York: Oxford University Press, 1979).

Washington Dept. of Wildlife, *Firearms Safety, The Law and You*, (n.p.: n.d.)

Weatherup, Roy G., "Standing Armies And Armed Citizens: An Historical Analysis of The Second Amendment", *Hastings Constitutional Law Quarterly*, 2:1 [Winter 1975], reprinted in *The Right To Keep And Bear Arms*, 130-70.

Webb, Walter Prescott, *The Great Plains*, (New York: Houghton Mifflin Co., 1936).

Webster, Noah, *An American Dictionary of the English Language*, (1828; reprinted New York: Johnson Reprint Corp., 1970).

Will, George F., "How to control guns", Santa Rosa (Cal.) *Press-Democrat*, March 21, 1991, B5.

Wilson, Theodore Brantner, *The Black Codes of the South*, (University of Alabama Press, 1965).

Wise, Terence, *Medieval Warfare*, (New York: Hastings House, 1976).

Wroth, L. Kinvin, and Zobel, Hiller B., ed., *Legal Papers of John Adams*, (Cambridge, Mass.: Harvard University Press, 1965).

Yahil, Leni, *The Holocaust*, transl. by Ina Friedman & Haya Galai, (New York: Oxford University Press, 1990).

INDEX

About the Author

CLAYTON E. CRAMER received his B.A. in History from Sonoma State University *cum laude* in January 1994. In addition to his previous book, *By The Dim And Flaring Lamps: The Civil War Diary of Samuel McIlvaine*, he has had numerous articles published concerning constitutional history, gun control, civil defense, and problems of media ethics.